Affect and Embodied Meaning in Animation

This book combines insights from the humanities and modern neuroscience to explore the contribution of affect and embodiment on meaning-making in case studies from animation, video games, and virtual worlds.

As we interact more and more with animated characters and avatars in everyday media consumption, it has become vital to investigate the ways that animated environments influence our perception of the liberal humanist subject. This book is the first to apply recent research on the application of the embodied mind thesis to our understanding of embodied engagement with nonhumans and cyborgs in animated media, analyzing works by Émile Cohl, Hayao Miyazaki, Tim Burton, Norman McLaren, the Quay Brothers, Pixar, and many others. Drawing on the breakthroughs of modern brain science to argue that animated media broadens the viewer's perceptual reach, this title offers a welcome contribution to the growing literature at the intersection of cognitive studies and film studies, with a perspective on animation that is new and original.

Affect and Embodied Meaning in Animation will be essential reading for researchers of Animation Studies, Film and Media Theory, Posthumanism, Video Games, and Digital Culture, and will provide a key insight into animation for both undergraduate and graduate students. Because of the increasing importance of visual effect cinema and video games, the book will also be of keen interest within Film Studies and Media Studies, as well as to general readers interested in scholarship in animated media.

Sylvie Bissonnette guest edited the special issue "Animating Space and Scalar Travels" for the journal *Animation*. Her writing on animation and cinema has appeared in *Animation*, the *Contemporary Theatre Review*, the *New Review of Film and Television Studies*, and *Screen*. She has published book chapters in *From Camera Lens to Critical Lens* and *Stages of Reality*, and a chapter on the Québécois filmmaker Denis Villeneuve in *Regards Croisés sur Incendies*.

Routledge Advances in Film Studies

58 **Collective Trauma and the Psychology of Secrets in Transnational Film**
Deborah Lynn Porter

59 **Melodrama, Self and Nation in Post-War British Popular Film**
Johanna Laitila

60 **Emotion in Animated Films**
Edited by Meike Uhrig

61 **Post-Production and the Invisible Revolution of Filmmaking**
From the Silent Era to Synchronized Sound
George Larkin

62 **New Approaches to Cinematic Space**
Edited by Filipa Rosário and Iván Villarmea Álvarez

63 **Melancholy in Contemporary Cinema**
A Spinozian Analysis of Film Experience
Francesco Sticchi

64 **Found Footage Horror Films**
A Cognitive Approach
Peter Turner

65 **Affect and Embodied Meaning in Animation**
Becoming-Animated
Sylvie Bissonnette

For more information about this series, please visit: https://www.routledge.com

Affect and Embodied Meaning in Animation

Becoming-Animated

Sylvie Bissonnette

First published 2019
by Routledge
52 Vanderbilt Avenue, New York, NY 10017

and by Routledge
2 Park Square, Milton Park, Abingdon, Oxon OX14 4RN

First issued in paperback 2020

Routledge is an imprint of the Taylor & Francis Group, an informa business

Library of Congress Cataloging-in-Publication Data
Names: Bissonnette, Sylvie, author.
Title: Affect and embodied meaning in animation: becoming-animated / Sylvie Bissonnette.
Description: London; New York: Routledge, 2019. |
Series: Routledge advances in film studies | Includes bibliographical references and index.
Identifiers: LCCN 2018057708 (print) |
LCCN 2018058662 (ebook)
Subjects: LCSH: Computer animation. | Body language—Computer simulation. | Affect (Psychology)
Classification: LCC TR897.7 (ebook) |
LCC TR897.7 .B566 2019 (print) | DDC 006.6/96—dc23
LC record available at https://lccn.loc.gov/2018057708

ISBN 13: 978-0-367-66037-6 (pbk)
ISBN 13: 978-1-138-48359-0 (hbk)

Typeset in Sabon
by codeMantra

Contents

	List of Figures	vii
	Acknowledgments	ix
	Introduction: Becoming-Animated	1
1	The Limits of Human Perception	23
2	Cyborg Viewers	62
3	Metamorphic Creatures	95
4	Muscular Augmentations	133
5	A Trek Across the Uncanny Valley	167
6	Algorithmic Couplings in Video Games	202
7	Becoming-Avatar	238
	Coda	269
	References	277
	Index	305

List of Figures

0.1 Hectic bodily movements produced by pixilation. *The Secret Adventures of Tom Thumb* (Dave Borthwick, 1993) 2
0.2 Mike and Sulley walking to work in *Monsters, Inc.* (Pete Docter, 2001) 5
1.1 Muscular man pushing a rock uphill. *Sisyphus* (Marcell Jankovics, 1974) 32
1.2 Imprisoned craftsman carving a hand into a large white block. *The Hand* (Jiří Trnka, 1965) 40
1.3 A penguin-looking creature stands on the ice and the shadows of a fish and a bird-fish appear below the surface. *Antagonia* (Nicolas Brault, 2002) 49
1.4 Animating a bouncing ball. *The Cabinet of Jan Švankmajer* (Stephen Quay and Timothy Quay, 1984) 52
1.5 The law of proximity represented with pearls. *Spheres* (René Jodoin and Norman McLaren, 1969) 55
2.1 The perspective of the mind-hacked cyborg. *Ghost in the Shell* (Mamoru Oshii, 1995) 64
2.2 RoboCop's perception associated with the degraded image of a TV monitor. *RoboCop* (Paul Verhoeven, 1987) 72
2.3 Android vision represented by the pixelated image of a cowboy reminiscent of video games. *Westworld* (Michael Crichton, 1973) 73
2.4 Aki wearing a head-up display system. *Final Fantasy: The Spirits Within* (Hironobu Sakaguchi, 2001) 78
2.5 Augmented perception represented with a superimposed grid. *Final Fantasy: The Spirits Within* (Hironobu Sakaguchi, 2001) 79
2.6 Briareos's body covered with metallic gear. *Appleseed Ex Machina* (Shinji Aramaki, 2007) 81
2.7 Flickering images representing Dr. Xander. *Appleseed Ex Machina* (Shinji Aramaki, 2007) 82
2.8 Aki's photorealistic eyes. *Final Fantasy: The Spirits Within* (Hironobu Sakaguchi, 2001) 88

3.1 The stalk of a flower transforms into an elephant's trunk. *Fantasmagoria* (Émile Cohl, 1908) 96
3.2 The Corpse Bride disintegrates into a flock of butterflies. *Corpse Bride* (Tim Burton and Mike Johnson, 2005) 111
3.3 Clay workers are hung by the neck and pushed into a bucket by a giant hand. *The Death of Stalinism in Bohemia* (Jan Švankmajer, 1990) 114
3.4 Combination of hand-drawn animation and 3D rendering to portray Ashitaka's curse. *Princess Mononoke* (Hayao Miyazaki, 1997) 119
4.1 Champion climbing a steep hill. *The Triplets of Belleville* (Sylvain Chomet, 2003) 155
4.2 Madam Souza massaging Champion's calves with a hand mixer. *The Triplets of Belleville* (Sylvain Chomet, 2003) 156
4.3 Champion's hypnotized gaze. *The Triplets of Belleville* (Sylvain Chomet, 2003) 157
4.4 The body of a superhuman runner splattering blood. *Black Jack: The Movie* (Osamu Dezaki and Fumihiro Yoshimura, 1996) 160
5.1 Uncanny look of the young boy. *The Polar Express* (Robert Zemeckis, 2004) 167
5.2 Ran's mask and her riveting gaze. *Texhnolyze*, Episode Stranger (Hiroshi Hamasaki, 2003) 174
5.3 Extreme close-up of Ichise's eye. *Texhnolyze*, Episode Stranger (Hiroshi Hamasaki, 2003) 174
5.4 Artifact emotion and the extreme close-up of Aki's eye. *Final Fantasy: The Spirits Within* (Hironobu Sakaguchi, 2001) 184
5.5 Erasing technological inscriptions on the computer-generated face of the elderly Benjamin Button. *The Curious Case of Benjamin Button* (David Fincher, 2008) 187
5.6 Malice's automated pupil and the robotic gaze. *Malice@ Doll* (Keitarô Motonaga, 2001) 191
6.1 The Insect Swarm Plasmid. Screen capture from *BioShock* (Ken Levine, 2007) 225
6.2 Genetic alterations and physical tonics are sold like cheap add-ons. Screen capture from *BioShock* (Ken Levine, 2007) 226
6.3 Seeing like a Big Daddy. Screen capture from *BioShock* (Ken Levine, 2007) 230
6.4 Anxiety-ridden atmosphere of Rapture. Screen capture from *BioShock* (Ken Levine, 2007) 233
7.1 Examples of female gestures available in the *Second Life* Inventory. Screenshot from *Second Life* 254

Acknowledgments

My ideas on the topic of embodied meaning are in constant mutation. This book only provides a snapshot of the chaotic neural exchanges the subject elicits in my mind. The thinking for this book started during my doctoral research at the University of California, Davis. I am particularly indebted to my dissertation committee members. Elizabeth Constable, Lynette Hunter, Colin Milburn, and Alva Noë contributed thought-provoking insights and enduring support during that initial phase of the project. Thank you for your intellectual generosity and motivation. The book project developed during my postdoctoral appointment at the University of California, Berkeley under the supervision of Alva Noë. I will keep fond memories of all the people I met in the Department of Philosophy at Moses Hall.

Parts of some of the chapters were presented at various conferences, including the SLSA 2010 Conference, the SCMS 2011 Conference, and the SCSMI 2014 Conference. Discussions with friends, collaborators, fellow panelists, and conference members were extremely inspiring. I also had the opportunity to participate in the Vision Club at UC Davis between 2008 and 2009. I am particularly grateful for the support provided by David Whitney and the members of his psychophysics laboratory who invited me to their meetings at UC Davis and then UC Berkeley between 2008 and 2012. Needless to say, I am solely responsible for any shortcomings resulting from my failure to draw on the numerous suggestions given to me along the way.

My warmest thanks, finally, goes to my family and close friends, who shared this animated adventure with me and provided their much appreciated love and endless encouragement.

Introduction

Becoming-Animated

Perceptual Entanglements

In our everyday life, animated figures and avatars cross our paths and touch us in surprising ways. We eagerly empathize with WALL-E, the robot in *WALL-E* (Andrew Stanton, 2008). The presence of synthespians in the computer-generated animation *Final Fantasy: The Spirits Within* (Hironobu Sakaguchi, 2001) arouses uncanny effects. Avatars in the synthetic world *Second Life* stimulate our social lives and engage us in the discovery of new sensory pathways. Moreover, synthetic worlds and video games awaken feelings in us we never knew we had and can even expand our physical skills. Because we interact more and more with avatars and animated characters, it is particularly pressing to investigate their effects on our embodied dispositions and our identity as humans. *Affect and Embodied Meaning in Animation* sets out to explore these questions in animated media, which includes a variety of screen-based media such as animation, cinema, video games, and synthetic worlds.

Some animated figures seem to toy with our bodies. I think of the jerky bodily movements in *The Secret Adventures of Tom Thumb* (Dave Borthwick, 1993) and the stretching limbs of Elastigirl in *The Incredibles* (Brad Bird, 2004). These distorted movements have a peculiar way of reverberating through my muscles when I watch them. In *The Secret Adventures of Tom Thumb*, I have the impression to feel inwardly the constant facial twitches of Tom's father and the creepy motion of the food in the plates. In this dark story loosely inspired by the original fairy tale, the small-sized Tom is abducted from his loving parents by strange men in black. The men take Tom to a laboratory where scientists perform bioengineering experiments. Live actors play the parents and the kidnappers, while Tom and the other creatures are portrayed by animated puppets. The actors are filmed with pixilation, a stop-motion technique. In order to animate the action, the actors remain still while one or more frames are photographed, and then they vary their pose slightly before the next frames are taken.

The combination of stop-motion animation and pixilation communicates the eeriness of Tom's world. In a sequence prior to Tom's kidnapping, a man in black prowls a dark alley. His slow, mechanized movements are produced by pixilation. A street lamp with oversized moths fluttering their wings around it stands in the background. Unexpectedly, the man forces himself inside Tom's house, and, with the help of an accomplice, he captures Tom. Unable to rescue their son, the mother and father gesticulate frantically (see Figure 0.1). Their grotesque and hectic bodily movements amplify their despair. When I watched this sequence, the expression of disarray in the mise-en-scène incited me to empathize with Tom's struggle, as I came to share his disorientation. The nightmarish street settings and the mechanical motion produced by pixilation not only conveyed the awkwardness of Tom's world but also toyed with my proprioceptive expectations. My interest in this book lies in such moments when the technologies of animation resonate by the viewer's body and thereby blur the frontier between the living and the animated.[1]

To understand how the entanglement between the spectator's body and the animated interface materializes, I query the bodily effects that may expose the permeability of the carnal envelope more forcefully. The focus is on affective responses evoked by metamorphic bodies in animation. Notably, metamorphoses disturb the character's appearance and the usual unfolding of its gestures.[2] Because our senses are attuned to the particularities of human physiognomy and movement, the hyperbolic distortion of the character's shape by various animated techniques

Figure 0.1 Hectic bodily movements produced by pixilation. *The Secret Adventures of Tom Thumb* (Dave Borthwick, 1993).

is more likely to cause interferences in our cognitive and physiological mappings. As I examine in the subsequent chapters, some affective and muscular experiences, currently unique to animated media, can help spectators reconsider the limits of their body.

Besides moving us, some animated pictures alter our body schema—the internalized landscape of all the movements that we can perform.[3] In certain video games, for instance, the scenarios we enact and our sensorimotor explorations of the game world stress the impact of technological extensions on the body. As the video game technology extends us toward the virtual environment, the avatar is a technology that transforms us from the "outside in." In the popular video game *BioShock* (Ken Levine, 2007), for example, the progressive metamorphosis of the avatar into a deadly cyborg is mirrored by the player's "real life" adjustments to bulky prosthetic extensions. Throughout the game, the player enacts the meaning of "genetic engineering" by performing a series of scenarios that involve painful mutations. The symbiotic relationship we develop with the genetically enhanced killers in *BioShock* redefines our usual understanding of the human.[4] Alternatively, in virtual reality-based therapies, interactions with avatars can "reprogram" the patient's neural networks and body schema. During some therapies, the patient's repeated engagement with his or her virtual limb can facilitate the recovery of the mobility that was lost in that limb after a stroke.

Viewer interactions with animated figures produce forms of cognitive and sensory extensions. These encounters highlight the human's complex perceptual entanglement with the animated interface. I call "becoming-animated" the idea that animation can bring out the permeability of our sensory boundaries and manifest our readiness to be extended by the interface. Simply put, animated figures not only move spectators but also expand their perceptual limits. This expanded model of cognition and sensory perception is no longer subordinated to the prevailing worldview of the liberal humanist subject, as indifferent or objective to the world. Instead, this "posthuman" perception reveals the human's complex perceptual entanglement with the animation apparatus. With this enactive approach to perception in animation, I revisit the notion that a film presupposes a liberal humanist subject as its spectator, suggesting that the technologies of animation extend the spectators' perceptual boundaries. Perception in animation does not happen in the head but at the intersection of the organic viewer and the animation apparatus.[5]

The Change Blindness Experiment

Affect and Embodied Meaning in Animation investigates the types of perceptual entanglements with the animation interface that call into question the limits between "viewer" and "viewed." The change blindness experiment in psychophysics is an exemplar of this kind of entanglement.[6] During typical change blindness experiments, participants are invited to look at a filmed scene or flickering images. While they are looking at the display, a prominent element of the scene varies, but participants do not realize it. These experiments demonstrate that there is a lot of information to process in our visual field, and that we cannot attend to every detail at once. I am particularly interested in animated versions of these experiments because they demonstrate that perception in animation is enactive; in other words, "seeing" requires an active engagement from the viewers.

Some animated films solicit the spectator's dedicated attention. For example, at the beginning of the animated film *Monsters, Inc.* (Pete Docter, 2001), Mike and Sulley walk to work. The bustling streets of Monstropolis present simultaneous activities happening everywhere around the frame (see Figure 0.2). There is so much going on that we cannot absorb all the details of the monsters' performances at once. On their way, Mike and Sulley say hello to a group of three young monsters who are playing in front of a house. The kids use the tongue of their friend as a jump rope. A blue car is parked in the foreground. Behind Sully, on the left-hand side of the frame, a small monster hides in the front staircase of the neighbors. In the background, another monster observes the scene from his window, filling out the window's frame with his huge eye. When jumping, one of the young monsters gets tangled in the rope and springs into the monster's eye in the window. This kind of busy sequence was disorienting when I saw it for the first time. I had to piece up together meaningful information from disparate audiovisual patterns. That is to say, the viewer's coordinated body-mind acts as a two-way membrane that performs different functions, including processes of selection, organization, inference, and analysis, depending on the level of meaningfulness solicited.[7] These functions vary across viewers, and from one viewing to another, thus accounting for different experiences.

Professor of philosophy Alva Noë carried out a public demonstration of the phenomenon of change blindness at the University of California in Berkeley. The film displayed a parked car that filled up a large portion of the frame's foreground. It was a usual street scene with nothing particularly outstanding going on, unlike the sequence in *Monsters, Inc.* Extremely slowly, the color of the car switched from red to blue, thanks to an animated transition.[8] After the screening, when audience members were asked whether they had observed anything peculiar happening on the screen, nobody mentioned that the color of the car had changed. During a second viewing, after the participants were told about this detail, everybody noticed the striking transformation and wondered how they could have missed it. This experiment demonstrates that there is more information in a film—even one with a very simple plot—than what we can grasp at once. How many times have we watched a film

Figure 0.2 Mike and Sulley walking to work in *Monsters, Inc.* (Pete Docter, 2001).

for a second time to notice that an important detail had escaped our attention the first time?

The change blindness demonstration reveals the particularity in our perceptual apparatus that allows us to be tricked into missing the change of color. During the first viewing, the transformation happened extremely slowly, and we did not know precisely what we were supposed to look at. The second time, the viewing conditions were similar, but because we knew where to devote our attention, the experience was totally different and revelatory. That time, we contributed to the transformation of the system by actively attending to the color of the car, thereby reshaping our body's boundary (increasing its filtering efficiency). I call this introspective process "becoming-animated."

Animations that highlight the particularities of the human perceptual system are crucial to this study. The change blindness experiment supplies evidence that vision is "attention-dependent" and that "we don't make use of detailed internal models of the scene (even if it doesn't show that there are no detailed internal representations)."[9] We have the impression that we can see in great detail the world or a scene from a film but this is a misconception. In fact, we easily miss important features of our environment if we do not specifically attend to them. Cognitive studies on the phenomenon of change blindness claim that our internal representation of the world may be incomplete and thus includes only central-interest information. This means that we rely on the world as an external memory and access it on a need basis.[10] The change blindness phenomenon, as O'Regan and his colleagues argue, is one phenomenon among others that support this hypothesis.[11]

Human perception is selective. We limit the flow of available information by attending to certain aspects of the scene presented in moving images. According to philosopher Henri Bergson, living beings are "centers of indetermination."[12] They suppress the parts from the scene under observation that have no interest to them. In *Cinema 1*, Gilles Deleuze draws on Bergson's findings to propose that the film (the movement-images) is the center of indetermination in the way that it selects a specific perspective from all the possible images available. In Deleuze's words, all "things considered, *movement-images divide into three sorts of images when they are related to a center of indetermination as to a special image*: perception-images, action-images and affection-images."[13]

Other phenomenological approaches posit the film as a perceiving body.[14] In this book, however, I consider the animation viewer as the center of indetermination, not the film. The viewer's perceptual system actively filters and selects perceptual information from the flow of available images displayed by animation technologies. In the change blindness example, even though we must know what to look for to attune ourselves to the transformation, it is the animation device that creates the slow transition of the color. Various combinations of viewing conditions and viewers' responses lead to the change blindness phenomenon, namely an "eye movement, a flicker, a blink, or a camera cut in a film sequence."[15]

The impression of movement through space that we experience when watching an animated cartoon depends on both the viewer's physiology and the animation apparatus, which comprises a variety of devices and "automatisms."[16] Film philosopher Stanley Cavell calls "automatisms" a series of genres and techniques that help distinguish the specificity of a medium. For instance, the speeds at which samples are recorded and then played back affect the smoothness of the character's locomotion in cinema. Some experienced spectators associate the jerky movements of black-and-white pictures with a sociohistorical framework or a cinematic tradition. When inserted in a contemporary film, they can be reminiscent of early silent films and the varying frame rate of that era. In contrast, the mechanical reproduction of the actors' movements using pixilation in *The Secret Adventures of Tom Thumb* can suggest the dehumanized worldview depicted in the storyline. Alternatively, slow-motion running in the TV series *The Six Million Dollar Man* (1974–1978) denotes physical augmentation.

Animation in the change blindness experiment is also a tool for helping viewers—and scientific observers—investigate the embodied nature of human perception. In *Techniques of the Observer*, Jonathan Crary studies the history of technical objects that revealed the "corporeal subjectivity of the observer" in the 19th century.[17] In *The Railway Journey*, Wolfgang Schivelbusch investigates train travelers who perceived the landscape as filtered through the machine ensemble.[18] For Crary and Schivelbusch, technical objects or train travels enabled new ways of seeing that underscored the embodied nature of vision and the mobility of the observer. Furthermore, Crary's book demonstrates that coinciding with the advent of new techniques to study vision, the observer's body became at once the spectator and the subject of empirical research. The last chapter returns to this topic. I approach the spectator as a subject for medical experiments in virtual environments and explore the use of the avatar as a medical technique. In the first chapters, however, I focus on the ways that the animation apparatus can extend the viewers' perceptual reach and the scope of their embodiment. In *Cinema's Bodily Illusions*, Scott C. Richmond claims that the "cinema's vocation of proprioceptive modulation demonstrates that proprioception is, at the very least, *open* to technics, susceptible to technical modulation."[19] The term proprioception refers to sets of perceptual modalities that inform us about our posture and position in space. *Affect and Embodied Meaning in Animation* probes the effects of this openness to technics on the perceptual assemblage between viewer and viewed and the possibility to extend the perceptual limits of the animation spectator. Proprioception is only one category of perceptual modalities that can modulate our affectivity, notably by toying with our experience of movement and space in moving imagery.

One of the foremost aims of this study is to illustrate that the animated interface is not separate from the viewer but an integral component of the perceptual system. The animation apparatus and the perceptual system of the viewer are part of an assemblage. As such, I consider our embodied engagement with the animated image as a new and larger functional system. While the viewers do not directly "redraw" or "manipulate" the content of the frame—unless they slow down or accelerate the projection speed with their remote, they participate in the audiovisual experience. During the change blindness demonstration mentioned earlier, the viewer's acute probing of the animated interface modifies the reception of the scene. As this phenomenon suggests, metamorphosis does not solely occur on the screen: the viewing body and the animation apparatus simultaneously transform the overall experience. Venturing further on this pathway, the next chapters flesh out what I mean by *enactive* perception in animation.

In *Cinema's Bodily Illusions*, Richmond sidesteps representational figures in his study of the relations between perception and technology in cinema. Although the change blindness experiment used as an example did not involve an elaborate narrative, I am interested in what narrative animations have to say about the technological body. More specifically, I explore the mechanisms deployed by several animations to attract our attention to these questions. Some of them use perceptual alignments with robots and cyborgs to envisage alternative perspectives on life and the human. Others bring to the fore the apparatus of mediation to complement the narrative's angle on the impacts of technology on the body.

As I suggest, we become animated when the mechanisms of mediation reveal the presence of the body's boundaries or when empathizing with an animated character causes reverberations throughout our body.

New Systemic Wholes and the Extended Mind

The spectators piece together the elements on the animated interface as they engage with the animation machine—the machine that animates bodies on the screen and animates the spectator's neural system. The spectator becomes part of a "functional ensemble" that interconnects his or her perceptions and sensations with the animated interface. First conceived by philosopher Gilbert Simondon, the idea of "technical ensembles" stresses the intertwined and productive relations between humans and machines in society.[20] After Simondon, philosopher Félix Guattari developed the concept of the "machine" in his theory of machinic heterogenesis.[21] Both concepts integrate technical objects, human bodies, and individual and collective subjectivities into functional ensembles, which form the basis for Lamarre's concept of the "animetic machine."[22] The "animation machine," the term I will use to adapt the animetic machine to animation in general, assembles animation automatisms, technologies, the animators' styles, traditions and conventions, and larger sociohistorical questions. While the "animetic machine" focuses on the collaboration between the animator and its technologies to create a unique vision, my approach prioritizes the spectator's body as a center of indetermination that interprets, filters, and interacts with the animated interface. The assemblage of bodies and technologies is central to the spectator's interpretation of the discourses produced by a particular animation.

Also part of the animation machine, animated bodies and avatars are tools that can extend our spatial reach beyond the surface of the screen. Philosopher Maurice Merleau-Ponty investigates the incorporation of technological extensions into the perceiver's body in *Phenomenology of Perception*. He refers to a blind man's stick as broadening the tactile reach and the scope of action:

> The blind man's stick has ceased to be an object for him, and is no longer perceived for itself; its point has become an area of sensitivity, extending the scope and active radius of touch, and providing a parallel to sight. In the exploration of things, the length of the stick does not enter expressly as a middle term: the blind man is rather aware of it through the position of objects than of the position of objects through it. The position of things is immediately given through the extent of the reach which carries him to it, which comprises besides the arm's own reach the stick's range of action. [...] To get used to a hat, a car or a stick is to be transplanted into them, or conversely, to incorporate them into the bulk of our own body.[23]

According to media scholar Mark Hansen, this form of prosthetic technicity gives priority to the body and technics comes only second.[24] From Hansen's perspective, technics does not befall the human from the outside. Drawing on late Merleau-Ponty's writing on the *écart* and Gilbert Simondon's work, Hansen's model of technics "refuses to divorce technicity from embodiment."[25] Although I elaborate on the ways that the animation apparatus can extend the viewer, I am less concerned with the "originary technicity" of the human. The emphasis is on the embodied viewer and the permeability of the junction between viewer and viewed. It is by engaging with the animated interface that the viewer gives life to the animated landscape. Following Merleau-Ponty's example from *Phenomenology of Perception*, I claim that the animated interface can extend the viewer's scope of embodiment to encompass the animated world. However, besides taking a phenomenological stance, I examine the mechanisms by which the animated interface extends the viewers' reach, notably looking at physiological extensions and functional systems. Philosopher of mind Andy Clark's extended approach to the mind, for instance, acknowledges that the perceptual system of *Homo sapiens* is preadapted to be extended by all kinds of tools.

Defying neat divisions between apparatus and bodies, the animation machine is essential to our understanding of the human and the self in our highly mediated contemporary world. I envisage the spectator as "a 'soft self,' a constantly negotiable collection of resources easily able to straddle and criss-cross the boundaries between biology and artifact."[26] The spectators' skills and cognitive faculties combine with the assemblage of elements that form the animation machine. The spectator's reach is extended by spreading the cognitive processes beyond the bounds of skin and skull. As Clark asserts, it is the brain's plasticity that makes humans natural-born cyborgs. This intrinsic capacity enables humans to extend their minds through internal rewiring and by distributing the cognitive load to external elements and structures. From this perspective, animated media extend our mind and are conducive to the creation of "new systemic wholes,"[27] not limited by our physical envelope.

As I argue in *Affect and Embodied Meaning in Animation*, the animation machine extends our perceptual perspectives by creating new cognitive wholes. I notably adapt Clark's extended approach to virtual environments, namely the symbiotic bonding of a player with a video game avatar can extend the player's practical and spatial reach into the game world. In addition, tool use reconfigures the webworks of neural connections mapping the intersections between body, mind, and apparatus. Such remapping of neural connections occurs when we find new strategies to negotiate the complex mise-en-scène of animated worlds or when we draw on media technology to facilitate analytical activities, such as puzzle-solving in video games.

To apply to media theory this expanded model of cognition and sensory perception, I employ the lens of posthuman theories for understanding the perceptual entanglements between the viewer and the animated interface.[28] From Donna Haraway's criticism of rigid boundaries in "A Cyborg Manifesto" to N. Katherine Hayles's insights into the posthuman, scholars have investigated the impacts of prosthetic extensions and cognitive ensembles on our conception of the liberal humanist subject. The effects of bioengineering, virtual reality, and artificial intelligence on the body are at the forefront of animated media. Yet, theories of spectatorship often neglect questions related to the progressive transformation of the human into the posthuman and the contribution of the media to this transformation. Generally, Film Studies theories have stressed the similarity between human perception and the cinematic apparatus. In contrast, I study animated films that challenge this analogy and reveal the nonhuman nature of perception. In encouraging spectators to transform into cyborg viewers, some animations help articulate an alternative to organism-bound approaches to perception in cinema.

Embodied Perception in Animation and Meaning-Making

Various theories posit cognition as emerging from the interaction between body, mind, and world, as illustrated by the theories of extended cognition and enactive approaches to perception.[29] More specifically, *Affect and Embodied Meaning in Animation* examines the sensory couplings that emerge at the interface between viewers and animated interfaces. In addition to the perceptual extensions produced by the technologies of animation, as shown in the study of the change blindness phenomenon, I investigate neural and physiological forms of extensions, such as empathetic responses, muscular resonance, and the effects of mirror neurons.

Some cognitive theories maintain that the mind is more than just the brain. They distinguish between embodied, situated, and extended cognition. Literature on embodied cognition claims that the mind exists in the entire body; it is not solely produced by the central nervous system. In addition, scholarship on situated cognition holds that the presence of particular environmental conditions or even social background contributes to the development of certain cognitive functions. From the perspective of the extended mind, cognition is embodied and situated, and the brain-body-world system is dynamically coupled. Proponents of this latter approach draw on either dynamic systems theory or wide computationalism to demonstrate that mental states and cognitive functions can extend spatiotemporally beyond the skin of the cognizer.[30]

The idea that visual meaning is embodied has already inspired a body of work in Film Studies.[31] Some of this scholarship finds its inspiration in the book on embodied metaphors *Philosophy in the Flesh* (1999), co-authored by George Lakoff and Mark Johnson. In it, the authors demonstrate that we use conceptual metaphors in our everyday language. Some metaphors, for example, express the concept of time in terms of space. We say that "life is a journey" or "time flies by." Their hypothesis is that our brain processes higher-level conceptualization with the same circuitry that it uses for locomotion or other motor activities. Lakoff and Johnson call image schemas the numerous patterns of interactions grounded in perceptual experiences that reactivate this embodied circuitry in the brain.[32] The SOURCE-PATH-GOAL schema, for instance, brings to mind the experience of moving from an initial condition A (source), following a pathway B (path) until reaching a destination C (goal). In an article that applies the embodied theory of mind to animation, Charles Forceville and Marloes Jeulink demonstrate the presence of the SOURCE-PATH-GOAL schema in the animated films *Father and Daughter* (Michaël Dudok de Wit, 2000), *Quest* (Tyron Montgomery, 1996), and *O* (Kireet Khurana, 1995).[33] This image schema, for example, facilitates the comprehension of audiovisual information in the animated short film *O* by reactivating the sensorimotor parts of the brain associated with metaphors such as TIME IS SPACE or KNOWLEDGE IS A BURDEN. As the time progresses in the story told in this animation, the protagonist matures and moves from the right of the screen to the left. The baby learns new concepts, becomes a knowledgeable young man, and then feels the burden associated with old age. The SOURCE-PATH-GOAL schema is represented by the metaphor TIME IS SPACE, as the right of the screen is associated with the protagonist's birth (past) and the left of the screen is associated with its end of life (future). Similarly, in their article on visual embodied meaning, Maarten Coëgnarts and Peter Kravanja analyze various film sequences to demonstrate the operation of a selection of image schemas from Lakoff and Johnson's list of basic image schemas.[34] They examine the metaphorical function of representative image schemas, some of which are: CONTAINER, SOURCE-PATH-GOAL, CENTER-PERIPHERY, VERTICALITY, and BALANCE. For instance, the CONTAINER schema represents our experience of physical delimitations and the separation between what is inside and what is outside. The authors associate the CONTAINER image with the filmic space (the space created within the film frame) in a scene of *Spartacus* (Stanley Kubrick, 1960). They demonstrate that the positions of the actors within the frame illustrate the metaphorical relations of power between the characters.

By drawing on the discovery of the mirror neuron system (MNS) and the concept of image schemas, Coëgnarts and Kravanja posit that the esthetic experience should be conjointly understood at the physical level and the conceptual level. Research on the MNS establishes that when we see someone performing an action, we mentally perform the same action. Following Lakoff and Johnson, Coëgnarts and Kravanja hypothesize that our innate understanding of others and abstract ideas is grounded in such biological mechanisms. The form of empathy witnessed by the MNS can link our neural activity with our physical experience of the different image schemas. In turn, these image schemas convey abstract ideas via the disposition of elements within the filmic space or camera movements.

Identifying the presence of image schemas, and showing how they reactivate neural structures in the brain from sensorimotor areas, is not the only way to describe the embodied nature of film spectatorship. As mentioned earlier, we can explore the perceptual entanglement between viewer and viewed in the light of research on the extended mind and enactive perception. In addition, I apply the work of David Freedberg and Vittorio Gallese on emotion and empathy in esthetic experience to animation.[35] They identify a sense of bodily resonance in the presence of works of art by showing figures struggling to free themselves, such as the male nudes sculpted by Michelangelo and known as the *Prisoners*. In Chapter 4, I further elaborate on the concept of muscular empathy by analyzing animations that encourage spectators to feel muscular pain. Following the steps of Freedberg and Gallese, art historian Barbara Stafford draws on cognitive research and the MNS to explain effects of resonance in the presence of artworks in *Echo Objects*. While these effects are not there to prove that the pictures are works of art, their evocation reinforces certain themes and moods that the works contain, as other motifs and figures of style would do.

The bodily empathy that an observer develops with figures in a picture also applies to animated characters.[36] One type of empathy involves the dynamic coupling of the spectator's body and the animated figure. Here, coupling "means an associative bonding or linking of self and other on the basis of their bodily similarity."[37] This similarity operates "at the level of gesture, posture, and movement—that is, at the level of the unconscious body schema."[38] I investigate the ways that bodily metamorphoses may elicit affective and sensorimotor couplings—or empathic resonances—between self and animated others. For example, this form of affective resonance happens for me in *The Incredibles* (Brad Bird, 2004) when Elastigirl stretches her torso and limbs beyond anything humanly possible. When she flips from one building to the other after meeting Mr. Incredible for the first time, the sensation of elongation surprisingly ripples through my muscles. Additionally, one may experience contagious laughter when characters on screen burst into laughter or when they giggle. Although the phenomena of empathetic resonance and emotional contagion initially alter our sensory breadth at an unconscious level, they nevertheless contribute to our engagement with animated characters in palpable ways.

Another type of empathy concerns the imaginary transposition of the spectator into the character's place. This cognitive perspective-taking process enables "one to imagine or mentally transpose oneself into the place of the other."[39] For instance, the empathetic sharing of the perspective of one's avatar often occurs when playing first-person shooters. In cinema, character simulation happens when the character's emotions transmigrate into the spectator, and alternatively, when we simulate the character's emotions and concerns from the character's own perspective.[40]

My emphasis on the embodied viewer shares affinities with haptic film theories.[41] As film scholars Thomas Elsaesser and Malte Hagener summarize in *Film Theory*, haptic theories critique the occularcentric paradigm present in film theories focusing on vision, including those of Rudolf Arnheim and Béla Balázs, and apparatus theory of the 1960s and 1970s.[42] Haptic approaches are "not predicated on a negation of the visual, but rather attempt to understand the senses in their interplay and perception as embodied, as well as to theorize this embodiment in its own complexity."[43] Vivian Sobchack, for example, puts the viewer's "corporeal-material being" at the center of her approach.[44] Other studies concentrate on the pleasurable effects and the empathic responses elicited by moving images. Steven Shaviro, for instance, explores mimetic contagion and the seductive pleasure of the image in *The Cinematic Body*. In *The Tactile Eye*, Jennifer Barker studies the ways that skin, viscera, and musculature are solicited by the content and texture of the film.

Drawing on these haptic theories and others, *Affect and Embodied Meaning in Animation* criticizes the limitations of Cartesian approaches and affirms the importance of embodiment for our understanding of cinema. Unlike these haptic studies, however, this book focuses on the specificity of animation.[45] The uncanny effects produced by near-human characters in CGI move us in different ways than live-action actors do. Likewise, animated figures bouncing around the frame may cause reverberating effects in the spectator's muscles that depart from usual patterns of affective responses. These unexpected effects underscore our perceptual entanglement with the technologies of animation. By constantly perturbing our perceptual expectations, animated media are therefore particularly suited to reveal the mutability of the body's boundaries.

We get a more rounded understanding of the message expressed by moving images when we consolidate the information conveyed by our sensual experience with the cues produced by audiovisual content. As film theorist David Bordwell attests in *Making Meaning*, interpretation is a constructive process that draws on materials that "include not only the perceptual output furnished by mandatory and universal bottom-up processes but also the higher-level textual data upon which various interpreters base their inferences."[46] The approach developed in Bordwell's book, however, focuses mainly on the latter. Similarly, many schools of film criticism rely on schemata, or high-level structures of understanding, for interpreting films.[47] My approach draws on higher-level textual data, such as character design and mise-en-scène, in order to provide a more comprehensive interpretation of specific animations. However, I foreground the role of bottom-up processes, such as facial mimicry and muscular empathy, on meaning-making.

Various empathic effects in moving images are akin to those we experience in the presence of living people. For instance, we have the unconscious tendency to produce expressions, postures, and movements by mimicking those of others. In the example of Michelangelo's *Prisoners* mentioned earlier, this form of affective mimicry covers muscular empathy and can find elements of explanation in the presence of the MNS. Moreover, scientific research shows a correlation between emotional contagion and facial mimicry. These multiple forms of resonance between the viewer and the animated world suggest the permeability of the invisible membrane separating viewers from viewed. These unconscious and conscious forms of mimicry contribute to our understanding of the characters' motivations and feelings. In addition, as we develop affinities with digital presences and avatars in video games and synthetic worlds, we discover our increasingly enmeshed identities.

Our physical movements through actual space and our interactions with physical objects inform the way we perceive virtual environments. Image schemas are grounded in sensorimotor experience and conducive of metaphorical meaning. This form of enactive knowledge is particularly important for video game theory. Beyond the animatic figures and literary figures, Ian Bogost identifies procedural figures in video games and describes their modes of operation in the monograph *Persuasive Games: The Expressive Power of Videogames*. By encouraging the players to perform particular actions or rely on specific procedures over others, some video games expose the operations of political structures to persuade us of their ideological ramifications. While some animated films convey audiovisual metaphors rooted in concrete physical experience, video games can use repetitive movements and conventions to reveal engrained ideologies grounded in discipline, which could otherwise pass as apolitical forms of behaviors.

Animation helps us see beyond the spatiotemporal limits of the body. Hybrid characters raise questions about the limits of the human in the light of accelerated transformations in bioengineering and information technology. This general approach to perception in animation invites deeper analyses of the ways that metamorphic figures may cause particular affective reverberations and imaginary transpositions in terms of gender, sexuality, and race. Using this framework, scholars could further investigate the manner in which diverse axes of identity shape the singularity of each individual experience.

The Animated Pathway

Our perceptual encounter with the animated interface involves body, mind, and world. As examined throughout the seven chapters of *Affect and Embodied Meaning in Animation*, some embodied interactions with animated figures induce neural, sensorimotor, and emotional reconfigurations. The main argument is that our engagement with animated media incites us to reevaluate what we know about our sensory boundaries and the limits of the human, a process that I call "becoming-animated."

Some animated films can draw on our specific modes of embodiment to transform what we think we see in them. The majority of my case studies concentrate on works that feature animated characters. Because animation shares empathic mechanisms with those found in live-action films, both the cinematic techniques and the particularities of animation are covered in the first three chapters. Then, animation specificity is explored throughout the remainder of the book.

The first chapter, "The Limits of Human Perception," shows that animation is particularly attuned to our human sensory system. The viewer's perceptual boundaries are permeable and can be extended by the animated interface. Obviously, the physical division formed by the screen, much like the constraints posed by the human anatomy, prevents the viewers from touching the animated images directly. Yet, this chapter presents different mechanisms by which animated films prompt spectators to revisit their assumptions about the human's perceptual limits. The chapter introduces the enactive approach to perception in animation under the light of other views on embodied cognition in cinema. I open with a discussion about Alva Noë's notion of model to suggest that animated figures are special models that functionally extend the viewer. I notably draw on Clark's extended approach to the mind to detail some ways in which animated figures engage us to think "out of our heads." The discovery of the MNS, for example, explains the mirroring effects between object and subject that inform the viewer's esthetic experience. Mirroring mechanisms support the idea that recurring patterns of sensorimotor experience called image schemas can convey metaphorical meaning in animation. In addition, empathic resonance can explain why we tend to mimic the posture of on-screen characters or "share" congruent feelings with them. Finally, the chapter turns to animated films that reveal the particularity of the human perceptual system. *The Cabinet of Jan Švankmajer* (Stephen Quay and Timothy Quay, 1984), for instance, shows us the trickery behind the perceptual illusion of continuous motion. *Spheres* (René Jodoin and Norman McLaren, 1969), for its part, accentuates the gestalt laws of perceptual organization.[48] As suggested by these last examples, the technologies of animation unsettle assumptions about the viewer's perceptual limits by exploiting the specificity of the animation medium.

In Chapter 2, "Cyborg Viewers," I posit that perception in animation is not human but posthuman. The enactive approach to perception presented in this chapter is contrasted with film theories that take human perception as their referent. Instead, I suggest that we perceptually assemble with the technologies of animation and become cyborg viewers. The cyberpunk genre is at the center of my inquiry, as it incites viewers to question the limits of the body and the dialectical positioning of humans and artificial creatures.[49] The chapter discusses this topic within the context of developments in cybernetics and the psychology of perception, as they challenge the concept of the liberal humanist subject. While cinema features many types of cyborgean extensions, animation is particularly self-reflexive about the nonhuman nature of perception. A constellation of motifs and representational strategies in cyberpunk animation alludes to the posthuman nature of perception in moving images. The chapter presents four categories of perceptual extensions in animations inspired by this genre. Taking *Final Fantasy: The Spirits Within* as a first exemplar of our becoming cyborg viewers, I demonstrate that synthespians in this animation are stand-ins for the augmented viewer. Secondly, I attend to flickering effects and cyborgean assemblages in *Appleseed Ex Machina* (Shinji Aramaki, 2007) and *Immortal Ad Vitam* (Enki Bilal, 2004), as these mechanisms incite viewers to reflect on the nature of perception and its hybridization with technology. Thirdly, the merging of subjectivity between multiple embodied virtualities and the viewer in a sequence of *Ghost in the Shell* (Mamoru Oshii, 1995) simulates the viewer's perceptual fusion with the animated world. Fourthly, the contrast between humans and posthumans in some animations underscore the challenge of empathizing with those who deviate from the accepted canon in our increasingly networked societies. Ultimately, the intersubjective alignments between spectators and cyborgs in these examples encourage viewers to embrace their posthumanity.

Chapter 3, "Metamorphic Creatures," probes the rhetorical possibilities offered by shape-shifting characters as they transgress the boundaries between the human and the nonhuman. The chapter first reviews the structure of engagement developed by Murray Smith in *Engaging Characters*.[50] Taking into account the particularities of metamorphic narratives, the rest of the chapter identifies processes that enhance character engagement such as recognition, alignment, and allegiance. Character design, for instance, directs our affect toward a bounded figure in ways that reactivate sensorimotor patterns of experience related to the inside and the outside of a container. *Corpse Bride* (Tim Burton and Mike Johnson, 2005) applies the IN-OUT schema to express metaphorically the state of alienation of the characters. Moreover, the use of clay, wood, or an articulated puppet for the design of a character provides additional rhetorical opportunities. In Jan Švankmajer's hybrid film *The Death of Stalinism in Bohemia* (1991), for example, the merciless disposal of the clay bodies decries political tyranny during a dark period in the history of Bohemia. Then, the chapter discusses themes and empathic mechanisms relevant to Japanese *anime* featuring hybrids and the work of Hayao Miyazaki in particular. In *Princess Mononoke* (Hayao Miyazaki, 1997), aligning with the perspectives of the wolf Princess San or the forest demons supports underlying themes of intercultural reconciliation and mutual respect. Alternatively, the representation of Ashitaka's infected arm using digital compositing invites parallels between the heterogeneous body of the animated character and the biological body of the viewer. A second example investigates the recurring transformations of the wizard Howl in *Howl's Moving Castle* (Hayao Miyazaki, 2004). The analysis of this *anime* draws on Deleuze and Guattari's concept of "becoming-animal."[51] As Howl morphs, his painful struggle sends ripples through the viewers' muscles. The character's transformation into a war machine and the process of becoming-animal incite spectators to reevaluate the meaning of the human in wartime. In summary, character engagement and empathic resonance enhance the understanding of a narrative.

When we empathize with cyborgs in *Appleseed Ex Machina* or the exploited cyclists in *The Triplets of Belleville* (Sylvain Chomet, 2003),[52] we apprehend the dangers of crossing the limits of the humanly possible. Chapter 4, "Muscular Augmentations," delves into the phenomenon of muscular empathy and the rhetorical possibilities of muscular effects in animation. The chapter examines technical and physical movements that rely on muscular memory to encourage muscular mimicry with the film's body and muscular simulation. The muscular sensations evoked by digital effects, for example, can modulate the interpretation of the filmic discourse. Alternatively, exaggerated familiar movements in 3D movies can disorient the spectator. The chapter also investigates the motivating appeal of extraordinary physical performances that defy the laws of nature in martial arts films. More specifically, the performances of strong female warriors in *Mulan II* (Darrell Rooney and Lynne Southerland, 2004) and *Kung Fu Panda: Secrets of the Furious Five* (Raman Hui, 2008) evoke empowering images and defy gender stereotypes. Additionally, nonhuman bodily motions and contortions expand our repertoire of motion schemas. By producing movements that deviate from usual sensorimotor patterns of experience, the modes of production can interfere with the mechanisms of engagement. For example, the defamiliarized movements produced by the pixilation and stop-motion techniques in *The Club of the Laid Off* (Jiři Barta, 1989) unsettle our muscular memories in ways that support grim narratives about alienation. Otherwise, the rotoscoped performances of Cab Calloway in the animations created by Max Fleischer produce eerie feelings when mapped onto grotesque characters. As the analyses of these rotoscoped performances suggest, the phantom presence of the black entertainer evokes various racial stereotypes. The last section tackles the ethics of muscular pain in tales about the negative effects of cybernetic technology, physical enhancement, and consumerism on health. As I contend, the effects of sensorimotor resonances evoked by distorted bodily movements in animation incite viewers to reevaluate their own contribution to discourses about man-machine symbiosis and superhumanity.

Chapter 5, "A Trek Across the Uncanny Valley," investigates the case of the uncanny valley in CGI. This phenomenon happens when our appreciation for a humanoid character drops as its likeness to the human increases above a certain threshold. Media theorists and neuroscientists have evoked several reasons for the responses that we have in the presence of synthespians. Certain scholars argue that our biological makeup is partly responsible for these uncanny feelings. Others, such as Alva Noë and Lawrence Weschler, prefer to attribute these effects to the animation medium or the narrative structure. Adopting a position at the intersection of these two approaches, I claim that uncanny feelings in animation help viewers identify the boundaries between the human and the nonhuman. First, I study defamiliarizing effects in hand-drawn animation. I show that technical elements besides digital technology can elicit discomfort in the presence of animated characters, including masks and distorted facial traits. Then, I briefly survey the literary origins of the uncanny and the conditions that foster eeriness in CG animation. Knowing about these conditions, the designers of *The Curious Case of Benjamin Button* (David Fincher, 2008), a film that depends heavily on CG technology, created a synthespian that is easily mistaken for a human. Although most films that replace live actors with CG characters aspire to suppress the presence of disquieting effects, I argue that these feelings may be desirable in some animations and video games. Uneasiness can amplify the spectators' anxieties toward bodily alterations, elicit their empathy for synthetic life forms, or even encourage creative "thinkering" about the consequences of toying with nature. Following this premise, the last section examines the process of engagement with CG characters in *Malice@Doll* (Keitarô, Motonaga, 2001). While uncanny effects are undeniably disturbing in this computer-generated animation, the process of defamiliarizing the human, imaginary transpositions with robotic gazes, and cross-modal effects provide opportunities to embrace the perspective of those who are different, including posthumans.

Chapter 6, "Algorithmic Couplings in Video Games," explores the ways that *BioShock* and *BioShock 2* draw on the players' modes of embodiment to convey their rhetoric. The scenarios they present encourage enactive forms of understanding of contrasted perspectives on optimized eugenics, a technique developed in Rapture to design the perfect soldier. The combination of somatic effects and what video game scholar Ian Bogost terms "procedural rhetoric" incites players to reflect on the dangers of genetic manipulation. The players develop new physical skills and cognitive abilities to resolve complex puzzles and become genetically enhanced warriors. In doing so, the games draw the players' attention on the effects of technology on their physical and moral agencies. Multiple techniques are used to create strong ties between the player and the avatar with the goal to persuade the player to follow Rapture's overarching ideology. First, the perceptual bonding with an avatar's perspective is an effective strategy to win the player's allegiance. Second, the progressive mastery of the interface contributes to the adaptation of the player's body schema. Indeed, juggling between weapons and fighting bloodthirsty creatures can become a second nature for the player. Third, underlying algorithms assert the video games' procedural rhetoric and "allegorize political power" in an informatic age.[53] By catalyzing a body-technology symbiosis between the player and a cyborg, the games suggest that life and the body are programmable entities. As players transform into genetically augmented warriors, they alternately embrace and then reject Rapture's posthuman ethics.

Chapter 7, "Becoming-Avatar," interrogates our relationships with online avatars. Scholars such as N. Katherine Hayles and Sherry Turkle have studied the effects of computers on our definitions of the self and reality with concepts such as the multiplicity of the self and the Computational Universe. Likewise, stories of avatars in literature and films have imagined ways to take control of our bodies and minds. Catching up with fiction, the advent of the Internet and the development of synthetic worlds have challenged views of the unitary self. As we become closer with our avatars, we begin to question unitary conceptions of personhood, the organic origins of life, the boundaries of reality, and other aspects of the liberal humanist view of the self. Computers and synthetic worlds have also contributed to shape a view of ourselves as programed beings. Residents of synthetic worlds, such as *Second Life* and *High Fidelity*, customize the appearance of their virtual selfhood and program their digital environment bit by bit, which conjures up elements of postvitalism—the idea that life can be reduced to organized arrays of computer code. Some *Second Life* residents can also multiply their virtual selves by experimenting with identity tourism. They can acquire new sensorimotor skills by learning to navigate between the real and the virtual. Moreover, residents adapt their emotional palette by expressing a modulated version of their feelings using computer interfaces. The last part of the chapter discusses how people suffering from partial motor disability after a stroke can use virtual reality-based therapies for sensorimotor rehabilitation.

Affect and Embodied Meaning in Animation investigates whether the symbiotic couplings between the spectators' bodies and the animated world can alter the ways in which spectators understand the body's boundaries and conceptions of life. With this book, I hope to demonstrate that animated media not only tell stories about metamorphic bodies, but also suffuse through the affective membranes of the embodied spectators. The spectators' affective responses to shape-shifting figures serve to incorporate the human body into a larger system of signification about technological extensions and the moving target that is the liberal humanist subject.

Notes

1 Other monographs investigate affects and embodiment in animation, including Jenkins, *Special Affects*; Richmond, *Cinema's Bodily Illusions*; Crafton, *Shadow of a Mouse*; and Wood, *Digital Encounters*.
2 The topic of metamorphosis in animation is widespread. Michael Barrier examines cartoon metamorphoses in *Hollywood Cartoons*. Sergei Eisenstein writes on the plasmaticness of Disney's animated characters in Eisenstein, *Eisenstein on Disney*. Contributors explore the topic of morphing in Vivian Sobchack's edited volume *Meta-Morphing*. On robots, cyborgs, and other metamorphic figures in *anime*, see Bolton et al., eds, *Robot Ghosts and Wired Dreams*; Brown, *Tokyo Cyberpunk*; Lamarre, *The Anime Machine*; and Napier, *Anime from Akira to Howl's Moving Castle*.
3 On the distinction between the body schema and the body image, see Tiemersma, *Body Schema and Body Image*. On the body image in culture, see Weiss, *Body Image*.
4 *BioShock* is followed by two other titles in the same series, *BioShock 2* (2010) and *BioShock Infinite* (2013).
5 Apparatus here simply refers to the screen and the technologies that produce the moving images.
6 For overviews on the phenomenon of change blindness, see Clark, *Supersizing the Mind*, 141–146 and Noë, *Action in Perception*, 51–53.
7 On the different levels of meaningfulness, see Persson, *Understanding Cinema*, 26–34 and Chapter 1.
8 Kevin O'Regan had originally conducted this demonstration. For a more detailed account of this experiment, see Noë, *Action in Perception*, 51–52.
9 Noë, *Action in Perception*, 52.
10 On the world as an external memory, see Clark, *Supersizing the Mind*, 76–81.
11 O'Regan et al., "Change-Blindness," 34.
12 Bergson, *Matter and Memory*, 28.
13 Deleuze, *Cinema 1*, 68 (emphasis in the original).
14 For examples on phenomenological perspectives in cinema, see Sobchack, *The Address of the Eye* and Barker, *The Tactile Eye*.
15 O'Regan et al., "Change-Blindness," 34. For a sample of experiments performed under alternate conditions, see Blackmore et al., "Is the Richness."
16 Cavell, *World Viewed*, 104.
17 Crary, *Techniques of the Observer*, 69.
18 Schivelbusch, *The Railway Journey*, 31.
19 Richmond, *Cinema's Bodily Illusions*, 164 (emphasis in the original).
20 On technical ensembles, see Simondon, *Du mode d'existence des objets*.
21 On Félix Guattari's theory based on machines rather than structures, see "Machinic Heterogenesis." On the concepts of assemblages and affects in relation to machines, see also Deleuze and Guattari, *A Thousand Plateaus*.
22 Lamarre, *The Anime Machine*, xxvii.

23 Merleau-Ponty, *Phenomenology of Perception*, 165–166.
24 Hansen, *Bodies in Code*, 100.
25 Hansen, *Bodies in Code*, 99.
26 Clark, "Re-Inventing Ourselves," 278. For a definition of "soft self" see Clark, *Natural-Born Cyborgs*, 138.
27 Clark, "Re-Inventing Ourselves," 265.
28 Some books explore posthuman forms of embodiment in animation. For examples, see Lunning, ed., *Mechademia 3*; Brown, *Tokyo Cyberpunk*; and Napier, *Anime from Akira to Howl's Moving Castle*. Other scholars have analyzed the signification of bodily transformations on-screen without considering them under the framework of posthumanism. For instance, Brian Massumi, Carl Plantinga, and Torben Grodal have studied the role of affect in shaping viewers' interpretations. Scholars Thomas Lamarre, Lev Manovich, and Alexander Galloway investigate the semiotics of animated media in relation with critical theory.
29 For general reviews of cognitive approaches in Film Studies, see Bordwell, "A Case for Cognitivism"; Plantinga, "Cognitive Film Theory"; and Smith, "Other Cognitivisms," in *Film Structure*.
30 For monographs on wide computational explanations for extended cognition, see McClamrock, *Existential Cognition*; Clark, *Being There*; and Wilson, *Boundaries of the Mind*. Among those who have endorsed dynamical systems explanations for the extended approach to the mind we find Port and Gelder, *Mind as Motion*; Kelso, *Dynamic Patterns*; and Thompson, *Mind in Life*. For reviews on embodied cognition, see Silberstein and Chemero, "Complexity" and Wilson, "Six Views."
31 For a range of views in film studies within the field of embodied cognition, see Coëgnarts and Kravanja, eds., *Embodied Cognition and Cinema* and Fahlenbrach, ed., *Embodied Metaphors*. On embodied cognition and cinema, see also Buckland, *The Cognitive Semiotics of Film*; Coëgnarts and Kravanja, "Embodied Visual Meaning"; and Forceville and Jeulink, "The Flesh and Blood."
32 On the definition of image schemas, see Lakoff and Johnson, *Philosophy in the Flesh*, 16–44.
33 Forceville and Jeulink, "The Flesh and Blood."
34 Coëgnarts and Kravanja, "Embodied Visual Meaning."
35 Freedberg and Gallese, "Motion, Emotion and Empathy in Esthetic Experience."
36 On empathy in cinema, see Barker, *The Tactile Eye*; Neill, "Empathy and (Film) Fiction"; Plantinga, *Moving Viewers*; and Zillmann, "Empathy."
37 Thompson, *Mind in Life*, 393. On motor mimicry and sensorimotor couplings, see Chapter 13 in Thompson, *Mind in Life*, Chapters 8 and 9 in Rosenblum, *See What I'm Saying*; and Bavelas et al., "Motor Mimicry as Primitive Empathy." On the phenomenon of emotional contagion, see Hatfield et al., *Emotional Contagion*; Rosenblum, *See What I'm Saying*; and Brennan, *The Transmission of Affect*.
38 Thompson, *Mind in Life*, 393.
39 Thompson, *Mind in Life*, 395.
40 On character simulation, see Chapter 8 in Grodal, *Embodied Visions*.
41 Many monographs present haptic theories of spectatorship or propose phenomenological approaches, including Sobchack, *Carnal Thoughts*; Sobchack, *The Address of the Eye*; Grodal, *Embodied Visions*; Shaviro, *The Cinematic Body*; Barker, *The Tactile Eye*; and Hansen, *New Philosophy for New Media*. A few monographs also examine affect in video games, including Perron and Schröter, eds., *Video Games and the Mind*.

42 See, for instance, Arnheim, *Film as Art*; Arnheim, *Visual Thinking*; Arnheim, *Art and Visual Perception*; and Balázs, *Theory of the Film*.
43 Elsaesser and Hagener, *Film Theory*, 110.
44 Sobchack, *Carnal Thoughts*, 55.
45 On the potential risks associated with animation specificity, such as claims that animation is superior to live-action films, see Darley, "Bones of Contention."
46 Bordwell, *Making Meaning*, 3.
47 For a summary of different approaches to narratology, see Persson, "Character Psychology and Mental Attribution," in *Understanding Cinema*; Thomas Elsaesser and Hagener, *Film Theory*, 42–45; Bordwell, *Narration in the Fiction Film*; and Branigan, *Narrative Comprehension and Film*.
48 On the different kinds of perceptual illusions in cinema, see Richmond, *Cinema's Bodily Illusions*.
49 On cyberpunk animation, see Brown, *Tokyo Cyber-Punk*.
50 Various monographs focus on emotions in cinema and draw on the psychology of emotions, including Plantinga, *Moving Viewers*; Tan, *Emotion and the Structure of Narrative Film*; Grodal, *Embodied Visions*; and Plantinga and Smith, eds., *Passionate Views*.
51 Deleuze and Guattari, *A Thousand Plateaus*.
52 *Les Triplettes de Belleville*.
53 Galloway, *Gaming*, 90.

1 The Limits of Human Perception

Introduction

Originally called the kineograph, the flip book was an optical novelty that received a patent in 1868. Early animator Winsor McCay claimed that the "flippers" that his son used as toys inspired him to create "cartoon movies."[1] Turning the pages of a flip book has always captivated me. I can turn the pages one by one and meditate on each photograph of a horse. Then, when I flip through the same images, the horse becomes alive and starts running. Like animation, the flip book produces the illusion of continuous motion when the series of images are presented at an accelerated rate. Because I manually turn the pages of the book, the process foregrounds the contribution of my body in giving the impression of continuous motion in the absence of actual movement.

The thaumatrope, another fascinating optical toy, started to gain some popularity around 1824. A friend once gave me a business card in the shape of a thaumatrope. A bird was drawn on one side of the disk and there was a cage on the other side. When I rapidly flipped the two sides back and forth, the thaumatrope produced the appearance of the bird imprisoned in the cage, a phenomenon attributed to the persistence of vision.[2] Unlike animations that create smooth, continuous movement, the thaumatrope and the flip book produce jerky motion. These devices also accentuate the principles of action in perception. I need to flip the pages of the flip book or spin the thaumatrope with my hands; otherwise, nothing moves. Because we can adjust the rate of presentation, these two devices stress the embodied nature of our perception of animated images.

Optical toys underscore the interrelated operations of the beholder's visual system and the device. Because the observers can alter the rate of display and thereby modify their perceptual experience at will, they can also identify the threshold at which the illusion of continuous motion appears or disappears. When beholders reach this threshold, they actively contribute to the transformation of the system to a state that enables them to see an object moving in the absence of actual motion.

This chapter focuses on our body-mind interactions with moving images. Drawing on Andy Clark's extended approach to the mind, the first section envisages animated figures as special tools that can expand our perceptual reach. In suggesting that the mind does not stop at the limit of our skin, Clark disputes the rigidity of the boundaries setting apart human cognizers from their animated tools. Then, I further examine the idea that we conceptualize the way we do, thanks to the body that we have. The experience of standing upright, the warmth of intimate encounters, or simply coming in and out of a room are patterns of sensorimotor interactions with our environment that help us conceptualize the actual world and the fictive worlds of animation. As the conceptual metaphor theory (CMT) suggests, our embodied mind enables the empathic exchanges between object and subject that we find in animation. The final section presents examples of the perceptual entanglements that arise between the viewer and the animation apparatus. As for the flip book and the thaumatrope, some animations compel spectators to recognize the embodied nature of human perception. One of the main themes of *The Cabinet of Jan Švankmajer* (Stephen Quay and Timothy Quay, 1984) is the production of optical illusions in animation. Another example, *Spheres* (René Jodoin and Norman McLaren, 1969), highlights the gestalt laws of visual perception. With the help of these case studies, I argue that we become animated when the mechanisms of mediation not only show that perception in animation is embodied but also make us realize the limits of human perception.

Animated Tools That Extend the Mind

Natural-Born Cyborg Viewers

As Alva Noë argues in *Varieties of Presence*, models "are tools for thinking about or investigating or perceiving something other than the model itself."[3] Animated bodies are visual models that can stand for people or grant us access to imaginary spaces. In order to be appropriate models, animated figures must be perceivable and understandable. On the one hand, as *Homo sapiens*, our perceptual systems enable us to distinguish between real objects, memories, live-action films, and animations. On the other hand, the animation apparatus is understandable because it follows a set of relatively well-established audiovisual conventions, as the field of semiotics demonstrates.

Animated figures are special models that can functionally extend us. According to Clark, we are "natural-born cyborgs" because the neural physiology of *Homo sapiens* is preadapted to be transformed by whatever technological prostheses we may develop.[4] We are "cyborgs not in the merely superficial sense of combining flesh and wires but in the more profound sense of being human-technology symbionts: thinking and reasoning systems whose minds and selves are spread across biological brain and nonbiological circuitry."[5] With his functional approach to cognition,

Clark does not want to characterize the cognitive solely on the basis of underlying causal processes because, according to him, the study of mind needs "to embrace a variety of different explanatory paradigms whose point of convergence lies in the production of intelligent behavior."[6]

Clark's extended model rejects the idea that brain equals mind and that mind is essentially inner. Clark's view on human cognizing involves feedback loops between the brain, the body, and the world.[7] Noë's strong enactive approach also supports the view that cognition does not happen in the head.[8] A crucial difference between the two models concerns the definition of "embodiment." According to Noë, human experience, and perception in particular, is body-dependent. Put succinctly, different bodily configurations yield different experiences. In contrast, Clark believes that there is no reason for experiences to be dissimilar when a different system processes a function that the brain usually performs. Clark's approach focuses less on the qualitative aspects of the perceptual experience, or the efficiency of the replaced components, than on the functional aspects performed by the new perceptual organization. In other words, a human body is not required for cognition to happen.

Clark distinguishes three grades of embodiment.[9] A "merely" embodied creature or robot is able to engage in a closed-loop interaction with the world but requires constant micromanaged control and uses pure reason to implement practical solutions. A "basically" embodied creature or robot actively exploits properties such as sensor placement and enhanced morphology. Both features allow for increasingly fluent forms of action selection and control. A "profoundly" embodied agent is one that can continuously reorganize the agent-world boundary by incorporating new resources.[10] Primates and humans are "profoundly embodied agents" because they are biologically configured in ways that allow "literal (and repeated) episodes of sensory re-calibration, of bodily reconfiguration and of mental extension."[11] They can renegotiate their boundaries and reconfigure their body schema when they grow or lose a limb, as opposed to current types of robots.

The spreading of the cognitive processes across resources can be achieved through the reassemblage of a variety of bodily controls in ways that promote fluid and efficient problem-solving methods and adaptive responses. For example, a specific bodily reconfiguration could apply the principles of biomechanics to harness the organism's morphology for its own advantage.[12] Instead of building a robot that micromanages every detail of its locomotion, the details of its embodiment, such as the use of springs to enhance running, "may take over some of the work that would otherwise need to be done by the brain or the neural network controller."[13] An organism may also choose to simplify a cognitive task by exploiting its immediate environmental structure.[14] For instance, laying out the ingredients necessary to make a recipe in the order that one will need them can simplify the cognitive load.

Clark's goal-oriented approach takes the perspective that cognitive processes are integrated into a larger system of information processing. Many functional organizations can lead to intelligent behavior, and they are not limited to brain circuitry. Therefore, for the purpose of identifying the material vehicles of cognitive states and processes, we should (normatively speaking) ignore the old metabolic boundaries of skin and skull and attend to the computational and functional organization of the problem-solving whole. From this perspective, parts of the overall perceptual processes can be distributed outside of the biological organism.

Because the brain performs a lot of tasks automatically, including many of the operations involved in solving a complex problem, Clark argues that scientists can physically extend the human mind without impacting the conscious agent. Possible cyborg-like extensions are not limited to "basic physiological homeostasis, but limb control, trajectory planning, and major components of the reasoning process itself may themselves be farmed out."[15] Although farming out reasoning processes appears very difficult to achieve, considering the complexity of the neural network, the possibility of physically extending the mind remains conceptually possible; certain processes could be bioengineered or even relayed to a computer.

Yet, these alternative implementations or brain "rewiring" may lead to different experiences. I am inclined to share Noë's doubts that dissimilar bodies can undergo qualitatively similar experiences.[16] For instance, I can place two different types of lenses in front of my eyes to look at the same movie. A sharply focused lens and a softly focused lens would enable me to see and recognize a close-up of Grace Kelly. Although from a functional perspective, both lenses allow me to understand the story, the experience is qualitatively different. In cinema, the soft focus lens produces a more glamorous and flattering image of a star, which thereby modifies one's appreciation of the character. If our visual system could not detect the difference, the effect would necessarily be lost. From the perspective of Film and Animation Studies, the conditions of production are important and "embodiment" matters and signifies.

New Systemic Wholes

Animated figures can be instrumental in the accomplishment of a cognitive process. Video game players sometimes integrate the physical manipulation of animated objects into their reasoning process to improve their strategy. *Tetris* players, for example, have to fill up rows with rotating zoids. Once a row has been filled up, it disappears from the display. The goal of the game is to make sure that no zoid exceeds the upper limit of the display, which can contain multiple rows. However, sometimes, expert players wait before filling a row up, and choose instead to physically rotate a zoid. For these players, previewing a rotating zoid can increase their mental capacity and enhance their performance.[17] This type of strategy, which is called an epistemic action, makes "mental computation easier, faster or more reliable."[18] Epistemic actions are opposed to pragmatic actions, which are oriented toward immediate results. Expert players do not solely use their minds to elaborate their strategies, but also rely on an effective combination of body, mind, and environment to cognitively extend their functional organization and improve their score.

In addition, the brain's plasticity enables neural reconfigurations that increase mental and physical skills. It is the brain's "plasticity that makes humans (but not dogs, cats or elephants) *natural-born cyborgs*: beings primed by Mother Nature to annex wave upon wave of external elements and structures as part and parcel of their own extended minds."[19] According to Clark, what is called "human perception" is a brain-bound model that happens to be an accident of the history of our technological development rather than an innate effect of our physiology. Thanks to our brain's plasticity, our embodied engagement with technology can reconfigure our body schema—the internalized map of all the movements that we can perform.

With his extended approach to the mind, Clark argues that the use of a tool can extend the brain's area allocated for the limb that handles the tool, which leads him to consider the combination of limb and tool as new and larger systemic wholes, not limited by flesh and skull.[20] Technological extensions can contribute to the creation of new systemic wholes, as the performance artist Stelarc has demonstrated with his "third hand," a device controlled by his brain via mental commands to muscles in his legs and abdomen. According to Stelarc, after some time, moving his "third hand" felt similar to moving his biological arms.[21] In this case, as when one becomes an expert violin player or when one drives a car, the tool had become "transparent" in use.

Neuroscientists have also demonstrated that the use of a tool for a specific goal can recalibrate plastic neural resources to reflect the new sensorimotor opportunities provided by the instrument. In one example, Angelo Maravita and Atsushi Iriki recorded the activity of bimodal neurons in the intraparietal cortex of Japanese macaques, while they were learning to manipulate a rake to reach for food. These bimodal neurons responded both to somatosensory information from a given bodily region, which corresponds to the somatosensory receptive field (sRF), and to visual information from the scene, which corresponds to the visual receptive field (vRF).[22] After five minutes of using the rake, the vRF of some of the bimodal neurons expanded to include the entire length of the rake in addition to the hand. According to Marivata and Iriki, such "vRF expansions may constitute the neural substrate of use-dependent assimilation of the tool into the body schema."[23] Interestingly, any "expansion of the vRF only followed active, intentional usage of the tool, not its mere grasping by the hand."[24] When a macaque handles a tool to achieve a goal, the whole system under examination temporarily includes the macaque and the tool.

Other scientific experiments confirm that the plastic reorganization of the brain can occur when an agent operates screen-mediated tools.[25] For instance, neuroscientists Jose Carmena and his colleagues recorded a monkey's neural activity across multiple cortical areas while it learned to use a joystick to move a cursor across a computer screen for rewards.[26] Then, they disconnected the joystick. Instead, the monkey was taught to use its neural activity—interpreted by a connected computer—to move the cursor. Subsequently, the same neural activity was used to control a remote robotic arm, whose actual motions were converted into on-screen cursor movements. The monkey had to learn to factor in the time delays created by the robotic arm.

In this case, the arm's motion, translated into on-screen cursor movements, was incorporated into the monkey's bodily structure. The researchers noticed significant changes in the response profiles of the frontoparietal neurons after the use of the brain-machine interface (BMI). The researchers noted that

> the gradual increase in behavioral performance during brain control of the BMI emerged as a consequence of a plastic reorganization whose main outcome was the assimilation of the dynamics of an artificial actuator into the physiological properties of frontoparietal neurons.[27]

In other words, this experiment demonstrates the plasticity of the monkey's brain and shows the possibility of improving mental skills by interacting with a computer-mediated interface.

Another attempt at extending the mind and the body's reach, and thereby creating a new systemic whole, concerns the neuroheadsets developed by EMOTIV™. This invention comprises a brain-computer interface that can decode brainwaves to control remote digital devices and digital media.[28] As demonstrated in Chapter 7, the possibility to interface with this computer system reflects a true incorporation of a tool into the body schema rather than its mere use.[29] In summary, both the neural plasticity of the brain and Clark's functional approach to cognition suggest that the human perceptual apparatus is already "posthuman."

Before Clark, Marshall McLuhan had investigated the impacts of technological extensions on human agency. In *Understanding Media*, McLuhan claims that we use electronic media to "translate more and more of ourselves into other forms of expression that exceed ourselves."[30] Indeed, powerful telescopes extend our reach into the cosmos, microscopes can touch the molecular realm and write with atoms, and the Internet distributes sparks of our consciousness at increasing speed. In addition, McLuhan mentions that by

> putting our physical bodies inside our extended nervous systems, by means of electric media, we set up a dynamic by which all previous technologies that are mere extensions of hands and feet and teeth and bodily heat controls—all such extensions of our bodies, including cities—will be translated into information systems.[31]

Although these translations and extensions imply a modification of the structure of our societies, the ways in which animated media can alter our minds are overlooked.

These approaches toward distributed cognition illustrate how animated tools may extend the spectator's mind. As seen in the examples earlier, the mental control of an animated cursor on a computer interface or the EMOTIV™ neuroheadsets can spread the cognitive load. Similar to canes or automobiles, animated figures can alter our body schema.

Mirror Neurons

The presence of mirroring mechanisms may also modulate the permeability of the animated interface. The discovery of the presence of a mirror neuron system in the human ventral premotor cortex and posterior parietal cortex reveals that understanding is a form of corporeal simulation.[32] The mirror neuron system may explain the apparently innate mimetic ability of infants. From birth, babies quickly learn to communicate with their bodies. Andrew Meltzoff and M. Keith Moore observed that "infants, even those less than an hour old, [can] imitate the adult gestures of tongue protrusion, mouth opening, lip protrusion, and finger movement."[33] These innate mechanisms intimate connections between the witnessed bodily acts of others and an internal sense of what we should do to imitate them. It appears that what "we see gesturally enacted in others, we can reproduce in ourselves, via our ability to make cross-modal connections and to realize patterns in our proprioception (our felt sense of our bodily posture and our joint and limb positions)."[34]

The body of studies on the mirror neuron system shows that we understand the behavior of others partly by imitation and simulation, even in the absence of any overt action on the part of the observer. When the mirror neuron system "is activated, the observation of an action—in particular, a goal-oriented action—leads to the activation of the same neural networks that are active during its execution."[35] Further summarizing the relation between mirror neurons and embodied understanding, neuroscientist Marco Iacoboni notes,

> [Y]ou understand my action because you have in your brain a template for that action based on your own movements. When you see me pull my arm back, as if to throw the ball, you also have in your

> brain a copy of what I am doing and it helps you understand my goal. Because of mirror neurons, you can read my intentions. You know what I am going to do next.[36]

Neuronal mirroring also indicates that embodied engagement is multimodal. In an experiment, neuroscientists showed that

> F5 mirror neurons in monkeys [...] discharged consistently under the following four conditions: (1) when the monkey *performed* a noisy action, such as breaking a peanut apart or tearing a sheet of paper; (2) when the monkey *saw* these same actions performed by someone else; (3) when the monkey *heard* these noisy actions being performed; and (4) when the monkey both *saw and heard* the same actions.[37]

Brain imaging experiments have identified the presence of these neurons in the human brain. Applied to cinema, these findings suggest that our visual and auditory experiences of an object depicted in a film or a video game can call other senses into play.

Although, as Iacoboni argues, mirror neurons work best in real life, when people are face to face, there is also evidence that still images, videos, and virtual reality can activate them.[38] The observation of actions represented in still images has led to action simulation in the brains of human observers. For instance, the "observation of pictures of a hand reaching to grasp an object or firmly grasping it activates the motor representation of grasping in the observer's brain."[39] The observation of graspable objects, such as a cup with a handle, activates both the visual areas of the brain and the motor areas that control object-related actions such as grasping, even when the observer is immobile. "Canonical neurons" are the neurons activated by both the visual features of a graspable cup and the action of grasping the cup.[40] As Freedberg and Gallese claim, the mechanism of motor simulation activated by the presence of canonical neurons, "is likely to be a crucial component of the esthetic experience of objects in art works: even a still-life can be 'animated' by the embodied simulation it evokes in the observer's brain."[41]

Accordingly, some sequences in the animated film *WALL-E* (Andrew Stanton, 2008) most probably stimulate the viewer's mirror neuron system. The beginning of the story depicts the learning experience of a sentient robot called WALL-E. Left alone on a polluted Earth after all humans have departed in a spaceship, the robot learns human behavior by repeatedly watching the movie *Hello, Dolly!* (Gene Kelly, 1969). One evening, after a day of collecting garbage, WALL-E plays the sequence where Cornelius and Irene sing a romantic song in the park after a dinner together. The two lovers join hands, and we see a close-up of their arms.

The image is reflected in WALL-E's eyes. He watches the sequence again and imitates the couple's gesture by holding one of his mechanical claws with the other. Later, WALL-E meets the search robot EVE. Longing for companionship and romance, WALL-E holds her "hand" like the man and the woman he saw in the film. In this self-reflexive sequence, the process of learning by imitation applies both to WALL-E and the spectators. The close-up of the couple joining hands and WALL-E's imitating gesture evoke embodied simulations, since what is important in the mirroring mechanism is that the action is goal-oriented, not that the gesture is performed by a biological actor.[42]

The presence of the mirror neuron system may also explain the feelings of empathy for another on the basis of bodily similarity. Providing a supporting example of empathetic coupling, Iacoboni says,

> [I]f you see me choke up, in emotional distress from striking out at home plate, mirror neurons in your brain simulate my distress. You automatically have empathy for me. You know how I feel because you literally feel what I am feeling.[43]

Mirroring phenomena also occur when we witness someone in pain. For instance, when a patient receives an unpleasant stimulus to his or her hand, neurons in the anterior cingulate cortex are activated. The same neurons fire when the patient watches a pinprick applied to the examiner's hand.[44] The perception of emotions in others also activates neural mechanisms that play a key role in simulating. People with lesions to regions that support these mechanisms have trouble judging other people's emotional states. For instance, damage "restricted to somatosensory cortex impairs the ability to recognize complex blends of emotions in facial expressions, and there is an association between the impaired somatic sensation of one's own body and the impaired ability to judge other people's emotions."[45] The activation of the mirror neuron system at the sight of emotional responses or actions performed in moving pictures has inspired a series of studies about the contribution of these neural mechanisms to the esthetic experience, which is the topic of the next section.

Extending Our Affective Boundaries

Scientific research has established correlations between the observation of actions in artworks and the mirroring processes happening at the level of our neurons. This phenomenon would suggest that our empathy for others in pictures is deeply rooted in our embodied minds. Furthermore, the discovery of these mirroring effects may partly explain how abstract concepts in moving images are transferred via embodied mechanisms to spectators.

Embodied Simulations

Sisyphus (Marcell Jankovics, 1974) appeals to embodied simulations to communicate the struggle of its protagonist. In this animation, a naked man rolls a very large boulder up a hill. The man is depicted with a gestural drawing on a white background. The large strokes of black ink emphasize the contours of his muscles as he pushes the rock with his arms, lifts it, and then leans on it to prevent it from rolling back down the hill. The varying width of the trembling lines, which changes from large to thin, expresses the alternation between pushes and rests performed by the muscles in the visual domain. The heavy breathing on the soundtrack stresses the man's exhaustion. As the slope gets steeper, the man's body is shown off balance and canted on the side. The muscular body, the large rock, and the long stroke of a pen standing in for the upslope separate the frame diagonally, further increasing the tension in the image (see Figure 1.1). As I watched the man pushing the rock, the multimodal combination of tensed muscles, breathing sound, and graphical tension aroused a vicarious experience of the man's weariness. It replayed in my mind similar situations where I had to push something very heavy, thereby causing the muscles in my calves and biceps to feel warmer.

Numerous studies in the field of "neuroesthetics" investigate the nature of the esthetic experience by drawing on findings in the neurosciences.[46] Freedberg and Gallese were among the first researchers to examine the neural mechanisms that underpin the empathetic power of images.[47] The mirror neuron system, according to them, could provide elements of justification for the proprioceptive sensations and mimetic

Figure 1.1 Muscular man pushing a rock uphill. *Sisyphus* (Marcell Jankovics, 1974).

reactions elicited by the sight of actions represented within a work of art. In some cases, proprioceptive impressions could provide a sense of our body's internal musculature and posture without having to look at our limbs or touch them.

Freedberg and Gallese maintain that the observation of certain gestures portrayed in pictures activates some muscles or induces forms of inward imitation. They distinguish two broad categories of feelings that contribute to empathetic engagement. On the one hand, the spectators may recognize and understand the emotional state of the represented other. On the other hand, the spectators may experience an embodied simulation, which is "a sense of inward imitation of the observed actions of others in pictures and sculptures."[48] These sensations are caused by figures that are in a state of intense struggle or horrific representations of wounded bodies. In these cases, "physical empathy easily transmutes into a feeling of empathy for the emotional consequences of the ways in which the body is damaged or mutilated."[49] This transmutation suggests that inward imitations and feelings of empathy are closely interconnected. In addition, implied gesture, such as the marks left by the painter on the canvas, can elicit physical responses in the spectators and encourage their empathetic engagement with the work.

While the discovery of mirror neurons is relatively recent, research on embodied simulation in the presence of artworks was already conducted in the 19th century. In his doctoral thesis published in 1873, Robert Vischer was one of the first to call attention to the physical responses evoked by the observation of particular forms in paintings.[50] We are also indebted to other scholars that followed Vischer's path, including Heinrich Wölfflin, Aby Warburg, Bernard Berenson, and Theodor Lipps.[51] Certain represented features, such as flowing draperies, can inspire a sense of imitating the movement or action seen, or implied, in the work. The latter scholars claim that the feeling of physical involvement can enhance the beholder's emotional response to a painting.[52]

Similarly, Freedberg and Gallese mention that observers who were looking at Michelangelo's *Prisoners* felt the "activation of the muscles that appear to be activated within the sculpture itself, as if in perfect consonance with Michelangelo's intention of showing his figures struggle to free themselves from their material matrix."[53] In addition, the horrific representation of punctured flesh in Goya's *Los desastres de la guerra* (*The Disasters of War*) caused pain in some viewers. The viewers' "physical responses seem to be located in precisely those parts of the body that are threatened, pressured, constrained or destabilized."[54] The mirror neuron system could explain why the sensations are often felt in the same region as the one that is afflicted.

The forms of simulation causing inward feelings of motion, muscular pain, or muscular sensations that are congruent with the action depicted are called muscular empathy. Not limited to muscular effort, this type of embodied simulation can also be associated with posture and physical movement.[55] Muscular empathy can occur, for instance, when viewers feel that they are traveling through the cinematic space, inwardly imitating the movements depicted on the screen. This conscious phenomenon is informed by both automatic responses—physical responses, such as the ones produced by motor mimicry—and proprioceptive feelings, such as the inward contortions that echo an actor's gestures. In addition to muscular pain, muscular empathy can produce a range of palpable affects, such as visceral discomfort and vertigo.

James Elkins refers to the more general term "sensation" to describe the effects of what he calls "psychomania." This word "denotes sensation produced by the sight of *bodily motion*: either in contorted faces (as in the practice of physiognomy) or in bodies that are twisted and turned about themselves (as in the practice of contrapposto)."[56] In the mid-15th century, visual artists had a renewed interest for the contrapposto. This practice facilitated the exploration of the possible motions of the human form in art. In *De pictura* (*On Painting*), Leon Battista Alberti distinguishes a type of contrapposto that evokes the balancing body found in dance and the one that expresses the displeasure of the body contorting itself. An example of dancing contrapposto, Donatello's bronze *David* in the Museo Nazionale del Bargello in Florence, demonstrates the balancing effort needed when one leg bears the figure's weight. The pose appears slightly uncomfortable, as the muscles on one side of the body appear tensed and the muscles on the other side are relaxed. The young man's trunk is delicately bent toward the leg that supports the weight, while the pose is balanced on the opposite side with the knee bending forward and the arm forming an arch on the hip. Filippo Brunelleschi provides an example of the second type of contrapposto in his competition panel of the Sacrifice of Isaac in Bargello, Florence. Isaac's torso is completely twisted on itself and distorted by pain, as his father is holding his neck with one hand and a knife is touching his throat. The tension in the pose and Isaac's contorted body reflect the intense mental struggle of the father who is about to sacrifice his only son and the physical distress experienced by the son. The expressive vocabulary of the body in motion can provide to the spectator a range of embodied simulations that are congruent with the mental states of the figures or support the mood of a scene.

Animation and video games exploit various forms of psychomania. They often showcase the balanced and twisted contrapposti, as the cartoonal body can effortlessly turn against itself and perform contortions. Each warrior in the *SoulCalibur* series of video games features a list of fighting movements that expand the catalogue of typical human gestures. When playing *SoulCalibur IV* in training mode, you can pick one character from the roster and explore the series of throws and attacks that are particular for its set of skills. The cyborg Voldo is a deft contortionist and an accomplished martial artist. When waiting for the player to command the next series of movements, Voldo deploys very ample gestures. His two arms repeatedly revolve away from his body and his spine is arched. This elegant posture, which makes Voldo look unsteady, recalls the balancing body of the dancing contrapposto. While his stationary walking is stylish, the sharp jamadhar katars he holds in his hands, the spikes coming out from his outfit, and the prosthetic lenses on his headset make him look quite menacing.

In contrast to Voldo's graceful dancing skills, his attacks exhibit impressive movements recalling crawling insects. With the Catacomb Throw move, Voldo jumps on the shoulders of his enemy and squeezes his or her neck between his legs. He then flips his opponent over him and throws him or her on the ground. At the end of the movement, Voldo finds himself in the Crawling Mantis posture, a type of back bridge that allows him to scurry away from his opponent using his arms and legs like a mantis. When I first observed the Catacomb Throw, I had to play back this unusual move multiple times until I could make sense of the series of gestures that were quickly unfolding. The physical contortions and curls he performed on the screen evoked inward contortions, as I tried to replay them in my head from the character's perspective. Perceived as a freak, Voldo's performances of both the balanced and twisted contrapposti can symbolize his hybrid nature. This character embodies the duality between good and evil played out in this video game. Voldo successfully wrestles opposites, namely grace and strength, human and cyborg, biped and insect, and dancing and contorting.

Similarly, *Howl's Moving Castle* features examples of contrapposti in the scene where Sophie and the Witch of the Waste arrive at the bottom of the immense staircase in front of the palace. On both sides of the staircase, soldiers in a row hold a rifle vertically while standing upright, which conveys authority and power. On the ground level, two large lions made out of stone are placed on the left and right sides of the stairs. Each lion has one of its legs standing on a large ball, while the other leg supports the weight of the body, thus representing a version of the balanced contrapposto. Numerous golden statues placed around the front of the palace present variants of the dancing contrapposto. Their relaxed postures contrast with the assertive and rigid stances of the soldiers. Alternatively, after being cursed by Madam Suliman, the wobbly movements of the two blob men carrying the Witch of the Waste recall the twisted version of the contrapposto. Also going to the palace, the elderly Sophie must climb the impressive staircase. Because of her old age, the bending and twisting of her body convey an impression of unbalance and inward discomfort, which are hallmarks of the twisted contrapposto. In the sequence, she bends her body forward to hold a heavy dog in her arms and painfully twists her body on the side to climb each stair. Her whining complements the visual depiction of her physical distress.

Embodied simulations, as mentioned earlier, can be partly explained by the presence of mirroring mechanisms in our brains. The inward imitation of movements on the screen can support the rhetoric of animated narratives. The display of muscles in *Sisyphus* reminds viewers of the struggles inherently associated with being human. The sequence analyzed from *Howl's Moving Castle* featured balanced and twisted examples of the contrapposto that express the power or vulnerability of the characters. The balanced bodies of the royal statues are visually contrasted with the depiction of Sophie's aching twists and the collapsing henchmen. In *SoulCalibur IV*, the variants of the contrapposto symbolize the duality between good and evil.

As addressed in this section, "low road" empathic mechanisms, such as muscular empathy, can contribute to character engagement. Unlike the emotions proper, which are called the "high road," affects are flows of sensations that often occur below the level of awareness of the person experiencing them. Although emotions seem to sometimes hit us with full force, a phenomenon that Klaus Scherer calls "affect bursts," they usually develop slowly over time.[57] Emotions often start as affects, which are more diffuse states of feelings or sensations. As psychologist Nico Frijda notes, in "emotional responding generally there is no succession of discrete events so much as flow of varying attitudes, acceptances, rejections, abandonments, and reserves; and that flow may be manifest in experience only."[58] We recognize emotions when the flow of processes produces a configuration that we usually associate with a particular emotion such as anger, sadness, or fear. Thus, emotion proper involves a higher degree of cognitive appraisal than do affects and also suggests ongoing mental activities that evaluate the significance of these affects during a situation of some concern for an individual or a character.[59] I return to the topics of character engagement and affects in Chapter 3, where I further evaluate rhetorical devices that intensify the spectator's empathy for animated characters.

Motor Mimicry

Motor mimicry is another "low road" empathic mechanism. Some scholars claim that understanding others via mimicry could have provided humans with an evolutionary advantage. Applying Giacomo Rizzolatti's research on the mirror neurons to the interpretation of artworks, art historian Barbara Stafford infers that our neural underpinnings may involve "a 'copy' in the brain that not only allows us to 'mind read' the emotions of others but that 'automatically' imitates their perceived joy, sadness, or distress and thus quickly allows us to understand what we see."[60] Moreover, we unconsciously integrate subtle information about other people through covert or overt motor mimicry. For example, an observer can overtly mimic the postures, facial expressions, and vocalizations of another person.[61] According to psychologist Lawrence Rosenblum, this unwitting mimicking "facilitates [our] perceptual, coordinative, and social success."[62] Motor mimicry can also involve a reaction by the observer that is similar to "one that the other person might make in his or her situation (e.g., Adam Smith's description of shrinking from a blow to another—whether or not the other does)."[63] Early theorists in this field include Jean-Baptiste Du Bos, David Hume, and Adam Smith. They distinguished various kinds of mimicry, which encompassed a variety of nondeliberate imitations of the others' movements or facial expressions.[64] At the end of the 19th century, for instance, French psychologist Theodule-Armand Ribot recalled "imitating the movements of a rope-walker while watching him."[65]

Motor mimicry is not limited to the observation of actual persons and is pertinent to the observation of represented behavior in photographs and videos.[66] Psychologist Dolf Zillmann integrates motor mimicry in his general review of various conceptual approaches to the phenomenon of empathy in cinema.[67] In one of their studies, Janet Beavin Bavelas and her colleagues studied participants taking part in scenarios likely to evoke motor mimicry. The participants were videotaped as they observed various situations happening live, on videotape, or in a narrative. The incidents that evoked motor mimicry included

> pain (caused in different episodes by an apparent cut, burn, shock, hammer blow, or crushed finger), laughter, smiling, affection, embarrassment, discomfort, disgust, facing a thrown projectile, ducking away from being hit, stuttering, word-finding, reaching with effort, and succeeding and failing at a timed task.[68]

According to their results, fictive events depicted on television can cause motor mimicry, especially when "the *plot* can become psychologically real and thereby cause considerable emotion."[69] From analyzing these findings, the scientists concluded that motor mimicry is a nonverbal communication act intended to express feelings congruent with those experienced by the person observed, even when watching a film.

The same scientists also proposed that motor mimicry applies to empathic responses from a third-person perspective. According to this view, the observer did not take the other's place or felt the other's feelings. Instead, they propose that the observer was portraying the other's reaction to the incident. The observer sent the message, "It is *as if* I feel as you do."[70] Although the researchers demonstrated that the observers' reactions to someone being hurt showed more care toward an injured person who made eye contact with them than in situations without eye contact, there was nevertheless evidence of some motor mimicry in the "no eye contact" situations. The study established that the participants' responses comprised both communicative intentions and involuntary mimicking.

While motor mimicry concentrates on the mimicking of gestures or facial expressions, other kinds of contagious phenomena arise during film viewing. For example, emotional contagion occurs when we "catch" the emotions of the members of the audience surrounding us at the theater.[71] People screaming in a large movie audience can amplify the intensity of the other viewers' reactions to a scary situation depicted on the screen. Similarly, we can also catch the emotions of the on-screen characters.

The phenomena of motor mimicry and emotional contagion attest that we are intimately connected with and influenced by the gestures and emotions of others, including those depicted in pictures. In *Echo Objects*, Stafford argues that these echoic systems define us as social beings. Identifying with another begins with the involuntary sharing of emotions, and this "primal impulse demonstrates that we are not autonomous agents but unconsciously mimic the mobile features and incorporate the implicit content in the facial expressions of those whom we behold."[72] Defining subjectivity should acknowledge the contribution not only of social institutions and the outer milieu on our agency, but also of the internal organizing phenomena that drive our physiological bodies.

While we exhibit some form of mimicry at the neural level via the mirror neuron system, we also experience muscular empathy with bodily movements and emotional contagion with a crowd. Our automatic mimicking of the positions of objects in our environment, as our embodied simulations, influences our moods, emotions, and responses toward a particular situation, and thus contributes to our understanding of it. By extension, these phenomena also influence our emotional engagement with animated figures exerting muscular efforts and goal-oriented bodily motions in animated media.

Embodied Meaning and Image Schemas

The transfer from the perception of bodily motions in pictures to our affective understanding of these movements is deeply ingrained in our neural circuitry and muscular experience. This mirroring mechanism could even explain the connections between perception and abstract understanding. Our understanding of metaphors, as the proponents of the CMT contend, is partly motivated by various embodied experiences. This section draws on studies in cognitive linguistics to explore the passage from embodied perception to abstract meaning, as patterns of interactions grounded in sensorimotor experiences become a source for visual metaphors and humor in a range of animated films.

The Corporeal Roots of Meaning-Making

Our individual interpretation of a film often shares elements of explanation with those of other spectators. The points on which we agree partly depend on similar physiologies, dispositions, and contexts of reception. We may disagree on other aspects because we have different cultures, upbringing, and tastes. Understanding how this process happens is very complex, and this chapter only provides some insights into embodied understanding in animation and cinema.

Drawing on empirical research in psychology, film scholar Per Persson argues that spectators usually strive to maximize meaningfulness when they watch a film.[73] Like "real-life" understanding, "discourse understanding seeks to integrate the textual cues into internal meaningfulness based on dispositions."[74] Despite sharing similar physiological make-ups, spectators' dispositions vary according to different axes of subject position, including gender, ethnicity, age, education, familiarity with cinematic conventions, religious beliefs, race, geographical location, political allegiance, and class. Because of these differences, spectators interpret some audiovisual cues given from the same film or animation differently.

Persson distinguishes six levels of increasing mental sophistication that are pertinent to the analysis of a filmic narrative.[75] The lower levels concern perceptual meaning, whereas the last level is relevant to interpretation and motivational inferences. To briefly describe this process, I take as an example the short animated film *The Hand* (Jiří Trnka, 1965). This puppet animation features a potter who makes pots for his unique plant. One day, a huge hand wearing a white glove erupts in his house and commands him to make pottery in the shape of a hand. Since the potter refuses, the hand locks him up in a birdcage and forces him to sculpt a hand statue with a finger pointing up (see Figure 1.2). At level 0, we experience moving imagery as formal patterns, rhythms, color configurations, and perceptual gestalts. The mirror neuron effects also fall into this pre-meaning level. In *The Hand*, the sequence where the potter is imprisoned has a blue background. A series of silver bars divides the frame vertically. Behind the bars, there is a white block. At level 1, we categorize objects and identify scene schemas such as "this is a cage" and "this is a hand." At level 2, spectators infer even more sophisticated meaning from what they perceive; they categorize characters and identify simple events. In this sequence, we see a string puppet sitting in a cage. A large hand above the cage manipulates the strings attached to the puppet's hands, forcing it to carve a hand into a white block. At level 3, the spectator attributes goals, beliefs, and emotions to the characters' behaviors. Separated from his beloved plant and pots, the craftsman appears alone and sad in the cage. He is forced to produce a likeness of his jailer against his will. Level 4 involves symbolic and metaphorical interpretations of the literal meanings conveyed by the events and objects identified on the lower levels. We can infer that the disruptive and manipulative hand symbolizes physical repression. As media scholar Charles Forceville argues, the abuse of power of the hand over the craftsman can be interpreted "in terms of the primary metaphors SOCIAL CONTROL IS PHYSICAL CONTROL, BEING IN CONTROL IS BEING ABOVE, and especially Lakoff's CONTROL IS CONTROL BY THE HANDS."[76] While level 4 operates at the intersection between comprehension and interpretation, level 5 is interpretative. At this level, the spectator makes inferences on the reasons that motivated the making of the film. This level also involves speculations on the purpose of certain stylistic elements or the use of particular techniques to support these judgments. In this example, the sociopolitical context of production can provide interpretative cues. Since this animation was made under the Communist regime in the 1960s in Czechoslovakia, the authoritative hand can allude to totalitarianism under this regime and its abusive control over creative production. Incidentally, it could be interpreted as Trnka's protest over the lack of freedom under which he had to produce his own animations.

This typology is only an overview of the kinds of meanings that spectators produce when they watch an animation or when they attempt to make sense of it afterward. These levels can also interact with each other. Bottom-up processes of perceptual meaning in conjunction with high-level hypotheses about the themes deployed in a film can guide the understanding of a particular sequence. Moreover, a film or an animation could invite preferred levels of understanding.[77] For example,

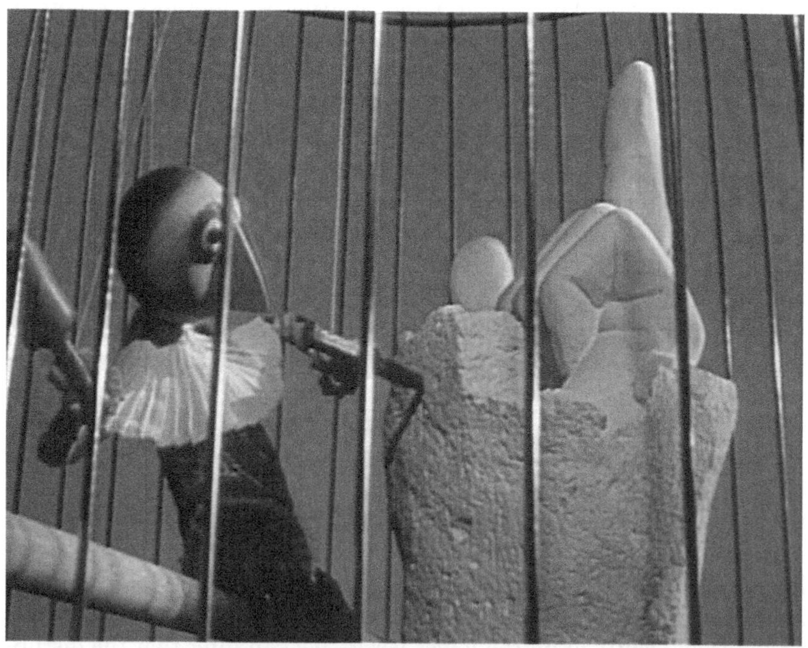

Figure 1.2 Imprisoned craftsman carving a hand into a large white block. *The Hand* (Jiří Trnka, 1965).

because they mainly contain formal patterns and rhythms, abstract animations such as *Rhythmus 21* (Hans Richter, 1921) and *Symphonie Diagonale*[78] (Viking Eggeling, 1924) constrain meaning on levels 0 and 1. The combination of curves and lines in the latter film evokes cubism. Although some of the series of diagonal lines resemble string instruments and other objects, the animated shapes do not invite metaphorical readings.

The enactive approach to perception in animation developed in this book also considers the mutual influences of cognitive, sensorimotor, and affective processes, as well as their reverberations on meaning-making during the viewing experience. As philosopher Mark Johnson demonstrates in *The Meaning of the Body*, meaning cannot be studied apart from its corporeal roots.[79] His approach to conceptual meaning rejects the representational theory of mind. According to Johnson, there are no disembodied "internal" ideas that represent "external" objects or events in the world. One popular version of representationalism, which is championed by Jerry Fodor and his supporters, posits that cognition is similar to a language of thought.[80] From this standpoint, people hold different beliefs or desires in relation to a proposition, and they call this attitude a "propositional attitude." We can entertain beliefs toward the proposition, or we can doubt it, or we can expect it, etc. This propositional attitude is in computational relation to an internal representation. Computations performed on these internal representations (or sets of symbols) successively determine the mental states of an organism. As we can interpret units of information in a text as sequences of words, we should be able to associate each propositional attitude with a causal state of the organism. From this exercise, we could develop a vocabulary of mental processes and ultimately build the language of thought. At the end, this computational program does not even need to be run on a brain, as it is completely independent of the "hardware."

One major problem with Fodor's approach to the mind is that the inner language of thought is not informed by our embodied relation to the world.[81] From Johnson's alternative view, "what we call 'body' and 'mind' are simply convenient abstractions—shorthand ways of identifying aspects of ongoing organism-environment interactions—and so cognition, thought, and symbolic interaction (such as language use) must be understood as arising from organic processes."[82] Although some laws in the structure of language contribute to our understanding of sentences, these patterns of experiential interactions with the world are necessary for the sentences to acquire meaning. The development of meaningful patterns of interactions with the environment requires social and cultural education, as well as perceptual, emotional, and sensorimotor explorations of this changing environment.

The neglect of the body and emotions in the study of conceptual meaning can originate from a traditional mind/body dichotomy in

Western philosophy. Johnson shows that a multitude of nonconscious bodily processes help us focus on the objects of our desire, consequently giving us the impression that our mind is separate from our body. The disappearance of our perceptual organs is instrumental to our fluid experience of the world. As philosopher Drew Leder puts it, "insofar as I perceive through an organ, it necessarily recedes from the perceptual field it discloses. I do not smell my nasal tissue, hear my ear, or taste my taste buds but perceive with and through such organs."[83] Moreover, nonconscious bodily processes govern posture and movement. It is "our body schema that hides from our view, even while it is what makes possible our perception, bodily movement, and kinesthetic sensibility."[84] Although nonconscious processes are not meaningful in themselves, they guide our actions and give rise to our thoughts.

Another misconception is the idea that the affects and sensations that we experience during a situation are separate from our conceptual understanding of it. Rejecting mind/body dualism, psychologist William James "denies any ontological separation between feeling, sensation, and perception on the one hand and conceptualization and thought on the other."[85] With other cognitive scholars supporting embodied cognition, including Rodney Brooks, Gerald Edelman, Vittorio Gallese, Edwin Hutchins, George Lakoff, Humberto Maturana, and Francisco Varela, Johnson claims that cognition is enacted by an organism embedded within its environment.[86] From this perspective, conceptualization interacts with the flow of our perceptual experience and is shaped by the nature of our embodiment. For the resourceful organism, cognition and emotion are integrated systems that engage in continuous cycles of problem-solving.[87] As philosopher Evan Thompson notes,

> cognitive and emotional processes modify each other continuously on a fast time-scale, while simultaneously being constrained by the global form produced by their coupling in a process of circular causality. This emergent form, the emotional interpretation, is a global state of emotion-cognition coherence, comprising an appraisal of a situation, an affective tone, and an action plan.[88]

Similarly, a combination of audiovisual elements in a scene transports us through a flow of affects that modifies our appreciation of the characters and their motivations. We constantly try to maximize coherence by evaluating the interactions between the audiovisual elements composing the scene and our past experience. We also go through episodes of assessing, questioning, and doubts that inflect the way we engage with upcoming events. Our interpretation of the scene is closely informed by our emotional inflections and draws on our prior experience of sensorimotor explorations of varied environments.

By drawing on the approaches of Thompson, Johnson, and Noë, this book examines the ways in which the particularities of our embodiment can contribute to our understanding of animation.[89] While the levels of perceptual meaning developed by Persson concentrate on the top-down integration of the disparate elements composing a scene, I propose to show how emotional processes and sensorimotor skills complete this picture. The following section examines how audiovisual representations of image schemas can translate physical experiences into metaphors.

Embodiment and Metaphors

Johnson demonstrates that our sensorimotor skills play a crucial role in grasping the meaning of things, experiences, and concepts. Rooted in embodied dynamicism, his philosophy of mind posits that body, mind, and environment are integrated into patterns of experiential interactions. Also an ally of embodied cognition, the CMT maintains that we conceptualize the way we do because of the type of body that we have. This section engages with what Lawrence Shapiro calls the conceptualization tenet of embodied cognition.[90] This tenet holds that the properties of an organism's body limit or inform the way it perceives the world. We could learn human spatial concepts because we move in erect position in a world where there is a gravitational field. In contrast, a spherical being with no acquaintance with gravitation would have some difficulty in grasping the concept of UP.[91] It is because we have walked on different types of roads that we are able to distinguish linear paths of motion versus nonlinear ones. Thanks to our practical knowledge of pathways, we easily understand the concept of trajectory.

Our physical embodiment teaches us about the "logic" of containment, exertion, and force. According to Lakoff and Johnson, our everyday experiences pervade the way that we speak and construct our sentences. For example, the phrase "Tell me your story again, but leave out the minor details" considers story events as containers. In this sentence, the word OUT, which applies to spatial orientation, "is metaphorically projected onto the cognitive domain where there are processes of choosing, rejecting, separating, differentiating abstract objects, and so forth."[92]

Various metaphors in the language bring into play our particular modes of embodiment. To characterize the process of transfer from sensorimotor experience to the metaphorical domain, Johnson develops the concept of image schema, which "is a dynamic, recurring pattern of organism-environment interactions."[93] In addition, image schemas "are abstract patterns in our experience and understanding that are not propositional in any of the standard senses of that term."[94] The patterns of interactions with our surroundings attach meaning to common bodily movements, namely left-right, up-down, into-out of, toward-away, and straight-curved. For example, from the experience of using containers, we have learned that they are three-dimensional objects that we can fill with things such as liquids and food. We also acquired the knowledge of spatial boundedness by entering closed rooms, riding a car, or hiding in a closet. From this firsthand experience of the "logic" of containment, we assimilated the CONTAINMENT schema. In film studies, scholars have extrapolated the notion of container to the frame.[95] Alternatively, the SOURCE-PATH-GOAL schema underlies our understanding of bodily motion along a path. We have walked on different kinds of paths, flat or steep, muddy or sandy. From these different perceptual patterns in our bodily experience, we understand the effort needed to complete a journey on foot. We also know that depending on the characteristics of the road, reaching the destination will take more or less time. Again, film scholars have associated this image schema with basic structures in storytelling. Looking at visual expressions of metaphors in *Father and Daughter* (Michaël Dudok de Wit, 2000), *Quest* (Tyron Montgomery, 1996), and *O* (Kireet Khurana, 1996), Charles Forceville and Marloes Jeulink demonstrate that the SOURCE-PATH-GOAL is a key concept to analyze journeys in animation.[96] As such, image schemas are not only useful to express abstract notions in language but also in audiovisual media.

Thanks to our intuitive knowledge of image schemas, we can attribute metaphorical connotations to audiovisual cues in an animation. In their initial inventory of image-schematic structures, Johnson and Lakoff include BALANCE, CENTER-PERIPHERY, CONTAINMENT/CONTAINER, PATH/SOURCE-PATH-GOAL, LINK, PART-WHOLE, and UP-DOWN. The force schemas encompass a range of forceful actions, including ATTRACTION, BLOCKAGE, COMPULSION, COUNTERFORCE, DIVERSION, ENABLEMENT, AND REMOVAL OF RESTRAINT. The list of image schemas is not a closet set and has expanded since the initial research by Johnson and Lakhoff.[97] These image-schematic structures can display distinctive qualities, such as explosive, graceful, halting, weak, and jerky. From this wide range of options, Johnson divides the qualities of organism-environment interactions into four broader qualities of bodily movements: tension, linearity, amplitude, and projection. As these different qualifiers and vectors are applied to movements implied in an image schema, they become a gestalt.

According to Lakoff and Johnson, human beings recruit image schemas to metaphorically structure abstract concepts. Image schemas are the building blocks for more elaborate metaphors. Among the different categories of metaphors, recent developments in CMT distinguish two main types: "correlation-based metaphors" and "resemblance metaphors."[98] "Correlation-based metaphors" are metaphors produced by correlating a physical sensation with an abstract concept. For example, in the metaphor EMOTION IS HEAT, emotion is a concept and heat is a thermal sensation that we can feel when we experience anger or hate. Alternatively, "resemblance metaphors" are concerned with metaphors based on similarity. When we say "he is a beast," we mean that his manners resemble those of a beast. Grady distinguishes "primary metaphors" from more complex ones. Primary metaphors are the simplest units of correlation metaphors. Examples of primary metaphors include HAPPY IS UP, AFFECTION IS WARMTH, DIFFICULTIES ARE BURDENS, SIGNIFICANT IS BIG, and BAD IS DOWN.

From the way we correlate object moving in space and temporal change, we produce MOVING TIME metaphors.[99] For instance, we say "Friday went by in a flash" and "the time flies by when you're having fun." Our experience of objects moving in space and the time it takes them to pass us by grounds in physical experience more complex metaphors about TIME IS SPACE. Various phrases express time in terms of space. We say "the deadline is ahead of us" and "we are nearing the end of the year." The animation *Flat Hatting* (John Hubley, 1946) provides a striking example of the TIME IS SPACE image schema. This US Navy training animation presents the risks and consequences associated with flying very close to the ground. At the beginning of the animation, the narrator is trying to understand the root causes of this precarious behavior. His saying "Let's go back a few years and see what makes him tick" is accompanied with movements from left to right. The airplane in which the pilot is sitting undergoes successive transformations into a car, a bicycle, a soap car, a tricycle, and finally into an axe held by a baby. The background scenery also changes from a modern city with electrical wiring to the rural area where the pilot grew up. This animation uses the right-hand side of the frame to represent the past and the left-hand side to symbolize the present. By converting time in terms of space, *Flat Hatting* represents visual metaphors grounded in our experience of riding different types of vehicles.

Images Schemas in Animation

Even though the relevance of image schemas is a source of debates among scholars in cognitive linguistics, they remain one of the most persuasive hypotheses to explain conceptual thought. As Johnson argues in *The Body in the Mind*, meaning is not only conceptual and rational; it is also perceptual and imaginative. Building on CMT and applying it to cinema, film scholars Maarten Coëgnarts and Peter Kravanja find "plausible to assume that non-verbal manifestations of conceptual metaphors exist as the metaphoric belongs to the realm of thoughts and not of words."[100] From this perspective, visual manifestations of image schemas help make the world depicted on the screen comprehensible.[101]

Orientational Metaphors in Boundin'

In *Metaphors We Live By*, Lakoff and Johnson introduce the idea of orientational metaphors.[102] As Lakoff and Johnson maintain, even though the image schemas that communicate oppositions such as UP-DOWN, FRONT-BACK, CENTRAL-PERIPHERAL, and IN-OUT vary from one culture to another, they all take root in physical experience. The use of spatial orientations to create metaphors "arise[s] from the fact that we have bodies of the sort we have and that they function as they do in our physical environment."[103] In the English language, for instance, we find an expression that says "I'm feeling up today." This phrase gives an orientation in space to a mood to express metaphorically the idea that HAPPY IS UP. In a different medium, the short computer-animated film *Boundin'* (Bud Luckey, 2003) expresses the metaphor HAPPY IS UP with uplifting banjo music and bouncing animals. We identify the idea HAPPY IS UP because when we feel happy, we have more energy. In contrast, lying down intimates the lack of vigor associated with sadness. Even though human legs cannot reproduce the extraordinary leaps that the sheep and the jackalope can achieve, we can extrapolate from our earthly background the kind of UP their bodies experience. The exaggerated bouncing of the sheep in this animation recalls the proprioceptive effects that one might have experienced when jumping on a trampoline or from a springboard.

Image schemas in animated films are pervasive. Spectators can use their body to develop virtual patterns of interaction with imaginary worlds. Although in reality the laws of physics limit the range of possible bodily movements, animation enjoys transgressing these limits. Animated films constantly challenge our expectations by presenting alien anatomies, worlds with natural laws of their own, and bodily movements that are impossible for human beings.

Elastigirl in The Incredibles

The Incredibles (Brad Bird, 2004) exploits a variety of image schemas to invite metaphorical interpretations. Since this animation is suitable for a diverse audience, including children, not every viewer will grasp the more complicated innuendos. Additionally, because we have different cultural backgrounds, certain allusions will be more salient than others. Assuredly, audiovisual metaphors can be interpreted in various ways, and this makes works of art even more interesting.

Since the image schema list is not a closed set, I propose to add FLEXIBILITY. People with flexible muscles can bend their torso and touch their feet. They may feel the tingling sensation associated with stretched muscles, but they are not completely blocked by a burning pain. In many ways, this image schema is an extension of the FORCE schemas. Flexibility is a kind of ENABLEMENT. Because human muscles have some degree of flexibility, by stretching them regularly, we can spread our arm to scratch the middle of our back. Frequently in cartoons, large, muscular bodies exhume brute force while slender bodies exhibit their flexibility.

Animators can create particularly able bodies that do not necessarily respond to anatomical constraints. I particularly appreciate animated films that transform the characters' bodies and broaden the range of possible movements. The gestures performed by Elastigirl in the animated film *The Incredibles* create a pleasurable form of imaginative disarray. I can inwardly feel the stretch of her limbs, but only up to a point. When I exceed this limit, I fill up the gap with my imagination. This computer-generated animation produced by Pixar Animation Studios features a family of undercover superheroes. Various patterns of experiential interactions and muscular abilities are metaphorically associated with the personality traits of the main protagonists. One sequence at the beginning of the animation introduces the physical abilities of the father and mother of this singular family when they were younger and not yet married.

At the beginning of the sequence, a thief is searching into a woman's purse on the rooftop of a building. Bob, aka Mr. Incredible, surprises the villain red-handed. He tells him, "You can tell a lot about a woman by the contents of her purse but maybe that's not what you had in mind." This sentence hints at a theme central to this sequence: the exterior of a person can reveal information about who they are inside. This sequence is a pun based on "undercover," which joins the image schemas UNDER and COVER. The first glimpse that we get of Mr. Incredible is a shadow of a muscular torso cast on the brick wall behind him, which suggests a large container closing around him.

Then, the sequence cuts back to a low-angle shot of Mr. Incredible's muscular stature standing erect with his two arms on the hips. The shot articulates the metaphor PHYSICAL APPEARANCE IS PHYSICAL FORCE. In addition, the camera position, by presenting a low-angle view of the subject, combined with the character's confident posture foregrounds the VERTICALITY schema. We often associate ideas of control and submission with this schema. Orientational metaphors built on this schema can articulate HAVING CONTROL or FORCE IS UP or BEING SUBJECTED TO CONTROL or FORCE IS DOWN. The scornful tone Mr. Incredible employs when he addresses the thief and the camera angle introduce the character's authoritative personality. The vertical schema in the superhero genre, where the opposition between good and bad is one of the important themes, can also symbolize that VIRTUE IS UP or GOOD IS UP. The position of a high-rise building located right behind Mr. Incredible reinforces the association between their sturdy postures, evoking the righteousness of the superhero.

As Mr. Incredible approaches toward the thief, the man pulls out his gun to menace him. At the same time, a thin arm appears on the right-hand side of the screen. The arm swiftly stretches across the frame to knock down the thief. We then discover Elastigirl holding her fists and ready to punch back. She approaches toward the camera with confidence. Her smooth gait and warm tone of voice contrast with the ruggedness of Mr. Incredible. When she tries to convince him that they could share the recognition for the arrest, Mr. Incredible responds, "I work alone." To which she replies, "You need to be more..." As she talks, she uses her two fingers to "walk" on his shoulder. Then, she agilely stretches her entire body over Mr. Incredible's shoulder, touches the ground behind him with her arms, bends her body to cross under him backward, and quickly stands back while whispering the last word of the sentence, "flexible." The flexibility she can achieve with her body also demonstrates one of her main personality traits. The physical appearance of these two characters, or their "cover," represents what is "under," or their inner self.

From the VERTICALITY schema and the UP-DOWN schema, we can construct primary metaphors that hint at the personalities of the protagonists. We easily recognize that Mr. Incredible is righteous but rough, while Elastigirl is flexible and conciliatory. The battle of the sexes played by the future husband and wife, which is common in classical romantic comedies, also illustrates the complex metaphor CONTRARIES ATTRACT EACH OTHER.

The World Is Upside Down in Antagonia

As we saw in the previous example, visual articulations of image schemas in animation play a vital role in determining meaning relations. While animation often presents bodily movements that are not humanly possible to perform, viewers can exploit their experience of moving in space or applying forces on objects to make sense of them. Even though we cannot quite know the effects of these superpowers on the internal organs and muscles of these characters, we extrapolate from what we know about flexible objects or bouncing on a trampoline.

Despite the deviations from anatomical expectations or the exaggerated powers of the characters, these animations reuse a set of cinematic conventions that increase their legibility and enhance character presence within the animated world. Variable framing and personal-space invasions, for instance, take advantage of our knowledge of real-life proxemics to suggest the porosity of the interface: when characters dangerously approach the camera at high speed, we perceive their threat.[104] Linear perspective, photographic realism, psychological realism, and markers of presence such as shading can also enhance a character's liveliness. Other animations, such as *Antagonia* (Nicolas Brault, 2002), present themselves like puzzle films.[105] This animation challenges our usual understanding of patterns of sensorimotor experience and requires more "mental processing" from the viewer to solve the visual riddles.

The beginning of *Antagonia* introduces the peculiar behaviors of creatures living in an icy world. The wind blows and the shadows of the ebbs and flows of large waves appear under the scratched surface of the ice. A creature that resembles a large gray penguin stands on the ice (see Figure 1.3). Under the penguin's feet beneath the ice, we distinguish the shape of a fish winding its tail. As the silhouette of a small bird approaches the shadow of the fish, it opens its mouth and swallows the bird. As the giant wave that forms below the surface comes back, it produces more birds that move under the ice.

One of the flows of the wave pushes on the surface of the ice a small penguin standing on its head. As for the large penguin, the shape of a moving fish shows up underneath it. The small penguin is more curious and expressive than the large one. It moves a little bit away from the shadow of the fish to see what will happen. The shadow of a small bird shows up and the small penguin jumps on it. The penguin taps its feet on the ice as if to play with the bird. While the penguin imitates the shape of the bird by spreading its wings, a fish passes by and gulps the bird. The small penguin displays a frown of disapproval and taps the ice above the wiggling fish with its beak until it goes away.

Figure 1.3 A penguin-looking creature stands on the ice and the shadows of a fish and a bird-fish appear below the surface. *Antagonia* (Nicolas Brault, 2002).

Viewers progressively learn about this mysterious world through the sensorimotor explorations of the small penguin. The laws of gravity and the effects of forces applied to objects, for instance, do not operate the same way as on Earth. As the small penguin cracks the ice with its beak, it creates a small hole from which the tip of a block of ice protrudes. The resurfacing of the piece of ice causes a large block of ice to fall down from the sky at a walking distance from the two penguins. It is as though the sky and the icy surface were folded together and could physically communicate. At one point, the small penguin flies above the upper frame. Surprisingly, its shadow shows up below the ice, surrounded by the silhouettes of small birds flapping their wings. When the small penguin falls back down from the sky, three birds are glued to his head. The large penguin removes two of the birds from its body and swallows them. The third bird flies up. As it disappears above the frame, its shadow reappears under the ice, thus confirming the theory that UP and DOWN in this world meet in the off-screen space.

At last, the final part of this animation pieces together the puzzle. The small penguin breaks the ice and creates a large hole. When the penguin peeks down the opening in the ice, it observes the birds flying around the hole. The viewer can see the shadows they cast on the ice above them. The large penguin also fractures the ice when it falls on its head. As an attractive force lifts the large penguin toward the top of the frame, the camera reveals again what is happening in the off-screen space. A group of birds catches the large penguin as it approaches them, and just above their heads, we can see the big hole the large penguin had just carved into the ice.

Antagonia, The Incredibles, and *Boundin'* provide examples of multimodal expressions of image schemas. While Persson's method helps viewers identify relations between patterns in an image, image schemas connect these patterns with the viewer's tangible existence. The medium of animation draws on the viewer's ability to experience emotions and apply his or her sensorimotor expertise to convey primary metaphors such as HAPPY IS UP in *Boundin'* or FORCE IS UP in *The Incredibles*. More complex metaphors can be articulated by combining technical devices specific to moving images, including camera movement, character's posture, and framing. While image schemas exploit patterns of sensorimotor interactions that are readily available to the human condition, the metaphors that we elaborate from them, such as CONTRARIES ATTRACT EACH OTHER, are often informed by culture. As illustrated by *The Incredibles*, the opposition of character traits between the protagonists of opposite sexes is a common formula in Western romantic comedies. The medium of animation also presents impossible movements that explore the limits of our earthly experiential patterns. As we saw in *Antagonia*, we can learn to extrapolate new image schemas from the sensorimotor explorations of unusual animated bodies.

Perceptual Entanglements in Animation

Animation can reveal basic features of our embodied perception, as demonstrated by the change blindness experiment analyzed in the introduction. This section turns to other animations that are attuned to the particularities of the viewer's visual system with its retinal photoreceptor cells and its excitable neural connections. The analyses of optical phenomena in *The Cabinet of Jan Švankmajer* and gestalt laws of perception in *Spheres* suggest that we can grasp the succession of animated images as a gestalt because of our specific anatomy. Animated images, as I argue, are neither on the screen nor constructed by the viewer; they emerge from the perceptual entanglement of the viewer's visual system and the animation machine that produces the illusion of apparent motion.[106]

Optical Tools

With the help of various formal techniques, animators often choose to foreground the "toolness" of the animated body and the instrumentality of animation. They employ audiovisual strategies that expand our perceptual boundaries and stress the limits of human perception. In the puppet animation *The Cabinet of Jan Švankmajer*, the Quay Brothers highlight the illusionary nature of animation and the spectator's perceptual attunement to animated images.

The section titled "Tarantella the Child Receives a Lesson in 1/24th of a Second" teaches a whimsical lesson on stop-motion animation. One of the puppets portrays the renowned Czech artist and filmmaker Švankmajer, and the other, a young boy, plays his student. Švankmajer looks like an anthropomorphized automaton. He has the legs of a compass at the place of his arms and wears an open book like a hat. The top of the apprentice's head has been chopped off and emptied, thereby readied to receive the teaching of his master. Around the beginning of the scene, Švankmajer turns a gear that opens a box, and a camera rolls out of it. Using the camera, the master shows the boy how to animate a bouncing ball. Švankmajer moves back and forth from the camera to the stand placed in front of the objective, above which a ball stays still, up in the air (see Figure 1.4). Instead of walking, Švankmajer abruptly jumps between the camera and the stand. His discontinuous movement underlines an "imperfect" use of the stop-motion technique, implying that no intermediary steps between the two positions were used to simulate "real" locomotion. In contrast, in full animation, the animator usually decomposes the movement into 24 images per second to create the appearance of a fluid movement. In limited animation, animators can reuse the same image twice or more to create the illusion of continuous movement, but this technique can introduce some jerkiness. In addition to observing the scene, the boy counts the takes. He activates a handle that increases a four-digit number on a board posted on the wall. At the same time that the shooting activities occur on the right side of the frame, there is a ball that strangely bounces down a staircase on the left side of the frame. The descending movements of the ball toward the bottom of the staircase mysteriously correlate with the manipulations of the camera. For instance, when Švankmajer turns the crank and the camera is in recording mode, the ball can freely fall down the stairs. But when Švankmajer stops the camera and walks next to the stand in order to adjust the position of the ball facing the camera, the ball that was rolling down the stairs stops in the middle of its motion, as if weightless. Tarantella's world of stop-motion animation responds to its own whimsical laws of physics. The *mise en abyme* of the lesson on animation self-reflexively alludes to the filmmaker's creative power over the images.

The Cabinet of Jan Švankmajer playfully reminds spectators that animation relies on optical trickery. The phenomenon by which we can be fooled into perceiving continuous motion from a sequence of still images has been called "short range apparent motion."[107] In stop-motion animation, frame-by-frame cinematography is an automatism that produces the illusion of movement, a process that differs from the continuous recording of images typical of traditional live-action

Figure 1.4 Animating a bouncing ball. *The Cabinet of Jan Švankmajer* (Stephen Quay and Timothy Quay, 1984).

cinema. A sequence of frames recorded with a movie camera represents chronological instances of a movement. When decomposed at the proper rate and then projected at the same rate, the movement appears as being continuous to the human eye.

Our specific neural configurations and sensorimotor skills are attuned to the automatisms of animation. Depending on the alternation rate between the static frames and our flicker fusion threshold for the given viewing conditions, we may see continuous motion or flickers.[108] As other optical devices that create continuous motion when they display a series of still images, stop-motion animation tricks us in seeing what is not there. According to Gregory Currie in *Image and Mind*, cinematic motion is real, not illusory, because we can track the movement of physical objects moving across the screen. More specifically, "cinematic images are real objects, reidentifiable across time and occupying different positions at different times during the viewing of the shot."[109] From Currie's perspective, no independent verification can undermine this fact; therefore, there is no illusion. I do not deny that the position of a ball that crosses the cinematic frame from right to left is "really" changing, since the position of the ball relative to the position of the surrounding frame varies. However, the impression of continuous motion in animated media arises from a combination of conditions. The experience of continuous motion is response-dependent; it relies on the visual acuity of the viewer. Moreover, for the illusion of continuous motion to be convincing, it also depends on the speed at which the still images are displayed, the speed at which the images were recorded, and the mechanisms by which the images are presented to the viewer. For example, motion picture technology achieves continuous motion with strategies different from those employed by video technology.

The Cabinet of Jan Švankmajer self-reflexively demonstrates the profound entanglement of the spectator's visual system and the animation apparatus. The discontinuous jumps performed by the master in *The Cabinet of Jan Švankmajer* emphasize the automatisms of animation by upsetting our expectation of fluid, continuous locomotion. In this example, the mechanical motion of the puppet is cocreated by the spectator, the animator, and the animation apparatus. Becoming-animated reveals a new systemic whole, one which acknowledges the posthuman nature of our extended perception.

The Gestalt Laws of Perception

Scientists have also studied the perception of biological motion and the embodied nature of the human visual system with the help of animated displays. In the 1970s, psychophysicist Gunnar Johansson devised a model of motion and space perception called "the visual vector analysis model."[110] Johansson's model outlines three principles that explain how disconnected dots can appear to move like rigid objects under certain conditions. The first principle states that "elements [...] in motion on the picture plane of the eye are always perceptually related to each other."[111] In animation, for example, we tend to group together outlined drawings located on the same plane. According to the second principle, "equal and simultaneous motions in a series of proximal elements automatically connect these elements to rigid perceptual units."[112] For instance, if we see three lined-up dots that move together in the same direction, we perceive them as being rigidly connected with each other. The third principle states that "when, in the motions of a set of proximal elements, equal simultaneous motion vectors can be mathematically abstracted (according to some simple rules), these components are perceptually isolated and perceived as one unitary motion."[113] In other words, when four dots arranged as a square move simultaneously toward their common center, these dots appear connected by the rigid, invisible structure of a shrinking square. Johansson used these three principles to devise a theoretical framework for the study of biological motion.

Intuitively, we organize groups of moving dots displayed on a screen according to these principles. Johansson's principles of biological perception belong to level 0 of Persson's model of understanding filmic discourse.[114] On this level, the gestalt effects of perceptual organization comprise the law of similarity, the law of proximity, the law of symmetry, the law of closure, the law of figure and ground, and the law of good continuation. In animation, our perceptual experience of these gestalt laws reflects the physiological particularities of our visual system. Moreover, these phenomena underscore the spectator's symbiotic assemblage with the animation machine; the simultaneous contribution of the perceiving body and the technologies of animation are necessary to experience the gestalt principles of motion.

Spheres, an animated short film made by René Jodoin and Norman McLaren, applies Johansson's principles in a harmonious choreography of translucent white pearls. They float weightlessly in a multihued landscape that alternates between representations of the cosmos and the sky.[115] The dancing pearls follow Glenn Gould's performance of the Well-Tempered Clavier by Bach in a synchronous fashion. The symmetrically arranged pearls create various geometrical structures in motion resembling cell division, celestial motion, and atomic patterns. At the beginning of the animation, a pearl in the center of the image splits into two pearls. Each of the two pearls separates into two new pearls, and, in turn, these two pearls divide into two more pearls. Because of the law of symmetry, we tend to assemble the individual pearls into pairs. Then, we perceive the resulting eight pearls as arranged into two rows of four pearls. Their organized linear motion suggests that they are attached together by an invisible thread. Later in the sequence, four lined-up pearls rotate simultaneously in the middle of a diamond-shaped structure of smaller beads (see Figure 1.5). Because of the law of proximity, the four pearls in the center appear to form one group connected by an invisible force. In these excerpts, our experience of geometry combined with the intuitive knowledge of Johansson's perceptual principles contribute to our automatic conversion of these independently moving pearls into geometrical gestalts and organized vectors.

This kind of experimentation with the gestalt principles of motion is present in earlier abstract animations, such as those created by Len Lye and Oskar Fischinger. The rhythms and repetitions in *Spheres* also evoke the mathematical precision of the graphic designs in motion found in Viking Eggeling's animations.[116] Yet, it is the animation machine that transforms abstracts geometry into meaningful patterns. Only the dynamic interactions between the spectator's perceptual system and the automatisms of animation can give birth to dancing pearls. Johansson's visual vector analysis model and the gestalt laws of perception help understand why even disconnected dots may appear imbued with a life of their own. The beautiful geometric arrangement and vectorial choreography come alive as we become animated by the encounter with abstract, algorithmic structures.

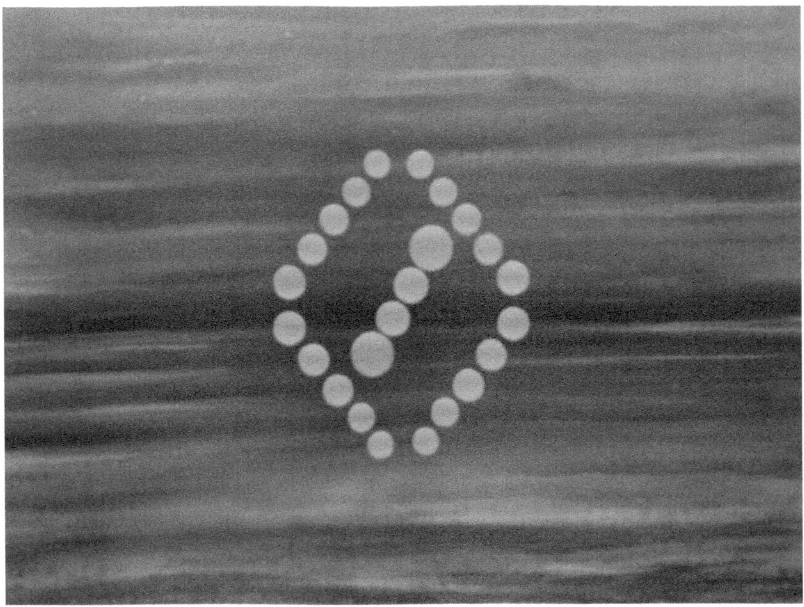

Figure 1.5 The law of proximity represented with pearls. *Spheres* (René Jodoin and Norman McLaren, 1969).

Conclusion

Our physicality shapes the way we experience animated worlds. We can enjoy optical toys and animated pictures because we are natural-born cyborg viewers. Our body and brain are preadapted to be transformed by technological prostheses. The repeated use of animated tools for a specific goal can alter our plastic neural resources and yield new cognitive opportunities. With the help of animated interfaces, humans and nonhuman animals enhance their strategic thinking, activate remote devices, or simply dive into the world of a video game.

The discovery of the mirror neuron system confirms that the boundary between viewers and animated characters is permeable. Research in neuroscience has revealed that the mirror neuron system is at the origins of embodied simulations, motor mimicry, and muscular empathy. When we see WALL-E holding EVE's "hand," his gesture activates neurons that would be stimulated if we were to reproduce a similar movement. The mirror neuron system confirms a lower-level form of empathy for the others' gestures, postures, and movements at the level of the unconscious body schema, a phenomenon also called sensorimotor coupling.

The empathic resonance underlying the physical relation between object and subject is useful to understand the esthetic experience of the spectator. Some viewers may feel inward sensations in the presence of figures exerting muscular efforts, such as the struggling man in *Sisyphus*. Muscular empathy, motor mimicry, and emotional contagion in the presence of animated characters help convey the feelings and emotions of the on-screen characters in both overt and covert ways. In addition, postures reproducing the balanced and twisted contrapposti provide rhetorical opportunities in *Howl's Moving Castle* and *SoulCalibur IV*.

Our understanding of visual metaphors in animation is partly anchored in our repertoire of sensomotoric experiences. The discovery of a relation between mirror neurons and embodied understanding strengthens this hypothesis. As examined in various animations in this chapter, the audiovisual manifestation of image schemas can articulate metaphorical associations grounded in physical experience. Camera position, music, and character movement are among the techniques that reactivate concrete patterns of sensorimotor interactions with objects. In *Boundin'*, the repetitive bouncing of the animated critters accompanied by cheerful music illustrates the primary metaphor HAPPY IS UP. Although the animated jumps are exaggerated, viewers can still piece together elements of past experiences to catch the metaphor. Image schemas can also combine into complex metaphors. In *The Incredibles*, the external appearance and skills of the superheroes reveal the internal traits of adaptability for Elastigirl and stubbornness for Mr. Incredible. The display of their flexibility and strength helps to convey the image schemas of UNDER and COVER that combine into the concept of "undercover." Alternatively, even though cartoon worlds do not apply the same laws of physics, we can still apprehend the unforeseen contours of their imaginary landscapes with our body. As we discovered in *Antagonia*, animation can sometimes invite us to be born again and see the world anew. By accompanying the small penguin in its exploration of a strange icy world, we experience the UP and DOWN schemas from a different perspective, one in which these concepts are folded together. These case studies demonstrate that we not only rely on our past experience of the world but also bring into play the power of imagination to make sense of hyperbolized animated feats.

The last part of the chapter focused on animation techniques and special effects that call the viewer's attention on the specificity of the human visual system. In *The Cabinet of Jan Švankmajer*, the master teaches his young apprentice how to use the animation apparatus to create the illusion of continuous motion. For its part, the animated film *Spheres* foregrounds the sensitivity of human vision to the gestalt laws of perceptual organization. By focusing on the uniqueness of some visual effects particular to animated media, these two examples underscore the simultaneous contribution of the spectator's perceptual system and the animation apparatus to the process of decoding the image content. These animations reveal that our visual system is not a clear window onto reality; we actively apprehend the complex organization of the world that surrounds us.

Finally, the animated films studied reconfigure the body's limits. Thanks to various mirroring mechanisms, they compel us to reevaluate our assumptions about our perceptual boundaries and acknowledge the permeability of the animated interface. Our assemblage with the animation machine extends our perceptual reach and redraws the limits of the human—a process that I call "becoming-animated."

Notes

1 McCay cited in Canemaker, "Winsor McCay," 15.
2 On the thaumatrope and the phenomenon of retinal afterimages, see Crary, *Techniques of the Observer*, 105–107.
3 Noë, *Varieties of Presence*, 13.
4 Clark, *Natural-Born Cyborgs*.
5 Clark, *Natural-Born Cyborgs*, 3.
6 Clark, *Supersizing the Mind*, 95.
7 Clark, *Supersizing the Mind*, xxviii.
8 Noë, *Action in Perception*.
9 Clark, *Supersizing the Mind*, 42–43.
10 Clark, *Supersizing the Mind*, 34.
11 Clark, "Re-inventing Ourselves," 263.
12 On the "principle of ecological balance" developed by Pfeifer and Bongard, see Clark, chapter 1, *Supersizing the Mind*, 3–9.
13 Clark, *Supersizing the Mind*, 7.
14 Clark, *Supersizing the Mind*, 64–66.

15 Clark, *Natural-Born Cyborgs*, 103.
16 Unlike Noë's strong sensorimotor account, Clark's view envisages the possibility that different sensory organs and bodily forms could "yield identical experiences despite surface dissimilarities," *Supersizing the Mind*, 205.
17 On epistemic action, see Clark's full explanation in *Supersizing the Mind*, 70–73.
18 Kirsh and Maglio, "Reaction and Reflection in *Tetris*," 3.
19 Clark, *Natural-Born Cyborgs*, 31 (emphasis in the original).
20 On the use of tools that cause plastic neural changes, see Carmena et al., "Brain-Machine Interface"; Maravita and Iriki, "Tools for the Body (Schema)"; and Berti and Frassinetti, "When Far Becomes Near."
21 On Stelarc's third hand, see Stelarc's website at stelarc.org, last accessed April 26, 2018.
22 Maravita and Iriki, "Tools for the Body (Schema)," 79.
23 Maravita and Iriki, "Tools for the Body (Schema)," 80.
24 Maravita and Iriki, "Tools for the Body (Schema)," 80–81.
25 Various experiments in the field of poststroke rehabilitation demonstrate the brain's plasticity in Bermúdez i Badia et al., "Virtual Reality for Sensorimotor Rehabilitation Post Stroke."
26 Carmena et al., "Brain-Machine Interface." For a more detailed description of this experiment, see Clark, *Supersizing the Mind*, 33–34.
27 Carmena et al., "Brain-Machine Interface," 205.
28 The EMOTIV's website at www.emotiv.com/, last accessed April 26, 2018 and Buhr, "Hack Your Brain."
29 For further details on the difference between true incorporation of a tool and mere use, see Clark, "Re-inventing Ourselves," 271–273.
30 McLuhan, *Understanding Media*, 57.
31 McLuhan, *Understanding Media*, 57.
32 For reviews on the mirror neuron system, see, for instance, Cook et al., "Mirror Neurons"; Rizzolatti and Craighero, "The Mirror-Neuron System"; and Rizzolatti et al., "Mirrors in the Mind."
33 Meltzoff and Moore, "Newborn Infants Imitate Adult Facial Gestures." See also Meltzoff and Moore, "Infants' Understanding of People and Things."
34 Johnson, *The Meaning of the Body*, 38.
35 Freedberg and Gallese, "Motion, Emotion and Empathy," 200.
36 Iacoboni quoted in Blakeslee, "Cells That Read Minds."
37 Johnson, *The Meaning of the Body*, 161 (emphasis in the original).
38 Iacoboni quoted in Blakeslee, "Cells That Read Minds."
39 Freedberg and Gallese, "Motion, Emotion and Empathy," 200. On the contribution of mirror neurons and canonical neurons to esthetic responses, see also Gallese and Freedberg, "Mirror and Canonical Neurons."
40 For experiments about hand manipulation and the human brain, see Chao and Martin, "Representation of Manipulable Man-Made Objects." For experiments on macaques, see Raos et al., "Functional Properties"; Sakata et al., "Neural Mechanisms"; and Murata et al., "Selectivity for the Shape."
41 Freedberg and Gallese, "Motion, Emotion and Empathy," 201.
42 Gallese, "Mirror Neurons and Art," 459. The repetitive action performed by robots may interfere with the mirroring mechanisms, see Gazzola et al., "The Anthropomorphic Brain" and Oztop et al., "Human-Humanoid Interaction."
43 Iacoboni quoted in Blakeslee, "Cells That Read Minds."
44 Hutchinson et al., "Pain-Related Neurons."

45 Adolphs, "Cognitive Neuroscience of Human Behavior," 172.
46 On different approaches to neuroesthetics, see Stafford, *Echo Objects*; Zeki, *Inner Vision*; Zeki, "Neural Concept Formation and Art"; McManus et al., "The Aesthetics of Composition"; Solso, *Cognition and the Visual Arts*; Ramachandran, "The Science of Art"; and Livingstone, *Vision and Art*.
47 For reviews of the influence of the mirror neuron system on art, see Gallese, "Mirror Neurons and Art" and Piechowski-Jozwiak et al., "Universal Connection."
48 Freedberg and Gallese, "Motion, Emotion and Empathy," 197.
49 Freedberg and Gallese, "Motion, Emotion and Empathy," 197.
50 Vischer, *On the Optical Sense of Form*.
51 Wölfflin, *Prolegomena su einer Psychologie der Architektur*; Warburg, *The Renewal of Pagan Antiquity*; Berenson, *The Florentine Painters of the Renaissance*; and Lipps, *Einfühlung*.
52 Gallese, "Mirror Neurons and Art," 459.
53 Freedberg and Gallese, "Motion, Emotion and Empathy," 197.
54 Freedberg and Gallese, "Motion, Emotion and Empathy," 197.
55 On muscular empathy in film, see Plantinga, *Moving Viewers* and Barker, *The Tactile Eye*.
56 Elkins, *Pictures of the Body*, 28 (emphasis in the original).
57 On the way that emotions change in response to events, see Planalp, *Communicating Emotion*, 51–52. On emotions as temporal processes that unfold in time, see Stein et al., "The Representation and Organization of Emotional Experience." On affect bursts, see Scherer, "Affect Bursts."
58 Frijda, *The Emotions*, 479.
59 On emotions in film, see Plantinga, chapter 2, *Moving Viewers* and Tan, chapter 3, *Emotion and the Structure of Narrative Film*. For a cognitive theory on emotion, see Lyons, *Emotion*. For a goal appraisal theory, see Stein et al., "A Goal Appraisal Theory of Emotional Understanding."
60 Stafford, *Echo Objects*, 81.
61 On mirror neurons and motor mimicry, see Rosenblum, chapter 9, *See What I'm Saying*.
62 Rosenblum, *See What I'm Saying*, 206.
63 Bavelas et al., "Motor Mimicry," 324.
64 See, for instance, Scheler, *The Nature of Sympathy*; Hume, *Human Understanding*; and Smith, *The Theory of Moral Sentiment*.
65 Ribot, *The Psychology of the Emotions*, 232. Ribot published his observations on three kinds of sympathy, one of which concerned motor mimicry.
66 Zillmann, "Empathy," 148.
67 On various approaches to the phenomenon of empathy in mass media, see Zillmann, "Empathy."
68 Bavelas et al., "Motor Mimicry," 323.
69 Bavelas et al., "Motor Mimicry," 331 (emphasis in the original).
70 Bavelas et al., "Motor Mimicry," 329 (emphasis in the original).
71 For scientific background on emotional contagion, see Hatfield et al., *Emotional Contagion*; and Brennan, *The Transmission of Affect*. On affective mimicry in cinema, see Smith, *Engaging Characters*, 98–102.
72 Stafford, *Echo Objects*, 76.
73 Persson, *Understanding Cinema*. On early film theorists who drew on psychological studies and gestalt theory to describe the filmic experience, see Hugo Münsterberg, *The Photoplay* and Rudolf Arnheim, *Visual Thinking* and *Art and Visual Perception*.

74 Persson, *Understanding Cinema*, 22.
75 Persson provides more details on distinguishing the particularities of each level of understanding in *Understanding Cinema*, chapter 1, 26–34.
76 Forceville, "From Image Schema," 250. Lakoff, "Mapping the Brain's Metaphor Circuitry," 3.
77 For more details on the ways that "preferred" levels of understanding, disposition, and "reading stances" may constrain the understanding to certain levels, see Persson, *Understanding Cinema*, 35–40.
78 *Diagonal Symphony.*
79 On Johnson's nonrepresentational view of mind, see Chapter 6 in *The Meaning of the Body.*
80 On Fodor's theory of mind, see *The Language of Thought*. In his book *Embodied Cognition*, Lawrence Shapiro validates the arguments put forward by the proponents of embodied cognition to replace the representational theory of mind.
81 For a discussion of other limitations of Fodor's language of thought and what Hilary Putnam calls functionalism, see Putnam, *Representation and Reality.*
82 Johnson, *The Meaning of the Body*, 117.
83 Leder, *The Absent Body*, 14–15.
84 Johnson, *The Meaning of the Body*, 5.
85 Johnson, *The Meaning of the Body*, 89. See James, *The Principles of Psychology.*
86 See Varela et al., *The Embodied Mind*; Maturana and Varela, *The Tree of Knowledge*; Edelman, *Bright Air, Brillant Fire*; Hutchins, *Cognition in the Wild*; and Gallese and Lakoff, "The Brain's Concepts."
87 See for instance, Johnson, *The Meaning of the Body*; Thompson, *Mind in Life*; and Lewis, "Emotion Theory and Neurobiology."
88 Thompson, *Mind in Life*, 371.
89 On the importance of sensorimotor skills for perception, see Noë, *Action in Perception.*
90 Shapiro, *Embodied Cognition*, 4.
91 Lakoff and Johnson provide the example of the spherical being in *Metaphors We Live By*, 57.
92 Johnson, *The Body in the Mind*, 34.
93 Johnson, *The Meaning of the Body*, 136.
94 Johnson, *The Body in the Mind*, 2.
95 Coëgnarts and Kravanja, "Embodied Visual Meaning."
96 Forceville and Jeulink, "The Flesh and Blood."
97 For a list of image schemas, see Hampe, "Image Schemas."
98 See Grady, "A Typology."
99 On the MOVING TIME metaphors, see Johnson, *The Meaning of the Body*, 29.
100 Coëgnarts and Kravanja, "Embodied Visual Meaning," 86.
101 For analyses of metaphors and image schemas in cinema and animation, see Fahlenbrach, ed., *Embodied Metaphors.*
102 See Lakoff and Johnson, *Metaphors We Live By*, chapter 4, "Orientational Metaphors," 14–21.
103 Lakoff and Johnson, *Metaphors We Live By*, 14.
104 For more on personal-space effects in cinema, see Persson, *Understanding Cinema*, 101–142.
105 On puzzle films, see Buckland, ed., *Puzzle Films.*

106 The debate on how to explain the illusion of apparent motion is still going on. See Aksentijevic, "Consciousness and Apparent Motion." For a summary of various scientific explanations given to the phenomenon of apparent motion in cinema, see Anderson and Anderson, "The Myth."
107 Petersik, "The Two-Process," 118.
108 The frame rate should be higher than the flicker fusion threshold to produce apparent motion with motion picture technology. For further details on this phenomenon, see Palmer, *Vision Science*, 471–474.
109 Currie, *Image and Mind*, 47.
110 Johansson, "Visual Perception of Biological Motion," 205–207.
111 Johansson, "Visual Perception of Biological Motion," 205.
112 Johansson, "Visual Perception of Biological Motion," 205.
113 Johansson, "Visual Perception of Biological Motion," 205.
114 Persson, *Understanding Cinema*, 27.
115 On YouTube http://www.youtube.com/watch?v=XiBiO66pOqg.
116 On Eggeling, see Russett and Starr, eds., *Experimental Animation*, 44–48.

2 Cyborg Viewers

Introduction

The chapter develops an enactive approach to perception in animation that distinguishes the embodied spectator from the abstract spectator of traditional film theory. Unlike abstract spectators, biological spectators experience animated media with their perceptual systems. From this perspective, the spectators construct meaning through their tangible engagement with the world viewed instead of decoding the semantic cues that emerge from the cinematic text. This enactive approach is also informed by a shift from a liberal humanist conception of the self to a posthuman one. Accordingly, there is no sharp distinction between the embodied viewers and the disembodied creatures performing on-screen. Instead, the animated interface broadens the viewer's perceptual scope because humans are naturally preadapted to be extended by technology. The chapter further explores how these interactions with the animated world can reshape the viewer's understanding of the body's limits. More specifically, the chapter gives specific examples of what I call "becoming animated," which happens when our encounters with animated figures reveal the frontiers between the human and the nonhuman.

Set in the globally networked Japan of the year 2029, *Ghost in the Shell* (Mamoru Oshii, 1995) explores many of these ideas. Its noirish style and postapocalyptic settings are reminiscent of *Blade Runner* (Ridley Scott, 1982) and *Akira* (Katsuhiro Ôtomo, 1988), two other seminal works of the cyberpunk genre. Following *Blade Runner* and its literary inspiration, Philip K. Dick's *Do Androids Dream of Electric Sheep?* (1968), *Ghost in the Shell* explores questions pertaining to posthumanism. The main protagonist, cyber cop Major Motoko Kusanagi, works for Section 9, a branch of the Japanese government that deals with counterterrorism. She is on the trail of a criminal called the Puppet Master. This dangerous computer virus hacks the minds of cyborgs to transform them into marionettes that unwittingly commit crimes for him. Kusanagi tracks the Puppet Master by jacking into cyberspace via ports located at the nape of her neck. Thanks to her neural extensions, Kusanagi can download useful data from the city's data banks;

however, it is also through these ports that the Puppet Master eventually gains access to her body and mind.

In particular instances, *Ghost in the Shell* aligns the spectator's perspective with those of electronic devices and cyborgs. The animation provides subjective point-of-view shots in the scene where the torso of a female cyborg watches men discussing in a factory. We soon discover that the partly organic brain of the cyborg has become a channeling device for the Puppet Master. Multiple point-of-view shots indicate that the ghost-hacked cyborg can see without the other people in the room realizing it. The rows of horizontal lines that cross the frame and the degraded quality of the image betray the machinic origins of her vision (see Figure 2.1). The repeated lines echo those on the images produced by the video camera in an earlier sequence. They also allude to a computer monitor, as the symbiotic relationship between the Puppet Master and the ghost-hacked cyborg parallels the interdependence between software and hardware in a computer system. The female torso channels a multiplicity of perspectives, since the Puppet Master and the viewers are simultaneously watching through her eyes. This is an example of embodied virtuality powered by the technology of animation and enacted by an embodied viewer.

The conspicuous splitting of the subjective viewpoint in this *anime* alludes to what I call "posthuman perception." This hybrid form of perception occurs when the film blurs the boundaries between the viewer and the animated interface. For instance, when the perspective of the mind-hacked torso coincides with the viewer's viewpoint, the technology of animation enables a subjective merging with monstrosities and otherness. This experience brings to life a hybrid body, one that composites the spectator into the animated world.

The chapter focuses on the cyberpunk genre, as this genre incites viewers to ponder about the limits of embodiment and the dialectical positioning of humans and artificial creatures.[1] Cyberpunk novels and films are peopled with digital subjects and cyborgs that challenge the boundaries between humans and animals, organisms and machines, and the realms of the physical and the non-physical.[2] This subgenre of science fiction reflects on the human condition in an era of accelerated developments in computer science and biotechnology. In her "A Cyborg Manifesto," Donna Haraway projected that the composite figure of the cyborg would resist opposing dyads and reject structures of power based on rigid boundaries.[3] However, depictions of cyborgs in the media wildly diverge from this vision; hybrid identities more than often reassert gender stereotypes, power hierarchy in the society, and class marginalization. Animation is not an exception. For instance, we notice numerous instances of victimization based on gender and class in the animated TV series *Aeon Flux* (Peter Chung, 1991–1995) and *Texhnolyze* (Hiroshi Hamasaki, 2003), the OVA

Figure 2.1 The perspective of the mind-hacked cyborg. *Ghost in the Shell* (Mamoru Oshii, 1995).

series *Malice@Doll* (Keitarô Motonaga, 2001), and the animated feature *Ghost in the Shell 2: Innocence* (Mamoru Oshii, 2004).[4] Yet, with their multiple references to perceptual extensions, cyberpunk animations foreground their preoccupation with the politics of the body in the digital era. For instance, they self-reflexively invite viewers to notice the impacts of developments in information technology, prosthetic research, and biotechnology on our understanding of the human.[5]

The viewer's embodiment is central to this approach to spectatorship. The chapter first examines the shortcomings of some theories of spectatorship that highlight the centrality of vision in cinema while they neglect the viewer's affect.[6] Then, it articulates an alternative to these theories, focusing on empathetic responses and intersubjective alignments between spectators and machines in cyberpunk films. Considering the perspectives of cyborgs, I suggest, helps challenge the notions of subjectivity and identity presupposed by occularcentric theories. In the second part of the chapter, I specify four methods in cyberpunk animations that accentuate the participation of the viewer's body to challenge the notion of a unitary self of liberal humanism. First, I identify examples of augmented perception in *Final Fantasy: The Spirits Within* (Hironobu Sakaguchi, 2001). Second, I explore techniques that simulate forms of perception extended by technologies such as avatarial experiences. Third, sequences where the subjectivity of human and nonhuman agents starts to fuse are analyzed. Fourth, I look at emotional engagements with nonhumans and the questions they raise about our acceptance or rejection of marginalized people. The case studies provided engage with notions of media specificity. They present applications of the technologies of animation that enable distinctive responses and rhetorical effects. The animated films studied reveal innovative assemblages between the viewer's physicality and the animation machine, thereby underscoring the posthuman nature of perception in moving images.

An Enactive Approach to Perception in Animation

Identifying with Posthumans in Cyberpunk Films

Cyborgs, AIs, informational constructs, and androids thrive in cyberpunk films. They behave like intelligent beings whose bodies consist in assemblages of parts open to a range of technological extensions. The posthuman minds and cognitive augmentations are featured in popular films such as *RoboCop* (Paul Verhoeven, 1987), *The Matrix Trilogy* (Lana Wachowski and Lilly Wachowski, 1999, 2003), *Chrysalis* (Julien Leclercq, 2007), *Elysium* (Neill Blomkamp, 2013), *RoboCop* (José Padilha, 2014), *Lucy* (Luc Besson, 2014), and *Ghost in the Shell* (Rupert Sanders, 2017). In animation, we find minds powered by computer technology in *Ghost in the Shell* (1995), dream machines in *Final Fantasy: The Spirits Within*, mind-control satellite technologies in *Appleseed Ex Machina* (Shinji Aramaki, 2007), and cyber viruses in the feature-length OVA titled *Ghost in the Shell: Stand Alone Complex – The Laughing Man* (Kenji Kamiyama, 2005), just to mention a few. These cyberpunk films and animations challenge the liberal humanist conception of the self, which presupposes a mind enclosed within an individual organic shell.

Many of these films present the conception of the posthuman described by N. Katherine Hayles in the book *How We Became Posthuman*.[7] According to this view, the information-processing power of the cyborg is privileged over a particular material instantiation. Because cognition is indistinguishable from computer processing, the cyborg's center of control can be seamlessly connected with computers and digital technologies.[8] Yet, despite an emphasis on brain-machine connections and avatarial forms of disembodiment, these cyberpunk narratives pay considerable attention to the organic body. They constantly stimulate physical and emotional responses in the spectator by multiplying titillating behaviors, violent altercations, painful journeys, and bodily mutilations.[9] Such vicarious arousal may be included on purpose to heighten the viewer's sympathy for posthuman characters. In turn, the spectator draws on these carnal stimulations to obtain a concrete grasp of the characters' motivations. When analyzing moving imagery that showcases the body, considering the spectator's affective responses is crucial for a complete understanding of the several rhetorical elements at play.

Theories of spectatorship that explore issues of identification tend to abstract the spectator to a liberal humanist subject. In doing so, they neglect films that envisage alternatives to the human. These theories are not oblivious to the dual nature of the spectator, which is to simultaneously be a biological being and a stand-in for a sophisticated viewer, one who can interpret cinematic conventions. In *Inside the Gaze*, for example, Francesco Casetti recognizes the difficulty of situating the spectator in Film Theory. In "one case, the interlocutor appears as a creature of flesh and blood, while in the other, as a profoundly symbolic phenomenon."[10] Although Casetti argues that subjectivity emerges as the intersection between a corporeal individual and the symbolic construction that the film implies as its interlocutor, his semiotic approach focuses on the ways in which films exchange gazes with an ideal spectator. The "ideal spectator" in Casetti's theory is a human knowledgeable of the multifold rules of communication. In the communication system he proposes, the spectator uses as its input the information produced by the interface. The spectator, as an organism, is kept separated from the interface and the moving images are considered similar to human perception. By stressing the analogy between human perception and the cinematic apparatus, organism-bound approaches such as that of Casetti neglect types of identification with robots and cyborgs, as they may challenge the assumption that the "ideal spectator" is human. Machinic perception in cyberpunk films could instead remind some viewers that cinematic images are nonhuman, a fact that the psychological realism of classical cinema wants to conceal.

Some organism-bound theories promote misconceptions about human perception. They falsely imply that an eye is like a camera objective or vision approximates the photographic process. The inaccuracy of these similes may lead to a misunderstanding of the nature of human perception, as they ignore the embodied viewer. For example, in Christian Metz's theory of identification, the spectator identifies with the camera, or via the camera, with the characters.[11] Elaborating on Metz's approach, the partisans of the suture theory and psychological realism argue that the use of shot/reverse shots and point-of-view editing encourage spectators to identify with characters by sharing their perspectives in the diegetic world.[12] This kind of psychological realism relies on cinematographic techniques that aim to convince spectators that the world depicted by the mise-en-scène mirrors real-life experiences.[13] The photographic image in live-action films simulates a linear perspective and a sense of depth, which approximate the experience of seeing a scene face-to-face. Cinematic conventions such as the 180° system and the photorealistic nature of the image help support the idea that the images projected—or displayed—on the screen are like images projected in the spectator's inner theater. For instance, when Metz describes the spectator's perception, he explains that there

> are two cones in the auditorium: one ending on the screen and starting both in the projection box and in the spectator's vision insofar as it is projective, and one starting from the screen and "deposited" in the spectator's perception insofar as it is introjective (on the retina, a second screen).[14]

This analogy falsely implies that we have pictures in our heads and neglects the dynamic interactions between body, mind, and world during film viewing. While Metz's theory does not totally abstract the embodied nature of the engagement between spectator and character, it does not account for the dynamic nature of the visual system.

Metz's and Casetti's approaches focus on the spectator as a symbolic concept that generally stands for a sophisticated and knowledgeable spectator. These theories envisage spectators as receptors; they intellectually process the outputs produced by an organized amalgam of signs on the screen without considering the interplay of the senses. They bracket out the dynamic nature of the visual system, and the constant feedback information generated by the body (skin, viscera, the senses, etc.) from the process of interpretation. Alternatively, Per Persson's approach in *Understanding Cinema* considers the contribution of the spectator's perceptual system to the process of cinematic understanding. Persson draws on the psychology of perception to argue that disposition and knowledge of cinematic conventions are closely involved in the process of interpretation. However, as other theories of spectatorship, such as those of Metz and Casetti, Persson's approach downplays the contribution of affect and emotion to the viewer's process of interpretation.[15] In contrast, haptic theories of spectatorship, such as those mentioned in the introduction, are more sensitive to the active contribution of the spectator's senses to the understanding of moving images.[16]

In their choice of corpus, organism-bound theories avoid films that create spatiotemporal distortions because these films draw the viewer's attention to their constructed nature. Indeed, these films reveal the gap between the viewer's perception and the moving imagery that represents perception. We find early examples of spatiotemporal distortions in the surreal films of the 1920s, including Fernand Léger's *Ballet mécanique* (1924) and René Clair's *Entr'acte* (1924). In the latter, the altered film speed modifies the viewer's experience of biological motion, coloring it with a mechanical character that destroys its natural feel. Like surrealist cinema, animated films constantly remind viewers of their constructed nature, even when they deploy various strategies to dissimulate their technological marks.[17] Animation often challenges the laws of physics or turns our points of reference topsy-turvy. The puppet animation *Street of Crocodiles* (Timothy Quay and Stephen Quay, 1986), for instance, presents the world from the perspective of an animated screw.[18] Many animated narrative films purposely break the conventions that encourage immersion in the story world.[19] As media scholar Aylish Wood demonstrates, spatiotemporal transformations in the animated films *Dough for the Do-Do* (Robert Clampett and Friz Freleng, 1949) and *Duck Amuck* (Chuck Jones, 1953) create a direct experience of spaces constructed for the viewer.[20] Pixilation, morphing, and rotoscoping are additional types of image manipulations that undermine an isomorphic connection between the actual world and the cinematic world and thus highlight the active contribution of technology to the construction of the animated world. Unconventional spatiotemporal manipulations constantly confront the idea that moving images are like stand-ins for human perception.

There are also approaches that neglect the dynamic interactions between body, mind, and world during film viewing. While Gilles Deleuze in *Cinema 1* acutely notes that perception in cinema is nonhuman, he explores the nature of perception in cinema from a disembodied perspective. Deleuze distinguishes three major types of perception that are not experienced by the spectator but suggested by the frame's content: the "perception-image," the "affection-image," and the "action-image." Drawing on Henri Bergson's philosophy of natural perception, Deleuze regards the film as if it were itself a center of indetermination that selects particular images from the abstract multidimensional flow of all possible images. This process differs from human perception, which is continuous, uninterrupted by film cuts, framed by eye sockets, and therefore presented from a unique perspective. Deleuze starts from the premise that cinema does not have human perception as its model, "because the mobility of its centers and the variability of its framings always lead it to restore vast acentered and deframed zones."[21] Since Deleuze also conceives of the brain as a device that frames and isolates an image from the flow of images that constitutes "total" perception, it is not difficult to understand why he envisages the camera as performing processes of framing that echo the operations orchestrated by the brain.

In contrast to Deleuze's disembodied approach to perception in cinema, Mark Hansen's theory of new media focuses on the embodied nature of the processes involved in new media production, including spectatorship; spectators are characterized by their bodily informed and affective interactions with animated images.[22] Hansen's theory draws on "embodied enaction," an approach to the mind that takes its inspiration from the work of Francisco Varela and his colleagues in *The Embodied Mind*. From this perspective,

> cognition is not the representation of a pregiven world by a pregiven mind but is rather the enactment of a world and a mind on the basis of a history of the variety of actions that a being in the world performs.[23]

The enactive approach to visual perception rejects the idea that perception is like having a picture in the mind.[24] Instead, as Alva Noë's enactive approach to perception asserts, perception is constituted in part by the possession and exercise of bodily skills.[25]

From the standpoint of embodied enaction, the cinematic image cannot reproduce human perception. A visual experience of a scene is not picturelike; it is enacted. The entirety of the scene depicted by a film is not in sharp focus and uniformly detailed, from the center out to the periphery.[26] Perception in this situation is about the progressive discovery of a scene based on our experience of what seeing feels like. Yet, a film can use certain strategies to represent the particularities of human perception. For example, Marcel Duchamp's short experimental film *Anémic Cinéma*[27] (1926) highlights the affective dimension of the visual experience. The spiraling image induces a sort of vertigo, especially if one tries to read the lines of the poem as they twirl around a revolving disk. As art critic Rosalind Krauss notes, as we look at the pulsating images that dissolve one into the other, the film "brings the news that we 'see' with our bodies."[28] In their approaches, both Krauss and Hansen consider "perception" as an experience that cannot be fully represented by an image, since perception also reverberates through the body. As such, the content of a scene or its particular editing can evoke the concept of human perception itself and its corporeal particularities.

The spectator's perceptual reach is augmented by the technologies of animation. As discussed in the previous chapter, the perceptual systems of *Homo sapiens* are preadapted to be extended by all kinds of technologies, including animated media.[29] Perceptual alterations in animation can unsettle the conventional mechanisms of identification with the characters. Yet, the simulation of machinic vision and the perceptual difference accentuated by the mechanisms of mediation can help viewers understand the feelings of estrangement that cyborgean characters experience. In addition, some cyberpunk animations can enable perceptual couplings with the animated interface that highlight the posthuman nature of perception in animation. Before presenting specific case studies of perceptual extensions, the next section explores underlying themes about extended forms of cognition in cyberpunk films and animations.

Posthuman Perception in Moving Images

A constellation of motifs and representational strategies in cyberpunk animation alludes to the posthuman nature of perception in moving images. Some subjective perspectives invite viewers to question the uniqueness of human vision, and the monstrous birth of animated creatures threatens the stability of the human as a category. In the animated films *Ghost in the Shell* and the OVA series *8 Man After* (Yoriyasu Kogawa, 1993), for example, identitary questioning underpins subjective shots and bodily transformations.[30] While cyberpunk films raise similar concerns, this chapter argues that animation is particularly effective in unsettling the limits between human perception and posthuman perception.[31] Moreover, cyberpunk animation often implies that the viewers themselves can experience posthuman perception because they are extended by the technology of animation.

While the core of the cyberpunk genre originated in American literature in the 1980s, it soon created offshoots in films and graphic novels.[32] The film *Blade Runner* (Ridley Scott, 1982) contains many of the iconographic elements archetypical of this genre, including references to cybernetic research and a futuristic, dystopian setting. Among the familiar characters featured in cyberpunk films, we find: AIs, cyborgs, virtual surrogates, and emergent cellular selves. Typically, digitally enhanced neural interfaces enable the augmented body to access cyberspace, a term that designates the transposition of disembodied realm of information into a three-dimensional space, or cyberspace.[33] William Gibson popularized the concept of cyberspace in his seminal novel *Neuromancer* (1984).[34] Set in a high-tech dystopian future, Case, the main protagonist, can jack into his computer console to rematerialize his disembodied self in the fractal geometry of pure information. Cyberpunk anticipates not only the symbiosis of the posthuman body with machines but also the city's ability to perform a kind of distributed cognition.[35] In cyberpunk narratives, vast data networks and video surveillance systems become the direct extensions of global corporations which use technology to monitor and discipline citizens.

The idea of assimilating the human nervous system to an information-processing machine draws some of its inspiration from the history of cybernetics after WWII and the computerization of the brain in scientific discourse.[36] During the Macy Conferences on Cybernetics, scientists such as Norbert Wiener, Claude Shannon, Ross Ashby, and John von Neumann studied algorithms of control and modes of communication to understand intelligent behavior in both animals and machines.[37] Then, following research on AI, the concept of information "lost its body" through processes of abstraction, as humans progressively became conceptualized as information-processing machines.[38] According to many transhumanists, "embodiment in a biological substrate is seen as an accident of history rather than an inevitability of life."[39] Roboticists Hans Moravec and Ray Kurzweil, for instance, believe that the equivalent of a conscious mind will eventually arise from an executed computer program.[40]

In addition, research in psychology associates human vision with information processing, a topic central to the research of cognitive scientist David Marr.[41] In *Vision Science: Photons to Phenomenology*, Steven Palmer describes visual perception as "the process of acquiring knowledge about environmental objects and events by extracting information from the light they emit or reflect."[42] Although knowledge is specific to people, information processing "allows vision scientists to talk about how people see in the same terms as they talk about how computers might be programed to see."[43] Since the brain is an organ that "produces" images, the computerized brain has become closely intertwined with digital image processing. Consequently, the linguistic shortcuts used to associate devices that automate vision with human perception are similar to the conceptual shortcuts that link digital images and perceptual "images." By assuming that the human body is accessory rather than necessary for perception to occur, cyberpunk films can fluidly cross boundaries between human and "machinic" forms of vision, a term that John Johnston uses to characterize various ways of seeing by means of machines.[44]

We find many exemplars of "machinic vision" in the cyberpunk genre. The term "machinic" is inspired from Deleuze who envisaged it as a working relationship between a perceiving body and technology. Various assemblages between bodies and machines "strive to surmount the human eye's relative immobility as a receptive organ."[45] The digital representations of mental images challenge the concept of machinic vision even further, as there is no seeing per se. As Johnston notes, "VR appears to offer the very antithesis of machinic vision, inasmuch as it replaces the act of looking with an electronically simulated experience of an entirely artificial visual world."[46] Johnston denominates "full VR," a system by which

> the entire sensory body is put in relation to a machine that only simulates external stimuli. But as the body is simultaneously displaced and replaced, the world collapses into the machine, and the eye becomes a vision machine operating in a closed loop. What it "sees" are only precoded signals or data from sensors that can be presented electronically.[47]

Final Fantasy: The Spirits Within, for instance, features cases of machinic vision and full VR. An electronic system can decode Aki's neural patterns and playback her dreams on a TV monitor. In a sequence featuring "full VR," Aki's colleague Gray can join her in one of her dreams via a wireless system. In cyberpunk-animated films, unlike in live-action cinema, both "human" vision and "full VR" are stylized, thus suggesting that human vision is already posthuman.

Additionally, the cyberpunk genre explores the challenge of representing the stability of personal subjectivity and the fragmentation of the self, which are themes also attributed to postmodernist literature. The concepts of the unitary self and the purely human are complicated as the body meshes with computer technology, or as it mutates, thanks to innovative biotechnologies. Major cyberpunk novels foreground their narrative strategies through "the modernist model of multiple, shifting points of view."[48] As literary scholar Brian McHale contends, although the disorganized forms of subjectivity extended by computer technology promoted by the cyberpunk genre are typical of postmodernism, cyberpunk novels continuously draw on the perspectivist narrative strategies of modernist fiction, which usually assume relatively stable subjectivities.

Cyberpunk films multiply perspectives to challenge the stability of the self, a narrative strategy that has often been adopted by modernist films to multiply points of view on the world. Yet, most film theories of the 1960s and 1970s assumed a rational, liberal humanist subject. In *The Cinematic Body*, published in 1993, Shaviro contests a solely rational conception of the self by examining both the affective experiences of the spectators and the irrational behaviors of some characters. Shaviro argues that viewers are not only rational thinkers but also deeply influenced by their affects. Moreover, cinematic bodies can be disorganized, and even brainless, if we take the case of cinematic zombies. Similarly, posthumans in cyberpunk films are often the victims of avatarial control, which may challenge the viewer's identification with rational, unitary selves.

Human and posthuman characters are hooked up to computer systems via neural portals in *Ghost in the Shell* (Mamoru Oshii, 1995), *Strange Days* (Kathryn Bigelow, 1995), *The Thirteenth Floor* (Josef Rusnak, 1999), *eXistenZ* (David Cronenberg, 1999), *The Matrix* (Lana Wachowski and LillyWachowski, 1999), and *Ghost in the Shell* (2017). Such films evoke a direct compatibility between electrical brainwaves and computer systems. *Sleep Dealer* (Alex Rivera, 2008), for instance, showcases applications of surveillance technology and augmented vision. Viewers can observe what Memo Cruz sees on the opposite side of the border when he controls a distant robot via a neural portal. The overlapped perspectives of human viewers and surveillance technologies reinforce Andy Clark's claim that the human is a "natural-born cyborg."

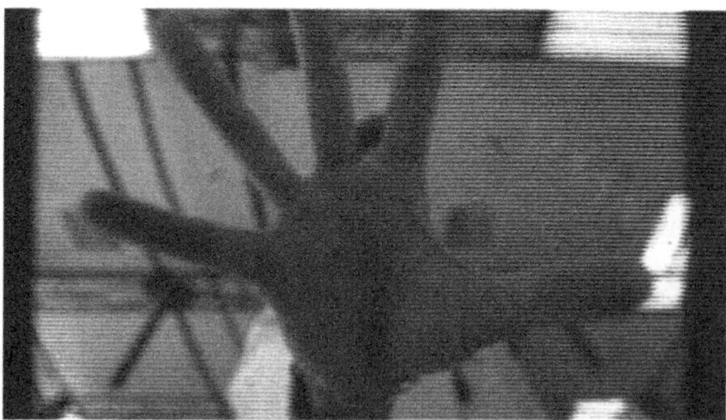

Figure 2.2 RoboCop's perception associated with the degraded image of a TV monitor. *RoboCop* (Paul Verhoeven, 1987).

Some cyberpunk films question the "purely human" nature of perception via the point-of-view shot.[49] By plugging the spectator's visual conduct into the flow of animated images "seen" by computer systems, cyberpunk films often simulate a mind-melding with the machines depicted on-screen. Spectators "see" from the perspective of RoboCop when he is switched on for the first time in *RoboCop* (Paul Verhoeven, 1987). The degraded image of a TV monitor, characterized by apparent horizontal lines, reveals Murphy's transformation into a cyborg (see Figure 2.2). Alternatively, *Westworld* (Michael Crichton, 1973) represents android vision with a pixelated image reminiscent of arcade video games. After a computer malfunction, a robot gunslinger is chasing one of the vacationers at the Westworld theme park. During the chase in the desert, one shot portrays the gunslinger sitting on the back of his horse with two mirrors at the place of his pupils. The subsequent shot presents his subjective perspective of the scenery. We see an eight-bit pixel portrait of a man horseback riding at the top of a mountain, showing the individual pixels that form the image (see Figure 2.3). In both films, point-of-view shots distinguish the posthuman and the human by highlighting the presence of the medium. The degraded image quality in these sequences implies that artificial intelligence can only approximate human perception.

The vanishing distinction between humans and machines is symptomatic of anxieties about the possibility that human perception will be taken over by automated machines. This concern, also expressed by Paul Virilio in *The Vision Machine*, is not unmotivated.[50] Our machines are becoming smarter and more affordable than human labor for certain tasks. Financial profit also motivates governments and industries to

Figure 2.3 Android vision represented by the pixelated image of a cowboy reminiscent of video games. *Westworld* (Michael Crichton, 1973).

transfer to intelligent machines some of the responsibilities traditionally assigned to humans. Yet, if robots acquire the ability to "perceive" one day, they may not be able to make sensible decisions based on the data given, as they would lack the savoir faire and ethical skills developed by embodied citizens. *RoboCop* (1987) explores this fear by featuring a gigantic robot that lacks the embodied ethics of the partly human RoboCop.

Photographic realism in cyberpunk films can obliterate the difference between the "real" and the "virtual." *The Thirteenth Floor* and *The Matrix*, for example, analogize induced forms of perception to visual perceptions experienced by a conscious character by minimizing the presence of the medium. Although the distinct color schemes in *The Thirteenth Floor* help distinguish between the different virtual worlds, Douglas Hall insists that the sensations he experiences in the body of his avatar in the virtual simulation of 1937 Los Angeles are the same as those he feels in the "real world" of the 1990s. We only discover at the end of the film that the world of the 1990s is also a simulation. Similarly, in *The Matrix*, there is no degradation of the image quality to distinguish inside the Matrix from the real world. As *The Matrix* and *The Thirteenth Floor*, the films *Avalon* (Mamoru Oshii, 2001), *eXistenZ*, *Possible Worlds* (Robert Lepage, 2000), and *Vanilla Sky* (Cameron Crowe, 2001) exacerbate anxieties about the "reality effect" and imply that we could all be brains in a vat or avatars living in cyberspace without knowing it.[51]

The difficulty of distinguishing real humans from androids is another source of anxiety in the cyberpunk genre. Because human eyes are often considered the windows to the soul, spectators scrutinize the expression of posthumans' eyes in order to evaluate the presence of some humanity in them. *Blade Runner*, for instance, opens with a huge close-up of an eye that reflects the burning flames of a dystopian cityscape. Despite its anatomical likeness to a human eye, this engineered replica belongs to a Replicant, a very intelligent type of android. As Peter Hutchings asserts, the eye in this film "is used as the site of the test of Humanity: it is the dividing line between Man and Monster, or between Man and Replicant, Model Nexus-6."[52] Instead of using the Voight-Kampff device to detect posthumans, as Deckard does in *Blade Runner*, cyberpunk films often use animated sequences to expose the difference between human vision and nonhuman vision. For example, when compositing charts and text messages are superimposed on a scene observed by a cyborg, they immediately reveal the posthuman nature of the onlooker. This strategy is employed by *Small Soldiers* (Joe Dante, 1998), *Malice@Doll*, *Parasite Dolls* (Kazuto Nakazawa and Naoyuki Yoshinaga, 2003), *8 Man After*, *Ghost in the Shell 2: Innocence* (Mamoru Oshii, 2004), and the animated series *Texhnolyze*. Because animation underlines the fabricated nature of perception for both humans and nonhumans, it reveals that vision in moving images is always posthuman, a fact that photographic realism in cinema tends to conceal.

Not bound to realistic, isomorphic representations of the world, animation often unsettles the viewer's spatiotemporal expectations. Lacking an indexical reference to the real, animated drawings do not pretend that they look like "human perception." As Roger Cardinal argues, "the whole ideal of the animated film is to suppress the categories of normal perception; indeed its logic might even be to suppress all differential categories."[53] The animated OVA series *Parasite Dolls*, for instance, uses various techniques to underline the defamiliarized nature of looking from the viewpoint of a robotic doll. In a sequence of this OVA series, the camera shows feet moving from a perspective taken at the ground level, which makes it difficult to attribute the gaze to a human beholder. In addition, bar charts, grids, and a moving target made out of multiple concentric circles overlay parts of the depicted scene. The strategies particular to the animation medium, such as the series of overlaid graphics, and the strategies shared with live-action cinema, such as unexpected framing, can heighten the defamiliarizing effect of seeing from the perspective of an intelligent machine. These multiple examples confirm that posthuman vision in cyberpunk animation cannot be mistaken for human vision, since animation wants to emphasize the constructed nature of perception.

The Birth of the Cyborg Viewer

The spectators can engage with a variety of hybrids in cyberpunk animation and cinema. While live-action films reassert the unity of the human figure through the body of the actor, the animated body is always on the verge of collapsing. The liminal state of the animated form is evocative of the monstrous body imagined by Mary Shelley in *Frankenstein; or, the Modern Prometheus* (1818). As Hutchings notes, the most abject and repulsive aspect of Frankenstein's monstrous creature originates from its assemblage of corpse fragments; the "living dead" idea is abject as it implies that death is infecting life.[54] Conjuring up similar abject symbols, animated films that deploy the theme of animation/reanimation "not only represent a melding of flesh and iron, life and death, but [also] the body of the films themselves are 'stitched' together through the editing process, technological composites, [and] hybrids of animation and live-action."[55] With its protean possibilities, animation is the perfect material to give life to ghosts, intelligent machines, and the other "centrifugal selves" of cyberpunk fiction. In piecing together heterogeneous elements produced by different technologies, animation is particularly suited to investigate the hybrid nature of the cyborg viewer.

Without the participation of the spectator, the creatures inhabiting the animated realms remain half-dead. It is when the spectator's gaze aligns with the perspective of the animated creature that their symbiotic relationship starts to have a life of its own. The psychological transformation that ensues triggers a cyborgean birth. On the one hand, the stitched bodies of the animated films and the spatiotemporal distortions enabled by the animated interfaces defamiliarize the "everyday" perceptual experience. On the other hand, the spectator is perceptually extended by the film's visual conduct. Through the intersubjective alignments between the viewer and the animated characters, cyberpunk animations not only highlight the presence of the monstrous body, but also suggest that it is not completely foreign to the spectator's body. This mediated experience, which I call "becoming-animated," attracts the viewer's attention to the continuum of sensations from their own to the animated ones.

Narratives that investigate themes related to posthuman perception encourage a reflection on alternative kinds of perceiving bodies. In stitching the spectator's perspective with that of a posthuman entity, cyberpunk films and cyberpunk animations prompt spectators to imagine the distinct visual experience that they could have if they were themselves equipped with machinic eyes or if they were neurally connected to cyberspace. This type of perspective-sharing invites viewers to question the indisputable nature of the differential categories of "human perception" and "nonhuman perception."

Cyberpunk animation often hybridizes the spectator's perceptual system with the animated interface. Also interested in mechanisms that extend embodiment, Hayles examined the kind of subjectivity that emerges at the junction between bodies and computer technology, a concept that she coined "embodied virtuality."[56] Elaborating on this topic, the next sections consider more particularly embodied forms of subjectivity powered by the animation machine. Specular identification with avatars, for instance, is a particular instance of "becoming-animated" that enables viewers to experience the interrelations of embodied and disembodied forms of spectatorship.

Four cases of embodied virtuality are examined in more detail. Some animations prompt spectators to imagine that they have acquired new modes of perception due to augmented devices or neural alterations. *Final Fantasy: The Spirits Within* illustrates this case with overlaid graphic displays that simulate augmented perception. In addition, certain animations employ distinct automatisms to underscore the posthuman nature of spectatorship, as revealed by: flickering effects in *Immortal Ad Vitam* (Enki Bilal, 2004), the merging of subjectivities in *Ghost in the Shell*, and empathic bonding with marginalized androids.

Hybridizing the Spectator's Perceptual System

Augmented Perception in Final Fantasy: The Spirits Within

Cyborg viewers perceive the liveliness of the animated world because their perceptual systems are naturally preadapted to distinguish shapes on the screen and register the succession of static images coming to life. Many animated films purposely spotlight the perceptual assemblage of the viewer with the animated interface by layering information on the screen in a manner that imitates augmented-reality devices. Although heads-up display systems or eyeglass-styled display systems are user-friendly devices, they are quite conspicuous. Yet, we progressively forget their presence after using them for a while. Clark terms these interfaces "human-centered products" because they "wear their functionality on their sleeve and exploit the natural strengths of human brains and bodies."[57] Similarly, even though animation technology creates eye-catching interfaces, viewers tend to forget their stylized designs when absorbed by the narrative. The animated interface—another form of human-centered technology—becomes a portal to fictive worlds.

The technology of animation appears to augment the viewer's perception in key sequences of *Final Fantasy: The Spirits Within*. At the beginning of the film, Dr. Aki and the other members of a military rescue team wear head-mounted displays (see Figure 2.4). Thanks to their augmented interface, the protagonists can detect the presence of a rare organic specimen. When Aki wears her head-mounted gear, she can identify alien phantoms invisible to the naked eye. The computerized device compiles and translates the information acquired from the environment into charts and schematic information, which are then superimposed over the landscape. Concurrently, the technology of animation integrates the spectator into a mixed-reality environment.[58] The prosthetic assemblage composed by the viewer's perceptual system, the screen, and the composited images thrusts the spectator into the fictive animated world. Other animated works, such as the animated series *Texhnolyze* and the animated OVAs *Parasite Dolls*, *Malice@Doll*, and *8 Man After*, employ composited interfaces to parallel the visual systems of cyborgs and AI with the windowed desktops of computer systems. Many science fiction films and TV series feature composited interfaces that represent mixed-reality environments, including *Iron Man* (Jon Favreau, 2008), *The Thirteenth Floor*, *Justice League* (Zack Snyder, 2017), and some episodes from the TV series *Eureka* (2006–2012). Animated films, however, motivate us to recognize that reality and mixed-reality environments do not need to be photorealistic. Unlike human perception, posthuman perception is free to reinvent and reshape its referent.

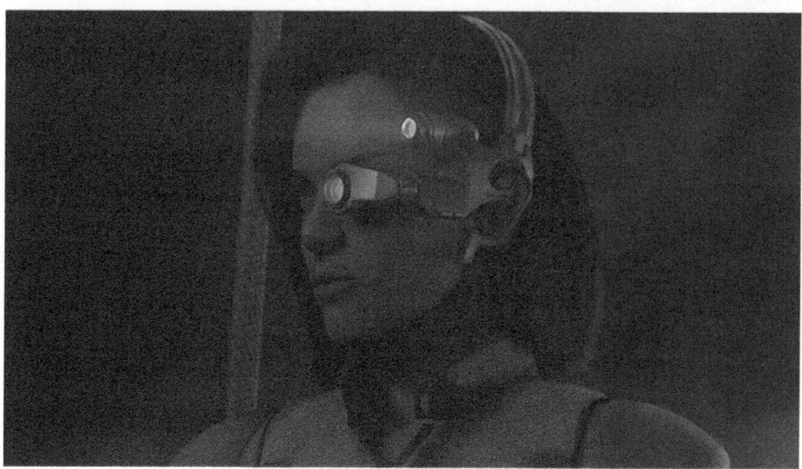

Figure 2.4 Aki wearing a head-up display system. *Final Fantasy: The Spirits Within* (Hironobu Sakaguchi, 2001).

Animation invites us to decode the unfamiliar world it creates rather than passively observe the flow of images that unfolds before our eyes. As examined in the previous chapter, animation can supplement the analytic capacity of the viewer. Rejecting the idea that perception is solely organism-bound, Clark argues that animated media and media storage can extend the mind.[59] For instance, we use notepads and calculating devices to help with the limitations of our human memory. Just as Clark extends the boundaries of the mind to external devices, since cognitive processes do not stop at the limit of our anatomy, the technology of animation functionally augments the spectator's access to the fictive world and thereby produces larger cognitive wholes. Because viewers have internalized many conventions of animated narratives, they can translate into meaningful information the stitches and seams that connect the heterogeneous elements composing the interface into a complex world. For instance, in *Final Fantasy: The Spirits Within*, the animated interface overlaid with charts and numbers guides the protagonists on their journey through the unfamiliar landscape (see Figure 2.5). The viewers understand that this is an extra layer that represents an "augmented" form of reality. The process of discriminating between the "augmented" world and the "real" world of the characters, which is a form of mental computing, has been internalized by the spectators. The augmented perspectives in this sequence can even function as extensions to the spectators' visions, as if they were themselves wearing head-mounted displays.

Cyberpunk animation often anticipates visions of a posthuman future in which humans have become seamlessly articulated with patterns of information.[60] The animated interface simulates the spectator's

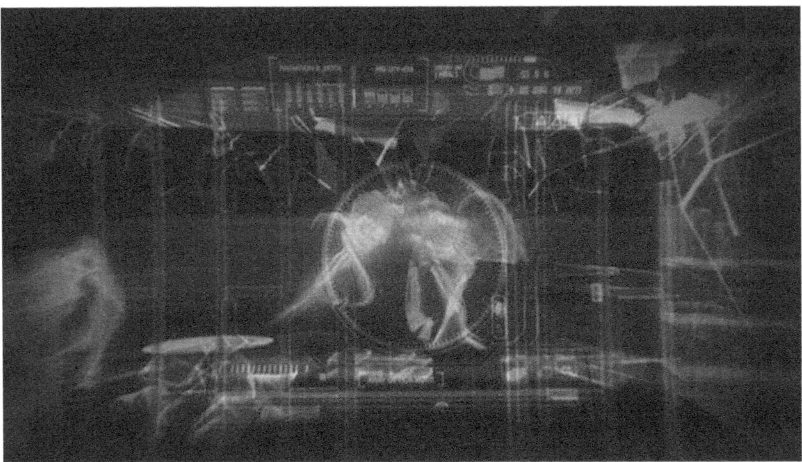

Figure 2.5 Augmented perception represented with a superimposed grid. *Final Fantasy: The Spirits Within* (Hironobu Sakaguchi, 2001).

environment in order to suggest that it will eventually extend it. In that sense, *Final Fantasy: the Spirits Within* blurs the boundary between the real and the Baudrillardian hyperreal. When the sun sets at the beginning of the film, the camera flares simulate a photographic effect despite the lack of a profilmic referent. The near-photorealism of the set designs evokes the possibility that our postapocalyptic future will be peopled by digital constructs.

Since the release of *Final Fantasy: The Spirits Within*, media productions rely more and more on synthespians for acting parts, thus further dissolving the differences between the human and the nonhuman actors. Although the synthespians' facial traits and their mouth movements were not absolutely perfect in 2001, the level of detail achieved by the CGI techniques and motion capture systems certainly started to convince viewers and the film industry that eventually they will not be able to distinguish photographic images from computer-generated ones. Arguably the first film to invest astronomical amounts of money and energy in its effort to design nearly photorealistic humans with computer technology, *Final Fantasy: The Spirits Within* encouraged speculations about the impacts of using synthespians instead of actors on the future of human labor. Why hire actors when cyberstars conform completely to the script and without any complaints? Noticing a change in the production practices since the advent of computer animation, actors started to voice their anxiety over the increasingly competitive role synthetic life was starting to play in the cinematic economy. As Hollywood prepared for the release of *Final Fantasy: The Spirits Within*, actor Tom Hanks, who would eventually "play" all the characters in the animated film *The Polar*

Express (Robert Zemeckis, 2004), started to fear that animated characters could replace actors in the future.[61] Even George Lucas was skeptical that one day he would use computers to portray human characters.[62] Although synthespians are increasingly present in recent blockbusters, humans are still very much involved in the creation of believable virtual performances, as it is the case for *Avatar* (James Cameron, 2009), *The Curious Case of Benjamin Button*, the film series *The Lord of the Rings* (2001, 2002, 2003), *Rise of the Planet of the Apes* (Rupert Wyatt, 2011), *Dawn of the Planet of the Apes* (Matt Reeves, 2014), *War for the Planet of the Apes* (Matt Reeves, 2017), and *Guardians of the Galaxy* (James Gunn, 2014).

We also witness an increase in the use of computer-skilled workers in the production of live-action films and animations. Even though many of the people usually hired for the production of live-action films were absent from the production team of *Final Fantasy: The Spirits Within*, teams of flesh-and-blood computer programmers, humans used for the motion-capture stage, and computer systems collaborated to form a whole new machinic assemblage.[63] Actors interact more and more with animated interfaces in special effects cinema. Depictions of mixed-reality environments in animation, such as those mentioned earlier, incite viewers to imagine themselves at the junction between the real and the animated, ready to be uploaded into the Matrix. The "real" world they depict is a multilayered world on which humans are composited, much like the animated characters featured in the mixed-media sequences of live-action films.

Extended Perception: Simstim, SQUID, and Flickering Effects

Many cyberpunk films simulate a somatic hybridization of the viewer with the interface. Viewers are incited to feel what the characters feel, not only what they see. Avatarial impersonation is one strategy to achieve this form of hybridization. In the novel *Neuromancer*, for example, when Molly wears a simstim broadcast rig, Case can remotely adopt her perspective and experience her sensorium by activating a switch. When she playfully touches her breasts to surprise Case, he can also feel them within his hands. Cyberpunk films often use avatarial impersonation and subjective perspectives as devices to engross viewers.[64] In *Strange Days*, when a character wears a SQUID, or "Superconducting Quantum Interference Device," on his or her head, the device records what the wearer sees and feels. The SQUID translates into digital information the electrical activity present along the scalp. It is then possible for another wearer to see and participate in the events that were recorded by someone else. The device enables the persistence of the flesh in digital space.[65] In many sequences, *Strange Days* shows exhilarating chases presented from the subjective point of view of the characters. The swift and jerky camera movements cause proprioceptive sensations in the viewers that mirror the sensations of the characters and thereby suggest that they themselves wear a SQUID.

Likewise, certain animation techniques transfer sensations experienced by the characters to the viewers. For example, a sequence of flickering images in *Appleseed Ex Machina* evokes the pain felt by the malfunctioning Briareos, a cyborg. *Appleseed Ex Machina* is set in the dystopian, futuristic city named Olympia, populated by an advanced civilization that comprises humans, bioengineered bioroids, and cyborgs.[66] Special police force officers and Deunan fight a mad scientist who invented a satellite-driven device, the Halcon system. When activated, this system can control the minds of humans and bioroids via a wireless Bluetooth earset. Halcon can also disrupt the brain functions of cyborgs from a distance, and among them Briareos, whose human body is partly covered with metallic gears (see Figure 2.6). His body had been cybernetically reengineered after having been severely injured in a shootout. Near the end of the animation, during a fight with a killing swarm of electronic devices, Briareos's brain is remotely hacked by the Halcon system. The damage inflicted to his neural circuits disrupts his visual system and causes him to see a succession of pixelated and distorted images. Made up of a series of thin horizontal lines, these flickering images resemble those produced by the cathodic screens of old televisions. The flickers induce visual pulsations, whose reverberating effects are amplified by Briareos's suffering moans.

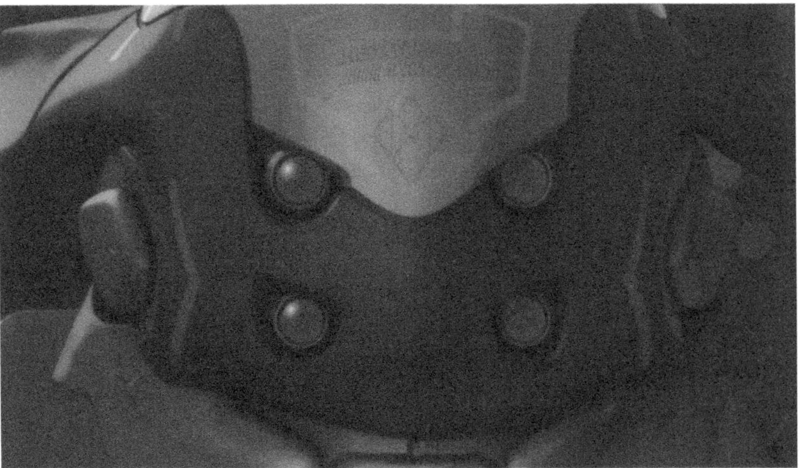

Figure 2.6 Briareos's body covered with metallic gear. *Appleseed Ex Machina* (Shinji Aramaki, 2007).

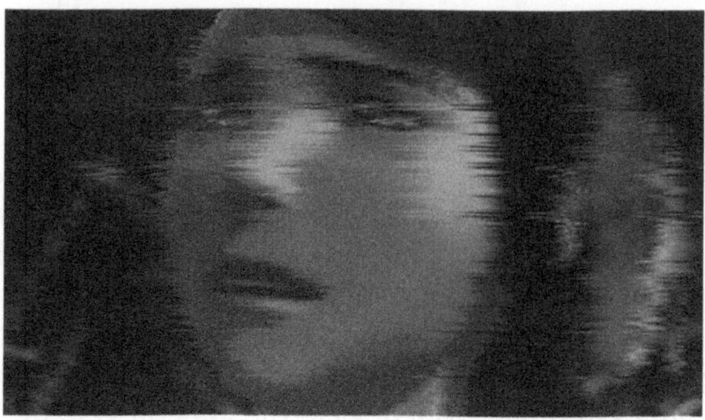

Figure 2.7 Flickering images representing Dr. Xander. *Appleseed Ex Machina* (Shinji Aramaki, 2007).

The flickering images translate the character's mental breakdown into the visual spectrum. They simulate Briareos's pain, albeit with a weakened intensity. In some rare cases, flashing lights and the stroboscopic effects generated by animated films have provoked health problems.[67] However, the flickering images in this sequence can unlikely elicit such extreme responses. The animation technique converts the disembodied perception of the cyborg into vicarious effects that remind viewers about the presence of their own body. In other words, the flickering images induce a coercive subjugation of the spectator's body to bolster our empathy for the cyborg character.

The rapid alternation of highly contrasted images makes them appear to flicker, since the human visual system cannot perceive individual images at this presentation rate. Indeed, the time-based effect disappears when the images are shown one photogram at a time. The flickering effect is caused by the particular coupling of the spectator's visual system with the animation apparatus. Moreover, because human perception is mostly continuous, the discontinuities introduced by the flickering images foreground the necessary contribution of the technology in the production of this perceptual effect. In brief, the animation takes advantage of the human visual system's limitations to arouse sensations congruent with those experienced by Briareos.

Later in this scene, *Appleseed Ex Machina* emphasizes the alignment of the spectator with the animation apparatus when the pulsating images indicate the merging of the consciousness of Briareos, Deunan, and Doctor Xander, whose body had been transformed into a cyborgean hybrid controlled by the Halcon system. At this point in the story, the Doctor holds captive Briareos and Deunan. With telescopic wires protruding from her body, the part human-part machine system can directly access their nervous systems. The flickering images of a woman that asks for help—presumably the Doctor before her transformation into a cyborg—represent the merging of Briareos's and Deunan's minds with what is left of Xander's memory (see Figure 2.7). Moreover, the mind-melding effect implicitly involves the spectators who are watching the sequence. When the viewers perceptually join the characters, they become "animated" as they realize that the place where their perception begins starts to run together with the characters' perceptions.

This perceptual alignment can expand the spectator's everyday perceptual repertoire. Hinting at posthuman forms of perception, the sequence alludes to the possibility of qualitatively experiencing forms of vision alternative to human vision. In addition, by sharing the distressing symptoms of the technologically hacked body, this animation warns viewers about the harm that can be caused by invasive technologies.

Since this animated film was made, companies have engineered retinal prostheses to restore sight. Although *Appleseed Ex Machina* does not explicitly describe the mechanisms by which Briareos comes to "see" his surrounding world, we can assume that information acquired from the environment, such as light reflected or emitted by objects around him, enters the green lenses on his metallic head, which is then processed by a computing device. Unlike the arguably high-resolution vision of Briareos, actual vision systems, such as the one built by the U.S. firm Second Sight™, enable blind people to distinguish the silhouettes of objects.[68] The reporter Josh Fischman divides the process by which Second Sight™'s system produces vision into four basic steps.[69] (1) The system first uses a video camera to send acquired video images to a computer worn on a belt, which then converts the images into a simplified signal. (2) A transmitter sends the signal wirelessly to an implant in the eye. (3) A receiver sends the signal to an electrode array to stimulate the retina. (4) The optic nerve carries the signal from the retina to the brain, which helps perceive the visual patterns corresponding to the stimulated area. Although this bionic eye extends one's perceptual awareness, it is less effective than Briareos's cyborgean prosthesis.

Similarly, the hybrid film *Immortal Ad Vitam* reveals the embodied nature of human vision with a sequence of animated images. In a scene set in a museum, Jill, the mutant protagonist, walks through a section about human physiology. By interacting with the exhibits on display, she learns about the human condition. Then, a body scanner reveals that her internal organs are now mapped in the same way as they are in a human. At the same time as Jill, we understand that her alien anatomy had mysteriously become human. A moment later, she watches a stop-motion animation featuring Eadweard Muybridge's experiments on human motion. Because she can perceive the flickering images as other humans do, the sequence self-reflexively underscores the particularity of human vision and echoes the condition of the spectators.

Immortal Ad Vitam highlights the distinctive experience that the automatisms of animation can arouse. Unlike classical narrative cinema, which privileges the transparency of the medium—the screen doubling itself as a porthole to the world—animation enables unique spatiotemporal experiences that result from the cyborgean assemblage of the spectator's body and the animated interface. Posthuman perception in animation, a kind of perception realized in conjunction with technology, challenges the liberal humanist idea that the human is self-contained within an organism and, consequently, that spectatorship is divorced from what happens in the animated world. When the spectator sees the flickering images, the symbiotic entanglement of their perceptual system with the technological apparatus provides an example of what Clark calls "extended cognitive wholes." When the spectators discover that Jill has become human, they also realize that perception in animation is posthuman.

The Merging of Subjectivities in Ghost in the Shell

The merging of distinct subjectivities in cyberpunk narratives destabilizes the conception of a central and stable self envisaged by liberal humanism. Fragmented bodies and "digital subjects" are typical of the Regime of Computation, a worldview where the Computational Universe is the engine at the source of both human behavior and physical reality.[70] As Hayles explains in *My Mother Was a Computer*, in

> the twenty-first century, the debates are likely to center not so much on the tension between the liberal humanist tradition and the posthuman but on different versions of the posthuman as they continue to evolve in conjunction with intelligent machines.[71]

As I argue, the cyberpunk *anime Ghost in the Shell* is filled with digital subjects and what Hayles denominates "embodied virtualities."

Merged perspectives and the sharing of one body by multiple people are two strategies that cyberpunk narratives employ to represent decentered selves. Some animations invite the viewer to mind meld with a cyborg character. This phenomenon is an animated variant to what McHale calls the "centrifugal self."[72] This term describes characters in cyberpunk novels that break up into multiple software "selves" or that become "diffused throughout the worldwide information network."[73] *Neuromancer*, for instance, uses an alternative to the literary point-of-view convention when Molly wears the simstim broadcast rig.[74] Narratively, the perspectives of the two characters are merged, which symbolizes the idea of a fragmented self. The switch between Case's reality plane and Molly's point of view produces an effect of "'split-screen' cinema or television—or indeed, that of multiple-point-of-view fiction."[75] In cyberpunk animation, point-of-view editing can replace the multiplicity of perspectives found in modernist novels.

Multiple representations of the centrifugal self in the animated version of *Ghost in the Shell* unsettle the Western humanist tradition. One occurrence is the perverse spectacle of Kusanagi's dismemberment when she is hacked by the Puppet Master before the finale. This scene threatens the idea of the unitary self, individual freedom, self-determination, and physical integrity. Additionally, the scene interrogates the limits of humanness. According to Batou, Kusanagi's colleague, having a minimum of human cells in the brain is sufficient to claim human identity, as long as society treats cyborgs like humans. For Kusanagi, however, the incapability to distinguish between perceptions generated by a human brain or synthetically induced is a reason for doubts; she has no way to compare what she experiences with what "real" humans experience. Similar philosophical questions pervade discussions about the Regime of Computation: how one could distinguish "real" perceptions from those simulated by the computer system to which one is supposedly connected? In *Ghost in the Shell*, stylistic strategies attempt to break this impasse and differentiate Kusanagi's vision from the vision of a ghost-hacked cyborg. Yet, the stylized rendering of animated vision clearly departs from the properties of human perception and casts into doubt the human nature of any of the characters.

The alignment between the spectator's gaze and the cyborg's gaze that occurs toward the end of *Ghost in the Shell* evokes a mind-melding of the viewer with posthumans. When Kusanagi's and the Puppet Master's minds merge, their coalesced "ghost" is subsequently incorporated into the body of a young girl. The story does not clearly explain why Kusanagi chose to fuse her mind with the Puppet Master's mind. Was it the Puppet Master's offer to share his unlimited knowledge that convinced Kusanagi to associate with him? An earlier conversation with Batou could imply so. She had told him, "I feel confined, only free to expand myself within boundaries." While this lament could justify her decision, the plot did not further develop this hypothesis, and the animation rather concludes in an open-ended way. In the final moments, the young girl, who affirms that she is neither Kusanagi nor the Puppet Master, looks at the shimmering lights of the city landscape with a totalizing gaze.

Media scholar Carl Silvio interprets this ending as "the recontainment of the radical cyborg within the paradigm of maternity."[76] Because the Puppet Master describes Kusanagi as the "bearer" of his offspring, Silvio argues that the narrative recodes the resistant cyborg body into the conventional, maternal trope of "passive and reproductive."[77] This interpretation of the ending simplifies the more complex representations of sexual identity and motherhood that the animation offers. For instance,

Kusanagi is not the sole bearer of the child. In fact, Kusanagi and the Puppet Master's "ghosts" combine to become the child of their union.

The merging of their subjectivities may refocus the spectators' attention to the sharing of their own visual perspective with that of a machinic entity. Toward the end, a moment of blackness precedes the climactic re-animation of the fused entity, neither human nor monster. A quick flash, reminiscent of the ones produced by old television sets when they are quickly switched on and off, marks the transition. The spark seems to "animate" the technological interface that separates the spectator from the newly born entity. The coming to life of the young girl can symbolize the spectator's own electronic transmutation. In other words, it evokes the possibility of the viewer's physical fusion with the animated world, a way of crossing of the boundary of the screen.

By creating a network of humans and machines, *Ghost in the Shell* unsettles the stability of the human promoted by liberal humanism.[78] On the one hand, posthuman perception is a theme explored in the narrative. On the other hand, the symbiotic relationship between humans and cyborgs is revealed by the perceptual overlap of the spectators' and the cyborgs' perspectives. This is a process of becoming enacted by the spectators. In the examples provided in this section, "becoming-animated" corresponds to the hybrid form of subjectivity that comes to life when the viewers' perceptions and sensations coincide with those experienced by animated cyborgs. Furthermore, becoming-animated is the sensation that the animated interface is not external to the viewer but an extension of the viewer's perceptual system.

Empathizing with Cyborgs

Seeing flickering images through Briareos's eyes in *Appleseed Ex Machina* or diving from a high-rise building with Kusanagi in the *anime Ghost in the Shell* arouse sensations congruent with those experienced by these cyborgean characters. Animation is particularly eager to address ambiguous questions about representing the affinities with and differences from nonhuman types of embodiment. This medium constantly boasts its ability to transform the body at will and imagine impossible forms of embodiment. As animation scholar Joanna Bouldin puts it, "[t]he medium of animation allows us to imagine the impossible—identities, capabilities, and bodies that exceed the limits of the flesh."[79] Although the viewer does not literally become the animated character, "there is a way in which some of the plasticity and strength of the utterly impossible animated body resonates with, or sends ripples of possibility through our own, more gravity-constrained flesh."[80]

At the same time, animated films ought to use various strategies to bypass the difficulties associated with the identification with the animated body. Indeed, some could argue that Kusanagi's bioengineered body can prevent viewers from engaging with her. Because of her acute reflexes and increased strength, Kusanagi performs feats impossible for humans, such as dives from high-rises and impressive acrobatics. While looking down from the top of a building can elicit thrilling sensations from some viewers, the lack of realism of the animated drawings can decrease narrative immersion for others. The next chapter further elaborates on a variety of strategies that contribute to making the animated world more familiar and engaging. As in cinema, various processes intensify the viewers' interest for a character, including the processes of recognition, alignment, and allegiance. Accordingly, viewers can empathize with nonhuman characters, but the processes of recognition and allegiance can be more demanding, especially when the animation stretches the limits of mimetism by depicting nonhuman bodies.

Nevertheless, the viewer's embodied vision provides an understanding of the perceived animated figure beyond the visual sphere, attaching a whole range of sensations around it based on prior spatial and physical experiences. It is thus possible to locate animated films along what Harald Stadler calls a "continuum of 'realities.'"[81] Live-action films and animations produce modulated intensities of spectatorial engagement that vary according to the sense of reality that the medium conveys. Drawing on the work of R. D. Laing, Stadler argues that "perception, imagination, fantasy, dreams, and memory are simply different *modes of experience*, all of which constitute a sense of reality."[82] The difference between these senses of reality is that some are "simply less imaginary than others."[83] As part of this continuum, *Ghost in the Shell* is more imaginary than a live-action science fiction film, but it is still concerned with preserving the structural consistency and the quasi-photorealism of the world it depicts. Kusanagi's human appearance also compels viewers to empathize with her and be inwardly involved in the action. Despite Kusanagi's animated embodiment, her impossible movements can elicit proprioceptive responses because feats of imagination can stretch the continuum of reality to accommodate new modes of experience. The depiction of sensational feats and Kusanagi's philosophical musing on her posthuman condition stretch the concept of the human and question the anatomical limits of what has been traditionally associated with the human body.

Anatomical differences can sometimes short-circuit empathetic responses. Some cyberpunk films use robotic eyes to evoke the android's lack of empathy, including *The Terminator* (James Cameron, 1984) and *Blade Runner*. The Terminator's eye and the replicant's eye are indicators of the presence of human emotions or the lack thereof. The robotic eye is also a recurring motif in cyberpunk animations and TV series such as *World Record* (Takeshi Koike, 2003), *Malice@Doll*, and *Aeon Flux* (1991–1995). In *World Record*, for instance, the metallic eyeball of a robot observes the body of a screaming sprinter immersed in a vat of liquid. On the one hand, the impassivity of the robotic eye intimates the robot's total lack of empathy for the suffering man. On the other hand, this disempowered condition of a man turned into a living battery compels viewers to sympathize with him. This allegory implies that empathy, an attribute usually reserved to humans, differentiates flesh-and-blood viewers from the emotionally impaired robots.

Unlike the soulless robotic eye of *World Record*, the computer-generated eye that looks into the camera at the beginning of *Final Fantasy: The Spirits Within* suggests the presence of a soul. The extreme close-up of Aki's eye is designed with subtle creases on the skin around the eye and realistic light reflection on the iris and pupil. The photorealistic rendering of the eyes lends Aki a human aura (see Figure 2.8). Additionally, the attention to details inspires viewers to "identify" with the character, or, in other words, feel sympathy for her. However, this type of identification is problematic. As Barbara Creed argues, when

> asked to identify with a cyberstar, the spectator [is] haunted by a sense of uncanny: the image on the screen appears human, and yet is not human. The glamorous other is a phantom, an image without a referent in the real, an exotic chimera, familiar yet strange.[84]

The uncanny effects expose the viewers' ambivalence toward the cyberstar, a topic that is further developed in Chapter 5. Indeed, although the animated form elicits affects in registers similar to those aroused by the human form, its uncanniness also reveals the difference in embodiment between the spectator's body and the animated character's body.

Anxiety toward difference underlies the stories of *Armitage III: Polymatrix* (Takuya Satô, 1996) and *Armitage: Dual Matrix* (Katsuhito Akiyama, 2002). These two *anime* anticipate the potential problems that cyborgs and androids may eventually pose for society. They are set

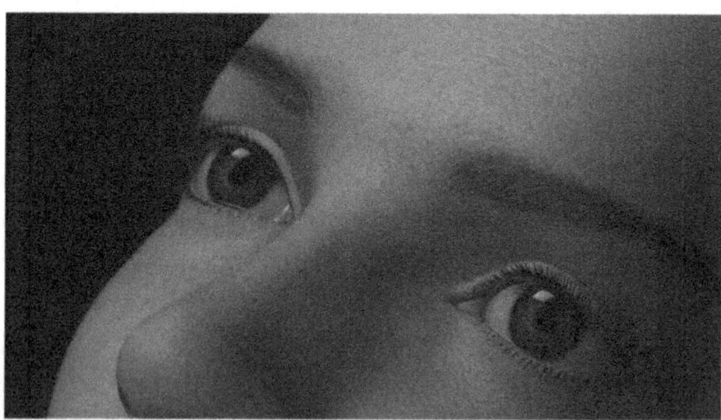

Figure 2.8 Aki's photorealistic eyes. *Final Fantasy: The Spirits Within* (Hironobu Sakaguchi, 2001).

in a futuristic society on Mars where humans cohabit with robots and androids. The main protagonist, special agent Naomi Armitage, is an android who looks completely human. She must hide her true identity because the society considers robots and androids as inferiors and subordinates. Androids of superior intelligence, such as Naomi, are seen as potential sources of threat because they can be hacked and controlled by criminals. The probing of the affinities and differences between humans and posthumans in these cyberpunk narratives raises questions about equity toward identities that deviate from the norm.

While the stories examined in this chapter occur in the realm of the imaginary, they may encourage some viewers to empathize with victims of marginalization in their everyday lives. Some characters in cyberpunk animation are substitutes for people falling outside the normative canon. Alternatively, as Sergei Eisenstein argues, the subversive potential of "the animated" cartoon could even encourage some viewers to embrace a different type of life:

> In a country and social order with such a merciless standardized and mechanically measured existence, which is difficult to call life, the sight of such "omnipotence" (that is, the ability to become, "whatever you wish") cannot but hold a sharp degree of attractiveness. This is as true for the United States as it is for the petrified canons of world-outlook, art and philosophy of eighteenth century Japan.[85]

Animation not only provides the opportunity to imagine impossible embodiments, but also conveys empowering images for those who look different.

Proprioceptive bonding, contrasting forms of embodiment, and the splitting of the viewpoint are methods employed by cyberpunk animations to blur the boundaries between the human and the nonhuman. Whether it is by showing supernatural feats of skill or by introducing eerie cyberstars, cyberpunk animations stretch the limits of the human in ways that are both familiar and uncanny. While the uncanny effects and dystopian themes can be symptomatic of a fear of the future anticipated by recent developments in bioengineering, they can also provoke uneasiness toward the social rejection of nonnormative bodies. Unlike CG cinema, which increases the viewer's engagement through modes of realism and photorealistic imaging, the defamiliarizing interface of cyberpunk animation underscores the challenges of engaging with those who are different from us or depart from the accepted canon.

Conclusion

Cyberpunk narratives depict varieties of embodiment that extend and redraw the limits of the human as envisaged by the liberal humanist tradition. As in cyberpunk literature, avatars, virtual constructs, and AI abound in cyberpunk cinema and animated films. In animation, more particularly, these posthuman characters are animated jointly by the viewer's perceptual system and the apparatus of animation. The focus on extended modes of perception and embodied vision in this book challenges traditional organism-bound theories of spectatorship that focus on the spectator as a disembodied stand-in for the biological viewer.

Although the animated world is conjured up by a combination of technologies that are independent from the spectator, the world "viewed" is enacted by an embodied spectator. This extended form of subjectivity powered by animated technologies expands Hayles's concept of "embodied virtuality." Although narratives in cyberpunk animation evoke a material/information separation, and thus a separation of the self from the body, they also grant viewers access to cyborgs' subjective perspectives, which enables the extracted information to be reembodied. I consider perception in animation to be an extended cognitive process that comprises inputs from the spectator's bodily sensations and the film's contribution to this process. The body of the cyborg viewer is part of a heterogeneous machine that orchestrates the eclectic automatisms of animated media, including their technologies, conventions, styles, and modes of production.

The chapter focused on four ways in which cyberpunk animations emphasize the contribution of the viewer's body to the emergence of embodied virtualities. First, the digital simulacrum produced by animation and CG cinema can be understood as an interface that augments the viewer's perceptual reach. Whether they depict augmented interfaces or mixed-reality environments, some animations and CG films suggest to viewers that they have been composited into the animated environment, as the characters they watch. The perceptual assemblage between the viewer and the animated interface in *Final Fantasy: The Spirits Within* enables a new cyborgean ecology in which viewers, machines, and synthetic life can coexist.

Sharing the perspective of posthuman characters and subjective camera movements can produce cyborgean assemblages that simulate avatarial experiences. Through perceptual hybridization with the animated interface, the viewer can experience spatiotemporal shifts and unfamiliar muscular sensations. Avatarial experiences with the SQUID in *Strange Days* and flickering effects in *Appleseed Ex Machina* cause emotional reverberations that extend the spectators' perceptual scope. What is special about animation is the fact that its non-photorealistic interface can simulate the defamiliarizing transformation of the human into the posthuman in ways that are not illusory. *Immortal Ad Vitam*, for instance, highlights the automatisms specific to animation in the sequence featuring an excerpt from Muybridge's animated experiments. While this sequence demonstrates in a literal way that Jill has become human, the discontinuous series of images subtly implies the posthuman assemblage between the viewer and the animation machine.

The cyborg viewer can be involved in a distributed cognitive system composed of human and nonhuman agents, another type of embodied virtuality. Point-of-view editing can incite viewers to identify with posthuman characters, a strategy also present in cyberpunk live-action cinema. The multiplicity of perspectives, overlaid text and bar charts, and degraded image quality intimate the perspective of the posthuman. In animation, more particularly, because the image viewed is dramatically different from human perception, the narrative often suggests that fictive machines have not only succeeded in tapping into the viewer's mind, but have also been able to completely rewire it.

Some of the cyberpunk animations studied incite viewers to investigate the limits between the human and the posthuman via their emotional engagement with animated characters. Their defamiliarizing interfaces underscore the difficulties accompanying any engagement with nonnormative kinds of embodiment.

Finally, novel spatiotemporal experiences, augmented perceptions, defamiliarizing engagements with roboticized bodies, or hybridized forms of subjectivity in cyberpunk animation can reveal the discursive and material practices through which differential boundaries between the "human" and the "nonhuman" are created. These different strategies make the case for an approach to spectatorship that considers the technology of animation as an extension to an embodied viewer, namely, a posthuman approach to spectatorship.

Notes

1 The history of the cyberpunk genre is explored in a series of essays in McCaffery, ed., *Storming the Reality Studio*. Cyberpunk in animation has been influenced by Japanese manga. The Japanese manga series *Akira* was published in *Young Magazine* between 1982 and 1990. French comic books also inspired cyberpunk authors. For instance, in an interview for *Details Magazine* in the October issue of 1992, William Gibson mentions that along with Ridley Scott, he had been inspired by the "lyrical sort of information sickness" found in the French magazine *Métal Hurlant* (*Heavy Metal*) that started to be published in January 1975. In this chapter, I do not distinguish cyberpunk from postcyberpunk, focusing instead on the more general characteristics pertaining to both eras. For insights into the postcyberpunk genre, see Person, "Notes Toward a Postcyberpunk Manifesto."

2 Haraway, *Simians, Cyborgs, and Women*, 151–155. On cyborgs, see also Gray, ed., *The Cyborg Handbook*. On the cyberpunk movement in cinema, see Gillis, ed., *The Matrix Trilogy* and Featherstone and Burrows, eds., *Cyberspace, Cyberbodies, Cyberpunk*. On cyborgs in cinema, see, for instance, Short, *Cyborg Cinema*; Clarke, *The Paradox of the Posthuman*; and Smelik, "Cinematic Fantasies of Becoming Cyborg." An examination of the

relations between spectatorship and the posthuman is found in Thomas, *Vertov, Snow, Farocki.*

3 Haraway, "A Cyborg Manifesto."

4 On cyborgs in animation, see Bolton et al., eds., *Robot Ghosts and Wired Dreams*; Brown, *Tokyo Cyber-Punk*; Lunning, ed., *Mechademia 3*; and Napier, *Anime from Akira to Howl's Moving Castle.*

5 On cybercultures, see Bell and Kennedy, eds., *The Cybercultures Reader.*

6 These theories include many of the proponents of realism in Film Theory, including Metz, *The Imaginary Signifier*; Cavell, *The World Viewed*; Casetti, *Inside the Gaze*; and Odin, *De la fiction.* Some neo-formalist frameworks also suppose an alignment between a human spectator and the camera's visual conduit, including Carroll, *The Philosophy of Motion Pictures* and Bordwell, "The Part-Time Cognitivist."

7 Hayles, *How We Became Posthuman.*

8 Hayles, *How We Became Posthuman*, 2.

9 On the multiple references to sexuality and the body in cyberpunk narratives, see, for instance, Cavallaro, *Cyberpunk and Cyberculture*; Gillis, "Cyber Noir"; McHale, *Constructing Postmodernism*; and Orbaugh, "Sex and the Single Cyborg."

10 Casetti, *Inside the Gaze*, 10.

11 Metz, *The Imaginary Signifier*, 56.

12 On the tenets of suture theory, see Silverman, *The Subject of Semiotics.*

13 On psychological realism, see Nichols, *Ideology and the Image*, 84.

14 Metz, *The Imaginary Signifier*, 51.

15 Psychoanalytic theories of spectatorship, for example, presume that the spectatorial experience corresponds to phases of subject formation. For a description of the analogy between the phases of subject formation and cinema, see Nichols, *Ideology and the Image.*

16 Many monographs explore embodiment and/or phenomenology in relation with spectatorship. For examples, see the note section in the introduction.

17 Technological marks can be more or less visibly inscribed on the interface, as Wood demonstrates in *Digital Encounters*, 12–16.

18 On the specificity of sharing the point of view of inanimate objects such as screws in puppet animation, see Buchan, "Animation Spectatorship."

19 On the distinction between visible inscriptions and active inscriptions, see Wood, *Digital Encounters*, 27–40.

20 For a discussion of these spatiotemporal transformations, see Wood, *Digital Encounters*, 28–29.

21 Deleuze, *Cinema 1*, 66.

22 Hansen, *New Philosophy for New Media.*

23 Varela et al., *The Embodied Mind*, 9.

24 On the differences between the cognitivist and connectionist approaches to the mind and the enactive approach, see Thompson, *Mind in Life.*

25 On the enactive approach to perception, see, for instance, Noë, *Action in Perception.*

26 Noë, *Action in Perception*, 35.

27 *Anemic Cinema.*

28 Bois and Krauss, *Formless*, 135.

29 See Clark, *Natural-Born Cyborgs.*

30 The character 8 Man is an early example of a popular cyborg character in Japan. It first appeared in the eponymous manga created by science fiction writer Kazumasa Hirai, which ran from 1963 to 1966. An animated series, also based on the manga, aired in Japan between 1963 and 1964.

31 On the topic of identity formation in cyberpunk films such as *The Terminator* (James Cameron, 1984), see Smelik, "Cinematic Fantasies of Becoming-Cyborg."
32 Brian McHale exposes various themes central to the cyberpunk genre in literature in the chapter "Towards a Poetics of Cyberpunk" in *Constructing Postmodernism.*
33 On the origins of cyberspace, see Benedikt, "Cyberspace: First Steps."
34 On the cultural themes and motifs featured in *Neuromancer,* see, for instance, Kellner, "Mapping the Present From the Future." The term cyberspace appeared in 1980, both in Vernor Vinge's novella *True Names* and John M. Ford's novel *Web of Angels.* It started being identified with online computer networks in William Gibson's short story "Burning Chrome" (1982) and then his seminal novel *Neuromancer* (1984).
35 William Gibson's short story "Johnny Mnemonic" (1981) alludes to distributed forms of cognition.
36 Hayles recounts the story of cybernetics by describing research communicated at the Macy Conferences on Cybernetics in *How We Became Posthuman.* The history of cybernetics is also summarized in Johnston, *The Allure of Machinic Life.* For the history of cybernetics in the UK, see Pickering, *The Cybernetic Brain.*
37 See Wiener, *Cybernetics*; Ashby, *Design for a Brain*; Shannon, "Presentation of a Maze-Solving Machine"; and von Neumann, *The Computer and the Brain,* 79.
38 For an introduction to the history of the AI, see Hayles, *How We Became Posthuman* and Johnston, *The Allure of Machinic Life.*
39 Hayles, *How We Became Posthuman,* 2.
40 Moravec, *Mind Children* and Kurzweil, *The Age of Spiritual Machines.*
41 For research on computational neuroscience in the early 1980s, see Marr, *Vision.* Bordwell's schemata approach applies Marr's naturalistic and constructivist approach to the psychology of perception in "A Case for Cognitivism." On the comparison between the human brain and a computer, see also Churchland, *A Neurocomputational Perspective.*
42 Palmer, *Vision Science,* 5.
43 Palmer, *Vision Science,* 6.
44 Johnston, "Machinic Vision."
45 Johnston, "Machinic Vision," 37.
46 Johnston, "Machinic Vision," 40.
47 Johnston, "Machinic Vision," 40.
48 McHale, "Towards a Poetics of Cyberpunk," 19. McHale identifies the modernist model of shifting points of view in many cyberpunk novels, including Pat Cadigan's *Synners* (1991), William Gibson's *Count Zero* (1986) and *Mona Lisa Overdrive* (1988), Lewis Shiner's *Frontera* (1984), and John Shirley's *Eclipse* (1985).
49 See Smelik, "Cinematic Fantasies of Becoming-Cyborg," 92.
50 Virilio, *The Vision Machine,* 59–60.
51 Virilio, *The Vision Machine,* 60.
52 Hutchings, "The Work-Shop," 169–170.
53 Quoted in Wells, *Understanding Animation,* 26.
54 Hutchings, "The Work-Shop," 165. For a discussion of the abject and the idea that "death is infecting life," see Kristeva, *Powers of Horror.*
55 Bouldin, *The Animated and the Actual,* 30.
56 On embodied virtuality, see Hayles, chapter 1, "Toward Embodied Virtuality," in *How We Became Posthuman.*

57 Clark, *Natural-Born Cyborgs*, 38.
58 In *Bodies in Code*, Hansen discusses mixed-reality environments in which the body is realized conjointly with technics.
59 Clark, *Supersizing the Mind*.
60 Hayles develops the history of how human subjectivity has been progressively associated with informational patterns in *How We Became Posthuman*, thus rejecting the conception of the self advocated by liberal humanism.
61 Anonymous, "Hollywood Stars to Be Replaced by Robots." In this article, George Lucas did not share Hanks' concerns, saying, "I believe that I have used more digital characters than anyone else but I don't think I would ever use the computer to create a human character. It just doesn't work. You need actors to do that."
62 George Lucas's 2D characters from the *Star Wars: Clone Wars* TV series (2003–2005) were adapted for the CG animated film *Star Wars: The Clone Wars* (Dave Filoni, 2008).
63 On the machinic assemblage in *anime*, see Lamarre, *The Anime Machine*.
64 For a discussion of disembodied forms of perception in cyberpunk films and the persistence of the flesh, see Cavallaro, "The Brain in a Vat in Cyberpunk."
65 See Shaviro, "Regimes of Vision."
66 *Appleseed Ex Machina* is the sequel of *Appleseed* (Shinji Aramaki, 2004). An earlier *anime* OVA titled *Appleseed* (Kazuyoshi Katayama, 1988), which was also loosely based on the *Appleseed* (1985) manga created by Masamune Shirow, was animated by Gainax.
67 On stroboscopic effects, see Plantinga, *Moving Viewers*, 118. When *Incredibles 2* (Brad Bird, 2018) came out, theaters posted warning signs for audience members with photosensitive epilepsy or other photosensitivities, as some scenes contained flashing lights. In 1997, flashing lights in the television series *Pokemon* caused convulsions and other symptoms among children in Japan.
68 Fischman, "The Blind Can See." The device described in this article can give limited vision capacity to people that possess certain types of blindness.
69 Fischman, "The Blind Can See," 45.
70 Hayles provides a definition of the Computational Universe in *My Mother Was a Computer*, 3.
71 Hayles, *My Mother Was a Computer*, 2.
72 McHale, *Constructing Postmodernism*, 247.
73 McHale, *Constructing Postmodernism*, 257.
74 McHale discusses the simstim technology in Gibson's *Neuromancer* in *Constructing Postmodernism*, p. 253–261.
75 McHale, *Constructing Postmodernism*, 260.
76 Silvio, "Radical Cyborg," 69.
77 Silvio, "Radical Cyborg," 68.
78 On posthumanism, see, for instance, Hayles, *How We Became Posthuman* and Graham, *Representations of the Post-Human*.
79 Bouldin, *The Animated and the Actual*, 63.
80 Bouldin, *The Animated and the Actual*, 58.
81 Stadler, "Film as Experience," 46.
82 Stadler, "Film as Experience," 46 (emphasis in the original).
83 Stadler, "Film as Experience," 46.
84 Creed, "The Cyberstar," 86.
85 Eisenstein, *Eisenstein on Disney*, 21.

3 Metamorphic Creatures

Introduction

Absurdly elastic, polymorphous, and dynamically plasmatic, animated bodies magically transform according to the whim of the animator. Since its earliest years, animation has relied heavily on metamorphic characters that squash and stretch their silhouettes at the flip of a switch. In *Understanding Animation*, animation scholar Paul Wells even claims that metamorphosis may be "the constituent core of animation itself."[1] Because metamorphosis is such an important aspect of animation, this chapter examines our engagement with metamorphic narratives and their specific rhetoric.

As briefly examined in the first chapter, in everyday life, we recruit image schemas to apprehend the meaning of concepts and metaphors of various levels of complexity, some of which are: CONTAINER, IN-OUT, and SOURCE-PATH-GOAL. Animation also helps us to envision the way our life would be if the details of our embodiment were designed otherwise. The spatiotemporal transformations and meta-morphings we encounter in animated media unsettle familiar image schemas.

Already at the beginning of the 20th century, animation was revisiting the distinction between the IN and the OUT of the body with surreal references to dream states. Oneiric hybrids and surrealist mutations abound in the animations of Émile Cohl, one of the first animators. Cohl was a member of The Incoherent, a group of artists that used laughter, humor, and gaiety as their sources of inspiration. Explicit references to dreams and nightmares appear in *The Puppet's Nightmare*[2] (1908), *The Hasher's Delirium*[3] (1910), and *Children's Dreams*[4] (1910). In *The Puppet's Nightmare*[5], for example, the claw of a lobster transforms into the legs and body of a walking man.

Alluding to hallucinatory states and phantasms, *Fantasmagoria*[6] (1908) features a series of nonlogical transitions between short quick-change events. Throughout the animation, the objects magically morph into new ones, as the white outlines enclosing them blend into each other. In addition to challenging the narrative chronology and the unity of space and time, this hybrid film creates whimsical composites. Arguably the earliest fully animated cartoon, this dreamlike animation mocks social pretensions by depicting a gentleman and a lady parading around a movie theater with her fancy hat covered with large feathers.[7] One member of the audience, a shape-shifting clown, is the victim of a series of calamities: he shrinks to the size of a puppet, inflates like a balloon, and has his head popped off. At one point, a champagne bottle swallows him up. Then, the bottle progressively transforms into a lotus blossom. When the lotus opens its corolla, it reveals the missing clown. Soon after, the petals wither and disappear, leaving the poor clown standing on the stalk. But—surprise!—the stalk suddenly metamorphoses into the trunk of an elephant (see Figure 3.1).

The variety of shape-shifting characters is wide; it ranges from Émile Cohl's stick figures in *Fantasmagoria*, to Popeye's augmented body after eating spinach, and the fantastic chimeras in the TV series *Fullmetal Alchemist* (2003–2004). Metamorphic characters compel viewers to feel their body stretching and moving in ways that are unfamiliar. I argue that certain animations use these alternative modes of embodiment as rhetorical mechanisms to upset the status quo. By redrawing the body's confines, the metamorphoses studied in this chapter invite philosophical questioning on the limits of the human and raise ethical concerns about marginalization.

The chapter adapts Murray Smith's structure of sympathy to the specific case of metamorphic narratives. The structure of engagement is combined with the conceptual metaphor theory to study empathic mechanisms and metaphorical understanding in animation. In a first case

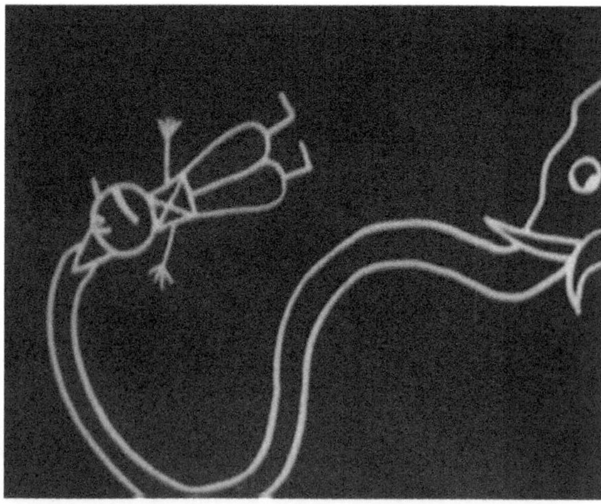

Figure 3.1 The stalk of a flower transforms into an elephant's trunk. *Fantasmagoria* (Émile Cohl, 1908).

study, I examine the animated film *Corpse Bride* (Tim Burton and Mike Johnson, 2005). The structure of engagement enhances the viewer's empathy for the Corpse Bride despite her unusual physique. Visual motifs and the IN-OUT image schema convey the contrasting themes of entrapment and freedom present in this gothic tale. In a second case study, I address the rhetorical opportunities presented by character design in stop-motion animation. In Jan Švankmajer's *The Death of Stalinism in Bohemia* (1990), for example, the malleable body of the animated character epitomizes the social alienation and political oppression experienced during the Communist era in Czechoslovakia.

The subsequent sections examine more specifically metamorphic bodies in Japanese animation, or *anime*. Characters in *anime* often challenge the unified body of liberal humanism and thereby probe ethical issues. The first example discusses viewer engagement with hybrid identities in Hayao Myazaki's tale *Princess Mononoke* (1997). A better understanding of our enemy's viewpoint, it intimates, can facilitate cross-cultural exchanges and reconciliation. The second example draws on Deleuze and Guattari's concept of "becoming-animal." By analyzing the metamorphosis of Howl in Myazaki's *Howl's Moving Castle* (2004), I demonstrate that the spectator's engagement with the shape-shifting wizard evokes the metaphorical transformation of the human into the nonhuman in times of war.

The intersubjective processes of seeing and feeling like hybrid characters, these animations suggest, lend insights into inclusive acceptance, personal growth, and social change.

Meaning-Making in Metamorphic Narratives

We are perceptually attuned to the motion of animated characters and extended by the animation machine. Our affective responses and embodied simulations contribute to our understanding of the necessary coupling of the viewing body and the animated interface. In this chapter, I integrate affective responses and empathy at the level of our neurons into the larger structure of character engagement. Engaging with animated distortions of ourselves, however, can be tricky. According to art historian James Elkins, all representations of the body are distortions. They flatten tri-dimensional objects, approximate particular traits, or exaggerate certain body parts. Elkins argues that pictures of metamorphoses and deformed appearances participate in processes of boundary formation that distinguish the self from the other. In fiction, monsters unsettle the limits between the human and the posthuman and androids challenge sharp divisions between the living and the dead.[8] Before examining the process of boundary formation and the rhetorical possibilities of metamorphic creatures, I first delve into the structure of engagement in animation.

The Structure of Engagement

The process of winning the allegiance of the spectator by extending their sympathy to animated characters involves both high-level psychological schemas and bottom-up affective responses. The spectators' active search for the coherence of form and content creates meaning by drawing on dispositions and physical experience. As examined in Chapter 1, from the creative sensorimotor interactions of our body and mind with the animated world emerge image schemas that help us make sense of acting, dialogues, cinematography, and mise-en-scène. Additionally, these preconceptual structures rooted in our perceptual and physical interactions with objects can be recruited to articulate audiovisual metaphors of various levels of complexity. In turn, these metaphors support the viewer's understanding of the plot, character traits, and themes.

In animated narratives, meaning-making is informed by character engagement. As Smith mentions in *Engaging Characters*, the spectator is

> an agent who knowingly fulfills certain institutional roles; whose mental life is constrained by particular beliefs and values, but whose imaginative capacities allow for change in what is assumed—automatized—and what is questioned; an agent for whom emotional response is part of a larger cycle of action, perception, and cognition.[9]

Our genetic makeup enables us to empathize with animated characters. Their actions and motivations elicit emotions that trigger changes in the flow of affects. Reciprocally, the variations in the flow of affects produce crescendos and decrescendos, staccatos and silences that multiply the layers of signifying motifs.

Interest in plot development and concern for characters are crucial elements for maintaining the audience's attention and sustaining emotional engagement as the story progresses. Narrative organization can manipulate the audience's concern for a character and foster interest in his or her objectives. Specific genres and narrative schemata capitalize on certain emotions more than others and thereby rely on audiovisual cues and elements of the mise-en-scène that will stir those emotions. For example, since horror films are designed to arouse fear in spectators, angst-ridden sequences in which the protagonist confronts a monster seek to elicit the audiences' concerns for the character's life. These concerns evoke a complex mixture of feelings and physical responses that depend on the perceived threat.[10]

As a strategy to quickly gain the audience's sympathy for the protagonists, the beginning of an animation can plunge them into life-threatening situations that make viewers feel anxious for their safety. The gravity of the consequences arising from a threat intensifies the spectator's concern and emotional response. The pursuit sequence at the beginning of *Howl's*

Moving Castle, for example, encourages spectators to develop concern and interest for the young Sophie and Howl. Sophie is introduced as a very conservative woman who rejects frivolous pleasures and prefers to dedicate herself to her work at a hat shop. One afternoon, on her way to her sister's bakery, Sophie meets irreverent soldiers who find it amusing to tease a frail young woman. Passing by, the flamboyant wizard Howl casts a spell on the soldiers to drive them away and offers to escort Sophie to her destination. Unfortunately, without a moment of respite, Sophie and her new companion must escape the ferocious pursuit of the evil henchmen of the Witch of the Waste. This peril is meant to elicit concerns about the couple's safety. Moreover, the work of iconography—a set of typifying traits—amplifies the audience's anxiety.[11] The portrayal of the Witch's henchmen as large black blobs aligns them with evil spirits. The color black is stereotypically linked with despicable protagonists and the oozing bodies suggest disorder and deviation from the norm, an overall portrayal that evokes dread. Their presence introduces suspense and intensifies the spectators' emotional responses; it makes them wonder how Sophie and Howl could possibly escape from their closing grasps. In this situation, suspense is another feeling that heightens the spectators' interest.

The anticipation of a romantic relationship in romantic comedies captures the spectators' attention and channels certain patterns of emotional responses. In *Howl's Moving Castle*, the dissimilarities between Sophie and Howl amuse and intrigue. Howl's ostentatious sartorial style contrasts with Sophie's simplicity. The differences between them may compel spectators to wonder how they could eventually fall in love with each other. As the persistent blobs are about to engulf the couple, Howl eludes the stalkers by unexpectedly getting off the ground. He chivalrously carries Sophie over the buildings' roofs, which produces immediate relief from the distressful situation. The sight of the city from a bird's-eye view amazes both Sophie and the audience with its lush colors and the proprioceptive feelings of weightlessness. The exalting adventure must also be an unsettling experience for Sophie, since she cultivates a restrained attitude and exhibits a taste for monotony. The mixture of uncertainty and visual delight that the situation provokes arouses the spectator's curiosity about the future of their romantic relationship. Evidently, not all spectators respond in the exact same way to the plot and its constructed discourse. Learned associations, memory, physiological responses, and dispositions influence the strength of character engagement. Yet, this romantic adventure is designed to produce a continuous flow of affects and emotions that alternates between periods of intense engagement and temporary relief.

As examined in Chapter 1, we can analyze a film according to specific levels of perceptual understanding. Cinema theorist Per Persson's model, however, neglects some aspects related to affect. *Affect and Embodied*

Meaning in Animation hinges on Smith's structure of sympathy because it accounts for empathic phenomena such as affective mimicry and emotional simulation—aspects that the original model of "identification" elides.[12] However, I replace the "structure of sympathy" with the "structure of engagement" because the term sympathy often excludes empathic engagements, while I consider that both processes are closely intertwined. Following Smith, my approach distinguishes three processes of engagement with fictional characters in order to refine the classical model of identification: recognition, alignment, and allegiance. For the sake of convenience, I summarize Smith's method in a few paragraphs later. Then, I foreground the importance of empathic engagements and various forms of imaginary transpositions, since these processes are particularly solicited in the metamorphic narratives studied.

During the stage of recognition, spectators construct a character by drawing on various visual, auditory, and linguistic cues. Lower-level psychological processes, namely those found on levels 0 and 1 of Persson's scale, inform the spectator's engagement with characters. Viewers tend to attribute agency to basic moving shapes and objects. For instance, psychologists showed a movie depicting triangles and circles moving around on a surface to selected participants.[13] Almost all the participants interpreted the motion of these geometrical shapes as the interactions of animated beings. The participants attributed intentions and personalities to the triangles and circles, and interpreted their behaviors as social activities. This tendency to anthropomorphize animated objects can partly explain the inclination to empathize with animated bodies that lack photorealism. In addition, animated films adopt many strategies to enhance the legibility of a character and attract the audience's sympathy or antipathy. The work of iconography and the attribution of physical traits pertaining to particular social or psychological types are convenient devices to influence the spectators. In the aforementioned example, the monstrous physiognomy of the Witch's henchmen and their masked faces associate them with the villains. Finally, live-action cinema, and to some extent animation, can rely on star persona to strengthen the audience's empathy for or antipathy toward the protagonists.

The second process involved in the structure of engagement is called "alignment." It concerns the camera's point of view and the narrative strategies that an animation or a film uses to provide spectators with access to the actions, thoughts, and feelings of the characters. When we watch an animation, we are "provided with visual and aural information more or less congruent with that available to characters, and so are placed in a certain structure of *alignment* with characters."[14] In the sequence described earlier, we first align with Sophie as she feels threatened by the two soldiers. The close-up of her face and her trembling voice betray her distress. Then, when Howl rescues her, we align with the couple as they run away from the army of blob men. The subjective perspective of the large oozing men blocking the couple's way and then approaching toward them creates a sense of urgency. The level of intimacy that we gain by being aligned with the young protagonists helps us evaluate their behaviors and motivations before we decide to give them our allegiance.

The strategies that enhance absorption and presence facilitate the spectators' access to the perceived feelings of the animated characters. The markers of presence, such as the projected shadow of a character on the floor, can enhance the spectator's feeling of its presence.[15] The simulation of a linear perspective and the use of a multiplane camera are other mechanisms by which animators can amplify absorption. These strategies reduce the gap between the visual perception of an image in an unmediated environment and an image perceived through a medium. Additionally, music could convey information about the mental state of a character. The affective meaning of music, style and technique, character engagement, and settings are all plot elements that can amplify affective congruence.

We can adapt many of the principles of continuity editing theory and the structure of engagement to animated films. By implementing the conditions on which psychological realism is based, live-action films compel spectators to share the perspective presented by the camera.[16] The simulation of spatial and temporal unity via establishing shots, point-of-view cutting, shot/reverse-shot patterns, the match on cut technique, and the respect of the 30° rule and the 180° system strongly encourage spectators to interpret the world presented to them as a coherent whole.[17] The similarity between the everyday spatiotemporal experience of a scene and the perceptual experience produced by continuity editing facilitates the development of sympathy or empathy for characters, as spectators spend less time reevaluating the rules and conventions of the world depicted. When a film operates within the framework of psychological realism, the use of shot/reverse shots and point-of-view cutting encourages spectators to identify with characters by sharing their visual perspective. A panoramic shot to the left or to the right, for instance, corresponds to a movement of the character's head to the left or to the right. By adopting these conventions, the spectators identify with the filmic perspective as it corresponds to their own.

Metz's notion of identification, which was influential for film studies, concerns the process by which viewers feel present within the cinematic space via a subjective camera point of view. In *The Imaginary Signifier*, Metz introduces a distinction between primary and secondary identification.[18] In the case of primary identification, the spectator identifies with the camera, which creates the illusion that one is actually present in the fictional world as an invisible spectator. Secondary identification implies identification with characters. In his structure of sympathy, Smith replaces "identification" with "engagement" because, according to him, identification connotes reconfirming and restaging the familiar. Smith suggests that we readily identify with characters that resemble us physically and ideologically. Theories of identification in cinema often neglect to explore the case of metamorphic narratives.[19] In contrast, character engagement requires an additional negotiation of a difference in allegiance and embodiment. In this context, engagement also derives "from the representation of the unfamiliar, the spectator's 'quasi experience' of the new."[20] The process of engagement may compel some spectators to adopt an "imaginative mobility" within the axes of identity, some of which are: gender, ethnicity, species, and social classes.[21]

Even though there is no camera movement per se in animation, it is still possible to simulate point-of-view shots and various camera positions. Animation relies on these mechanisms to induce experiences of personal-space invasion and deictic-gaze situations.[22] Many conventional narrative animated films and even video games rely on psychological realism and point-of-view cutting.[23] Although the lack of verisimilitude can arguably hinder empathetic engagement with animated characters, it does not necessarily prevent embodied simulation.

The third and last stage of character engagement, "allegiance," encompasses the strategies a film or an animation takes to marshal our sympathy or lack of sympathy toward the characters.[24] In evaluating the protagonists' actions, spectators draw on the information they have gathered from the plot by sharing the aspirations and concerns of different characters. Animation influences our understanding of the semiotically constructed discourse by modulating our attraction or repulsion for the characters within the structure of engagement. In the aforementioned example, we are inclined to give our allegiance to the romantic couple. Reciprocally, we despise the Witch of the Waste and her henchmen. Even though Sophie's sister warns her of the danger of having her heart stolen by the flamboyant wizard, we nevertheless fall under his charismatic spell.

In summary, the higher levels of character engagement include the conscious processes of recognition, alignment, and allegiance. Forms of empathic engagement at these levels may include imaginary transpositions and emotional simulations of the emotions experienced by a character.[25] Emotional simulations are mental simulations of the emotions that someone else may be experiencing in a particular situation, and they involve speculating on how one would act in a similar situation. As discussed in Chapter 1, we also find automatic and pre-reflexive empathetic responses, including embodied simulations, motor mimicry, and emotional contagion. These low-road mechanisms, conjointly with subjective access to the inner lives of characters, strengthen character engagement in animation.[26]

The Rhetoric of the Metamorphic Body

Animation shares its interest in metamorphic characters with literature. Early tales of mutation, including Ovid's *Metamorphoses* and Charles Darwin's *On the Origin of Species* (1859), cross the divide between species or depict processes of dehumanization.[27] In *Metamorphoses*, Ovid explored the limits of the human in stories of humans transforming into animals, plants, and stones. Before the 20th century, most fantastic creatures were *grylli*.[28] As described in medieval and Renaissance texts, the *gryllus* is a composite of recognizable animal parts, or a combination of human features and animalistic traits. For example, the centaur joins the upper body of a man and the legs and the tail of a horse. These mythical creatures were found in tales of metamorphoses, medical treatises on monstrous bodies, and depictions of demons in religious art. Literary texts around the world and in a variety of genres pursued this ancient fascination for transmutations, including African and West Indian tales of zombies and the canonical *Strange Case of Dr. Jekyll and Mr. Hyde* (Robert Louis Stevenson, 1886). These various narratives transgressed physical laws, shaped discourses on selfhood, and ran "counter to notions of unique, individual integrity of identity in the Judaeo-Christian tradition."[29]

Grylli and composites of all sorts were featured in Cohl's *Fantasmagoria*. Metamorphoses also take center stage in animations featuring Otto Messmer's Felix the Cat. With his expressive body parts and individualized personality, the Chaplinesque cat was a favorite in the 1920s. Because of his polymorphous plasticity, Felix can mold himself into a suitcase in *Felix in Hollywood* (Otto Messmer, 1923) or draw digits with his tail in *Felix Finds Out* (Otto Messmer, 1924). Alternatively, his tail "can be an umbrella, a sword, a clarinet, or Chaplin's cane."[30] All this shape-shifting amused audiences while making fun of the limitations of classical film conventions, which usually left the body intact and the laws of nature untouched.

The short animated film *Felix the Cat Switches Witches* (Otto Messmer, 1927) experiments with the figure of the *gryllus*. On Halloween each year, one can delight in cross-dressing in an extravagant costume for an evening. Enjoying the festive ambience at the farm, Felix decides to play some pranks on his fellow animals and invents some *grylli* of his own. While the rooster and the rabbit were sleeping, Felix swapped their heads. Furious, the creature with a rabbit's head and the body of a rooster starts to chase the creature with the rooster's head and the body of a rabbit. Looking for other tricks to play, Felix gets an idea when he sees a donkey standing next to a bicycle. This time, Felix invents a new means of transportation by replacing the hind legs of the donkey with the rear wheel of the bicycle. As Cohl did with *Fantasmagoria*, Messmer experiments with the metamorphic possibilities of the medium. While the hand of the animator responsible for the magical trick appears in

Fantasmagoria, it stays concealed in *Felix the Cat Switches Witches.* Instead, Felix stands in for the avatar of the animator, the actual practical joker behind the scene.

Many animations self-reflexively play with the metamorphic possibilities afforded by the medium. Notably, stories of mutation "offer a way of imagining alternatives, mapping possibilities, exciting hope, warding off danger by forestalling it, casting spells of order on the unknown ahead."[31] By crossing species, mutating bodies, and recasting membranes, animation stimulates the intellectual remapping of traditional worldviews. Much like contemporary literature, animation imagines stories and characters "against the normative models of the unified self."[32] Literary scholar Marina Warner classifies forms of metamorphosis into four major categories: hatching, mutating, doubling, and splitting. While references to "hatching" and "mutating" mainly draw on biological phenomena, examples of "splitting" and "doubling" explore metaphysical associations between body and soul. The term "splitting" describes the severance of the spirit from its mortal husk, an idea that underpins stories of roaming zombies and eerie specters. Alternatively, "doubling" suggests the coexistence of a second self or a second existence. Doubling can involve the permutations of inner and outer selves and is featured in certain soul migration plots. Tales about *doppelgangers*, alien creatures living inside an individual, and fusions with avatars are other familiar examples of "doubling."

Such supernatural transformations express the fragility of the borders between matter and mind. According to literary scholar Tzvetan Todorov, author of *The Fantastic*, metamorphoses allude to the multiple roles and personalities that we can adopt in our life. We are simultaneously an actor and a spectator, a teacher and a student, or a child and a parent. In a sense, "the multiplication of personality, taken literally, is an immediate consequence of the possible transition between matter and mind: we are several persons mentally, we become so physically."[33] The animations featuring Superman, who doubles the introvert Clark Kent, imply that with physical strength comes self-confidence and extroversion. In the animated film *Pinocchio* (Hamilton Luske and Ben Sharpsteen, 1940), Pinocchio's nose grows in length when he acts disobediently. He also transforms into a donkey as a punishment for his inappropriate conduct on Pleasure Island.

Our physical responses to images of distorted bodies and composites provide glimpses of wisdom about the distinctions we draw between self and other. Instead of limiting the choices of "body images," animation invites viewers to align with characters that experience identity mobility caused by shifts of embodiments and bodily mutations. However, since their otherness challenges our assumptions, the particularities of the embodiment of the animated character may potentially hinder the process of engagement. Nevertheless, because they are situated on the threshold between humans and others, they may function as catalysts that could invite spectators to adopt alternative subject positions. Moreover, spectators can always choose the character with which they want to sympathize. As Smith claims, a "narrative text can attempt to regiment the viewer's experience, it can encourage the activation of certain schemata over others, but it cannot 'position' the spectator."[34]

Some animators have exploited the malleability of the animated bodies so as to communicate a political message of inclusion for marginalized people. Filmmaker and film theorist Sergei Eisenstein, for instance, recognized the revolutionary potential of animation. He was fascinated by the "plasmaticness" of the cartoonal body and its ability to deviate from the expectations of the evolutionary ladder.[35] Moreover, metamorphic characters can introduce viewers to a variety of embodiments and thereby shift their assumptions away from simplistic distinctions between dominant and marginalized subject positions. When aligning with such characters, the subject position of each spectator may be invested with various degrees of power depending on the intersecting axes of identity at play.[36] Any of the subject positions, whether virtually embodied, physically augmented, identified by a gender, racially marked, or the member of a social class or a species, can combine to empower spectators or make them feel vulnerable, depending on the surrounding network of forces.

Animation challenges the coherence and stability of typical human and animal anatomies. The "plasmaticness" of the cartoon body unsettles the traditional views that consider the self a unified and self-contained entity. According to these views,

> selfhood is predicated on a carefully maintained distinction between the outside (of the person) and the inside, a distinction materialized in/through the structure of the human body. The body is conceived as being self-contained, autonomous, with the skin serving as its outer boundary—both holding in the person's "insides" and preventing (or at least hindering) the invasion of elements from the outside.[37]

The population of protean organisms, mutants, reincarnations, spirit doubles, and migrating souls in animation playfully contests the individual integrity of identity and prefers to explore other paths than those set in real life.

Empathy and Character Design in *Corpse Bride*

The Corpse Unsettles the IN-OUT *Schema*

Emily, the Corpse Bride in *Corpse Bride* defies the unspoken rules of a fictive Victorian-era village whether they are those of the living or those of the dead. Despite her state of advanced decomposition, this charismatic zombie fascinates audiences with her extravagant personality. This section further explores the empathic mechanisms that marshal our sympathies for her. Additionally, it investigates recurring motifs that challenge the IN-OUT schema and thereby articulate tropes of alienation.

Our understanding of others is facilitated in part by the mirror neuron system. When we see an action performed by a character in a film, we mentally perform the same action. This biological mechanism could facilitate our understanding of multimodal metaphors. It also enables us to feel what James Bond feels when the tarantula crawls on his chest in *Dr. No* (Terence Young, 1962). As neuroscientist Christian Keysers argues, the mirrors in our brain can make our hands sweat and our skin tingles under the creature's legs just as this scary sight happens on the screen.[38] While these automatic reactions suggest a hardwired form of empathy, mechanisms of mediation such as camera position and character design also enhance our attraction to animated characters.

Character design in animation and video games communicates values and norms. Superheroes, in particular, represent ideals cherished by the American society. Captain America and Superman, for instance, promote patriotism and heteronormativity. Alternatively, *The Incredibles* (Brad Bird, 2004) reflects traditional American values such as the nuclear family and the American dream. As described in Chapter 1, character design and bodily reshaping in this animation facilitate various metaphors based on embodied gestalts and image schemas. In *Corpse Bride*, the design of Emily's external appearance unsettles expectations. We can see parts of her rib cage through her tattered dress, and some of her bones are not covered with flesh. The recurring motifs of entrapment associated with the body of the characters suggest that flesh and bones can symbolize a cage. Yet, her lively and open personality contrasts with those of Victor and Victoria who are introvert and express self-restraint in their manners.

Bodily hybridization and metamorphoses transgress the IN-OUT schema.[39] We understand our body as bounded and separated from the world by the surface of our skin. This bounded body is experienced as a stable container that holds bones, organs, and blood. What is located outside of the confines of our skin is considered outside us. The opening credits and the closing scene of *Corpse Bride* draw on character design, settings, and patterns of movement in space to correlate feelings of alienation with images of containment, including one's corporeal envelope.[40]

This stop-motion animation was codirected by Tim Burton and Mike Johnson, because Burton was directing *Charlie and the Chocolate Factory* (2005) at the same time and could not personally oversee both productions alone. As with other films by Burton, *Corpse Bride* shows his "penchant for characters who suffer from alienation and are outsiders."[41] *Corpse Bride* expresses the malaise of living and the depressive state of the Victorian characters with embodied gestalts and audiovisual motifs. Classical music provides the supporting ambience for the austere Land of the Living. The bleak cityscape is covered with teal monochromatic tones. In contrast, the colorful world of the Land of the Dead, with its lack of etiquette and upbeat jazz music, emphasizes the "antiestablishment message of most of Burton's films."[42]

The Opening Title Sequence

The beginning of *Corpse Bride* evokes the rigidness of the Land of the Living with motifs of confinement. In the opening credits, the young Victor draws a butterfly with black ink in a sketchbook. The frame within a frame is a recurring motif in the composition of his sober bedroom. Several objects in the room feature series of vertical and horizontal bars. The crossbars of the brass bed, the multiple panels dividing the window, and the butterfly drawings hung on the wall communicate the idea of being trapped. The steadiness of Victor contrasts with the frenzied flutter of the wings of the blue butterfly held captive under a bell-shaped glass. Victor's position in front of the closed window parallels his situation with that of the trapped butterfly. However, the formal contrast between the curved shape of the butterfly's prison and the straight bars within the window behind it emphasizes the difference between the butterfly's state of alienation and Victor's: the butterfly struggles and fights to get its freedom back, whereas Victor appears resigned.

When Victor opens the windows to set the butterfly free, the music accelerates and the number of instruments on the score increases, which conveys the intensity of emotion felt by the butterfly. It twirls around the room, making wide turns that embrace the open space. When the butterfly exits through the window and soars in the sky above the city, the camera follows it, waltzing up and down with fluid movements, thereby communicating to the spectator a sort of vertigo from the heights. While the butterfly flies around freely among the space left between slender houses, we hear the monotonous and repetitive ticking of a clock. Although the constant ticking brings to mind a heartbeat, its stiffness conflicts with the fluidity and lightness of the butterfly's flight. At one point, the butterfly passes by a shop with clocks aligned side by side in its front window. The shopkeeper stands stiffly on the porch, sweeping the floor rhythmically, the handle of his broom following the backward and forward motion of the clocks' pendulums. The symbolic usage of a heartbeat to represent liveliness is subverted and instead evokes the "body is a clock" metaphor.[43]

During this stage of recognition, the animation provides information about Victor's personality. Elements from the settings and his expressionless eyes evoke sadness. In contrast, the liveliness of the butterfly and its bright blue hue, which is also the skin color of the Corpse Bride, symbolize hope. By showing Victor's feeling of detachment and his longing for freedom, the animation starts by aligning the viewer with him. The music, the mood, and character design invite the spectators to empathize with Victor, who himself showed compassion for the butterfly and released it. However, when the butterfly soars in the sky, we leave Victor behind and align with it. Thanks to the butterfly's freedom of movement, we can discover the villagers' surroundings and witness the monotony of their lives.

Additionally, this animation explores motifs about the imitation of life via character design and mise-en-scène. The liveliness of the animated butterfly is stylized. The flapping of its wings appears slower and less smooth than the motion of real butterflies. Furthermore, the traits and gestures of the human characters are caricatural. For instance, Victor has very long and slim legs and moves stiffly. Most of the characters in the opening scene have very limited facial expressions, which signals their apathy. Yet, facial expressiveness in the Land of the Living can represent dubiousness. The villain Lord Barkis expresses his feelings with a variety of expressions and postures, which stands out from the humdrum monotony exuding from the other characters. He can move parts of his face, such as when he frowns his eyebrows to convey his discontent with the presence of the butterfly. Lord Barkis's detailed facial expressions, as well as the intensity and the precision of his gestures, contrast with the limited emotional palette of the other characters.

Tête-à-Tête with the Bride

During the production process, cinematographer Pete Kozachik realized that with "a storyline that was more about a quirky relationship than action and adventure, the project held the challenge of engaging the audience on a personal level with animated characters."[44] In the sequence where the Corpse Bride confides in her spider and worm friends about her broken heart, the animation self-reflexively acknowledges the difficulty of empathizing with nonliving entities, namely a corpse and animated puppets. To overcome this challenge, *Corpse Bride* implements various strategies to move viewers. In his book *Acting in Animation*, Ed Hooks explains that animating the thought process, showing an emotional range, and revealing internal negotiations are effective ways to elicit empathy.[45] Moreover, the development of character personality and the clarification of the character's motivations help strengthen the spectators' level of engagement.

Emily experiences a whole range of emotions in the sequence where she retires to her room to sulk after having discovered Victor's affair with Victoria. After she throws her wedding bouquet on the ground to show her frustration, the sequence cuts to a head shot lit from the top, making her face glow. Her head is slightly tilted down; her eyelids stay closed for a moment and the position of her eyebrows conveys her sadness. When she says to her spider friend: "Maybe he's right. Maybe we are too different," her voice expresses disheartenment. The tone lightens up when the worm hiding in her ear speculates, "Maybe he should have his head examined. I could do it." Indifferent to his humor, Emily replies, "Or perhaps he does belong with her," emphasizing the word "does" in an angry way, and calling Victoria "Little Miss Living" with a funny face that discloses her jealousy. She then starts singing while walking gracefully across her bedroom, with her entire body glowing. Trying to comfort Emily, the spider and the worm remind her: "The sole redeeming feature from that little creature is that she's alive. Everybody knows that's just a temporary state." Despite the fact that she cannot feel the pain of a burning candle or the cut from a knife, the Corpse Bride sings: "Yet I feel my heart is aching, though it doesn't beat, it's breaking. And the pain here that I feel, try and tell me it's not real. I know that I am dead. Yet it seems that I still have some tears to shed."

This emotional wandering with the Corpse Bride initiates a privileged connection with her as she opens up her heart. The presentation of her facial traits in close-ups and her expressive tone of voice provide the opportunity to understand her despair from an intimate perspective. The intensity of emotion during this sequence creates a bond between the audience and the character. The spectator is not trying to figure out what will happen next in the story, as it is the case in an action sequence, but is engaged in the present moment with Emily, following the train of her thoughts and trying to understand how she will overcome this depressing phase. Because we are experts in decoding the feelings and intentions of the others, we apply our expertise when we watch audiovisual media. We intuitively attempt to decode a character's expressions. The perceived feelings may give us clues about the intentions of the characters, their personality, and the significance of the events that happen to them. Trying to understand how characters feel and what they really want grabs the viewer's attention and evokes an array of sensations that can elicit compassion, pity, admiration, and sympathy, just to name a few.[46]

These emotions elicit changes in bodily states and automatic responses that participate in the feedback loops that alter the flow of affects. Antipathetic emotions, such as the viewer's anger directed at Lord Barkis, are "feeling against" emotions.[47] In contrast, empathic emotions compel viewers to engage with the characters and stay interested in their adventures. It is not easy to sharply distinguish sympathy from empathy, as they evoke a mixture of what scholars commonly call "feeling with" and "feeling for."[48] "Feeling for" evokes sympathetic feelings such as caring about characters without sharing their experience. In contrast, "feeling with" is usually associated with empathy and involves sharing emotions congruent with those experienced by the character.[49]

Despite the fact that we know that characters are not living entities, we can develop empathetic feelings for them, although they may be less intense than those we experience for people. Not being able to feel physical pain or having no heart may be difficult to conceptualize. However, most of the spectators can understand what it is to have a broken heart and can sympathize with Emily on this ground. Victoria and the Corpse Bride also attract the compassion of the spectators because they feel helpless in getting a grip on their tragic situations. In the excerpt analyzed earlier, when the Corpse Bride opens up, she makes it possible for the spectator to share part of her sorrow. Even though we do not have a broken heart, some spectators can still experience the deflated mood conveyed by the music and the grim setting. While it may be difficult for some spectators to share the physical pain experienced by a puppet, this sequence eases this process with moving dialogues and the intimate atmosphere of the mise-en-scène.

The Final Scene in the Church

In the last scene of *Corpse Bride*, Emily meets a tragic end, as she was the third in the love triangle formed by Victor, Victoria, and herself. While we have aligned with her throughout the narrative, this special bond is severed when her body splits into hundreds of small blue butterflies. The beginning of the scene puts in place the standard mechanisms of engagement. Tricked by Victor, the man she loves, Emily has crossed over to the Land of the Living to marry him. In the church, when the Corpse Bride is saying her vows, she notices Victoria hidden behind a pillar. At that moment, Emily finally realizes that Victor is in love with Victoria, not her. Even though Victor wants to keep his promise to marry Emily, she prefers to leave and gives him back the ring he had mistakenly put on her finger when they first met. She tells Victor, "You kept your promise. You set me free. Now I can do the same for you." The close-up of Victor and Emily's juxtaposed faces, just as she turns her back on him, and before she exits the frame, are particularly moving, as it is the last time we will see them together. What she means when she says that he set her free is left ambiguous. She deeply loved Victor, and the moments she spent with him taught her the importance of caring for someone. Emily chooses to sacrifice the possibility of a future with the man she loves. Instead, she prefers to give Victoria the chance to find happiness with him.

The end of the final scene questions a simplistic identification with the Corpse Bride. The sequence shifts from a view of her entire body to the splitting of her body at the end. On her way toward the exit, Emily stops near the arch at the back of the church. Illuminated by a dazzling moon, she briefly glimpses back at Victor and Victoria who are standing next to the altar. Emily throws the bouquet of blue flowers she was holding in her hands toward them. The low-angle shot and the high-key lighting emphasize the expressiveness of her face. Her look toward the left of the frame and her delicate smile suggest a mixture of bittersweet resignation and relief. As she continues to walk toward the exit, she looks up at the moon. Multiple butterfly-shaped cutouts separate from her bridal veil and take flight, leaving holes in the translucent fabric (see Figure 3.2). Progressively, her entire body disintegrates into a flock of blue butterflies fluttering frenetically toward the moon.

This form of doubling disrupts the usual structure of engagement because it fragments the character's destiny. This moment ruptures the demarcation between the inside of the body and the outside of the body, as well as the image schemas linked with Emily's corporeality. While Emily repeatedly shared her inner thoughts and feelings, spectators lose this perspective as her body splits into many new lives. For the spectators who have grown fond of Emily's personality by understanding her motives and sharing her thoughts, this abrupt ending can be puzzling.

The closing sequence parallels the opening credits. This cyclical narrative form connects the last breath of Emily at the end of the film with the newly freed butterfly at the beginning. Other motifs that confuse life and death resurface at the end. The Corpse Bride's dematerialization alludes to the animation of the inanimate by blurring the physical and conceptual distinctions between the dead corpse and the animated butterflies. When the butterflies are released from the vanishing body of the Corpse Bride, these underlying ideas coalesce to evoke a renewal or a reincarnation. Since the last scene is set in a church, the dematerialization of Emily can insinuate a spiritual living-on as her soul quits her undead body.

The magical transfiguration in the realm of the story, which emphasizes the simultaneity of life and death, crystallizes the essence of animation. Various references to animation techniques in *Corpse Bride*

Figure 3.2 The Corpse Bride disintegrates into a flock of butterflies. *Corpse Bride* (Tim Burton and Mike Johnson, 2005).

suggest the action of imparting life to inanimate objects. For instance, a combination of stop-motion animation and computer-animated effects simulates the fusion of life and death as the butterflies bloom out from the wedding veil. In addition, the opening title sequence alludes to hand-drawn animation by associating the outline of a butterfly in Victor's drawing pad with the animated blue butterfly held captive under a glass dome. The emphasis on "animating" a drawing encourages viewers to draw further connections between the animate and the inanimate throughout the film.

The opening title sequence of the *Corpse Bride* draws on the IN-OUT schema to evoke the "body is a cage" metaphor. When the blue butterfly flies around the city, the combination of sound, character design, and movement brings to mind the resemblance metaphors "the heart is a clock" and "the body is a machine." By aligning the spectators with the bounded body of the puppet and using camera techniques and aspects of the mise-en-scène, this animation encourages empathy to develop with the Corpse Bride despite her quirky appearance. When the animated body of the Corpse Bride becomes simultaneously alive and dead during her transformation into a frenetic flock of butterflies, our alignment with Emily disappears. Among other possible interpretations, the transgression of the IN-OUT schema can camouflage spiritual undertones or a Cartesian division between body and soul. Likewise, it can symbolize an individual's rebellion against societal barriers. While Victor and Victoria settle back into the matrimonial ritual, the Corpse Bride chooses her own path, one that defies the usual patterns of behavior set by society. She would be remembered as an ephemeral spark of joy in the drab Land of the Living.

The Clay Body in *The Death of Stalinism in Bohemia*

The materiality of the animated body and the modes of production are important rhetorical tools. The variety of shapes and materials used to design the animated figures can reveal underlying themes or provide information about the character's intentions. In the pursuit sequence of *Howl's Moving Castle*, the garish clothing of the blob men serves to elicit fear in accordance with psychological typage. Alternatively, *The Incredibles* unsettles the viewer's expectations when Elastigirl extends the length of her arm to punch the thief. Her physical strength causes surprise and comic relief because the "frail" woman is cast against type. In Trnka's *The Emperor's Nightingale* (Jiří Trnka and Miloš Makovec, 1949), the trope of alienation is expressed with the materiality of the characters' bodies. This hybrid film tells the story of a Chinese emperor who preferred the singing of a mechanized bird to the pleasure of hearing a real nightingale. The wooden puppets and their rigid expressions embody the tale's motif of entrapment and the emperor's fascination for mechanized objects that resemble living creatures.

Metamorphic bodies in Jan Švankmajer's animations convey feelings of social alienation. Švankmajer critiques social issues by harming, dissecting, splattering, and deconstructing the animated body. Some of his animations viscerally shake up the audience's complacence with grim allusions to cannibalism in *Food* (1992), the stages of decomposition of a strange creature in *Flora* (1989), and torture in *The Pendulum, the Pit and Hope* (1963). This section analyzes the short hybrid film *The Death of Stalinism in Bohemia*, as it provokes embodied responses that encourage a reflection on the harsh reality of Czech life after 1968. After joining the Prague-based Surrealist Group in 1970, Švankmajer actively criticized the Czech government. As Michael O'Pray notes, there is

> little doubt that Czech Surrealism's critical and subversive role must be perceived as a response to the crushing of the Dubček government by the Soviet Union in 1968, after which there was a period of silencing "difficult" voices in Czechoslovakia.[50]

Open criticism was severely punished during those days and Švankmajer personally experienced this coercive reality. After having made unauthorized postproduction changes to *Leonarduv deník*[51] (1972), which underlined the repression during that period, Švankmajer had to stop making films until the late 1970s. After the "Velvet Revolution" in 1989, Švankmajer was finally free to openly criticize the regime and decided to make the "propaganda" film *The Death of Stalinism in Bohemia*.[52]

Švankmajer produced a provocative critique of Stalinism with nauseating depictions of bodies at the edge between life and death. Two atypical C-sections are featured in this film. The first C-section, which happens at its outset, reveals a small bust of Klement Gottwald (1896–1953), a former leader of the Czech Communist Party, covered with blood. According to film scholar Wakagi Akatsuka, the "'birth' of Gottwald [was] accompanied by the implantation of Stalinism."[53] Although the partisans welcome the birth of the bust of Gottwald with a round of applause, his dictatorship was eventually considered to be a deadly one. The ending repeats a similar C-section, but this time the birth coincides with the death of Stalinism. A clay bust of Stalin is divided into three equal sections and painted with the colors on the flag of the Czech Republic: white, red, and blue. The gloved hands of a surgeon cut open the face of the bust, revealing actual bowels within it. As film scholar Jan Uhde notes, this disturbing experience is reminiscent of the extreme close-up of a razor slicing an eye in Luis Buñuel and Salvador Dalí's surrealist film *Un chien andalou* (Luis Buñuel, 1929).[54] The cold, inert, white clay contrasts with the bloody surplus of flesh inside the cavity. The sight of the hand manipulating the bowels may elicit disgust from some viewers. These images could be cognitively disturbing, even for physiologically unaffected viewers, since, as Elkins notes, "the inside of the body is a powerful sign of death."[55] Then, after a cut to black, we hear the first cry of a newborn baby on the soundtrack, and the film ends on this touching note. In this open-ended film, the second C-section implies that history often repeats itself. Consequently, the abrupt cut to black may indicate that it would be premature to rejoice about the death of Stalinism, as we have to see the future baby first.

Tangled viscera not only unsettle our senses, but also stimulate our minds. The mutilation of Stalin's bust is Švankmajer's way of denouncing the criminal deeds of Czech Stalinism, including the systematic purge of its dissidents.[56] Another sequence of this film alludes to this dark period and seeks to elicit the viewers' pity for the workers that were exploited by the regime. A series of bodies made of clay are assembled and put on a treadmill. After they fall from the assembly line, they walk to the end of a table where they are hung by the neck and pushed into a bucket by a giant hand (see Figure 3.3). They end up squashed with other clay figures, ready to be molded into new bodies of clay—once again. *The Death of Stalinism in Bohemia* decries the standardization of the individual and the limitations of freedom of expression under Stalin. This endless cycle

Figure 3.3 Clay workers are hung by the neck and pushed into a bucket by a giant hand. *The Death of Stalinism in Bohemia* (Jan Švankmajer, 1990).

of death emphasizes the meaninglessness of existence and elicits hostile reactions against the regime's cruelty.

The viewers' empathic and antipathetic feelings influence their allegiance to the political ideas that *The Death of Stalinism in Bohemia* promotes. The prior experience of the repugnant images of tangled viscera inflects the newsreel footage with a negative valence. The lacerations inflicted on Stalin's bust may release pleasurable feelings for those who were opposed to his political practices. The spectator's body acts as a medium that alters, transforms, and filters the moving images, or refocuses attention on certain details. As such, our emotional responses to bodily distortions can become central to our understanding of the filmic discourse.

Corpse Bride and *The Death of Stalinism in Bohemia* stir feelings that enhance the paradox of the simultaneity of life and death. On the one hand, Emily's transformation into a flock of butterflies is unexpected and puzzling, which potentially increases the cognitive load required for understanding its metaphorical relevance. On the other hand, the flight of the butterflies is liberating and their feathery lightness may relieve muscle tension in some viewers. In *The Death of Stalinism in Bohemia*, the hands of the surgeon not only penetrate the malleable flesh, but also churn the viewers' viscera. Hence, when the first cry of the newborn baby resounds, the proximity of life and death may compel some viewers to search for greater meaning. These examples highlight the importance of the medium in the creation of meaning in metamorphic narratives. However, this process does not occur without the participation of the spectator's own body, whether through intellect or feeling.

The Origins of Species in *Anime*

Many Japanese animated films tackle issues of identity related to the limits of the human, the monstrous, speciesism, and companion species.[57] Populated by hybrids of human animals and nonhuman animals, multifarious spirits, shape-shifting wizards, postvital cyborgs, mutant telekinesis, and electronic life forms, *anime* fluidly cross boundaries and facilitate shifts of identity by "redrawing" new appearances. The hybrid identities often cross-pollinate personal identity crises with broader local, national, and historical issues. According to Napier, the body in *anime* interrogates the dominant constructions of identity in modern society—be they gender-based or even human species-based.[58] Metamorphoses in *anime*, she argues, highlight the schism between generations, the tension between genders, the problematic relationship between humans and machines, and the position of Japan vis-à-vis the modern world.

Hayao Miyazaki's work abounds with *grylli* and amalgamations of diverse stylistic influences. Famous for his luxuriant worlds of stunning visual poetry, Miyazaki draws on a variety of myths to create hybrid characters that can cross between the natural and the supernatural realms. Myazaki's hybridizations borrow from diverse sources, including science-fiction robots, Eastern art, ancient Shinto mythology, Western mythology, fairy tales, and Gothic imagery.[59] As Dani Cavallaro points out, "the Totoros—a hybrid species combining characteristics of the cat, the raccoon and the owl—are Miyazaki's own personal creations and the very epitome of his passion for fantastic bestiaries and zoologies."[60] The Fire Demon in *Nausicaä of the Valley of the Wind* (Hayao Myazaki, 1984) "evinces Pre-Columbian features intermingled with elements of *matsuri* masks and of classic icons of the grotesque and the carnivalesque."[61]

The magician Howl in *Howl's Moving Castle* morphs into a composite of a human and an owl. In this animation, the progressive morphing of the human body into a fantastic creature helps distinguish this type of metamorphosis from the *gryllus*, which depicts a specific stage of the transformation of a body but does not explicitly depict the morphing process. As for other characters in Miyazaki's work, the reversibility of Howl's shape may symbolize the character's ability to work through his identity problems. Metamorphic narratives are often tales of individual change and growth, in which bodily alterations evoke other familiar processes, such as maturing, psychological enlightenment, and religious conversion. These developments in a story seek to mirror psychological and physiological changes in the spectators. The character's mutability is also symptomatic of secret causes that the spectators must progressively discover along with the character.

Mutating animated characters are assortments of lines and colors that struggle to redraw their outlines. Although people are made of flesh and bones, textual and filmic references to people usually neglect these aspects. Instead, they rely on mimetic strategies to establish a lifelike association between characters and people. In film, the "person schema" is a convenient way to connect a character with the physical characteristics normally associated with a person, including a discrete body (human or not), individuated and continuous, and persisting visual and aural attributes.[62] We decode characters by piecing together the various parts that compose the panoply of cloths, speech patterns, accents, ethnic and gender features, and gestures. In *Spirited Away* (Hayao Myazaki, 2001), the uncouth No-Face is as much an assemblage of visual features as it is a collection of bodily movements. No-Face's magical transformation into a gigantic digestive organ that can run like a lizard suggests that a character consists of assembled pieces that can vary, expand, and shift, while a core self persists. We intuitively learn to fear or like animated characters by looking at the way they move within their environment and interact with others.

Infectious Digital Effects in *Princess Mononoke*

The *anime Princess Mononoke* tells the story of Ashitaka, a young prince whose arm has been infected by a curse after a fight with a dangerous demon. Set during the Muromachi era in Japan, this tale features crossings between species and clashes between tradition and modernity. By entering into a symbiotic relationship with the host's body, the curse challenges neat separations between the human and the nonhuman. Furthermore, Ashitaka's infection underlines the intersection between traditional hand-drawn animation and computer-generated imagery.

Crossings Between Species

This historical fantasy considers the difficulty of maintaining harmonious relations between the humans, the gods, and the forest animals.[63] At the beginning of *Princess Mononoke*, the young warrior Ashitaka sets out to find the cure for a deadly curse cast by a Tatari-gami, a kind of boar demon, who attacked his village. On his journey, he encounters a mining colony at war with the forest gods and meets the princess wolf San. Raised by the wolf god Moro, San can communicate with the wolves. The princess wants to protect the forest against the destructive effects of the mine. Even though Ashitaka assures San of her humanness, she refuses this categorization, arguing that living like a wolf and having been raised by one does not make her completely human. San shows the limits of analogizing with the way she moves. Although she may look like a human and can express herself with human gestures, she runs with the speed of a wolf and performs supernatural leaps. In the sequence where she attacks the mining colony, she wears the fur of a white wolf on her shoulders and a mask with the features of a wolf on it. She swiftly runs on the top of the roofs and easily jumps between the buildings. Her ruthless fighting with armed men and her sharp reflexes also convey her otherness. *Princess Mononoke* defamiliarizes clear divisions between the human and the nonhuman by underlining the hybrid nature of San's bodily motions and attitudes.

In *Princess Mononoke*, the hybrids can allude to motifs of cross-cultural exchange and personal growth. While San was hostile to all humans at the beginning of the story, she eventually opens up to Ashitaka and learns to appreciate her human identity. As with his other animated films, Miyazaki promotes respect for all living organisms, including animals, humans, and plants. Miyazaki explains that he finds inspiration in rural Shinto myths to promote a philosophy of respect for everything that surrounds us:

> In my grandparents' time it was believed that [*kami*] existed everywhere—in trees, rivers, wells, anything. My generation does not believe this, but I like the idea that we should all treasure everything because spirits might exist there, and we should treasure everything because there is a kind of life to everything.[64]

As journalist Susan Bigelow claims, Miyazaki draws on Zen-Shinto religious imagery to create a cinema "that is culturally specific while also transcending cultural specificity to speak to a simple, universal concern—the dignity of life."[65]

Digital Infections

Princess Mononoke interrogates the limits of the human with depictions of bodily infections.[66] The effects of the Tatari-gami's curse challenge the idea of a self in perfect control of its body. When Ashitaka experiences hate or he is angry, his cursed arm swells and snakelike feelers crawl over it. In the sequence where San infiltrates Irontown to kill Lady Eboshi, Ashitaka experiences the effect of the curse when a man attempts to block his way. A close-up shows Ashitaka closing his hand to make a fist. Then, with his facial expression showing determination and rage, he walks toward the camera in the direction of his opponent, one of Eboshi's guards. The translucent blue feelers enveloping his right arm are neither inside nor completely detached from Ashitaka's body; they symbiotically interact with their host. This new bodily assemblage of affects, molecular structures, and organs suggests that the "human" as a category is not only a cultural invention, but also the product of a precarious chemical balance of affects. Ashitaka's loss of control over his emotions and bodily reactions compel him to become "inhuman" and harm fellow "humans" without considering the damaging consequences of his impulsive actions.

Later in the scene, Ashitaka separates Lady Eboshi and San as they were fighting to death in the middle of an agitated crowd of workers. Furious, San bites Ashitaka's arm. Ashitaka tells Lady Eboshi, "There's a demon inside of you. It's inside both of you." As he finishes his sentence, a medium shot of San and Ashitaka's arm shows glowing tentacles protruding and growing at the place where she was biting (see Figure 3.4). Then turning toward the people of Irontown, Ashitaka shouts, "Look everyone. This is what hatred looks like." This shot makes visible the otherwise invisible negative forces destroying the forest's spirit. San stands on the left side of the frame holding her knife. In the middle of the frame, the cursed Ashitaka holds San with one hand and pushes Lady Iboshi's sword with his own sword. Around them, the astonished workers are ready to give their life to protect their Lady. The digital effect represents the enemy within, the hatred that must be defeated at all cost.

In a more subdued way, the curse's invasion of Ashitaka's body underlines the permeability of the body's membranes. The digital compositing breaches the conception of a clear distinction between the outside of the person and the inside. From this perspective, which holds that the person is self-contained, the skin acts as a peripheral membrane that hinders foreign elements from contaminating the person's "insides."[67] The person's brain processes the information acquired from the sensory modes of access—eyes, hears, nose, skin—which can give the impression that the confines of the body can keep strict control over the flow of incoming stimuli. This careful monitoring of the flow of information that circulates through the skin bag conveys the sense of an interior self. Additionally, the person can communicate his or her internal affective states via information that manifest on the body's surface—facial expressions, blushing, and goose bumps. However, this animation reminds us that our body's membranes are porous. According to Theresa Brennan, who explores the effects of pheromone molecules and the mechanisms of transmission of affect in *The Transmission of Affect*, the human body experiences physiological changes in response to both chemical stimuli and visual imagery. For instance, when the body ingests pheromone molecules, they activate neurological networks, which, in turn, release chemical components such

Figure 3.4 Combination of hand-drawn animation and 3D rendering to portray Ashitaka's curse. *Princess Mononoke* (Hayao Miyazaki, 1997).

as corticosteroids that influence our affective responses. Similarly, the spectators in movie theaters release those pheromones, which, in turn, permeate the orifices of the other members of the audience and thereby modulate their emotional responses.

Ashitaka's mutation combines the traditional hand-drawn animation for drawing the body and a 3D rendering technique for producing a composite of the snakes swirling around his arm and the background environment (see Figure 3.4). Established in 1995, the CGI department at Studio Ghibli produced 15 minutes of CGI for *Princess Mononoke*, of which approximately ten minutes are sequences that only use digital ink and paint. The remaining five minutes include visual effects produced by various digital techniques, such as "3D rendering, morphing, particles, digital composition, and texture mapping."[68] The layering of the arm in full visibility with the snakes in semitransparency illustrates the mixture of old and new techniques, which self-reflexively highlights the hybrid nature of the animated body. The composite nature of the visual effect reveals the dual identity of the young man—both human and nonhuman—who must vanquish the nefarious effects of his infectious and virulent disease to regain control over his instincts and impulses.

The body of the animated character is analogized with a technological hybrid and a molecular assemblage. Although *Princess Mononoke* is set in a fantastic world, its mimetic approach incites viewers to compare it with the "real" world and their own living conditions. By depicting animated bodies with permeable membranes, virulent infections, and symbiotic leakages, this animation threatens the assumption that selves are easily contained, in perfect control of their impulses, and unalienable wholes. Rather, animated bodies are complex assemblages of affects and cultural behaviors that resist definite categorization. The character identities in this *anime* are understood in terms of assemblages and they question the concept of a "pure" human, a species divorced from the animal kingdom or in absolute, rational control of all its bodily actions.

The meshing of infectious digital effects with traditional inked cels also evokes infectious organisms invading the human body. Media scholar Sharalyn Orbaugh maintains that images of contagion in *anime* represent our anxiety toward the loss of stable boundaries. Because our interfaces are permeable,

> "invasions" of the body effected by external substances may be of any of these three characters: parasitic/pathogenic, commensal, or symbiotic/beneficial. Contemporary science and medicine recognize that the bodies we tend to think of as autonomous, clean, and purely *human* are, in fact, multiply invaded, radically hybrid. The "insides" we imagine as producing our *human* subjectivity and affect are, in fact, inhabited by millions of nonhuman creatures.[69]

In Ashitaka's case, the parasitic snakes are pathogenic substances that inhabit and invade not only his body, but also alter his mind and his agency. Neuroscientist Antonio Damasio demonstrates the influence of the body over the mind in *Descartes' Error*. In his book, Damasio provides examples of patients with brain damage who underwent radical personality changes. These behavioral transformations provide evidence that there is no "soul" separate from the body that maintains the integrity of the human's personality. The hybrid nature of the animated body in *Princess Mononoke* also evokes the multifaceted nature of human subjectivity, which resembles more a complex system that relies on variable chemical flows, molecular exchanges, and neural circuitry to maintain its balance than a homogeneous whole.

Meta-Morphing and the Limits of the Human

Digital morphing often displays molecular transformations that unsettle fixed notions of identity. "Morphing" refers to visual effects that smoothly transform an object or a shape into another. Unlike "blurring" effects, which immediately betray the presence of the medium, the digital morphing technique can either hyperbolize its effects or blend in with the background as an "invisible manipulation of the photorealist image."[70] In many recent live-action films, human characters "transparently" morph and take the shape of extravagant bodies, such as the masked joker in *The Mask* (Chuck Russell, 1994), or completely malleable bodies, as illustrated by the melting T-1000 in *Terminator 2* (James Cameron, 1991).[71] In *Princess Mononoke*, the morphing technology produces the accelerated decomposition of the Tatari-gami's body and the magical regeneration of the depleted forest at the end of the movie.[72] The process of morphing bodies entails a complete structural reorganization of matter at the molecular level.[73] This manipulation of matter echoes the processes used in the production stage to produce digital characters. Digital tools can shuffle the pixels composing the images of the characters' bodies and redraw their shapes at will.

Composite bodies and digital morphing can evoke a "loss of stable boundaries."[74] By amplifying our uncertainty about the body's limits, the composite animated bodies, which are assemblages of techniques, conventions, and practices, stress the composite nature of the human. The animation machine is an assemblage of devices, automatisms, bodies, and larger sociohistorical questions that not only echoes popular discourses on "the human," but also engages in reinterpreting, reinventing, and transforming its limits in productive ways. As I further explore in the next section, spectators actively participate in the cobbling together of new cultural images of the human. While they watch the animated bodies metamorphose, they become animal and reinvent the meaning of what it is to be human.

Becoming-Howl in Miyazaki's *Howl's Moving Castle*

In *Howl's Moving Castle*, the two main characters, Sophie and Howl, undergo multiple physical transformations. This section investigates various strategies used to ensure that spectators can develop an affective attachment with characters that persistently change their physical form while keeping their core identity. First, I examine the effects of personal-space invasions and subjective perspectives on character engagement. Then, I draw on Gilles Deleuze and Félix Guattari's concept of "assemblage" to examine processes of proprioceptive adjustment with the character's perspective.[75] I argue that the mutable symbiotic relationship of the spectator and the character can heighten empathic resonance. Finally, drawing on Deleuze and Guattari's concept of becoming-animal, I examine the effects of morphing on the production of resemblance metaphors such as HUMAN IS AN ANIMAL and HUMAN IS A WAR MACHINE.

Personal-Space Invasions and Subjective Perspectives

Howl's Moving Castle reflects on the power of emotions to change someone and the people around them. This theme is explored through fantastic changes in character design. This animation tells the coming of age story of Sophie, an 18-year-old woman who manages a hat shop. At the beginning of the story, Sophie receives the visit of the Witch of the Waste at her shop. Enraged and jealous of the wizard Howl's fondness for the young woman, the Witch casts a spell that transforms Sophie into an old lady. Feeling like an outcast, Sophie decides to leave the city and heads toward the mountains where only witches and wizards live. Looking for a dwelling, she hops on Howl's castle, a motley collection of rusty junk flanked by four metallic chicken legs. As eccentric as its lodgers, the modular castle is covered with assorted protruding pipes and encrusted with enigmatic tiny bungalows. A demon in the shape of a fire, Calcifer, propels the castle and protects its lodgers from intruders. Unfortunately, the kingdom is at war against the neighboring kingdom. Howl must adopt the shape of a monstrous predatory bird to defend his King against savage air raids.

On multiple occasions, Miyazaki enhances or hinders the spectator's sympathy for a character by simulating personal-space invasions. According Persson, "shot scale and framing have the ability to suggest distance and thereby in what personal-space zone the 'meeting' between character and spectator takes place."[76] Drawing on culture-dependent conventions corresponding with proxemic patterns, film and animations across eras have elicited emotional responses through variable framing, editing patterns, and camera movements.[77] Depending on the behavior of the character approaching the camera objective or the type of object that is invading the spectator's personal space, the spatial invasion creates either a sensation of intimacy or one of a perceived threat.[78]

Howl's Moving Castle uses personal-space invasions to elicit a congruence of experience between the spectators and Howl. In a sequence where large aircraft attack the kingdom, Howl has transformed into a huge bird of prey to protect the city. Howl's face is unchanged, but his body is covered with gray feathers and large wings have replaced his arms. At the beginning of the sequence, Howl swiftly glides toward the camera with a fierce gaze that conveys the urgency of the situation. The illusion of a progressively decreasing distance between the character and the space where the spectator stands intensifies the effect of the invasion of personal space and produces a chilling ambience. Images of houses in flames that collapse, series of bombs detonating, and the shrilling sounds of firing cannons also aggravate the atmosphere. Above Howl in the dark sky, flying boats launch bombs and burning aircraft debris fall dangerously toward him, leaving behind them vertical trails of smoke. Both the rapid movements of objects across the various axes of the frame and the framing of Howl against a background of objects in flames intend to intensify the spectators' affective responses and enhance their engagement with Howl's challenging experience. In this sequence, the invasion of personal space and the mise-en-scène compel spectators to share the character's fearful experience.

The animation machine aligns the spectators with Howl's perspective on the war, thus reinforcing their allegiance to his cause. During the sequence described earlier, we often accompany Howl as he glides in the sky without seeing what he sees. We imagine being alongside him, which is a form of acentral imagining. In contrast, subjective perspectives can compel some viewers to mentally put themselves in the character's place in their imagination.[79] This form of imaginary transposition resembles the weak version of central imagining mentioned in *Engaging Characters*.[80] Central imagining implies a kind of fusion between spectator and character. From a central perspective, the spectator vicariously experiences the thoughts and feelings of the protagonist. Moreover, in perceiving and comprehending the character's motives and the situation, the spectator can experience congruent emotions and can envisage being the character in that situation.

This sequence sometimes confuses central imagining and ballistic vision. In the fighting scene mentioned earlier, a bird's-eye view camera angle shows Howl flying over the city in flames. A closer view of the blazing buildings follows. Then, a medium shot of Howl looking down confirms that the preceding shot was a point-of-view shot. The high angle in this sequence induces a sense of empowerment over the situation by simulating a totalizing gaze. This ballistic vision relates to Virilio's concept of cinematism.[81] As Lamarre explains,

> cinematism is part of a more general optical logistics that ultimately serves to align our eyes with weapons of mass destruction, with the bomb's-eye view. The eye becomes one with the bomb, and everywhere in the world becomes a target.[82]

By aligning the viewer with Howl's perspective above the blazing buildings, the animation machine strengthens the exchange between the spectators and the protagonist, as they partner up against a common enemy. As Deleuze and Guattari note, an assemblage "is a composition of speeds and affects involving entirely different individuals, a symbiosis."[83] Assemblages are amalgams of objects, functions, questions, and feelings that characterize the parties that enter into relations of becoming. The spectators' proprioceptive adjustments to reproduce Howl's flying movements and the adoption of Howl's perspective in imagination elicit a congruence of speeds and affects that strengthen the symbiotic coupling between the spectators and the animated character.

Affective Assemblages and Becoming-Animal

A sequence of *Howl's Moving Castle* highlights the painful transformation of Howl to intensify character engagement. As mentioned earlier, the mechanisms of recognition, alignment, and allegiance enable spectators to understand the characters' motivations and thereby empathize with them. The affective assemblage of the spectators and Howl also strengthens when Howl progressively transforms back into a human figure after the savage fight against the evil wizards.

In this sequence, Howl's expression of suffering and his tone of voice convey his pain and state of exhaustion. Back to the castle after the battle, Howl materializes at the top of the stairs with his shoulders slumping and his head hanging down. Weary, he flops down and sprawls in a chair by the fireplace. A profound sigh and his dawdling gestures communicate an inward depletion of tension that parallels his apathy. Feathers cover his wings and three claws have grown on each of his feet. In contrast to before the battle, feathers cover parts of his head and cheeks, indicating an advanced stage of his becoming-animal. When Deleuze and Guattari define a "becoming" in terms of the dynamic assemblage of a human animal with a nonhuman animal, they reject figures of analogy.[84] For example, the wasp's participation in the orchid's reproductive process involves not only luring the wasp by imitating its shape, but also initiating a molecular form of becoming. The becoming-wasp of the orchid and the becoming-orchid of the wasp are informed by "the relations of movement and rest, speed and slowness that are *closest* to what one is becoming, and through which one becomes."[85] While Howl literally "becomes-animal," the spectators "become-animated" as they are engaged in the amplifying affective feedback loops that result from their observation of facial expressivity and muscular activity during his morphing.

A first close-up details Howl's closed eyes and frowning face. A groan of pain accompanies Howl's efforts to recover his human shape. Another close-up focuses on his claws morphing into shoes. Simultaneously, the feathers covering his legs progressively disappear. The same close-up of his face that was previously shown confirms that his hair has grown back and his cheeks have retrieved their smoothness. In this sequence, the close-ups on Howl's facial expressions facilitate empathy via facial mimicry and facial feedback.[86] Facial mimicry is an automatic process that contributes to the complex operations associated with empathy. Covert or externalized, affective mimicry occurs when we involuntarily imitate the affect or facial expressions of others. Hearing people laughing or screaming, or seeing moving images of people expressing fear or happiness with their body postures can influence covert facial reactions. For example, if "you were first put into a scared mood by watching a horror film, your covert reactions to seeing a fearful face would be amplified."[87] Our own covert reactions and facial expressions can also play a role in determining our emotional state, a phenomenon called "facial feedback." While facial feedback is unlikely to cause full-blown emotions such as fear or anger, they can intensify our emotional response to a situation depicted on the screen or affect our mood.

Drawing on motor mimicry and facial feedback, Carl Plantinga calls "scene of empathy" a sequence "in which the face of a favored character is dwelt on for some length in a close-up, and at emotional high points in the narrative."[88] Most of the time, these scenes occur at the end of the narrative because spectators have been given the opportunity to become acquainted with the character's motivations and to develop an allegiance to them. The extended length of the sequence of transformation and the use of the close-up encourage the spectator to "catch" some of Howl's affect. Spectators not only recognize the pain endured by Howl, but also come to experience congruent affects via facial mimicry and embodied simulations.

The morphing of Howl into a fantastic bird not only strengthens our empathy for the young wizard but also provides a more rounded depiction of his personality. Until this scene, Howl acts like an immature, haughty, and frivolous young man. After seeing his participation in the war effort, some spectators may revisit their opinion about him. Howl's transformation demonstrates that he can feel pain. The war has taken its toll on his body. Like Sophie, who appears younger when she is happy, the variations in Howl's anatomy reflect the conflict of emotions within him. He aspires to protect innocent people but for achieving this goal, he needs to take violent means.

The Human as a War Machine

Howl's metamorphosis into an animal also sends a message about transgressing the limits of the human in wartime. His dramatic mutation insinuates that war can force humans to become inhuman. Because he is a hybrid—a human, a wizard, and an owl—Howl can transgress the limits between these categories, but not without consequences. Becoming-animal is a particularly risky business. Calcifer reminds him, "You shouldn't keep flying around like that. Soon you won't be able to turn back into a human." Howl assumes the risk to lose his human shape not out of vanity or pure wickedness, but because of his beliefs. He fights to protect Sophie's nation against the attack of his neighboring kingdom, which is looking for their missing prince. Howl tells Calcifer about the dubious wizards who also participated in the battle, "My own kind attacked me today. [...] Some hack wizards who turned themselves into monsters for the King." Calcifer answers him, "Those wizards are going to regret doing that. They'll never change back into humans." With cynicism, Howl replies: "After the war, they won't even recall they were human." Howl's appearance makes visible the way that war can transform one's fundamental nature. In addition to highlighting the horrors of war, the "plasmaticness" of the animated body underlines the risks of crossing borders. Howl's painful transformation symbolizes the struggles resulting from the necessity to change our habits, roles, and behaviors to fulfill our social responsibilities and thereby respect our personal convictions.

The human in *Howl's Moving Castle* is never natural, but always metamorphic. The instability of Howl's physical shape may evoke playfulness, flexibility, ability, and vitality. At the same time, the instability of shape may symbolize chaos, unpredictability, dubiousness, or madness. War in this animated film pushes the characters to explore the negative side of their persona. As media theorist Antonia Levi notes, "Howl is a wonderful metaphor for what happens to soldiers—even antisoldiers—in war. He fights only to defend others, especially those he loves, but the act of fighting is turning him into a monster."[89] The analogy between Howl's figure when he flies and the shape of an aircraft deepens this monstrous association, eroding the gap between the monster, the machine, and the animal. As other wartime animations do, turning characters into animals is a strategy "to strip away their very humanness, their humanity."[90] When Deleuze and Guattari talk about the animal peopling of the human being, they claim that the "hunting machine, the war machine, the crime machine entail all kinds of becomings-animal that are not articulated in myth."[91] The transformations that our environment imposes on us, or the makeovers that we choose to undergo, are not without contradictions. On the one hand, Howl's painful metamorphosis may symbolize his self-sacrifice for a good cause. A positive representation of the chivalrous wizard encourages allegiance with the character's noble combat against evil. On the other hand, Howl tells Sophie that both sides are wrong in participating in the war. The pain evoked by Howl's transformation into a war machine and the repulsive war sequences appeal to the spectator's affect to promote an anti-war message. Upsetting somatic effects can suggest that warfare entails negative consequences for individuals and for society.

With *Howl's Moving Castle* and *Princess Mononoke*, Miyazaki warns us about the dangers of war and ethnocentrism on the individual, the environment, and society. The reshaping of the protagonist into a bird of prey and then back to its human form engages spectators not only in the process of becoming-animal, but also in the process of becoming-animated. The process of becoming-animal raises questions about the fixity of categories such as "human" and "animal." As with San's becoming-animal in *Princess Mononoke*, embodied engagement with hybrid characters has the potential to involve the spectators in processes of becoming that disrupt culturally derived divides by creating new assemblages. The symbiotic relationship established between the spectator and the animated body of Ashitaka involves more than just empathic resonances: it explores intersubjective interactions with composite images of the self. Represented as composite bodies that can stretch, disassemble, and collapse beyond recognition, metamorphic characters invite spectators to reevaluate the uniquely organic boundary of their own body as they enter into resonating linkages with distorted figures. While becoming-animated reveals the productive intersubjective relationships we develop with our animated mirrors, it can also highlight the consequences of machinic transformations.

Conclusion

The traditional structure of sympathy conceives the self as a self-contained, unalienable whole, in perfect control of its body. The possibility for animated bodies to change embodiment with their transmutable outlines challenges the rigidity of this structure. Drawing on the protean abilities of the animated figures, metamorphic narratives tell stories about social transformation and individual enlightenment. In the metaphorical domain, the character's metamorphosis incarnates mocking the establishment in *Fantasmagoria*, the problem of fitting in for Emily in *Corpse Bride*, intercultural exchanges in *Princess Mononoke*, and personality growth in *Howl's Moving Castle*.

The structure of engagement replaces the vague notion of identification with character engagement, which involves three main processes: recognition, alignment, and allegiance. Normally, these processes are facilitated by our tacit knowledge of the IN-OUT schema and all the patterns of physical interactions associated with it. In *Corpse Bride*, the body of the puppets is a bounded structure that helps to identify the various resemblance metaphors evoked in the opening title sequence, including the BODY IS A CAGE, THE HEART IS A CLOCK, and THE BODY IS A MACHINE. Despite Emily's idiosyncrasies, viewers can empathize with her, thanks to engaging dialogues and intimate scenes. Alignment with her becomes problematic when she metamorphoses into a flock of butterflies and the points of reference connected with the IN-OUT schema vanish. Her transfiguration encourages new metaphorical interpretations where life and death meet.

The materiality of the animated body can also be political. The hybrid film *The Death of Stalinism in Bohemia* moves the spectators outside of their comfort zones by mutilating, fragmenting, and threatening clay bodies. The shocking images of bloody flesh and viscera call the viewer's attention to the cruelty of the Czech regime after the implantation of Stalinism. The succession of recycled bodies of clay falling into a bucket evokes the numerous dissidents that were executed by the regime. The unexpected juxtaposition of life and death in this animation seeks the viewers' allegiances by appealing to both their intellects and emotions.

The hybrid creatures of Japanese animation are often means to bridge personal identity struggles with broader familial or national issues. In *Princess Mononoke*, Ashitaka's body mutates after he has been infected by the curse of the bore demon. San, the princess wolf, is a hybrid between a wolf and a human. The collection of affects and violent behaviors represents both internal conflicts and political tensions in the fabric of their fictive societies. Themes and motifs at the level of the narrative also relate to the healing power of love and aspire to reconciliation among fellow humans, animals, and plants. Composite bodies and digital morphing in this animation parallel the highly modular structure of the animated characters with the heterogeneity of the viewer's body.

Alternatively, the animated film *Howl's Moving Castle* creates empathic resonances between spectators and animated characters that cross categories between the human and the animal and the human and the machine. Through empowering proprioceptive assemblages and perceptual alignments, this animation invites viewers to empathize with Howl's struggle. His transformation into an animal symbolizes the monstrous effects of war on people. Processes of empathic reverberations and affective mimicry rewrite the bounds of the animation machine to include a two-way bandwidth that links a spectator to an animated body during the viewing process—a dynamic system of interactions that I have termed "becoming-animated." Embodied simulations and empathic resonances cause molecular transformations that echo the flow of affects that accompanies the metamorphosis of Howl.

In the reshaping, remixing, and repurposing of the human and nonhuman bodies, metamorphic narratives encourage a self-assessment of our "body images" and constant reevaluations of the delimitation between "self" and "other." When creating this distinction, we use others as mirrors, looking for similarities and differences in their traits, beliefs, behaviors, and underlying structures. An examination of our intellectual contrapposti and visceral responses to distorted figures can expose our implicit tolerance thresholds and encourage a reevaluation of these arbitrary limits, a subject particularly relevant as we encounter different axes of identity and ways of seeing in our everyday lives.

Notes

1 Wells, *Understanding Animation*, 69.
2 The original title is *Le cauchemar du fantoche.*
3 The original title is *Le songe du garçon de café.*
4 (my translation). The original title is *Rêves enfantins.*
5 *Le cauchemar du fantoche.*
6 The original title is *Fantasmagorie.*
7 This film is not fully animated, since there is live-action footage showing a hand at the beginning and at the end. On Cohl, see Crafton, *Emile Cohl.*
8 In *Representations of the Post/Human*, Graham argues that representations of the posthuman in cultural texts reassert the boundaries of the human. Sue Short comes to a similar conclusion in *Cyborg Cinema and Contemporary Subjectivity.*
9 Smith, *Engaging Characters*, 63. For general theories of emotion, see Frijda, *The Emotions*; Izard, *Human Emotions*; and Ortony et al., *The Cognitive Structure of Emotion.*
10 On concern-based construals, see Roberts, *Emotions.* On their application to film, see Plantinga, chapter 2, *Moving Viewers.* For a list of common concerns, see Planalp, *Communicating Emotions*, 19–22.
11 On iconography, see Smith, *Engaging Characters*, 192.
12 For details about the structure of sympathy, see Smith, chapter 2, *Engaging Characters.*
13 Heider and Simmel, "An Experimental Study."
14 Smith, *Engaging Characters*, 75 (emphasis in the original).
15 On markers of presence in animation, see Wood, chapter 1, *Digital Encounters* and Crafton, *Shadow of a Mouse.*
16 On psychological realism, see Nichols, *Ideology and the Image.*
17 On continuity editing, see Bordwell and Thompson, *Film Art*, 236–246.
18 Metz, *The Imaginary Signifier*, 56.
19 On identification in cinema, see, for instance, Metz, *The Imaginary Signifier* and Mulvey, "Visual Pleasure and Narrative Cinema."
20 Smith, *Engaging Characters*, 93.
21 Smith, *Engaging Characters*, 94.
22 On point-of-view conventions and deictic-gaze ability, see chapter 2 in Persson, *Understanding Cinema.*
23 On the subjective point of view in video games, see Galloway, *Gaming.*
24 For psychological studies on the phenomenon of allegiance and perspective sharing, see Hoffner and Cantor, "Perceiving and Responding to Media Characters," 87–89.
25 On emotional simulation, see Smith, *Engaging Characters*, 96–98.
26 On subjective access, see Smith, *Engaging Characters*, 150–152. On depth of story information, see Bordwell and Thompson, *Film Art*, 95–100.

27 On fantastic metamorphoses in literature, and the ways in which they alter popular perceptions of the self, see, for instance, Forbes Irving, *Metamorphosis in Greek Myths* and Skulsky, *Metamorphosis.*
28 On the *gryllus*, see Elkins, *Pictures of the Body.*
29 Warner, *Fantastic Metamorphoses*, 2.
30 Crafton, *Before Mickey*, 329.
31 Warner, *Fantastic Metamorphoses*, 212.
32 For various examples of metamorphoses in literature, see Warner, *Fantastic Metamorphoses*, 203.
33 Todorov, *The Fantastic*, 116.
34 Smith, *Engaging Characters*, 171.
35 Eisenstein, *Eisenstein on Disney*, 21.
36 On intersectionality and the continuum of subject positions, see Crenshaw, "Mapping the Margins."
37 Orbaugh, "Emotional Infectivity," 152.
38 Christian Keysers examines the physiological relations between mirror neurons and empathy in *The Empathic Brain.*
39 For a discussion of the IN-OUT schema and its association with CONTAINER metaphors, see Johnson, *The Body in the Mind*, 29–32.
40 Fahlenbrach and Schröter detail the process of mapping from metaphoric source domains in the design of player-controlled characters to metaphoric target domains in the video games *Arkham City* and *InFamous*, "Embodied Avatars in Video Games," 251–268. While the process these authors describe is specific to video games, I apply many elements of this process to the interpretation of character design in *Corpse Bride.*
41 Page, *Gothic Fantasy*, 30.
42 McMahan, *The Films of Tim Burton*, 7.
43 Neumann, "Machina."
44 Kozachik, "Reanimating Romance," 48. See also Fordham, "Pete Kozachik on *Corpse Bride.*"
45 Hook, *Acting in Animation*, 54.
46 Tan defines compassion, sympathy, and admiration as the three major empathetic emotions felt toward film protagonists. See Tan, *Emotion and the Structure of Narrative Film*, 177–182.
47 Plantinga, *Moving Viewers*, 73.
48 For a distinction between "feeling with" and "feeling for," see Coplan, "Empathetic Engagement with Narrative Fictions."
49 On the distinction between sympathy and empathy in film, see Carroll, *The Philosophy of Horror*, 88–96; Grodal, *Embodied Visions*, 181–204; Neill, "Empathy and (Film) Fiction"; Plantinga, *Moving Viewers*, 97–111; Smith, *Engaging Characters*, 102–106; Tan, *Emotion and the Structure of Narrative Film*, 153–193; and Zillmann, "Empathy."
50 O'Pray, *Jan Švankmajer*, 48.
51 *Leonardo's Diary.*
52 During an interview, Švankmajer mentions about this film, "I never pretended that it was anything more than propaganda," in Hames, "Interview with Jan Švankmajer," 100.
53 Akatsuka, "The Wager of a Militant Surrealist."
54 Uhde, *Jan Švankmajer*, 64.
55 Elkins, *Pictures of the Body*, 109.
56 See Akatsuka, "The Wager of a Militant Surrealist."

57 On speciesism in American animation and Japanese *anime*, see Lamarre, "Speciesism, Part I." Richard Ryder coined the term speciesism in the early 1970s to designate a discrimination against nonhuman animal.
58 Napier, *Anime from Akira to Howl's Moving Castle*, 33.
59 On a similar process of cultural hybridization in Disney's *Fantasia* (1940), see "Eye-Candy and Adorno's Silly Symphonies" in Leslie, *Hollywood Flatlands*.
60 Cavallaro, *The Animé Art of Hayao Miyazaki*, 71.
61 Cavallaro, *The Animé Art of Hayao Miyazaki*, 54.
62 See Smith, chapter 3, *Engaging Characters*.
63 Napier, *Anime from Akira to Howl's Moving Castle*, 241. On the exploration of the limits of the human, see Lunning, ed., *Mechademia 3*.
64 Miyazaki, quoted in Boyd and Nishimura, "Shinto Perspectives," 4. Originally published in *Japan Times Weekly*, September 9, 2002. See Boyd and Nishimura's article for a description of the Shinto worldview. They explain that kami is a vital power that "harmoniously pervades the whole phenomenal world."
65 Bigelow, "Technologies of Perception," 56.
66 On the limits of the human in anime, see Lunning, ed., *Mechademia 3*.
67 On the conception of the self-contained self, see Orbaugh, "Emotional Infectivity," 152. For an overview of theories of mind that address the divide between body and mind, see Rifelj, "Minds, Computers, and Hadaly."
68 Cavallaro, *The Animé Art of Hayao Miyazaki*, 127.
69 Orbaugh, "Emotional Infectivity," 167–168 (emphasis in the original).
70 Fisher, "Tracing the Tesseract," 103.
71 On the history of morphing, see Sobchack, ed., *Meta-Morphing*. On morphing in *The Mask*, see Bukatman, "Taking Shape: Morphing and the Performance of Self," 237–244.
72 Cavallaro, *The Animé Art of Hayao Miyazaki*, 128.
73 On control at the molecular level of the image, see Fisher, "Tracing the Tesseract," 120.
74 Orbaugh, "Emotional Infectivity," 167.
75 Deleuze, and Guattari, *A Thousand Plateaus*, 257.
76 Persson, *Understanding Cinema*, 110.
77 On proxemics, see Hall, *The Hidden Dimension*.
78 Persson, *Understanding Cinema*, 110.
79 On imaginary transposition, see Thompson, *Mind in Life*, 395. For a discussion of this empathetic process in film, see Hoffner and Cantor, "Perceiving and Responding to Media Characters." On character simulation, a process similar to imaginary transposition, but adapted to moving images, see Grodal, chapter 8, *Embodied Visions*. Tan calls "imagine-self empathy," the process by which viewers imagine the situation as though it was happening to them, *Emotion and the Structure of Narrative Film*, 185.
80 For further details on central and acentral imagining, see Smith, *Engaging Characters*, 74–81. Richard Wollheim originally developed these concepts in *The Thread of Life*, 74.
81 Virilio, *Pure War*.
82 Lamarre, *The Anime Machine*, 5.
83 Deleuze and Guattari, *A Thousand Plateaus*, 258.
84 Deleuze and Guattari, *A Thousand Plateaus*, 272.

85 Deleuze and Guattari, *A Thousand Plateaus*, 272, (emphasis in the original).
86 On emotional contagion and facial feedback in film studies, see Plantinga, *Moving Viewers*, 126–128; Smith, *Engaging Characters*, 98–102; and Dimberg, "Facial Reactions to Facial Expressions." On affective mimicry, see Hatfield et al., chapter 2, *Emotional Contagion*. Studies argue that response to faces is more than mere mimicry. The recognition of an emotion in the face triggers motor structures in the brain, see Moody et al., "More Than Mere Mimicry?" and Magnee et al., "Electromyographic Responses to Faces."
87 Rosenblum, *See What I'm Saying*, 189.
88 Plantinga, *Moving Viewers*, 126. On the scenes of empathy, see also Plantinga, "The Scene of Empathy." On the effects of extended close-ups, see Tan, *Emotion and the Structure of Narrative Film*, 183–184.
89 Levi, "*Howl's Moving Castle*," 262.
90 Lamarre, *The Anime Machine*, 75.
91 Deleuze and Guattari, *A Thousand Plateaus*, 242.

4 Muscular Augmentations

Introduction

With the advent of digital cinema, blockbusters increasingly engage audiences with breathtaking action scenes and impossible feats such as the digitally enhanced backflips and jumps performed by Neo and Trinity in *The Matrix* (Lana Wachowski and Lilli Wachowski 1999). The choreography in this film synthesizes the muscular abilities of the actor and the augmented performances of the synthespian.[1] The slowed-down movements of the gravity-defying bodies cause unexpected muscular resonances throughout the spectator's body. The hyperbolized movements in animation can also impress the viewers muscularly. In *The Incredibles* (Brad Bird, 2004), Dash becomes a human propeller for the inflatable boat made by his mother's body by rapidly moving his legs in the water. Muscular excess and muscular augmentations are not new expressive devices. Early on, animators developed a cartoonal logic that defied the biological limitations of human characters. For instance, after eating spinach, the famous sailor Popeye transforms into a human airplane in *I Never Changes My Altitude* (Dave Fleischer, 1937). In the same vein, the chapter investigates animation technologies that unsettle our understanding of the limits of the human body in animation by stirring effects in the muscular domain.

Camera movements and subjective perspectives can prompt a range of muscular experiences of space. Truck rides and car races in *Cars* (John Lasseter, 2006), for instance, evoke muscular memory of riding a vehicle or playing a racing video game. Other techniques focus on enhancing character performance to elicit muscular sensations. Some camera movements and awe-inspiring feats in martial arts animated films communicate heroism and seek to empower the spectators. The chapter examines the special case of female martial arts characters and their demonstrations of womenpower. Then, I tackle the politics of the defamiliarized muscular sensations induced with the help of animation technologies. For example, the introduction of temporal discontinuities in bodily motion propelled by technology heightens existential angst about modern urban life in the puppet animation *The Club of the Laid*

Off (Jiří Barta, 1989). The pixilation and puppet animation in *The Secret Adventures of Tom Thumb* (Dave Borthwick, 1993) produce uncanny bodily movements that communicate anxiety about technological progress. The rotoscope technology can also perturb the muscularity of the cyborg viewer in a meaningful way. In *Minnie the Moocher* (Dave Fleischer, 1932), for example, the rotoscoped dance of Cab Calloway haunts the spectators with questions about racial representation. The last section of the chapter explores the ethics of muscular augmentations in *The Triplets of Belleville*[2] (Sylvain Chomet, 2003) and the consequences of superhumanity in *Black Jack: The Movie* (Osamu Dezaki and Fumihiro Yoshimura, 1996). These two animated films elicit vicarious effects to engage viewers in contemporary debates on enhanced athletic performance and their ethical ramifications.

The Muscular Experience of Space

Muscular Memory

Movement in animated media is engaging and thrilling in and of itself. The Lumière brothers understood its appeal in their early films. *Employees Leaving the Lumière Factory* (Louis Lumière, 1895), for instance, captivated audiences with images of ordinary people walking.[3] Another example, the experimental film *La Région Centrale* (Michael Snow, 1971), mesmerizes spectators with repetitive camera movements. The spectator's response to movements is in large part automatic and pre-reflexive, and as such belongs to direct affect.[4] Film scholar Lisa Fehsenfeld divides movements in moving images into two large groups: technical movements and physical movements.[5] Technical movements include the nondiegetic movements produced by camera movements, editing techniques, and special effects. The movements performed by the characters on the screen are called "physical movements." Camera work and the speed and the direction of the characters' motion can induce visceral, physiological, and emotional responses in the spectators. Some of the direct physiological effects of movement include "dizziness, nausea, motion sickness, autonomic reflexes, perception of effort responses, classic conditioning, mimicry, and basic stress responses."[6] Although these effects may sometimes produce discomfort, they also increase the appeal of certain films by eliciting vicarious thrills. While animated films are exempt from camera movement and physical movement per se, they can simulate camera movements and muscular efforts. These simulations also produce physiological effects, as described in the analysis of *Sisyphus* in Chapter 1.

Muscular mimicry with the film's body and embodied simulations can occur in any film or animation that involves camera movements, objects moving within the frame, or muscular efforts. Scholars have pondered whether some genres could arouse the spectators' empathy more forcefully than others, and could thereby manipulate the spectator's affective experience in more persuasive ways. In "Film Bodies: Gender, Genre and Excess," film scholar Linda Williams singles out certain "body genres," including melodrama, horror, and pornography as being conducive of empathic responses. Unlike Williams, who focuses her analysis on character-centered mimicry, film scholar Jennifer Barker prefers talking about the mimicry of the film itself. This form of mimicry can happen when the viewer shares the character's perspective via point-of-view shots, first-person narration, or linear perspective. Muscular mimicry occurs when our "bodies orient and dispose themselves toward the body of the film itself, because we and the film make sense of space by moving through it muscularly in similar ways and with similar attitudes."[7] Mimicry of the film's body is a way for viewers to organize and understand the space depicted in a film by drawing on their muscular experience of space, consciously or not. As Barker notes in *The Tactile Eye*,

> every film, regardless of genre, evokes some kind of bodily response, even those films we find dull and uninspiring (the ones that "bore us to tears"). Viewers' responses to films are necessarily physical, full-bodied responses, because our vision is always fully embodied, intimately connected to our fingertips, our funny bones, and our feet, for example.[8]

Although I agree with Barker that bodily responses are not limited to certain genres, kung fu fights in animation are more likely to induce muscular stimulations than some of the sequences of *Waking Life* (Richard Linklater, 2001), an animated film that portrays talking heads. Even though the characters remain still for extended periods while they meditate on the meaning of consciousness, this animation can still stir up bodily responses. The vibrating outlines of the images produced by the rotoscope can be visually attractive in some sequences or viscerally annoying in others. However, the subdued physical movements and camera movements in the interview sequences serve other purposes than eliciting muscular empathy, such as maintaining the viewer's attention on what the character is saying.

Film scholar Geoff King has called the increased reliance on spectacle and affect in Hollywood films "impact aesthetic."[9] These films favor intense, physical action to a greater extent than the ones made prior to the 1960s.[10] An example of this cinematic style, which showcases fast-paced editing and pronounced movement toward the camera, can be found in *Mad Max: Fury Road* (George Miller, 2015). Fascinating technical and physical movements are not just achieved by spectacular visual effects. In addition, the intensity of their physiological, emotive, and visceral effects on the spectators varies widely. Some movements entail effortless travel through space, while others underline the bumps along the way. For example, the experience of smooth movement forward or backward in the film *Cosmic Voyage* (Bayley Silleck, 1996) conveys an incredible lightness.[11] During the cosmic exploration, I do not sense any muscular tension that could strain my muscles. Rather, the journey arouses the sensation of a smooth, gravity-free ride in the backseat. The experience of weightlessness in outer space in *Gravity* (Alfonso Cuarón, 2013) evokes a slightly increased range of muscular intensities. Film scholar Scott Richmond theorizes the cinema's disordering and reordering of the viewer's perception in this film as a modulation of our proprioception. In Richmond's words, the movements across the screen were "accompanied by a series of bodily responses: a lump in my throat, a tightening in my chest, the involuntary engagement of the musculature of my core, pushing into the back of my seat, my hands gripping my armrests."[12] In his analysis of the films *Gravity* and *2001: A Space Odyssey* (Stanley Kubrick, 1968), Richmond mentions that "the sensation of moving through space in both films is not manifest, really, in a sense of space as such but rather in sensations of self."[13] As an alternative to these mostly effortless rides, the animated film *Boundin'* (Bud Luckey, 2003), in which the fluffy sheep gracefully bounces up and down, amplifies the contrast between tensed and relaxed muscles. When I watch it, the repetitive rebounds ripple through my musculature as my eyes attempt to keep up with the high leaps of the animal. In a way similar to associations and moods, such embodied effects can strengthen character engagement and immersion—a sense of being there where the action happens.

Our muscular experience of the on-screen space brings to mind prior physical experiences. For instance, it approximates the experience of walking forward or backward, jumping up or down, turning our torso from side to side, or tilting our head up and down. Although the camera movements may revive bodily memories, the vividness of the sensations appears modulated. In order to amplify the mirroring effects, some animations adopt a first-person perspective. For instance, when I watched the Super Silly Fun Land roller coaster ride from the perspective of the characters in *Despicable Me* (Pierre Coffin and Chris Renaud, 2010), I felt my viscera going up and down, an impression that can induce motion sickness in some viewers. There are evidently limits to the resemblance between both experiences. While the feeling of dizziness produced by the animated roller coaster ride approximates what I feel when I ride a real roller coaster, I never mistake my body for the film's body.

Recent 3D movies multiply not only digital camera movements and physical movements that stimulate bodily memories, but also disorienting computer-generated effects. For example, the animated feature *A Christmas Carol* (Robert Zemeckis, 2009) piles up stirring camera movements that encourage motor mimicry with the film's body. When Scrooge flies over the city at a fast pace, closing in on some buildings or abruptly diving head first into the void, it may compel some viewers to sway to the side to avoid hitting a building or lean toward the back of their seat when rapidly approaching the ground. These immersive 3D effects amplify the sensation of personal space invasion found in traditional live-action films and animations, a topic examined in the previous chapter.

In addition, some movements in depth can convey emotional distress. Virilio calls "cinematism" a camera alignment that emphasizes speed and movement in depth in his mobile apparatus theory.[14] For example, when we adopt the perspective of the conductor of a train, we become

> an apparatus-subject, whose eyes and other senses are aligned with the apparatus, with the speeding train. As speed introduces a sense of separation between the world and the subject, the eye becomes a kine-eye, desirous of greater velocity and mobility, bent on its own destruction.[15]

A comparable condition occurs when I adopt Scrooge's perspective as he skims over a weathercock or when the image quickly zooms in on approaching objects. I feel aligned with the apparatus and Scrooge's destructive drive. The swift penetration of the landscape from his perspective occasions a physical discomfort that also brings to mind past experiences of hitting a wall or approaching a dangerous place. The apparatus defamiliarizes the cognitive familiarity with thrills that reverberate through my viscera. These vicarious sensations heighten the apparent sense of danger provoked by the loss of firm ground.

Similar to digitally augmented movements that travel into depth, the impossible nature of some camera movements in animation and special effects cinema can induce estrangement effects. The swings of Spider-Man between skyscrapers in the video game *Spider-Man 3* (2007) or the flutter of Tinker Bell's wings in *Tinker Bell* (Bradley Raymond, 2008) produce sensations that "we can't have experienced ourselves, and yet we feel them in our muscles in a way that exhilarates us."[16] By exacerbating the difference between human movement and digital movement, some visual effects films make "clear that the 'action hero' body is an impossible one, and that the action film places impossible demands on the bodies of the characters and its viewers."[17] In "Virtual Actors, Spectacle and Special Effects," film scholar Dan North argues that the use of special effects enables filmmakers to work around the limitations of the actor's body and to amplify the viewer's fascination.[18] When experienced for the first time, the backflips in slow motion may heighten one's sense of awe while inducing a pleasurable sensation of disorientation as Neo defies the gravitational forces. The extreme slow-motion effect produces a discrepancy between the real body and its virtualized double that modulates the familiar process of motor mimicry. By underscoring the gap between the impossible bodily movements and the spectator's natural sensorimotor abilities, the spatiotemporal manipulations expand the spectator's repertoire of image schemas.

While viewers can enjoy the muscular sensations caused by digital effects and animated camera movements for themselves, these affects also carry additional connotations. Technology-induced sensations may invite spectators to speculate about the effects of technological innovations on global politics. For example, the scalar travel toward a satellite perspective in *Appleseed Ex Machina* (Shinji Aramaki, 2007) implies a potential subjection to global telecommunication networks, as this posthuman perspective is controlled by a megalomaniacal scientist. On a more positive note, Spider-Man's delirious swings in the *Spider-Man* trilogy (Sam Raimi, 2002, 2004, 2007) compel spectators to revel in the newest technological innovations in CGI, while the plots celebrate scientific progress and warn viewers about the evil schemes of unscrupulous scientists.

Hyperbolized Physical Movements and Martial Arts Animation

Popular animated films such as the *Kung Fu Panda* trilogy (2008, 2011, 2016), *Kung Fu Panda: Secrets of the Furious Five* (Raman Hui, 2008), *Mulan* (Tony Bancroft and Barry Cook, 1998), and *Mulan II* (Darrell Rooney and Lynne Southerland, 2004) enthrall spectators with action-packed sequences of kicks, leaps, and punches. While the performances of martial artists in live-action films feature physical performances that defy the laws of nature, the animated characters redefine these laws in terms of cartoonal logic. Camera movements and physical movements in martial arts animations portraying strong female characters produce subjective positions of empowerment for the spectators by borrowing strategies from live-action cinema and freely adapting them.

Even though physical movements on the screen can engage the senses of the spectators with no frills, filmmakers often adopt strategies to amplify their impact. Examples of techniques that enhance the fighters' skills and muscular strength include group fight sequences, display of an individual warrior's skills, the use of special effects, and impossibly mobile camera movements. In kung fu live-action films, combatants "can appear to transcend the limits of plausibility to fight, for example, with superhuman speed (under-cranking the camera during shooting makes the projected film run slightly faster) or skill (supporting wires can help them to defy gravity)."[19] However, cinematic technique is often all it takes to draw the viewer's attention on the performer and elicit embodied simulations. In "Aesthetics in Action: Kung Fu, Gunplay, and Cinematic Expressivity," David Bordwell explains that Sergei Eisenstein put expressive movement at the core of his cinematic mise-en-scène. According to Eisenstein's theory,

> the filmmaker had to devise ways of framing (*mise en cadre*) and editing (*montage*) which would sharpen and further dynamize the [actor's] expressive movements. And at key moments these techniques could cooperate, double, and intensify one another in massive assault on the spectator's senses. If the effort was successful, the force of the movement and its onscreen presentation would stir in the viewer's body a palpable echo of the actor's gesture.[20]

Eisenstein would also add that

> it is precisely expressive movement, built on an organically correct foundation, that is solely capable of evoking this emotion in the spectator, who in turn reflexively repeats in weakened form the entire system of the actor's movements; as a result of the produced movements, the spectator's incipient muscular tensions are released in the desired emotion.[21]

In other words, framing and editing can both heighten emotional response and produce muscular reverberations that echo the actor's movements. For instance, the use of tight framing can more easily trigger motor mimicry by affording a closer view of the movements performed on-screen and by clarifying the character's emotions.

Duels in martial arts animated films can induce feelings of empowerment. As *Secrets of the Furious Five* demonstrates, nonhuman characters that have no visible muscles can also mesmerize viewers with their fighting styles. In this animation, an overweight panda called Po tells the story of how Mantis, Viper, Crane, Tigress, and Monkey had to deal with their personal issues before becoming renowned kung fu masters. Po motivates his rambunctious pupils by telling how the warriors overcame the obstacles they encountered on their journeys toward excellence of self. In the sequence about Viper's story, we learn that she was born without fangs. Consequently, she could not carry on her father's legacy as the protector of the village. Yet, when the village was under the attack of a giant gorilla bandit, she found the courage to confront him. Thanks to her dexterity with ribbons, she managed to tie the arms and feet of the gorilla and vanquish the beast. This sequence opposes the deceptive dancing skills of Viper to the brute force of the muscular gorilla wearing a poison-proof metallic armor. Despite her small stature and thin body, Viper proved herself to be a quick, agile, and very determined warrior.

The fight sequence assaults the spectator's senses with the speed at which Viper can twirl her ribbon in the air. The red color of the ribbon stands out from the dark buildings and the gray skin of the gorilla. When she twirls it with her tail, it fills the frame with colorful spirals. At one point, Viper surprises the overconfident bully by wrapping the ribbon around his huge arm and quickly pulling on it. As the gorilla falls on the ground, the impact shakes the image and produces a large cloud of smoke. The contrast in size between the two opponents is another aspect that makes Viper's success even more satisfactory. A series of high- and low-angle shots emphasize the disparity in size. Once Viper is victorious, a shot of her tiny silhouette sitting on the top of the wrapped up gorilla, followed by a close-up of her smiling face, brings to mind the story of David who vanquished Goliath. This finale claims that success does not reward bullies but those who like Viper demonstrate great courage in defending the ones they love.

The group fights on the rooftops in *Kung Fu Panda 3* bombard the senses by dividing the frame into multiple sites of attraction. This sequence is reminiscent of the chase scene on the rooftops in *Crouching Tiger, Hidden Dragon* (Ang Lee, 2000). Yet, the cartoon extrapolates the height of Po's jumps and the impact of his falls for humorous purposes. Another reference to cinema is made when the Furious Five warriors freeze their motion. Tigress's posture when she holds one of her knees bent in the air and lifts her two arms resembles Daniel LaRusso's kick pose in *The Karate Kid* (John Avildsen, 1984). One of the most graceful moves in this animation involves Tigress when she does a flash kick and then falls on the top of a high-pitched roof. Because of her stature and gait, her arm movements and kicks look like those of human fighters. While some of the martial arts movements Tigress performs can awake muscular memories, the extravagant movements of the other warriors and the fantastic settings transport the viewer into the imaginary world of cartoonal logic.

As an alternative to heighten emotional impact, *Mulan II* employs a training sequence and a variety of camera positions to plunge the viewer into the action. In the introductory sequence, Mulan motivates the young girls in her village to become successful warriors. She teaches them the first rule, "One should be gentle and at the same one should be tough." Mulan does not have to cross-dress or behave like a man to display her strength in this sequel to *Mulan*. The songs and the representations of female characters in *Mulan* had been criticized for reinforcing "a binary understanding of gender stereotypes that privilege men over women."[22] Although *Mulan II* still portrays a society in which gender inequality is part of women's lives, Mulan does not need to abandon her femininity to be a successful heroine and a powerful martial artist.[23]

Mulan's demonstration of the basic kung fu movements is turned into a musical choreography. Martial arts fights, as Aaron Anderson argues, are stylized like a dance and convey a "romanticized empowerment relative to a displayed level of skill and training."[24] The alternation between Mulan's fluid dance movements and quick punches concretizes her feminine approach to martial arts. Unlike *Enter the Dragon* (Robert Clouse, 1973) and *Birth of the Dragon* (George Nolfi, 2016), two movies featuring the muscularity of Bruce Lee, or the character playing his role, Mulan's muscles remain dissimulated under her ample clothes. Skillful juggling between fluidity and strength is the key element of Mulan's fighting style. As Po also explains to his pupils in *Secrets of the Furious Five*, muscularity is not the secret ingredient of successful kung fu warriors. Everyone can develop his or her particular aptitudes to achieve excellence of self.

Since the spectators also witness Mulan's kung fu lesson, they can experience motor mimicry. Eisenstein saw "motor mimicry as susceptible to conditioning, [...] such that filmmakers could create new associations—new links between movements and responses—and could thus manipulate the spectator's affective experience for persuasive purposes."[25] A vicarious engagement with martial arts fighters can even translate into physical empowerment in reality. When watching Bruce Lee exhibit astonishing martial arts prowess in *Enter the Dragon* (Robert Clouse, 1973), Anderson recalled its empowering effect on him and his fellow student soldiers: "Our mental association with the invincible character we saw on screen expressed itself through our own physical actions as we consciously attempted to recreate elements of Lee's movement within our own bodies."[26] The belief that Lee's on-screen movements could be performed in reality was a motivating force for Anderson's fellow soldiers, and arguably other spectators. However, some mirroring effects can be hindered by the cartoony appearance of the fighter. For example, if Viper's prowess could be a source of motivation and a lesson of courage for the young rabbits listening to Po's story, her extravagant abilities remain impossible to reproduce in real life.

The departure from tradition is a theme explored in *Mulan* and *Mulan II*. While the girls from Mulan's village adhere to the sartorial customs and respect their traditions, they express their individuality when they train with Mulan. When the girls imitate Mulan's kung fu movements, they introduce a touch of humor into their interpretations. Moreover, by following Mulan's instruction, the village girls implicitly learn that a woman can also demonstrate leadership, not only a man. *Mulan II* reinterprets certain conventions of martial arts films that are detrimental to female characters. It breaks from the tradition of many Chinese martial arts films that reward male kung fu teachers and relegate female teachers to less successful statuses.[27] For instance, when General Shang and Mulan are dangling from a rope loosely attached to a broken bridge, it is Shang who "sacrifices" his life to save Mulan—even though Shang does not really die after falling into the river. The sacrifice of a man's life in martial arts films is unusual considering the higher percentage of women who sacrifice themselves compared to men. The film *Crouching Tiger, Hidden Dragon* features the famous example of Jen Yu who jumped into the abyss to grant her lover's wish.[28] In contrast, *Mulan II* suggests, no one's life should be sacrificed by the plot.

Distorted Bodily Motion

While some camera movements and bodily gestures in the animated films studied evoke muscular memories, others can expand our repertoire of motion schemas. By motion schema, I mean a tacit list of the possible bodily motions and contortions that human and nonhuman bodies can produce. This section first examines the rhetorical effects of hindering the process of muscular empathy in the puppet animations *The Club of the Laid Off* (Jiřì Barta, 1989) and *The Secret Adventures of Tom Thumb* (Dave Borthwick, 1993). Then, I study the rotoscoped dances performed by Cab Calloway in Fleischer's animations. Their evocative settings and character designs, I argue, are haunted by racial stereotypes.

Defamiliarizing Everyday Gestures in Puppet Animation

The Club of the Laid Off quirkily reveals the gaps between usual patterns of human locomotion and animated contortions. The awkward movements of muscleless puppets defamiliarize everyday gestures and communicate angst about the humdrum of urban life. Made by the Czech animator Jiřì Barta, this short hybrid film features live-action and puppet animation sequences. The opening sequence sets the action in a gloomy city. It shows a noisy street scene with tramways crossing the frame in the foreground and old dark apartment buildings in the background. Several broken mannequins live together in one of the abandoned apartments. The camera roams around the messy rooms. Suddenly, a male mannequin with squeaky joints wakes up in his bed. He manages to stand up by tilting his body forward. His joints and limbs are stiff and his movements spasmodic. Because he sleeps with a briefcase attached across his body, he is ready to leave for work. Just before departing, he clumsily hugs his female partner. When he walks across the hallway, he cannot bend his knees. His locomotion lacks the smoothness of a human gait, which may provoke unsettling muscular tensions in some viewers. He takes unusually long strides and hesitates before going down the staircase. As expected, after attempting to get down onto the first step, he tumbles noisily down the stairs.

In addition to highlighting the difference of embodiment between humans and mannequins, this animated film exaggerates spatiotemporal discontinuities. In stop-motion animation, the sequential juxtaposition of a series of still images of an object taken from slightly different angles or positions simulates the continuous movements of live-action cinema. The subtler the change of position, the smoother the gesture appears. When presented at the right speed, the gaps between the individual poses become imperceptible to the naked eye. However, some stop-motion animations can purposely design jerky motion or discontinuous gestures, as demonstrated by the analysis of *The Cabinet of Jan Svankmajer* in

Chapter 1. Camera tricks that highlight the gap between human perception and the simulation of human perception reveal the posthuman nature of perception in animation. When the puppets' gestures diverge from our expectations, they may also cause discomfort because we are expert at recognizing the human gait, as psychophysicist Gunnar Johansson has demonstrated in his research on the perception of biological motion.[29]

Likewise, we easily notice when an actor's lips are out of sync, or when someone is not really playing the piano. The discrepancy is deeply felt into our viscera and confirms that something is wrong. *The Club of the Laid Off* accentuates the discontinuity of movement produced by the stop-motion process in the sequence where a female mannequin plays the harp. Although she produces a series of harmonious notes by plucking loosely hanging strings, each time I watch it I can't help but notice her stiff fingers. Her irregular gestures are accompanied by cacophonic sound effects that attract the viewers' attention to the modes of production. Moreover, she has a broken neck, which she abruptly tilts up while making a loud squeaky noise. Because these audiovisual discrepancies trigger muscular memories that are incompatible with the movements depicted, they amplify the uncanny feelings elicited by the cavernous warehouse. The cross-modal stimulations hinder muscular empathy and the discomfort they cause may perturb the audience's desire to sympathize with these strange outcasts.

Scientists have tried to explain the processes by which the brain interprets discontinuity in bodily motion. One hypothesis posits that the brain interpolates or fills in the blanks between series of discontinuous images. For instance, an animated film consists of two frames, one with a dot to the left, and the other with a dot to the right, both of them positioned at the same height. When a viewer is presented with repeated sequences of these two frames at the appropriate interval, these dots will appear to move from left to right and back to the left. When the dots are replaced by images of a human body holding two different positions, a classic study by psychology scholars Maggie Shiffrar and Jennifer Freyd reveals that the brain chooses an anatomically possible route to connect the two positions.[30] Moreover, Jennifer Stevens and her collaborators

> showed that motor areas in the brain become active when people watch two rapidly alternating body positions, but only if the connecting movement is physically possible and the interval between the two frames long enough for the unobserved movement to have been made.[31]

These studies establish that the brain can connect successive body positions whether anatomically correct or not. However, when the alternating body positions correspond to a movement that is biomechanically possible, the primary motor area in the brain cortex is activated, which suggests that successful embodied simulation and motor mimicry may depend on the nature of the physical movement.

Stop-motion animation usually takes advantage of the brain's ability to fill in the blanks between gestural increments to produce a smooth movement. *The Club of the Laid Off*, however, does not always display fluid motion. The distance between the poses taken by the mannequins during the recording is often too wide or their joints cannot bend. Despite the brain's attempt to fill in the blanks when the worker gets out of the bed or falls down the stairs, his movements are rigid and mechanical, lacking vitality. The stiff fingers of the harp player also fail to display the mobility we expect from the music we hear. Yet, the mannequins' choppy movements may increase the viewer's attention and interest because of their peculiarity. As Ivar Hagendoorn notes in his study of the relations between neuroscience and dance, if "the brain fails to predict correctly the unfolding of a movement, we are taken by surprise."[32] Alternatively, if "the movement trajectory predicted by the brain coincides with the actual movement, we are filled with pleasure."[33] Stop-motion animation exploits these two cases. While *The Club of the Laid Off* surprises the viewers or creates discomfort with jerky movements, *Dog* (Suzie Templeton, 2001) excites the compassion of the spectators with delicate gestures of the hands, the touching gaze of the boy, and the expressive postures of the suffering dog.[34]

Some animated films produced with the pixilation technique also present exaggerated discontinuities in bodily gestures that can unnerve some viewers. The production of pixilation requires the motion of the actor to be photographed frame by frame. As Aylish Wood notes, this

> technique not only allows the integration of live action and puppets, but also creates an estranged interface where the movement of live action is rendered curious as the normal and often overlooked motion of even the simplest of gestures is reconfigured and stylized through the process of pixilation.[35]

In *The Secret Adventures of Tom Thumb*, the defamiliarized movements produced with pixilation induce uncanny feelings. They reflect anxieties about the possibility that synthetic doubles may eventually replace the human as we know it. *The Secret Adventures of Tom Thumb* and *The Club of the Laid Off* both exploit the estrangement of the interface and uncanny bodily motion to provoke a general malaise suited to the pessimistic worldviews they depict. Both hybrid animations express anxieties about technological advancements and their detrimental consequences for social and familial relations. The multiple contrasts between the traditional and the modern in *The Club of the Laid Off* also suggest that humans in the contemporary society resemble worn-out mechanical puppets. The traditional gender division of labor offers an acerbic view of conformity, with the stereotypical smiling housewife controlled by patriarchal ideology. Even after breaking free from the repetitive gestures of their everyday life, the mannequins are subjected to the influence of their television set.

Watching the odd movements produced by pixilation and stop-motion animation produces sensations akin to what dance scholar John Martin calls a kinesthetic "revulsion for abnormality."[36] According to Anderson, such revulsion is caused by watching the exaggerated or distorted movements created by cinema, such as the ones found in horror films.[37] This genre employs "special visual effects to create grotesque monsters and horribly mangled bodies that still move and kill."[38] Without being horrible monsters, the pixilated parents in *The Secret Adventures of Tom Thumb* and the harp player in *The Club of the Laid Off* can arouse a similar "revulsion for abnormality." The revulsion is caused by the viewer's inability to reconcile his or her expectation for normative bodily movements with the grotesque movements they see.

The Secret Adventures of Tom Thumb and *The Club of the Laid Off* choose the poetics of muscular sympathy to express their critique of modernity rather than take a purely intellectual approach. Mirroring effects transfer the awkwardness of mechanically produced movements to sensations in the viewers' limbs and joints. When they see the jerky movements of the puppets, they can imagine what it feels like to be an automaton. These nonnormative muscular engagements produced by animation techniques remind the cyborg viewers that invisible forces, whether technological or ideological, can manipulate or even control their everyday behaviors.

Cab Calloway's Rotoscoped Performances

While the stop-motion technique can make us feel like automata, the rotoscope technique injects a dose of human likeness into the movements of the animated characters created by Max Fleischer. Max Fleischer and his brothers Dave and Joe developed a process to animate motion from a live-action film called the rotoscope.[39] The device included a film projector to project the footage frame by frame onto a transparent drawing board placed on an easel. The animator could then trace the outline of the performer on paper and capture each pose with a motion-picture camera. Max Fleischer was granted a patent for this invention in 1917.[40] This technique was popularized by the initial *Out of the Inkwell* series (1918–1921) produced at Bray Studios, a series of short animations featuring a clown who will be known as Koko by 1923.[41] Fleischer also used the rotoscope technique to capture the dance routines performed by Cab Calloway, a famous band orchestra director during the 1930s and 1940s. The rotoscope technology can interfere with the structure of engagement and its various subprocesses, including the processes of recognition, alignment, and allegiance. As I argue, depending on the external appearance of the animated body mapped onto the rotoscoped gestures, we can detect life, the uncanny, or racial stereotypes.

First, the rotoscope technique informs the process of engagement by facilitating the process of recognition when the rotoscoped movements are traced from a human-looking character. As an example, this section examines the lifelike gestures of Koko the Clown and their effects on the spectators. Second, when an animation alternates between the realism of rotoscoped motion and cartoonal physics, as in the cartoons featuring Superman, it can underscore the tension between normal and augmented muscularities. Third, in *Minnie the Moocher* (Dave Fleischer, 1932) and *Betty Boop's Snow White* (Dave Fleischer, 1933), the discrepancy between the cartoony appearance of the character mimicking Cab Calloway's moves and the uncanny resemblance injected via rotoscoping is disturbing. The lifelike gestures enter in conflict with our muscular understanding of cartoonal motion. The eeriness produced by this muscular discrepancy is amplified by the inclusion of ghosts and skeletons in the mise-en-scène. The haunting presence of the black performer produced by the rotoscope technique in these precode animations, I suggest, rehearses stereotypical associations between race and perversion.

The rotoscope technique can induce a semblance of liveliness in the gestures performed by human cartoons. For example, critics of *The Moving Picture World* claimed that the process of rotoscoping could produce lifelike motion. Fascinated by the clown's athletic ability and Dave's performance underneath, they wrote,

> We saw him display athletic propensities such as might shame the star performers of the city's "gyms," and manly attributes not the least of which is the personal directing of the coloring and fashioning of his clothes. And while enjoying the novelty of these animated pen drawings, how many of us stopped to consider the hours of thought and concentration that made possible the lifelike action of the Max Fleischer animated cartoon.[42]

The critics marveled about the effect this novel technique had on them. Comparatively, contemporary viewers perceived animated movements reproduced from memory as mechanical and unnatural.[43] For some, the sense of liveliness could have been heightened by the knowledge that the Fleischer's mystery process involved movements drawn from life. Although Fleischer relied on motion-picture footage as a reference for sketching the movements performed by Koko, it did not prevent him from morphing the clown's body into different shapes in *Betty Boop's Snow White* or exaggerating his physical abilities in *Modeling* (Dave Fleischer, 1921).

Fleischer probably mapped the gestures of Koko onto the frame-by-frame poses of a skater in *Modeling*, one of the *Out of the Inkwell* short animations. Just after the animator played by Max Fleischer in the diegesis has drawn skates under Koko's shoes, the poor clown loses his balance, slides backward, and falls. He goes on gesticulating and turning around himself, as someone learning to stand on skates would do. While the hand-drawn images do not reproduce the realism of motion pictures, the timing and precision of some of the clown's gestures are particularly convincing. Even though the movements looked somewhat accelerated in the version I watched, they appeared natural, and as such stood out from the cartoony background.[44]

Although the clown has difficulty standing on his skates at first, he quickly learns to master complex turns. Like a professional skater, he successfully traces the outline of the face of a man with his skate blades. For carving the circle of one of the man's pupils, Koko jumps and quickly spins around like an Olympic medalist. As noticed by the *Moving Picture World* critics, the animator not only drew lifelike movements but also enhanced Koko's physical abilities in ways that asserted his masculine fitness. While the rotoscoped performance was most probably altered to achieve the impressive art piece on ice, its cartoonal rendering stretches the boundaries of plausibility for humorous purposes.

When I watched *Modeling* for the first time, the timing of the skates sliding on the icy surface and Koko's gesticulating arms when he loses his balance produced palpable reverberations throughout my body. The likeness to human motion achieved by the rotoscope technique was felt in my muscles because Koko's athletic achievements and failures reactivated routines that I had myself performed or seen performed. Certain innate dispositions may unconsciously contribute to my impression of seeing likeness to "life" in these animated drawings. One of Nikolaus Troje and Cord Westoff's experiments on the perception of biological motion provides some evidence that the human visual system behaves like a "life-detector."[45] Their experiment uses the motion capture technique, a process that reproduces in the digital domain the motion performed by humans or animals. Unlike the rotoscope, which captures the information about the motion in 2D, the motion capture system records spatial coordinates in 3D. As Christian Uva suggests, the rotoscope is an analogical form of motion capture; it is a direct parent to the motion capture technique in the way in which it translates motion from the indexical domain into the iconic domain.[46] While the animator traces the body of the performer on paper via transparency in the case of the rotoscope, a computer program draws the characters on a flat screen by digitizing the 3D coordinates that correspond to the participant's joints.

Troje and Westoff's motion study can be traced back to Gunnar Johansson's early experiments on biological motion, which I introduced in Chapter 1. He notably studied walking and running patterns by analyzing dynamic point light displays. This technique avoids interferences from the other perceptual cues produced by the body of the moving human or animal. The moving light spots help distinguish the visual information produced by biological motion from the shape of the body. The "ten points moving simultaneously on a screen in a rather irregular way [gave the participants in his experiment] a vivid and definite impression of human walking."[47] With this technique, Johansson wanted to explain the psychophysical mechanisms that compel humans to perceive moving bodies instead of moving dots.

Instead of recording the motion of the light spots placed on the walking subjects, as Johansson did, Troje and Westhoff employed the motion capture technique to study the stationary locomotion of humans and animals. They placed markers on the joints of the participants and then captured their 3D coordinates in a computer system as they were walking on a treadmill. Using a computer program, they displayed the subjects' locomotion on a computer screen. Despite the small number of markers to reference the movements of the subjects, the participants could accurately report the perceived direction of the figure. Even when some of the points were inverted, the participants' judgment was correct, as long as the local motion of the points associated with the feet remained intact, and these points were located at the bottom of the display. The inversion effect in biological motion perception suggests that the presence of gravity, combined with clear cues about the direction of motion, are necessary factors to accurately interpret the information about the motion of a body.

Evolutionary dispositions can explain the "life-detection" phenomenon. Since a variety of adaptive behaviors, including filial attachment and prey hunting, rely on the accurate detection of the direction of the motion of other animals, this ability is critical for a variety of terrestrial animals, including humans. According to Troje and Westhoff, the typical movement of a terrestrial animal in locomotion, which propels its limbs away from the ground and then plays with gravity as efficiently as possible, has the potential to provide a reliable indicator for the presence and the location of an animal in the visual environment.[48] They suggest that animals possess a visual filter that is tuned to this cue. More specifically, they support "the view that some vertebrates, including humans, have primitive brain systems for the visual detection of other legged vertebrates."[49] They call this general detection mechanism a "life-detector."

Similarly, when viewers watch Koko's locomotion, their visual filter may detect the human form from which the moving outlines were produced. Our innate life-detector compels us to see life in the animated drawings and distinguish the effects of gravity on Koko's body. However, our experience of dynamic patterns of sensorimotor behavior can also call into question this innate life-detector when movements deviate from familiar patterns. For instance, when Koko manages to draw the face of the model on the ice, we can feel and deduce that he crosses the boundary of the plausible to access the realms of the extraordinary.

Max and Dave Fleischer also relied on the rotoscope technique for their cartoons featuring Superman, a character renowned for his strength and muscular excess. The large budget for the Superman series allowed the Fleischer animators to use rotoscoping to add believability to the character.[50] For the production of the rotoscoped footage, "wrestler Karol Krauser was hired as the live action model for *Superman*."[51] Seeing Clark Kent at the office could help the viewers recognize themselves in his everyday problems at work. As Wells points out, Clark Kent "was often rotoscoped from the actions of an actor to properly authenticate his identity as real human being *not* subject to cartoonal logic."[52] In comparison, when Superman performs extraordinary feats, the mise-en-scène magnifies his muscularity. For instance, *Superman* (1941) features several extreme long shots that underscore his strength. In spite of Superman's small stature among the city high-rises, he can easily push back up a huge building threatening to collapse. His tight costume also reveals the curves of his muscles as he stops a glowing ray aimed at a building.

The Fleischer animators also employed various techniques to design natural movements for Popeye. In an article titled "Vintage Popeye is Good Popeye" published in the newsletter of the International Popeye Fan Club, the animator Gordon Sheehan explained that "there was in each animation room a large piece of carpet, which could be rolled out onto the floor whenever an animator wanted to 'get the feel' of a falling down or rolling around action."[53] When a special dance step was needed, Sheehan added, the animators would ask the former vaudevillian dancer Jack Ward to perform for them. He "would go through the routine, freezing occasionally for the animator to make quick pencil sketches to be later transposed into the cartoon character's action."[54] During life-threatening situations or to save those he loves, Popeye's body transforms and morphs into various objects and machines. In these situations, the powerful cartoonal logic is preferred over realistic motion. During a battle with Sinbad in *Popeye the Sailor Meets Sinbad the Sailor* (Dave Fleischer, 1936), Popeye acquires the strength of multiple factory machines after eating spinach. A close-up of three spinning motors superimposed over his bicep reinforces this analogy. Thanks to Popeye's increased strength, he can twist his arm around itself to produce a powerful rotor that can spin Sinbad's heavy body like a propeller. In this animation, Popeye proves his masculine superiority over the exotic Sinbad, a monstrous two-headed man, and a crowd of fantastic creatures.

With their superpowers, Popeye and Superman served to secure the American white man as the dominant mode of masculinity. During the years preceding WWII, their heroism contributed to galvanizing audiences' patriotism. In *The Mighty Navy* (Dave Fleischer, 1941) and *Fleets of Stren'th* (Dave Fleischer, 1942), Popeye is recruited for war propaganda. The Superman cartoon *Jungle Drums* (Dan Gordon, 1943), for its part, conflates Nazi practices with native rituals.[55] On a basic level, the fusion of the lifelike gestures with the "cartoony" body facilitates the viewer's engagement with the hero, thanks to the realism of his everyday body language.[56] In time of war, seeing these heroes cope with their weaknesses and overcome them with their augmented powers could also unite white audience members against a common foreign enemy, but not without racial prejudice against native people.

The metaphorical association of Popeye's body with a machine evokes the trope of the cyborg before the term was coined by Nathan Kline and Manfred Clynes in 1960.[57] In *Popeye the Sailor Meets Sinbad the Sailor*, Popeye's entire body morphs into a drill to pierce a wall of rock. The rotoscope itself, by enhancing Koko's athletic performances, could also be interpreted as a form of animated prosthesis. Mark Langer used this analogy to describe the way that the rotoscope "became a prosthesis that overcame the physical limitations of the human body on the screen."[58] According to Langer, by

> incorporating live-action (the organic) with the mechanical (cel method drawing), the rotoscoped image was a hybridized product that overcame the limitations of both the machine and the human body, while at the same time erasing the borders that separate them. The result was that human capabilities were augmented through fusion with the machine.[59]

On the one hand, the animator-cyborg is augmented by this new technique. The hand of the animator is guided by the technologically produced image of the performer projected on the drawing board. On the other hand, the cyborg trope describes the way that the rotoscopic process hybridizes the animated cartoon and the live performer together. In her seminal "Cyborg Manifesto," Donna Haraway considers the blurring of the boundaries between the organic and the technological as a political tool against essentialism. She saw in "the illegitimate fusions of animal and machine" a way to disrupt fixed cultural identity categories and dualisms such as male/female, self/other, and culture/nature.[60] The unstable trope of the cyborg could serve to bring together people of different races, genders, and classes. As Bouldin argues in her study of *Betty Boop's Bamboo Isle* (Dave Fleischer, 1932), despite the potential of the cyborg to unite people against the domination of fixed categories, the representation of hybridized bodies in animation can still fall into the trappings of exoticism and racial stereotypes.[61] While my analyses of the animations featuring the rotoscoped movements of Cab Calloway are informed by these various takes on the animator-cyborg and the extended animated character, I am particularly interested in how the hybridization between the organic and the technological informs the experience of the cyborg viewer. The rotoscope technology modulates our multisensory experience and tricks us in seeing the haunting presence of the performer thanks to our innate life-detector.

When the rotoscoped movements are mapped onto grotesque shapes, the unexpected crossings between a live performer and a fantastic creature can trick our life-detector and promote uncanny feelings. The sequence where Koko the Clown sings and dances in the Mystery Cave of *Betty Boop's Snow White* exemplifies this phenomenon. While in the spooky cave, the evil queen transforms Koko into a ghostly creature whose elastic legs can elongate and twist to create multiple knots and hooks. When Koko reproduces Calloway's signature spins, the uncanny surfaces, as the rotoscope technique turns the familiar into the unfamiliar. According to Norman Klein, the repetitive rotoscoping of Koko lent him a "phantom presence."[62]

> Koko practically inhabited two bodies at once, from cartoon clown who shuffled (buttery head, sacklike body) to a leaner man who ran gracefully (more angles to his chin; a stiffer spinal column). Koko was designed to be haunted, wrapped in billowy cloth that was ideal for a ghost dancing between bodies.[63]

The creepy settings and the illicit behaviors of the shape-shifting Koko imbue the sequence with racism. In the background of the Mystery Cave, for example, skeletons play poker and dice. Ghost Koko morphs into a bottle of wine and pours himself a glass. As Klein notes, the "skulls of African Americans reenact the greasy underworld of back-alley and saloon life in Harlem."[64] The dreadful representation of Koko in the sequence hinders the viewer's sympathy for this darker version of his personality.

Racial prejudice and uncanny performances are also portrayed in *Minnie the Moocher*, a hybrid film featuring the rotoscoped motion of Cab Calloway. In the opening footage, Calloway dances in front of members of his orchestra who play the score of "Minnie the Moocher" with their trumpets and saxophones. Calloway's hips are balancing while he performs ample gestures with his arms and intricate foot movements. When later on Calloway is conjured up under the traits of a walrus, contemporary audiences must have been as thrilled as I was when the ghastly animal spun around itself, thus mimicking one of Calloway's signature moves presented in the lead-in sequence. The presence of the live-action footage at the beginning confirms the authenticity of Calloway's animated performance. Yet, instead of making the performance lifelike, it reveals the forced assemblage between the animated envelope in the shape of a walrus and the human-inspired propelling muscles underneath. We can sense the residual traces of his living presence before it was captured by the rotoscope. The known discrepancy between the ghostly body and the propelling spirit inspires eeriness, as the apparent match between body and voice is called into question by our body and mind.

The animated sequence following the live-action footage employs gothic imagery. The mise-en-scène perpetuates racial stereotypes linking black people to criminality. Betty escapes from home with her friend Bimbo. As her feet touch the ground outside the house, the classical music playing on the background score switches to the jazz song "Minnie the Moocher." The further Betty and Bimbo stray away from the house, the darker the sky becomes. Black ghosts start threatening them. Afraid, they hide inside a cave where a menacing walrus materializes from a cloud of smoke. The walrus starts singing the song that was played by the jazz orchestra at the beginning of the film. As the lyrics reveal that Minnie is a "red-hot hoochie-coocher," Betty's presence in the scene facilitates the association of the sexually provocative belly dancer with the sexy flapper. Betty's running away from home at night in company of a male companion can imply her promiscuousness. Afraid from the walrus, Betty wiggles her body and squeaks as he makes his lascivious moves. The song also alludes to Smockey's criminal behavior when he showed Minnie "How to kick the gong around," a slang reference to smoking opium. The background images of ghost prisoners taken to the electric chair emphasize the illicit innuendos. As Austin Collins notes in an article about horror cinema, the motif of the black ghost is haunted with references to slavery.[65]

As *Betty Boop's Snow White* and *The Old Man of the Mountain* (Dave Fleischer, 1933), two other animations featuring Calloway's performance, *Minnie the Moocher* reflects racist stereotypes in vogue from the 1910s until the 1950s. Watkins identifies similar stereotypes in black caricatures of the period that magnified the perceived sensuality and abandon of African Americans.[66] Wells interprets them as "a deep ambivalence about 'otherness,' half-attracted to its freedom, half-frightened of its ultimate repercussions."[67] In *Minnie the Moocher*, the danger and cultural threat are expressed by the combination of nightmarish imagery, jazz music, and blackness.

As suggested in this section, the disturbing effects produced by the rotoscoping process can convey different meanings depending on the mise-en-scène. Once the live performance is mapped onto human characters, such as the performance of Dave Fleischer under the traits of Koko the Clown, some viewers detect lifelike motion, a phenomenon supported by what Troje and Westoff call an innate life-detector. By giving flesh and gravity to the animated character, this technology facilitates the process of recognition, as we feel the echo of the human performance beneath the shell of the animated cartoon. The rotoscoped performances can also be combined with other animation techniques. In the Superman cartoons, the realism provided by the rotoscoped movements assists in winning the viewer's allegiance; the superhero is not so different from us after all. At the same time, the augmented physical prowess of the white superhero can empower members of the audience in times of insecurity. For instance, in the years before WWII, Superman and Popeye helped confirm white masculinity as the dominant form of masculinity. The rotoscope technology can arouse uncanny feelings when it reanimates the dead corpse of a live performance captured on film. As he returns under the traits of various fantastic creatures, Cab Calloway is experienced as a phantom presence in *Minnie the Moocher* and *Betty Boop's Snow White*. The haunting presence of the black performer furthers stereotypes of raciness especially when they are underscored by sexually explicit jazz music, gothic imagery, and taboo graphics.

In summary, when animation techniques such as pixilation, stop-motion, and the rotoscope enter in assemblage with the cyborg viewer, they significantly inform our appraisal of the performance and reveal a web of uneven relations between performance, technology, gender, race, and sexuality.

Muscular Pain and Ethics

As seen in the previous section, mechanical movements in puppet animation can be symptomatic of ideological control in modern societies or fear of corporate despotism. Physical prowess enhanced by the mise-en-scène in science fiction animation can also reflect anxieties about the obsolescence of the body in the future. Still concerned with the impacts of technology on the body, this section concentrates on mediated representations of muscular effort in *The Triplets of Belleville* and *Black Jack: The Movie*. With their representations of the body in pain, these animated films expose the dangers associated with transgressing the limits of the human.

The athletes featured in these animations are the victims of corrupt organizations or criminal tyrants: the mafia in *The Triplets of Belleville* and a bioengineering corporation in *Black Jack*. As victims who aspire to survive despite their more or less desperate conditions, the protagonists in these animations react differently toward their state of victimhood. In her study of survival modes in Canadian literature, Margaret Atwood distinguishes four basic victim positions that can be useful for understanding the loss of agency of these characters.[68] A victim in position one denies the fact that he or she is a victim. When in position two, a victim acknowledges that he or she is persecuted, but puts the blame on the Will of God or other vague sources of oppression. Victims in position three acknowledge that they are victims, but they refuse to assume that their condition is inevitable. In this position, the victim has identified the cause of exploitation and can find the means to repudiate it. In position four, we find creative non-victims or ex-victims who have successfully eliminated the abusive tyrants. As Atwood notes, in "an oppressed society, of course, you can't become an ex-victim—insofar as you are connected with your society—until the entire society's position has been changed."[69]

These two animations align the spectators with protagonists that adopt one or more of these victim positions. This form of imaginary transposition appeals to the spectator's empathy. Reciprocally, self-reflexive strategies and echoing mechanisms invite spectators to envisage their potential position as a victim.

Muscular Augmentation: The Triplets of Belleville

The Triplets of Belleville tells the story of Champion, a professional cyclist kidnapped by the French mafia. Set in the 1960s in France and Belleville, a city reminiscent of New York, it analogizes the cyclist to a mass of muscles and a racehorse.[70] The animation compares the human body to an animal and a machine. These comparisons underline the degenerative transformation of the human under the pressure of consumerism and success in our modernized societies. The monstrosity of the super athlete's body can also symbolize the limits of humanity. Comparable analogies between nonnormative individuals and beasts find their roots in a long literary tradition. In *Frankenstein; or, The Modern Prometheus* (Mary Shelley, 1818), for instance, deviance from the dominant norms is metaphorically associated with decay and threat to the established order. Associating the human with the animal can also connote various forms of exploitation, such as human trafficking and unbearable working conditions. Turned into slaves, the cyclists exhale like racehorses after the French mafia villains have imprisoned them. As I argue, *The Triplets of Belleville* employs muscular empathy and self-reflexive strategies to refine these analogies and convey its social critique.

The representation of muscular efforts solicits the viewer's empathy for the dedicated athletes. When Champion trains for the Tour de France, the animation emphasizes the difficulty of climbing a steep hill on his bicycle. He balances his body with effort, transferring his weight from one leg to the other. A close-up of the character's face conveys his intense fatigue. A side view of his frail upper body accentuates the curves of his back and his bulging calves. The side perspective also underlines the sharpness of the hill (see Figure 4.1). When I watch Champion's painful ascent, I imagine myself ascending the slope. Additionally, I experience his exhaustion in my own muscles.

Studies in cognitive sciences have attempted to explain motor imagery and its physical effects on the observer. An experiment has shown that when people imagine walking from point A to point B, it takes them longer in their imagination to walk between the two points when the

Figure 4.1 Champion climbing a steep hill. *The Triplets of Belleville* (Sylvain Chomet, 2003).

distance is increased. When the same subjects were asked to mentally walk between the two points while carrying a heavy box, they spent 30% more time than what it actually took them to perform the task.[71] In a different situation, when the participants were asked to imagine running, their heart and respiration rates increased.[72] Although the physiological mechanisms underlying motor imagery are still investigated, some studies in neuroscience show evidence that common neural mechanisms are activated regardless of whether you perform a mental rehearsal of a movement without performing any overt action or you actually perform that movement.[73] As mentioned in the previous chapters, studies on the mirror neuron system have also demonstrated that observing human movements activates the same muscle groups and motor circuits in the brain than executing the movements does, although there may be variations according to the context.[74] Moreover, neural mechanisms underpin the empathic power of images and can explain our visceral responses to depictions of muscular pain. Tania Singer and her colleagues at the University College of London found that "part of the pain network associated with its affective qualities, but not its sensory qualities, mediates empathy."[75]

In addition to depicting muscles in action, *The Triplets of Belleville* details the athletes' facial expressions to enhance our understanding of their struggle. The animation distorts the facial traits of one of the cyclists when he reaches his physical limits during the Tour de France. The black streaks under his hazy eyes, his extremely extended neck, and his gasps for breath illustrate his extreme fatigue. His shaking head and his repetitive movements toward and away from the camera while he is panting can even reverberate in the chest of some viewers.

This animation may also evoke a "revulsion for abnormality" when it associates the human body with a piece of machinery. In one sequence, Champion returns home after an intense training. His muscular legs are trembling. Stiff like a wooden mannequin, he collapses on the dinner table. Mme Souza, his grandmother and trainer, uses a hand mixer and a vacuum cleaner to massage his calves (see Figure 4.2). Later, during the escape from the mafia, when Mme Souza releases the stand on which the bicycles were attached, the cyclists mechanically continue to ride their bicycles, as though they were automata. The degrading image of the servile athlete with a hyper muscular body departs from the heroic representations of comic book superheroes, often depicted as hyper masculinized man-machines in symbiosis with their weapons. In an article, Mark Oehlert groups contemporary cyborg characters into three categories: simple controllers, biotech integrators, and genetic cyborgs.[76] *The Triplets of Belleville* tones down these science fiction ideas. The man-machine symbiosis does not bring to mind a warrior but a degenerated species on automated mode that has completely lost affect.

In addition to visual analogies and muscular empathy, the animation employs self-reflexive strategies to communicate its social critique. The body in *The Triplets of Belleville* is an indicator of the advanced state of degeneration of society. Obese people and unhealthy muscular athletes abound in France and Belleville. Images of the athletes' exhaustion and muscular pain metaphorically associate the modern society with a tired and worn-out body hypnotized by recycled media images.[77] When the

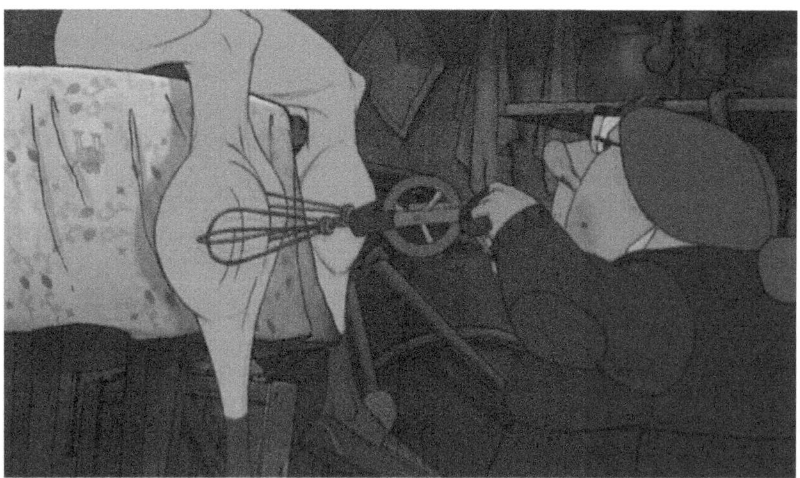

Figure 4.2 Madam Souza massaging Champion's calves with a hand mixer. *The Triplets of Belleville* (Sylvain Chomet, 2003).

kidnapped athletes compete for the French mafia, we see a high-angle view of gamblers holding dollar bills as they watch the cyclists riding their stationary bicycles in front of projected images of a country road. The exploitation of the athletes evokes the barbarian spectacles performed by Roman gladiators or the 19th-century freak shows.

This animated film self-reflexively comments on its absorptive nature. It prompts viewers to reflect on their own hypnotized gaze. After the kidnapping, the cyclists had transformed into docile racehorses. According to Atwood's scale, Champion's hypnotized gaze places him in the first position of victimhood. The distorted low-angle perspective on his face conveys his extreme fatigue and thus appeals to the viewer's sympathy. Moreover, attached to their stand in front of the large screen, the human racehorses become part of the cinematographic assemblage. The self-reflexive references to spectatorship in *The Triplets of Belleville* symbolize the viewers' own subjection to the media (see Figure 4.3). Self-reflexivity could help one realize the presence of oppression and thereby escape from a state of victimhood.

The viewer's embodied simulations and the self-reflexive mirroring of the cyclists' victim positions bring to mind Deleuze and Guattari's discussion on molecular becoming in *A Thousand Plateaus*, a concept introduced in the previous chapter. Champion becomes a man-machine, thanks to assemblages of speed and affects, as well as functional exchanges between the body and the bicycle. The mirroring effects experienced throughout the animation expand the viewer's possible range of sensations. On the one hand, like Champion, the viewers can experience the worn-out body of modernity within their struggling muscles. On

Figure 4.3 Champion's hypnotized gaze. *The Triplets of Belleville* (Sylvain Chomet, 2003).

the other hand, like Mme Souza, the viewers can experience technological bliss when she effortlessly rides her tricycle and whistles the tempo. Muscular empathy with these two contrasting body types forms different symbiotic relationships: whether you experience the pain of each propelling stroke until you reach the top of the hill, or you just enjoy the ride.

Superhumans: Black Jack: The Movie

The animated film *Black Jack* raises questions about eugenics and the research experiments performed by pharmaceutical corporations. At the beginning of the animation, highly successful superhumans meet unexplained violent deaths. Brane, the pharmaceutical company that designed Endorph A, a drug that can transform ordinary people into superhumans, needs help to identify the cause of their demise and find a cure. Their chief researcher, Joe Carol, hires Black Jack, a gifted surgeon without a license who performs complicated operations for large sums of money. As I demonstrate, gory imagery produces affective responses that compel viewers to consider ethical questions about the creation of enhanced humans.

Black Jack approaches Brane's illegal experimentations on humans from different angles. On the one hand, the Medical Soldiers for Justice decry the violation of human rights by the Brane Corporation. They also condemn the deteriorating effects of their refineries on the environment. On the other hand, the first volunteers in the project Endorph A never complained. As Joe Carol told Black Jack, there is no shortage of people who want to become wealthy and famous. Yet, hundreds of people were infected by the virus and were going to die if not treated.

The idea of altering the human makeup for the benefit of mankind is not new. Creating an improved human species was the aim of the American Eugenics Movement, a social movement particularly active between 1900 and 1929. Its members hoped "to eradicate societal problems through the application of evolutionary theory to humans."[78] By the early 1930s however, several factors led to the decline of this movement. Four decades later, successful genetic experiments at Stanford University and the University of California, San Francisco were at the origin of a "new eugenics." Teams of researchers developed a method to combine and transplant genes between species. The results evoked fears in the population and contributed to reactivating public debates on the ethics of genetic technologies. While the "old" eugenics relied on the socially unacceptable regime of selective breeding, the "new" eugenics depended on technological experiments to directly manipulate genetic material. Some films made in the 1990s critique the consequences of "new" eugenics and genetic determinism, including *Gattaca* (Andrew Niccol, 1997) and *The Island of Dr. Moreau* (John Frankenheimer, 1996).[79] In *Black*

Jack, the Brane Corporation does not directly alter human genes, but instead infects its victims with a virus that increases the secretion of endorphins in the brain. Brane's endeavor is similar to that of the "new" eugenics while its means are different.

Black Jack multiplies the violent images of blood splattering in *Black Jack* to condemn the transgression of human rights in medical research. The superabilities witnessed around the world turned out to be the symptoms of a deadly disease. The affliction has caused the organs of its victims to deteriorate very rapidly. The gold medal winner and record holder for 100 meters, Ellen Shryer, was among the firsts to fall sick. During an episode of hysteria while she was running medical tests at the Brane Research Institute, she ran toward a wall and crashed into it. In the sequence, as she approaches the wall, the animation replaces the image of her exterior body with an X-ray vision of her degenerated muscles and bones. The garish colors of the body's interior and the sound of her crushed skull combine to increase the horror of her disintegration (see Figure 4.4). In a later sequence, the heart of a superhuman bursts and splatters blood all over the operating room, just as Black Jack is about to slice it with his scalpel. The mouth of another victim expels torrents of blood after the mysterious syndrome has impaired the proper functioning of his organs. In his book *Splatter Movies*, John McCarty defines splatter films as a subgenre of the horror film genre that aims "not to scare their audiences, not to drive them to the edge of their seats in suspense, but to mortify them with explicit gore."[80] Similarly, in *Black Jack*, the gory sequences elicit a mixture of affects in the viewer, including disgust, shock, revulsion, and pity. The quantity of blood expelled from their frail bodies amplifies their suffering. The portrayal of these people in a state of complete disarray inspires pity. These highly successful athletes, who had astonished the world a few days before the epidemic started to spread, have now completely lost their vitality and strength. By appealing to the spectator's affect, the animation associates distress and disgust with the medical alterations performed on "the human."

In contrast to the images of hectic patients and unstable bodily membranes, *Black Jack* showcases the clinical precision of medical imaging to distinguish the human from the superhuman on various levels of magnitude. *Black Jack* shares its fascination for dissected organs, brain scans, and enlarged viruses. When Black Jack operates on Joe Carol's brain, he has augmented abilities. Joe had forced him to unwittingly absorb the new formula of Endorph A, a drug ten times more potent than the original one. While dramatically improving Black Jack's visual skills and the precision of his hand, the drug also engenders side effects that include extreme sweating and fever. As Black Jack starts to experience these symptoms, the animation presents a close-up of the underlying muscles and bones of his face, which confirms the presence

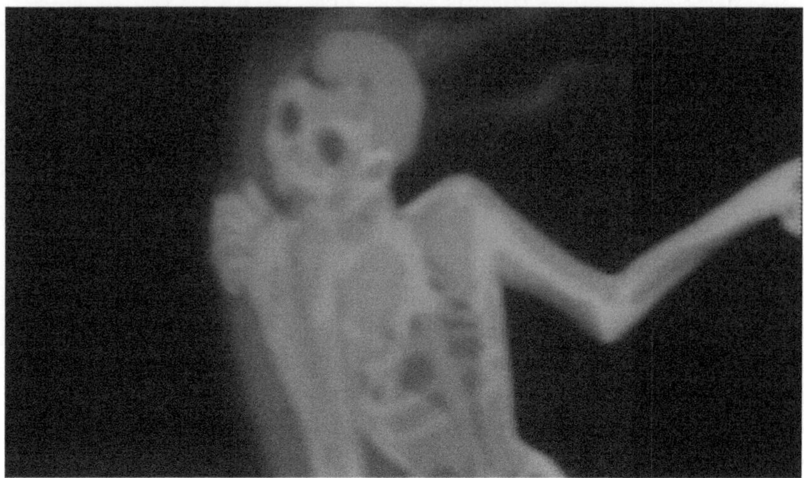

Figure 4.4 The body of a superhuman runner splattering blood. *Black Jack: The Movie* (Osamu Dezaki and Fumihiro Yoshimura, 1996).

of the drug in his veins. An enlarged image of Joe's blood cells suggests that he has a superhuman vision. Thanks to his new skills, the talented surgeon can easily excise the green glowing brain tissue from Joe's brain. This site locates the limit between the human and the posthuman, as it is the source of both her disease and her superabilities. Aligned with Black Jack's perspective, the viewers can participate in the removal of the source of Joe's affliction. This sequence has also replaced the revulsion caused by the splattering super bodies with awe-inspiring pictures of the body's interior.

The uncontrollable bodies of the superhumans demonstrate the scientists' loss of control over the outcomes of their creation. Although some of the victims volunteered to take part in Brane's experiment, the majority of the victims of Endorph A are collateral damage. While some enjoyed a short period of extraordinary performances and success, they soon faced the complete degeneration of their body and an agonizing death. When infected by the virus, Joe Carol and Black Jack had to join their efforts to find a treatment. At the end, Black Jack managed to cure Joe Carol with his scalpel and a tribe of nomads saved Black Jack with an extract they prepared using a flower with medicinal properties. In this story, science was both the cause of and the remedy for the epidemic. However, the battle was not actually over at the end of the animation, since the remedy was ineffective against the mutations of the virus. As Baudrillard claims in "Prophylaxis and Virulence," physical constraints, computer viruses, and biological viruses limit the immense possibilities of science and technology. The threat of the virus is another way to warn us about the dangers associated with posthumanism. In an allegorical way, *Black Jack* implies that there is no easy way to transcend our human finitude and natural limitations. Echoing the ethics of filmic adaptations of H. G. Wells' *The Island of Dr. Moreau* (1896), including *The Island of Dr. Moreau* (Don Taylor, 1977), and *The Island of Dr. Moreau* (1996), *Black Jack* condemns scientists—and also corporations—that attempt to impose their vision of what is human and who can be enhanced, genetically and otherwise. When blinded by greed for power and money, scientific progress can only bring doom to humanity.

Yet, *Black Jack* resists clear oppositions and blurs the distinction between the victims and the persecutors. The superhumans underwent excruciating pain for having achieved wealth and popular success. Notwithstanding her power and wisdom, the deadly virus did not spare Joe Carol. Her splattering body could be read as a mark of punishment for having attempted to play God. Even though Joe Carol might have had altruist intentions when she gave superabilities to a little girl, her illegal medical experiments on children and unwilling patients ultimately killed many innocents. However, the woman was not simply portrayed as a monster; she was also the victim of a difficult upbringing. Joe Carol was one in a series of test-tube babies bioengineered by her adoptive father. His only interest lied in hiring the most gifted child to join him at the head of the company, and he chose Joe Carol. The other children were coldly eliminated. Because of his tyrannical parenting, Joe became an insensitive surgeon and business manager, led by the sole ambition of creating a new race of super achievers.

Black Jack deploys different strategies to foreground the importance of empathy. This animation contrasts Joe Carol's lack of compassion with Black Jack's strong desire to protect the sick and the weak. It also compels spectators to empathize with the superhumans in gory sequences depicting their advance state of degeneration. Finally, the horrific deaths united the scientific community against a common enemy of humanity.

Nevertheless, the ending of *Black Jack* shows that there is no possible return to humanism. Black Jack and the Military Soldiers for Justice have only won the first battle against the Moira disease and the superhumans will continue to suffer. This open ending borrows some conventions from the horror genre. As media scholar Judith Halberstam notes in *Skin Shows*, the figures

> that emerge triumphant at the gory conclusion of a splatter film are literally posthuman, they punish the limits of the human body and they mark identities as always stitched, sutured, bloody at the seams, and completely beyond the limits and the reaches of an impotent humanism.[81]

Black Jack's external appearance reflects his split identity at the limit of the human. His hair is divided between a black side and a white side. His skin is also covered with large scars. After an accident, part of the skin of his half-African friend was grafted onto the left side of his face. Black Jack's surgical skills are also extraordinary and at the limit of the possible. However, although he demonstrates great devotion to his patients, he is far from being perfect; he charges millions of dollars for his services. Despite this darker side of his personality, Black Jack did not hesitate to risk his life to save Joe Carol. Finally, even the viewers were invited to become superhuman when they aligned with his perspective during the surgery on Joe Carol's brain. At the conclusion of the animation, the identities that were stitched and sutured were those of the spectators who embraced the limits of the human.

Conclusion

The previous chapter was concerned with character design and the rhetorical possibilities offered by the metamorphic body. This chapter examined the specific case of animated movements that underscore the gap between dull everyday gestures and unsettling irregular movements. Whether they portrayed muscleless puppets in *The Club of the Laid Off* or images of bulging muscles in *The Triplets of Belleville*, the animated films studied probed the muscular domain to comment on the pervasive effects of technology in society. By presenting characters with more or less muscles, these animations either invited spectators to be empowered by augmented bodily motion or crippled by pain.

Some animations contrast the viewer's everyday muscular experience of space with hyperbolized movements. Martial arts animations, for instance, enthrall spectators with stupendous feats. While often inspired by cinematic strategies, they usually downplay the importance of naked muscles in action and boast various fighting skills grounded in cartoonal logic. The filmic references can be made for humorous reasons. Po's extraordinary jump in the air and catastrophic fall on the roof in *Kung Fu Panda 3* parodies sequences from *Crouching Tiger, Hidden Dragon*. *Mulan*, *Mulan II*, and *The Secrets of the Furious Five* provide feminist twists on conventional tropes in cinema. Mulan and Viper demonstrate that untypical female fighters can display feminine strength, ability, and wisdom.

Alternatively, *The Club of the Laid Off* and *The Secret Adventures of Tom Thumb* present impossible bodily movements as a way to reflect anxieties about the changes introduced by modernization. The jerky movements performed by the wooden mannequins amplify the alienating aspects of their lives in the abandoned warehouse. At the end, their attraction to the television set suggests that this invention may be the new opiate of the masses. The disquieting effects of technology on traditional modes of living are also expressed with mechanized motion in *The Secret Adventures of Tom Thumb*. Technique and style support a critique of biogenetics and corporate polluting. The pixilated movements transpose the evil effects of biotechnology into the muscular domain. Additionally, the animation borrows the iconography and conventions of film noirs to reveal the corruption of the research laboratory and its henchmen. Drawing on their unique styles, these two animated films unsettle the viewers' expectations in terms of muscular memory to support their somber depictions of society's progress.

Our innate life-detector can be tricked in seeing life beneath the rotoscoped performance of Koko the Clown in *Modeling*. Alternatively, when the animated gestures take the shape of fantastic creatures, the mismatch between the realism of human motion and the cartoony appearance can be disturbing. For example, the rotoscoped performances of Cab Calloway in *Minnie the Moocher* and *Betty Boop's Snow White* echo the lifelike gestures of the band director in an uncanny way. The grotesque appearances of the performer and the scary settings contribute to racist associations between blackness and danger.

The last section looked at two animations concerned with the risks of crossing the athletic limits of the human body. By transposing the spectator's audiovisual experience to its muscular domain, the subjective perspective on suffering invites the spectators to show compassion for oppressed characters. They display the pain and extreme anguish experienced by protagonists finding themselves into one or more of the victims' positions on Atwood's scale of victimhood. *The Triplets of Belleville* conveys the sensation of intense muscular effort as Champion ascends the steep hill on his bicycle. The framing induces embodied simulations, and possibly motor mimicry, that communicate the character's struggle. After his kidnapping, Champion appears oblivious to his state of oppression. In the self-reflexive sequence in which he races in front of a projected film, the spectators exchange their perspective with that of the victimized protagonist by an effect of mirroring.

Finally, *Black Jack* contrasts the gory sequences of collapsing superhumans with the clinical precision of medical imagery of the body's interior. Thanks to these images, the viewer can alternately share the point of view of the victim and the point of view of the hero. On the one hand, the mise-en-scène and direct affect communicate the brutality conveyed by the splattering bodies. On the other hand, the spectator visualizes the ascepticized standpoint adopted by the Brane Corporation. Unlike *The Triplets of Belleville*, this animation demonstrates the possibility of rejecting the source of oppression with the intervention of the Military Soldiers for Justice. In addition to presenting the perspectives of the victim and the oppressor, *Black Jack* includes the hero's subjective gaze. Despite his personal flaws, the talented surgeon demonstrates compassion for the victims and helps to find a cure to the Moira disease.

In the sequence where Black Jack operates Joe Carol's brain, himself infected by the virus, spectators adopt the subjective perspective of the superhuman by entering into an assemblage with the animated interface, thus becoming the victim and the hero simultaneously.

The Triplets of Belleville and *Black Jack* elicit the spectator's empathy for characters in pain and present self-reflexive references to the viewer's own state of victimhood. In other words, the other's suffering can have tragic consequences for one's own safety. By producing effects in the muscular domain and awakening muscular memories, these case studies engage the viewers in debates about the effects of consumer society on health, cybernetic technology, and physical enhancement.

In the animations studied in this chapter, the viewer's muscular domain is extended by the animated interface through mirroring effects. Viewers become animated by a wide range of sensorimotor couplings with impossible bodily gestures that are specifically conceived by animation. The hyperbolized movements in martial arts animations unsettle muscular memories and empower viewers. Pixilation and puppet animation create disquieting bodily movements that underscore the gap between human and nonhuman bodily motion. The phantom presence of black performers produced by the rotoscope can conjure up the uncanny ghosts of slavery and racism. These animations encourage viewers to draw on their muscular experience to weigh into the debates about urbanization, man-machine symbiosis, and superhumanity.

Notes

1 On Baudrillard's hyperreality and its relationship with cyberpunk literature and cinema, see Kellner, "Mapping the Present From the Future."
2 *Les Triplettes de Belleville.*
3 On early film and its spectator, see Gunning, "The Cinema of Attractions."
4 More details on direct affect are found in Plantinga, *Moving Viewers*, 117–120.
5 Fehsenfeld, "Motion Analysis Overview."
6 Plantinga, drawing on Fehsenfeld's talk "Motion Analysis Overview" in *Moving Viewers*, 119.
7 Barker, *The Tactile Eye*, 75.
8 Barker, *The Tactile Eye*, 74.
9 King, *Spectacular Narratives.*
10 Plantinga, *Moving Viewers*, 137.
11 According to Vivian Sobchack, animations depicting lack of gravity and sensations of lightness often lack the "incredible effortfulness of being" and foreclose the living makers who created the works, Sobchack, "Animation and Automation."
12 Richmond, *Cinema's Bodily Illusions*, 8.
13 Richmond, *Cinema's Bodily Illusions*, 8.
14 Virilio, *Pure War*, 85.
15 Lamarre, *The Anime Machine*, 5.
16 Barker, *The Tactile Eye*, 117.

17 Barker, *The Tactile Eye*, 116.
18 North, "Virtual Actors," 56–60.
19 North, "Virtual Actors," 59. On the authenticating strategies employed in kung fu films to resynthesize the presence of the body, see Hunt, *Kung Fu Cult Masters*.
20 Bordwell, "Aesthetics in Action," 88 (emphasis in the original).
21 Eisenstein and Tretyakov, "Expressive Movement," 187.
22 Fung, "Feminist and Queer Analysis of Disney's *Mulan*." On gender inequality in *Mulan*, see also Bellmore, "Who Is This Girl I See?"
23 On the misrepresentation of Chinese culture in *Mulan*, see Goh, "(Mis)representation of the Chinese Culture in *Mulan*."
24 Anderson, "Action in Motion."
25 Plantinga, *Moving Viewers*, 129.
26 Anderson, "Action in Motion."
27 On gender inequality in martial arts films, see Chen, "Phallocentric Teacher-Student Complex" in *Women in Chinese Martial Arts Films*.
28 For other examples of women who sacrifice themselves in martial arts films, see Chen, "Let's Make a Wish" in *Women in Chinese Martial Arts Films*.
29 Johansson, "Visual Perception of Biological Motion." On the perception of human motion, see also Blake and Shiffrar, "Perception of Human Motion."
30 Shiffrar and Freyd, "Timing and Apparent Motion." On the distinction between "structure from motion" and "motion from structure," see Orgs et al., "From Body Form to Biological Motion."
31 Hagendoorn, "The Dancing Brain," 4. See also Stevens et al., "New Aspects of Motion Perception."
32 Hagendoorn, "The Dancing Brain," 3.
33 Hagendoorn, "The Dancing Brain," 3.
34 On the production of movement and expression in puppet animation, see Buchan, *The Quay Brothers*, 103–110.
35 Wood, *Digital Encounters*, 14.
36 Martin, *The Modern Dance*, 12.
37 Anderson, "Violent Dance in Martial Arts Films," 3.
38 Anderson, "Violent Dance in Martial Arts Films," 3.
39 On the history of the rotoscope, see Pointer, *The Art and Inventions of Max Fleischer*; Fleischer, *Out of the Inkwell*; Cabarga, *The Fleischer Story*; Langer, "Introduction to the Fleischer Rotoscope Patent"; and Crafton, *Before Mickey*.
40 Fleischer, "Method."
41 On the initial *Out of the Inkwell* series, see Pointer, *The Art and Inventions of Max Fleischer*, 37–41. In 1923, Dick Huemer assumed the role of Animation Director of the Inkwell Studio and named the Clown Ko-Ko, see Pointer, *The Art and Inventions of Max Fleischer*, 46. Between 1924 and 1927, the name was hyphenated and the hyphen was dropped after that, Pointer, *The Art and Inventions of Max Fleischer*, 286.
42 "Fleischer Advances Technical Art: Puts Life Action Into His Wonderful Series of Animated Pen Drawings, 'Out of the Inkwell,'" *The Moving Picture World*, June 7, 1919, 1497. On the use of the human body as a basis for comparison for the animated body, see Bouldin, *The Animated and the Actual*, 65–77.
43 "The Inkwell Man," *New York Times*, September 13, 1920, 21.
44 The two DVD set "Max Fleischer's Famous Out of the Inkwell" made in 2003 and produced by Ray Pointer.
45 Troje and Westoff, "The Inversion Effect."

46 Uva, "La performance numérique," 43. Bouldin also describes the motion capture technique as the "rotoscope's recent digital 3D incarnation," *The Animated and the Actual*, 91.
47 Johansson, "Visual Perception of Biological Motion."
48 Troje and Westhoff, "The Inversion Effect," 823.
49 Johnson, "Biological Motion," R376.
50 Cabarga, *The Fleischer Story*, 174.
51 Pointer, *The Art and Inventions of Max Fleischer*, 217.
52 Wells, *Understanding Animation*, 193 (emphasis in the original).
53 Sheehan, quoted in Grandinetti, *Popeye*, 68.
54 Sheehan, quoted in Grandinetti, *Popeye*, 68.
55 Wells examines the representation of masculinity in the Popeye and Superman cartoons in *Understanding Animation*, 190–195.
56 Culhane quotes Max Fleischer on the "cartoony" effect, *Talking Animals and Other People*, 62.
57 Clynes and Kline, "Cyborgs and Space."
58 Langer, "Cyborgs Before Computers," 8.
59 Langer, "Cyborgs Before Computers," 8.
60 Haraway, "A Cyborg Manifesto," 54.
61 Bouldin, *The Animated and the Actual*, 110.
62 Klein, "Animation and Animorphs," 27.
63 Klein, "Animation and Animorphs," 27.
64 Klein, "Animation and Animorphs," 27.
65 Collins, "Horror Movies."
66 Watkins, *On the Real Side*.
67 Wells, *Understanding Animation*, 216–217.
68 Atwood describes the four basic victim positions in *Survival*, 36–39.
69 Atwood, *Survival*, 38.
70 On this animation, see for instance Rouyer, "*Les Triplettes de Belleville*" and Ciment, "Sylvain Chomet."
71 Decety, "Imagined and Executed Actions," 88.
72 Decety, "Imagined and Executed Actions," 90.
73 See Grèzes and Decety, "Functional Anatomy of Execution."
74 For a review of these studies, see, for instance, Rizzolatti and Craighero, "The Mirror-Neuron System." A study also explores the ways in which different contextual situations impact the stimulation of mirror neurons, Rizzolatti et al., "Mirrors in the Mind." The neural regions activated differ whether one sees point light displays representing locomotion or succession of bodily postures in photographs, Decety, "Motor Cognition and Mental Simulation," 480.
75 Singer et al., "Empathy for Pain," 1157.
76 Oehlert, "From Captain America to Wolverine," 221.
77 On the way *Les Triplettes de Belleville* critiques French modernity, see Fauvel, "Nostalgia and Digital Technology."
78 Kirby, "Are We Not Men?" 94. On the history of eugenics, see Kevles, *In the Name of Eugenics*.
79 The characteristics of the new eugenics in cinema are examined in Kirby, "The New Eugenics in Cinema" and Graham, chapter 5, *Representations of the Post-Human*.
80 McCarty, *Splatter Movies*, 1.
81 Halberstam, *Skin Shows*, 144.

5 A Trek Across the Uncanny Valley

Introduction

It is Christmas Eve and a young boy is restless in his bed. At 11:00 pm, he wakes up and hears the humming sound of a distant train. As the train approaches near his house, everything in his bedroom starts shaking. Objects begin to fall around him. The boy decides to sit on his bed to look out of the window and find out what is causing all the trouble. While he is observing the scene, a close-up calls attention to his surprised reaction. Despite having detailed eyelashes and reflecting pupils, his eyes look lifeless and peculiar (see Figure 5.1).

The stiff gaze of the young protagonist of *The Polar Express* (Robert Zemeckis, 2004) has evoked dread in audiences.[1] Similarly, the cyberstar of *Final Fantasy: The Spirits Within* (Hironobu Sakaguchi, 2001), Aki, has elicited a mixture of awe and eerie feelings from film critics.[2] With careful attention to skin texture and hair details, this computer-generated (CG) animation pushed the limits of photorealism at the time it was released. However, despite the careful digital rendering of the characters' facial features, many reviewers complained about their disquieting aspects. Aki looked strange because her face expressed a limited

Figure 5.1 Uncanny look of the young boy. *The Polar Express* (Robert Zemeckis, 2004).

palette of emotions and the slight imperfections in the synchronization of her voice distracted audiences from the storytelling.

Defamiliarized facial expressions such as those found in *Final Fantasy: The Spirits Within* and *The Polar Express* give rise to the phenomenon commonly known as the "uncanny valley" effect. This effect is produced by verisimilar synthespians when they start looking *human* and our appreciation of them begins to drop.[3] As various experts argue, the catalyst for the feeling of dread could be rooted in our expert ability to distinguish anomalies in human expressions.[4] The difficulty to decipher the emotions that the synthespian's behavior and facial traits convey may also cause mixed feelings.

The chapter investigates the phenomenon of the uncanny in animated media. The uncanny valley effects, some have claimed, may reveal an innate ability to detect the boundaries between the human and the non-human in pictures. I further investigate this hypothesis by describing the psychological mechanisms and the particularities of human biology that can predispose to these effects. However, eeriness can occur in 2D animation as well, which I will argue by looking at the disquieting sensations created by masklike faces in the animated TV series *Texhnolyze* (Hiroshi Hamasaki, 2003). Before zooming in on the more specific case of the uncanny in CG animation, I consider Freud's approach on the topic, as it reveals cultural aspects related to the phenomenon. Then, I revisit the esthetic mechanisms that are more likely to induce disquieting effects in CG animation. Thanks to a better understanding of their influence on audiences, the production team for the film *The Curious Case of Benjamin Button* (David Fincher, 2008) developed strategies to overcome these effects. In the final section of the chapter, I analyze the animated series *Malice@Doll* (Keitarô Motonaga, 2001), to show the esthetic implications of the uncanny and its relation to empathy. The presence of mechanized dolls in this CG animation blurs the boundaries between the animate and the inanimate. Notably, it presents the uncanny from the perspective of sentient machines that have been infected by humanness. Various mechanisms of alignment with synthespians evoke the unsettling effects of the human. This reversal of perspective also engages with preoccupations about the representation of marginal people. I suggest that uncanny feelings can analogize negative responses toward what is queer and different. By revealing the thresholds between the human and the machine, and the normal and the queer, these esthetic figures contribute to the impression of becoming-animated.

Facial Empathy

Research in the psychology of perception can help elucidate how certain facial traits or expressions in animated films induce effects of estrangement. Numerous factors influence patterns of looking at a picture and justify our attraction to the face. The composition of the various elements in a picture also contributes to enhancing the appeal of some of the elements over others.[5] The scholars J. Anthony Deutsch and Diana Deutsch contend that "the weighting of importance of messages" is a main factor in visual attention.[6] In an environment that includes various competing visual elements, some are more salient than others and are more likely to influence our intellectual and visceral responses. Generally, the eyes and the mouth have a higher weighting than other features. Because the human brain has the capability to process information conveyed by the face, we are particularly tuned into changes in facial expressions and apt to decode their meanings.[7] For example, when we look at pictures depicting people performing various tasks, we are naturally drawn to the webwork of their gazes.[8] We may attempt to guess what emotions the figures are expressing or speculate about their intentions. From this perspective, the lifeless looks of the protagonist in *The Polar Express* are particularly noticeable because of the visual weight we give to the face. Since we expect useful information from the character's face, the subdued expressions and zombie gazes in this animation are puzzling because they are not justified by the context.

Besides conveying a wealth of useful information about a person or a character, faces in pictures also appeal to our emotions and affects.[9] When we watch a film, facial mimicry and facial feedback, two concepts introduced in Chapter 3, can unconsciously influence our emotional responses, cognitive processes, and psychological impressions.[10] Facial mimicry can contribute to eliciting affective resonances in response to emotions conveyed by audience members that surround a viewer, a phenomenon commonly called emotional contagion.[11] Facial mimicry and emotional contagion can be explained in part by neurological predispositions, such as the presence of mirror neurons.[12] However, unlike conscious judgments that affect allegiance, these processes almost always operate in an automatic and unconscious way. Nevertheless, the action of facial mimicry and emotional contagion can enhance the processes of sympathy or empathy to sway one's allegiance to a character. Although facial mimicry and facial feedback can occur in relation to any type of close-up, genre or narrative context can enhance their emotional impact. In melodrama, for instance, weeping characters are likely to arouse feelings of empathy or elicit a congruent mood from the audience.[13] Cognitive empathy tends to occur more intensely during what Carl Plantinga calls "scenes of empathy," a topic mentioned in Chapter 3. The increased duration of the close-up allows viewers enough time to decipher the facial emotions of the character and to anticipate the character's reactions through emotional simulation. Scenes of empathy, along with genre and camera position, are effective ways to amplify affective responses and to contribute to the dynamism of the flow of affects.

While drama and melodrama can absorb viewers in emotionally intense situations, certain genres privilege superficial engagement.[14] Unlike extended close-ups, which clarify for the viewer the emotions expressed by a character, fast-paced, action-packed films rarely permit the spectator to develop an appropriate empathetic response. As psychology scholar Dolf Zillmann argues, "the pace that characterizes contemporary audio-visual storytelling and reporting is likely to produce affective confusion and shallowness in both children and adults."[15] To nuance this tragic prognostic, it is fair to say that action films are not completely devoid of emotions. They display and evoke a range of emotions congruent with stress, anger, and awe. Moreover, the media are not the only sources of reinforcement in matters of sensible emotional and social behavior.

The vantage point and the spectators' observational attitudes are other factors that may influence affective responses. The mirror neurons are particularly excited when the observer and what is observed are positioned face-to-face. Art historian Barbara Stafford argues that the webwork of avoidance and facing in pictures influences our affective responses to depicted figures.[16] Displaying the back of a character can elicit curiosity or annoyance. In contrast, the face-to-face positioning can prompt viewers to speculate about the figures' motives and feelings. Film theorist Ed Tan distinguishes between two main observational attitudes of film spectators. Those vary according to the position of the character in relation to the camera. In the case of the *attitude en-face*, where the spectator faces the camera, the spectator studies the character's reaction to events, as the complete array of facial expressions as described by Ekman and his colleagues in the Facial Action Coding System (FACS) is available.[17] Alternatively, in the case of the *attitude en-profil*, when the character is seen from the side, the viewer can reconstruct the situational meaning from the diverse cues given by the character's gestures and voice intonations within the context depicted.[18]

Although certain psychologists argue that there are pan-cultural similarities for the expression and recognition of certain emotion categories, there are inevitable variations.[19] Many factors influence our appreciation of a character and modulate the continuous flow of affects.[20] Those factors include physical traits, narrative cues, editing techniques, filmic conventions, and social pressure. Disposition and technical elements can prompt us to evaluate whether a character conforms to social expectations, and if it is worthy of our allegiance.[21] In film noir, for instance, the partial lighting of one half of the face, while leaving the other half in the shadow, can intimate the character's dubiousness. In contrast, the physical appearance of Mulan in *Mulan* (Barry Cook and Tony Bancroft, 1998) does not conform to what we expect from a typical martial arts hero. At first, she appears unfit for the challenge that awaits her during the battle. Yet, as we gradually learn to appreciate her determination, courage, and good heart, we finally choose to vouch for her and hope she will succeed.

Cultural, technical, and psychological factors influence the emotional investment of the spectator. The next section explores more specifically eerie close-ups in animation and the effects of distorted facial traits on character engagement.

Eerie Close-ups and Masks in 2D Animation

The close-up has aroused the viewers' sympathy for many beloved characters since the beginning of the history of cinema.[22] The famous close-up at the end of *City Lights* (Charlie Chaplin, 1931) produces a lasting impression, touching viewers with the subtle blend of love and embarrassment on Charlie Chaplin's face. The close framing seems to facilitate the understanding of his inner thoughts. It also intensifies our connection with him. Additionally, the expression of emotions in close-ups is "critically involved in the elicitation of empathy and discordant affect."[23] The series of contemplative close-ups in Carl Dreyer's *The Passion of Joan of Arc* (1928) elicits the spectator's empathy for Joan's suffering.[24] Contemporary films and animations continue to draw on this popular framing device to intensify emotions or emphasize the dramatic importance of a scene. Around the beginning of *WALL-E* (Andrew Stanton, 2008), a close-up of WALL-E shows the reflection of Irene and Cornelius from *Hello Dolly!* (Gene Kelly, 1969) holding hands in his two lenses. Despite his complete lack of facial expressions, the romantic music and the framing arouse the spectator's sympathy for the lonely robot.

Alternatively, the greedy Ebenezer Scrooge in Zemeckis's 3D adaptation of the popular tale *A Christmas Carol* (2009) is dreadful. The character design achieves a high degree of likeness to Jim Carrey, the actor who lends his voice to the despicable protagonist. The near photorealism of Scrooge's face does not make him more attractive, on the contrary. When he is anxiously waiting for the visit of the spirit of his former business partner, he sits in a chair by the fire. With a squinted look, he stares toward the camera. His partially lit face and the chiaroscuro lighting foreground the whiteness of the sclera, while his pupils disappear in the shadow. The combination of his darkened look and frowning eyebrows is particularly disquieting. The mysterious music and the noises of clinking chains create a spooky ambience. The uncanny in this animation is heightened by the presence of multiple *doppelgangers* or doubles. The ghost of the Christmas past appears in the shape of a flame dressed into a white nightdress. The masklike shape of Jim Carey's face amplifies the feeling of dread. The ghost's head is flattened, and in a close-up approaching the camera objective, his two enlarged eyes with dead pupils purposely attempt to scare both Scrooge and the viewer. In *A Christmas Carol*, the ghosts reanimate Jentsch's uncertainty principle. Intellectual uncertainty occurs in the presence of "doubts whether an apparently animate being is really alive; or conversely, whether a lifeless object might not be in fact animate."[25] Before tackling the special topic of the uncanny valley, I demonstrate that eerie close-ups are not limited to CG animation and that some masks and distorted facial expressions can evoke congruent feelings in 2D animations.

The line that separates a sympathetic face from an antipathetic one can be thin. By masking characters and hiding their facial expressions, some animations increase the viewers' suspicion concerning their motives and feelings. We find masked characters in many superhero animations. Often, the mask serves to preserve the heroes' secret identities and distinguish their private lives from their public lives, as in the animations featuring the comic book characters Catwoman, Batman, Spider-Man, and Iron Man. The mask enables them to explore a darker side of their persona thanks to the veil of anonymity. This symbolic and physical doubling of the hero's personality falls into the spectrum of the uncanny.

In *Spirited Away* (Hayao Miyazaki, 2001), the ghastly face of No-Face is unnerving as this character blurs the lines between life and death with its translucent body.[26] Likewise, the plot suggests the porous boundary between life and death. Chihiro fears that her parents will be eaten, since the witch Yubaba has transformed them into pigs. Moreover, if Chihiro forgets her name, she may not be able to leave the spirit world. The eerie figure of the double is also expressed with *doppelgangers* such as the twin sisters Yubaba and Zeniba and the mask of No-Face doubling his face. The flatness of his white mask and the painted triangles above and below his eyes are reminiscent of Japanese Noh masks. In Noh theater, the mask can represent the instability of identity.[27] When the actors put on the mask, they not only see themselves in the mirror but also become the represented deity or demon that will be incarnated on stage.[28] The mask designer can produce many facial expressions by creating different shapes of eyes, styles of eyebrows, and mouth openings. The actor can also control these expressions by playing with the direction of the light falling on the mask and by revealing or concealing the parts of the face perceived through the small openings. This assemblage of gestures and shapes produced by the actor and the mask reinforces the duality of the mask and the face.

The science fiction TV series *Texhnolyze* also explores questions about the instability of identity. The close-up is a way to emotionally engage viewers who could otherwise feel estranged from the high-tech world it depicts. For example, the first episode of this animated series, entitled "Stranger," features close-ups of various durations. Some of the close-ups solicit the viewer's sympathy for rejected characters and outsiders. Alternatively, close-ups of masked faces help sustain the eerie mood of the peculiar city of Lukuss. The *anime* series *Texhnolyze*, I argue, uses the mask to defamiliarize faces and emphasize the nonhuman characteristics of a character, thus helping viewers feel the boundary between the human and the nonhuman.

The story of *Texhnolyze* is set in the underground city of Lukuss, a place where a corrupted organization, the Organo, imposes its rule with violence and terror. The city supplies the population with Raffia, a special material that prevents the body's rejection of transplanted organs. However, since it has overthrown the old government, the Organo controls the supply of the substance and only allows its members to get transplantation, or become "texhnolyzed." The film noir style of the first episode of the series conveys anxiety and alludes to the criminality implied by this style. Low-key lighting, canted frames, and the precisionist graphic style stress the loneliness and alienation of many of the citizens of this off-kilter world. The audience can only gather glimpses of information about this world from a few lines of dialogue and backdrops cropped by the frame. The film's emphasis on the fragmented perspectives on reality and the opaqueness of the power structures are also common features of cyberpunk and postmodern culture.[29]

Masklike expressions in this episode can evoke mixed feelings because they prevent viewers from deciphering facial expressions. Consistent with the anxiety-ridden atmosphere, many of the close-ups in the first scene of the first episode are asymmetrical and underline the graphical elements of the face, thus avoiding the reassuring cuteness present in numerous *anime*. In one scene, Yoshii, a man who came down to Lukuss from the surface, meets Ran, a young girl who can predict the near future. At one point, a canted angle shows Ran's face covered by a white mask with pink and blue line strokes painted on it that vaguely suggest the features of a fox (see Figure 5.2). When she removes the mask, her facial traits are immobile, and the shape of her wide eyes echoes the shape of the fox's eyes on the mask. Her face is emotionless, suggesting that she wears a second mask under the first one. Ran's gaze is particularly riveting in this sequence and prompts viewers to speculate about her intentions. Hypnotic, her eyes elicit a strange feeling of discomfort, perhaps caused by the impossibility of decoding her expression. Although the depicted face clearly represents a young girl, this sequence highlights the constructed nature of the representation by comparing her face with a mask, a gesture that purposely associates the living with the inanimate.

A close-up shot of Ichise in a later sequence parallels Ran's empty gaze. The camera shows an extreme close-up of his right eye, staring into space. He does not blink. His facial traits are static, thus conjuring up the idea of a mask. Like tears, drops of water slide down a tuft of hair next to his eye, conveying sadness (see Figure 5.3). The lack of depth in the composition and the limited textures in the image enable the parallel between drops of water and tears. More generally, the flat graphical similarity between human skin and the surrounding objects blurs the line between the subjecthood of objects and the objecthood of subjects.

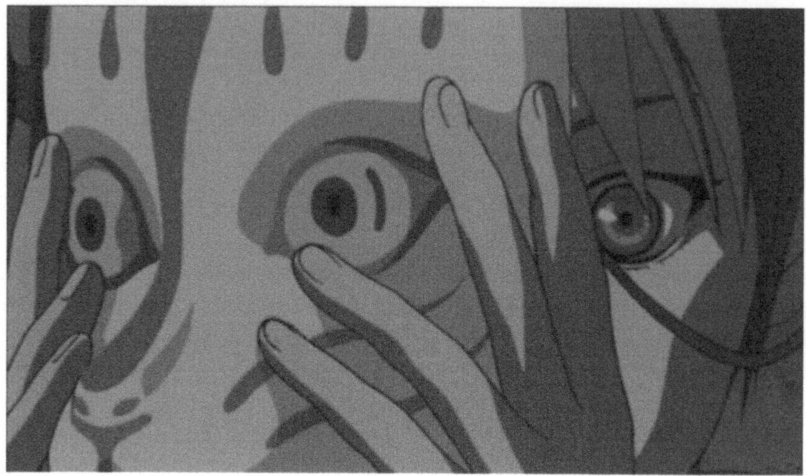

Figure 5.2 Ran's mask and her riveting gaze. *Texhnolyze*, Episode Stranger (Hiroshi Hamasaki, 2003).

Figure 5.3 Extreme close-up of Ichise's eye. *Texhnolyze*, Episode Stranger (Hiroshi Hamasaki, 2003).

These two close-ups emphasize the characters' lack of emotions instead of making their intentions more legible. Not all masks and animated faces are eerie; by blurring ontological oppositions between the organic and the graphic, the living and the nonliving, the masklike faces in these sequences harmonize with the off-kilter mise-en-scène to inspire anguish. Moreover, as mentioned earlier, facial mimicry may unconsciously influence emotional responses. In the case of Ran's face, the stiffness of her gaze and her limited facial movements can cause confusion that may interfere with the viewer's empathetic response to her apathetic state. In this episode, the masklike expressions support the eerie ambience and maintain the narrative's mystery.

Some close-ups in the mayhem sequence of the same episode of *Texhnolyze* heighten the viewer's empathy for Ichise. The sequence begins with one of the Organo gangsters raising his sword toward Ichise. The actual slicing of his limb is omitted, which forces the spectator to imagine it. The canted shots of his elongated facial muscles and open mouth convey his pain. The composition creates tension between the vertical edges of the frame and the diagonal lines formed by Ichise's stretched face.

The cross-modal similarities between the effects produced with sound, montage, and color produce a highly stylized depiction of his agony. The spasmodic series of images and the purple hue underscore the restlessness of the sequence. The repeated "cuts" in the montage also allude to the violence of the butchery. As the camera quickly moves the focus on different parts of Ichise's face, the character's groaning amplifies his suffering and may even reverberate within the viscera of some spectators. The correspondences across different domains of sensory experience have been termed "weak synesthesia."[30] Someone may find cross-modal similarities between increasingly high-pitched sounds and increasingly bright lights. As such weak synesthesia may be distinguished from strong synesthesia, which happens when a stimulus perceived by one sense is also perceived by another sense, as when hearing musical notes evokes seeing certain colors. In cinema, we refer to "synesthetic affect" when we find the response to one sensory modality to fit with the response to another one.[31] In this sequence, the combined effect of stylistic elements maximizes the emotional impact of the distorted facial expressions. At the end of the sequence, the splashing sound of an arm falling in a pool of blood may accentuate the discomfort of some spectators. By bombarding the spectator's senses with intense editing, unusual hues, and disturbing sounds, this sequence uses familiar fields of sensation to communicate Ichise's agony and expands them with synesthetic affect.

Although spectators may not be particularly concerned for Ischise's faith before this mayhem, mainly because his motivations were still unknown, his mutilation evokes mixed feelings of indignation, pain, and anger. The cruelty of his punishment can also appeal to the spectator's innate sympathy for the suffering of others. Many spectators could feel repulsed by the insensibility with which the Organo henchmen cut off Ichise's arm while he screams to death. Moreover, the criminals leave him bathed in his own blood in an empty street, reducing the chance that somebody passing by could rescue him. Here, the animation appeals to the spectators' basic sense of justice to condemn the Organo's organization. Part of the series' moral and ideological project resides in presenting the various sources of power and oppression in Lukuss. The defamiliarizing effects produced by the distorted facial traits and the masklike expressions not only support the plot's esthetic but also influence the spectator's allegiance.

The Curious Case of the Uncanny Valley

While the masklike expressions in *Texhnolyze* were sought for their eeriness, the zombie-like gazes of the characters in the animated film *The Polar Express* were certainly unwanted by the production team to avoid scaring young children. CG animation produces facial expressions that elicit a continuum of emotional responses, ranging from awe to repulsion. This section maps the origins of the expression "the uncanny valley" and surveys explanations given about the causes of the sensation of strangeness elicited by synthespians.

Automata and Synthespians

Animated faces are particularly engaging in *Avatar* (James Cameron, 2009), a Hollywood blockbuster that examines the cross-ethnic tensions between the humans and the Na'vi, the native inhabitants of a moon called Pandora. The details in Neytiri's facial expressions, her large golden eyes, and her strange glowing blue skin all combine to produce a fascinating digital star. Despite the strangeness of this CG creature, her mysterious gaze and photorealistic blue face successfully avoid the zombie-like appearance of near-realistic humans. Her expressive looks simultaneously elicit both empathy and admiration.

In contrast, the human characters in the video game *Alan Wake* (Remedy Entertainment, 2010) look creepy because their eyes lack focus and intensity. In this story about a successful writer of horror stories, the characters' gestures are stiff and their movements limited to the eyes and mouth. Nevertheless, the character design successfully contributes to the frightening mood conveyed by the surreal landscape filled with murderous "dark presences." The feelings experienced toward digital cyberstars are diverse. The wide range of empathetic responses depends on factors such as photorealism and degree of humanness. Accordingly, not all films and video games will deal with uncanny effects in the same way: some will prefer to avoid them, while others employ them to create a particular atmosphere.

Some critics complain that the technology distracts them from engaging with the character performances in CG animation.[32] However, this reproach had been initially voiced for cel animation and proved wrong. As Dan North claims, we "know from the way audiences have responded emotionally to characters in cel animated features such as those of Walt Disney, that there is no essential reason why emotional responses should be given exclusively to live actors (human or animal)."[33] Moreover, since many CG characters have successfully engaged audiences, including the protagonists of *The Incredibles* and the recent Oscar winner *Toy Story 3* (Lee Unkrich, 2010), technology is not necessarily the only cause of the limited appeal of some CG performances.

Some synthespians produce disquieting feelings akin to the uncanny valley effect, a phenomenon studied by roboticist Masahiro Mori in the 1970s. The uncanny valley describes a drop in a hypothetical curve that plots the appeal of a humanoid form in relation to its similarity to the human figure. The more a robot or an animated character possesses human characteristics, the more it is appealing, until it becomes too humanlike. The drop in empathy for the near-human figures corresponds to the "uncanny valley" on the curve. For instance, when shaking a prosthetic hand that has achieved a high degree of human verisimilitude, we are surprised by the lack of soft tissue and its cold temperature.[34] A strange feeling has replaced the sense of familiarity projected by the common act of shaking a hand. In his article "The Uncanny Valley," Mori warns that advances in robotics and prostheses may be undercut by their own success, since designs that are too humanlike often produce eerie sensations.[35]

This experience can generate the kind of dread described by Sigmund Freud. In his essay "The 'Uncanny,'" Freud assembled the different meanings attached to the word uncanny and collected events and situations that can arouse the feeling of uncanniness in people. He defined these feelings as that "class of the frightening which leads back to what is known of old and long familiar."[36] Freud rejected the hypothesis that having doubts that something is alive is sufficient to produce the chilling effect of the uncanny, a position held by Ernst Jentsch, a contemporary scholar. Drawing on E. T. A. Hoffmann's short story "The Sand-Man" (1816), Freud identified a strong relationship between the uncanny and the anxiety belonging to the castration complex of childhood. In the story, the Sand-man is a mythical creature that tears out the eyes of children who would not go to bed. Freud reads Nathanael's dread of losing his eyes as a fear of the punishment of castration. He draws on his study of dreams and myths, such as the Greek myth of Oedipus who blinded himself for having married his mother and killed his father. Freud also associates the uncanny with the queasiness caused by events that unexpectedly repeat themselves. Among other sources of the uncanny, he included the resurfacing of old animistic beliefs, such as wishful thinking. For instance, when a person wishes the death of someone, if that someone dies, the person may believe to have caused her death because of the power of her mind. Many studies have deconstructed Freud's reading of Hoffmann's story and explored the psychoanalytic ramifications of the uncanny.[37] While I acknowledge the insights provided by Freud and Jentsch into the phenomenon of the uncanny valley in CG animation,

I focus on recurring motifs that evoke that class of feelings and their implications for the cyborg viewer.

When we see too-humanlike synthespians, unconscious animistic beliefs about the possibility of inanimate objects to come alive may resurface. Multiple reviews on photorealism in *Final Fantasy: The Spirits Within* suggest that highly verisimilar synthespians can elicit anxiety toward the replacement of actors with digitized humans.[38] According to North, "the synthespians represent a contemporary manifestation of the Frankenstein myth, embodying our own fear of replication and obsolescence, our replacement by digital constructs capable of outstripping our every capability and nuance."[39] While this anxiety is not usually present in cel animation or cartoonish CG animated features, eeriness can still be present in images that are not generated by a computer, especially when they unsettle ontological categories between human bodies and nonhuman bodies.

The unnerving effect of characters that fall within the uncanny valley influences character engagement. As media scholar Barbara Creed notes, the viewer's identification with cyberstars is "marked by a sensation of strangeness."[40] Because cyberstars have no unconscious and no "real" life, the idea of wanting to take their place and become like them, as it could be the case when we identify with a superhero played by a flesh-and-blood actor may seem odd. If one day filmmakers succeed in producing images that are so realistic that no one would be able to tell the difference, the sensation of strangeness would theoretically disappear. Only a spectator who is aware of the presence of a synthespian would be unsettled. Spectators in that situation may inhibit their empathetic feelings for the cyberstar, just because they find the idea repelling or inappropriate. In addition, a synthespian that evokes the traits of a dead person can amplify the discomfort. It is also possible to imagine that actors would eventually sell digitization of their performance to studios so that they could create new digital performances even after their death, a topic explored in the hybrid film *The Congress* (Ari Folman, 2013). As Creed speculates, the "spectator might well feel engulfed by a sense of the uncanny as she/he watches the dead reanimated."[41] The sensation of strangeness is amplified by the idea that we can empathize with animated entities that are dead or simply nonliving. This singular sensation of doubt relates to the definition of the uncanny given by Jentsch. Wax figures, dolls, and automata are examples of objects that can produce the impression of intellectual uncertainty.

Many animated films explore angsty territories by self-reflexively referring to reanimating dead bodies or giving the spark of life to automata and dolls. Both *Corpse Bride* (Tim Burton and Mark Johnson, 2005) and *Coraline* (Henry Selick, 2009) intertwine the idea of semblance of life produced by puppet animation with the theme of reanimation. Their gloominess inspires the type of uncanny feelings that Freud identified in relation to corpses and the return of the dead. In addition, Jentsch's theory is relevant to the cases of films featuring synthespians. *Blade Runner 2049* (Denis Villeneuve, 2017) transparently replaces the character of Rachel originally present in *Blade Runner* (Ridley Scott, 1982) with a cyberstar, thus conjuring up a younger version of actress Sean Young in the sequel.

The Science of the Uncanny

Scientific studies provide evidence that the phenomenon of the uncanny valley may elicit anxiety or aversion.[42] Computer scientists Karl MacDorman and colleagues identified possible scientific explanations of this phenomenon. Three categories of explanations involve automatic and specialized perceptual processing in humans.[43] First, evolutionary mechanisms incite us to avoid threat. We fear defects perceived in human-looking entities as they can suggest a potential disease or a decomposing corpse. Second, our shared circuits for empathy are sensitive to human likeness and can be disturbed by the presence of roboticized motion. Third, the biological basis of attractiveness reveals that certain biological markers have selective advantage for a species and those lacking them can elicit the feelings of aversion associated with the uncanny valley. Two more categories involve conscious appraisal of the eerie figure. On the one hand, the human-machine hybrid can be terrifying because it makes us wonder where the machine ends and where the human begins. On the other hand, the spine-chilling image is a subliminal reminder of our inevitable mortality.

The evolutionary thesis is supported by evidence showing that macaque monkeys can detect the uncanny. Neuroscientists Shawn Stekenfinger and Asif Ghazanfar have compared the reactions of macaque monkeys when they were looking at realistic synthetic monkey faces to their reactions when looking at real monkey faces. They discovered that the monkeys spent less time looking at realistic synthetic monkey faces than looking at realistic or synthetic monkey faces. Their conclusion to explain this difference is that the "monkey visual behavior fell into the uncanny valley."[44] According to Stekenfinger and Ghazanfar, this finding indicates that the response to the phenomenon is evolutionary and not based on human-specific mental structures. Other scientists, who also associate our reaction to slightly distorted human features with evolutionary mechanisms, attempt to demistify the phenomenon. Lawrence Rosenblum claims that our "visceral reaction to the zombie-like appearance of near-realistic humans could be a by-product of evolutionary pressures to avoid corpses, and their possible diseases."[45] Similarly, drawing on Christian Keysers's view that the uncanny valley is the result of an evolved mechanism for pathogen avoidance, MacDorman and his colleagues assert that the perception of "defects in a human-looking entity could trigger an aversive response automatically by activating an evolved mechanism for self-preservation."[46]

The unnerving sensation occurs because our expertise in facial detection tells us that something is not quite right. Scientists tested the effects of near-human figures displayed on a screen on participants. Among the key emotions that the test helped identify were: fear, anxiety, disgust, dislike, and shock.[47] Many scholars seem to agree that we experience uncanny effects because we are face experts.[48] Our brain is attuned to faces because they quickly communicate vital information about the other person's feelings and intentions, as well as about potential threats in our environment. As Rosenblum notes, by looking at "a face, you can rapidly determine an individual's identity, gender, emotional state, intentions, genetic health, reproductive potential, and even linguistic message (through lip-reading)."[49] An experiment that slightly altered the distance between Mao's eyes demonstrated that observers familiar with his face could notice a shift of just one-tenth of an inch, which represented 1% of the full width of the face in the photo.[50]

In addition to brain specialization for face perception, mirror neurons could also explain the sensitivity of the humans to distortions in a facial image. As Rosenblum suggests, perhaps "this reflexive mirroring is involved in making face perception that much more sensitive to distortions in a facial image. If so, the uncanny valley experience may be a by-product of [our] brain's disposition to mirror human actions."[51] The mirror neuron system (MNS), which is activated when one attentively watches another perform an action, seems to require some anthropomorphic realism in order to be responsive. Some studies have demonstrated an increased activation of the MNS when the motion is performed by a human or a human-looking figure.[52] Moreover, the walking of a humanoid figure engages mirror neuron sites, while stick figures do not.[53] Studies have also compared robot motion with human motion. According to Erhan Oztop and colleagues, mirror neurons are activated when a humanoid robot performs a task but not when a non-humanoid robot performs the same task.[54] In contrast, according to another study, the MNS responds to robotic actions when the movement is not repetitive.[55] It has also been suggested that human likeness is not the only factor that determines likability. Other aspects of robots' design influence our empathy for them and their perceived threat, including height, color, and form.[56] These studies on the MNS and the uncanny valley bring to light a complex combination of factors that may hinder our empathic response toward synthespians and robots.

While the effects have been experienced in humans and macaque monkeys, there are variances in responsiveness to the uncanny valley.[57] When one is sensitive to the eerie effects, aspects of the physiognomy of a cyberstar or an animated character can give rise to discomfort or antipathy. As mentioned in Chapter 3, the recognition process is an important aspect of the structure of engagement. A character with deformities or physical characteristics that depart from the norm can elicit defiance and therefore hinder the process of allegiance.[58] To avoid this problem, animators often design cheerful cartoons with cuddly faces to win the sympathy of children.[59] Alternatively, they reserve facial distortions for antagonists; asymmetrical features, scars, and prostheses can elicit disgust or anxiety, which are feelings often experienced in the presence of nonnormative bodies and strangers. As an example of the work of iconography, the prominent teeth and large forehead of Cruella De Vil in *The 101 Dalmatians* (Clyde Geronimi, Hamilton Luske, and Wolfgang Leitherman, 1961) classify her as a suspicious character.

The inability for some human-looking animated characters and avatars to express accurate emotions with their face can produce eerie feelings.[60] For example, the lack of smoothness of Aki's gestures in *Final Fantasy: The Spirits Within* and her restrained palette of facial expressions may signal a lack of emotions or a limited ability to express herself. Since emotional ability is a characteristic that cinema often uses to distinguish androids from humans, her coldness may raise suspicion. Like cinema, animated films often associate physical attributes with the moral status of a character.[61] In the case of Aki, her unfocused eyes and stiff gestures could make her appear untrustworthy. Whether "we consciously assent to the moral associations of iconography or not, they are part of the 'automatized' level of filmic comprehension."[62] The responses produced by character representations that fall within the uncanny valley are also partly automatic. These responses could influence the process of allegiance since the mechanisms of moral orientation influence one another. Disposition also alters the viewer's judgment of situations involving CG characters.[63] Finally, in CG animation as in live-action films, spectators can rely on character action and voice to confirm or revise their first impression about the physiognomy of a character.

Overcoming the Uncanny Valley in *The Curious Case of Benjamin Button*

Because uncanny valley effects can suppress sympathetic feelings toward synthespians and thereby hinder the process of allegiance, many animators prefer to get around them. The presence of eerie characters in some productions set in futuristic worlds, however, can revive questions about bodily alteration and bioengineering, as it is the case in *Final Fantasy: The Spirits Within*, *Immortal Ad Vitam* (Enki Bilal, 2004), and *Appleseed Alpha* (Shinji Aramaki, 2014), just to name a few. Alternatively, as this section examines, some animations embrace their uncanniness to question a lack of empathy for nonnormative bodies and people who are different, including cyborgs and sentient machines.

The Design of Cyberstars

The design of verisimilar humans in animation is a difficult challenge, as Brad Bird, the writer-director of *The Incredibles*, mentioned during an interview. Because we are extremely familiar to how humans look, we have high expectations in relation to the rendering of simulated human shapes and behaviors. As Bird notes, there is "a certain way a person's weight shifts, how expressions go down, and little 'tells'—visual cues as to what people are actually thinking as opposed to what they are saying."[64] For these reasons, many animated films avoid CG humans in main roles to prevent triggering disturbing effects. Pixar has used toys, fish, insects, cars, robots, and monsters as their heroes in *Toy Story* (John Lasseter, 1995), *Finding Nemo* (Andrew Stanton, 2003), *A Bug's Life* (John Lasseter, 1998), *Cars* (John Lasseter, 2006), *WALL-E* (Andrew Stanton, 2008), and *Monsters, Inc.* (Pete Docter, 2001). These effects are not limited to humans as "very realistic virtual pets tend to cause a similar aversion as humanlike characters."[65] When animators need to feature CG humans and photorealistic animals, they bypass the problems posed by the uncanny valley phenomenon with cartoony stylizations. Following this tip, *Monsters, Inc.*, *Toy Story*, and *The Incredibles* (Brad Bird, 2004) exaggerate the features of their human characters and emphasize their comical traits. In *Shrek* (Andrew Adamson and Vicky Jenson, 2001), which did not follow this recommendation, "the ogre Shrek has an appealing warmth, [while] the royals he interacts with seem embalmed."[66] Similarly, when designing the characters for *Final Fantasy: The Spirits Within* and *The Polar Express*, animators used the motion capture technique to enhance the photorealism of facial expressions and gestures. However, neither photorealism nor highly verisimilar representations are sufficient to create familiarity. As "a visit to Madame Tussaud's proves," John Canemaker points out, "masses of highly specific visual information don't necessarily result in a higher degree of believability—in fact, the results can be downright creepy."[67]

The animated film *Final Fantasy: The Spirits Within* achieved a high degree of photorealism and certainly raised the bar for the productions that followed. Yet, perfection was not the ultimate objective. Jun Aida, the producer, claimed, "Our goal was not to create photo-real characters. I don't think technically it's possible with animation. In still photos, we can."[68] The production team created proprietary programs to produce realistic-looking skin, hair, and clothing textures. Aki's looks cost millions of dollars because "the 60,000 hairs on [her] head took a fifth of Square's graphic rendering capacity to produce."[69] The motion capture process was also used to transfer information about the motion of actual performers to the animated cast. Nevertheless, despite the incredible effort put behind the creation of this entirely CG universe, the animation left the production company, Square Co., with a debt of $113,000,000. According to North, the fact that the characters fall into the uncanny valley could be one of the reasons that explain the film's failure at the box office.[70]

While the production team of *Final Fantasy: The Spirits Within* was unable to avoid the sensation of strangeness produced by synthespians, it attempted to alleviate the unnerving feelings by marketing a star image for Aki, the main protagonist. Many productions use "star personae" as a means to attract audiences.[71] As film scholar James Naremore claims, the "surge of recognition and pleasurable anticipation most viewers feel [in recognizing stars in a film] constitutes the most elemental form of identification, and it has obvious value for the filmmakers."[72] The pre-publicity team for *Final Fantasy: The Spirits Within* invested a great amount of energy in creating a star persona for Aki. Showing pictures of the cyberstar wearing only a pink bikini reinforced her similarity to a real actor. These photoshoots were "designed to suggest a celebrity life outside the confines of the diegesis."[73] Websites dedicated to Aki, which were inspired by fan sites for real actors, featured biographies and photo galleries.[74] Like actors, cyberstars are products that are sold to an audience. Unlike actors, as Creed judiciously claims, cyberstars are "perfect products."[75] Indeed, they can work extended hours and never complain.

The many close-ups in *Final Fantasy: The Spirits Within* also demonstrate an intention to increase emotional depth and engage viewers' affect. The close shots clarify Aki's facial expressions and show the details of her skin and hair. In order to increase photorealism, her "face has one hundred separate controls for facial movements."[76] As one of the animators explains on the interactive documentary provided with the special DVD edition of *Final Fantasy: The Spirits Within*, they carefully hand-keyed the characters' hands and facial expressions. Animators also looked at themselves in the mirror to guide their animation of her eyebrows, eyes, and mouth movements. The animators also watched video recordings of the actors who provided the characters' voices to mimic their lip movements and adjust them frame by frame when the automated results were not convincing. However, the slight asynchrony between audio and visual stimuli is irritating. It can even distract some viewers from the story. As an animator mentions in the making-of documentary of *Final Fantasy: The Spirits Within*, despite the team's efforts to produce realistic movement, "there are subtleties that are very hard to achieve."

The transfer of negative affect into positive artifact emotions is another strategy that can minimize discomfort in films and animations featuring synthespians. Spectacular visual effects or camera movements produce artifact emotions such as awe and surprise. Various sequences of *Final Fantasy: The Spirits Within* underscore its technical achievement in computer imagery. The first few shots present aerial views of monumental cliffs and a colorful sunset peering through the openings between the tops of the rocks. Following this magnificent landscape, an extreme close-up of Aki's left eye pops up. Small wrinkles, brown spots, and pores are visible on the skin. The reflection on her cornea and the details of her iris and eyebrow attain a high degree of photorealism. The extremely close shot was possibly intended to elicit awe from spectators and fascinate them (see Figure 5.4). Its near-perfect photorealism, which was considered a novelty at the time the animation came out, produces artifact emotions that enhance the sequence's limited appeal. However, the mesmerizing effects of many of the shots were not sufficient to sustain the spectators' absorption. Film critic Michael Tunison claimed that the digital people in *Final Fantasy: The Spirits Within* were "a little too eerily realistic to be interesting as animation and quite a bit too animated-looking to pass as real—an awkward middle ground that proves endlessly distracting."[77] Moreover, Aki's exceptionally detailed eye and her procedurally modeled hairdo invite "the eye to inspect closely, to seek out pixilation, jerkiness, or other vestiginal traces of its computed origins."[78] Similarly, even though the visual effects were impressive, film critic Peter Travers was disappointed by the lifelessness of the characters and settings:

> At first it's fun to watch the characters [....] But then you notice a coldness in the eyes, a mechanical quality in the movements [....] The dark backgrounds leave you with the deadening feeling you get after too many hours of playing cybergames. You miss something. It could be the joystick, the interaction. More likely, it's the human touch from those pesky actors.[79]

Figure 5.4 Artifact emotion and the extreme close-up of Aki's eye. *Final Fantasy: The Spirits Within* (Hironobu Sakaguchi, 2001).

For these reviewers, the technological wonders did not compensate for the flaws in the appearance and movements of the CG characters. The traces of computer origins were too distracting and prevented them from being engrossed by the photorealistic achievement.

Digital Captures of Benjamin Button

For many animators and software developers, the uncanny valley effects are the undesired by-products of a race to attain photorealism in the film industry; they are the last obstacles in the way to achieve the "perfect" animated human. The production of a flawless imitation could potentially eliminate the defamiliarizing effects produced by human-looking CG characters. The character supervisor for the film *The Curious Case of Benjamin Button*, Steve Preeg, claimed that his team had virtually obliterated these effects with meticulous renderings of the aging character played by Brad Pitt. When speculating about the future of synthespians, Creed argued that "the presence of the synthespian in film is not meant to be perceived by the audience as a 'special effect' nor to draw attention to itself: the virtual or synthetic origins of the star will have to be rendered invisible by the text in order for the character to offer a convincing, believable performance."[80] Unlike *Final Fantasy: The Spirits Within*, which capitalized on the spectacular appeal of technological innovations, the makers of *The Curious Case of Benjamin Button* followed Creed's advice and chose to erase the technological inscriptions to enhance photorealism and thereby increase the spectator's absorption.

For Preeg and his team, when a spectator experiences eerie feelings, it is an indication of a technological failure. Although they are convinced of their success in bypassing the uncanny valley, some critics voiced some doubts. For example, cultural writers Lawrence Weschler and Clive Thompson argued that Ed Ulbrich, who developed the CG effects with Preeg, did not "scale the deepest part of the valley. Old, wrinkled skin reacts to light differently and is easier to digitally render. And the conceit of a human aging backwards is inherently unreal, a fantasy, so we're more likely to forgive the uncanny effect."[81] When I watched the film, I certainly recognized the high level of photorealism. However, I first thought that sophisticated masks were responsible for the aging effects, which signaled that there were still details in the design that seemed fabricated.

Preeg and his team put a lot of energy into perfecting every aspect of Benjamin's face and paid special attention to the appearance of his eyes. They kept in mind the principle that "enhancing the realism of one feature [makes] other less realistic characteristics more conspicuous."[82] He claimed that avoiding the uncanny valley "was a constant process of fixing one problem and then noticing something else."[83] As an inspiration, Preeg scrutinized images of real eyes to animate a convincingly naturalistic gaze that avoids the zombie-like looks of the characters in *The Polar Express*. When explaining his process, Preeg said,

> When a real eye moves, the thin film of moisture covering the eye builds up more on the side toward which the eye is moving. Moving your eyes to the right produces more moisture on the right side of your irises than the left. This difference in the amount of moisture creates different glimmers on the two sides of your eyes—and this difference changes whenever your eyes move. It turns out that these changing glimmers give the eyes a more natural, soulful look. If the eyes shift to the right, but then don't glimmer a bit more on the right than left, they just don't look as real. So we added this detail to every animated shot.[84]

This attention to detail was important because many of the shots in the film were dialogue-driven and filmed in close-ups to amplify the actors' emotional subtleties. When Benjamin meets Daisy for the first time, he looks as though he is 70, and she is 9. In that scene, his face was completely CG from the neck up (see Figure 5.5). Because of the oddness of the situation, Preeg wanted to achieve the right tone for this scene. When clarifying his intention, Preeg mentioned: "We had to make it innocent enough that it feels like a 15-year-old that is confused about things and still has to be Brad. We were trying to make a dirty old man feel innocent and do it in computer."[85] By seemingly integrating CG and real-life acting, Preeg and his team wanted to foreground the character's performance. As Preeg put it, "It was just a character in your face, giving his line and—hopefully—conveying the emotion Brad wanted to get across."[86]

Erasing the technological inscriptions on facial expressions required extensive work and a careful hybridization of the real and the animated.[87] For the older version of Benjamin, the production team filmed a small actor who was wearing a blue hoodie with tracing markers placed on it. The hoodie would later be replaced with a CG head. To create the computerized model, they used a realistic-looking cast of an aged version of Brad's head made by Rick Baker Studios. Then, they digitally analyzed Brad's facial expressions with a motion capture system called Contour Reality Capture. These digital captures enabled them to store highly detailed facial reconstructions in the computer. Brad first practiced about 200 facial expressions. When Brad was well rehearsed, as Preeg explains, they

Figure 5.5 Erasing technological inscriptions on the computer-generated face of the elderly Benjamin Button. *The Curious Case of Benjamin Button* (David Fincher, 2008).

> applied a luminous speckled paint to his face and filmed him making the expressions with 28 cameras. This allowed us to very carefully track the movements of thousands of points on his face. The tracked movements were then used to build an animation program. This allowed our animators to move Benjamin character's face in the same way Brad would move his face. When the animators lifted an eyebrow, they would be lifting it the way Brad lifts his eyebrow. In fact we noticed that, like all of us, one side of Brad's face moves a bit more than the other. Retaining these sorts of imperfections helped with the realism.[88]

With this extensive digital library of Brad's facial movements, animators could eventually match the required expression with the CG head model of the old-looking Benjamin. As this tedious process suggests, it was important to erase the boundary between live and animated, and thus conceal from the spectators any trace of technological inscriptions.

Empirical studies attempt to elucidate the psychology underlying the defamiliarizing effects of the uncanny valley. According to MacDorman and colleagues, "eeriness is not the result of a certain degree of human likeness, but the result of a discrepancy between more human-looking and less human-looking elements."[89] When using a human photorealistic texture, it is important to maintain the proportions of the computer-animated face within human norms. To support this claim, scientists Seyama and Nagayama discovered that the combination of a 50% increase in eye size for a figure having a photorealistic skin texture resulted in much greater eeriness than the same increase in eye proportion for a doll.[90] Their study revealed that in the presence of human-looking faces, we are less tolerant of deviations in facial shape, size, and location. As a rule of thumb to prevent eeriness, it is advisable to "avoid mismatches in the degree of human likeness of [computer generated] elements."[91] Even though *anime* characters and cartoons often feature abnormally large eyes, they mimic the cuteness of toys and childish faces. The idea that unearthly characters, such as Neytiri in *Avatar,* can avoid the uncanny valley does not seem to be universal. For instance, Golum in *The Lord of the Rings* resembles an old man but his weird stare and manners can evoke uneasiness. Similarly, Tiwa's fix gaze and enormous red eyes in *Fantastic Planet* (René Laloux, 1973) can give shivers down the spine. In this last case, the lack of visible response in the eye region and "aberrant facial expression may evoke the Uncanny Valley phenomenon."[92] When characters are animated, other factors such as the story, settings, and personality seem to contribute to the perception of uncanniness. The uncanny, as Robyn Ferrell suggests, "is a type of moment rather than a class of objects; an effect of a process of perceiving rather than of an image perceived."[93] I would argue that the process by which the uncanny emerges requires a savant mixture of viewers' dispositions, facial proportions, storytelling, and mise-en-scène.

In summary, the focus on technological prowess in *Final Fantasy: The Spirits Within* can hinder the spectator's empathetic responses for synthespians. Instead of being absorbed by the narrative and the characters' performances, spectators tend to turn their attention toward the materiality of the image, its modes of production, or its apparent flaws. Those unaware of the CG processes that generated the aging Brad Pitt in *The Curious Case of Benjamin Button* most probably experienced the film as they would experience a live-action film. However, for the spectators aware of the technical accomplishment, their involvement may shift from getting absorbed in the action and sympathizing with the characters to scrutinizing the image for potential imperfections. While uncanniness may not have been justified by the plot of *The Polar Express*, other animated films may exploit unsettling effects to support a specific mood or incite viewers to reexamine their responses toward queerness, a topic investigated in the next section.

Queerness in *Malice@Doll*

In his article on the uncanny, Jentsch had identified dolls and automata as sources of spookiness because they can make us doubt about their aliveness.[94] Various animated films explore the effects of the "*mechanical* uncanny."[95] Geppetto's desire for Pinocchio to come alive in *Pinocchio* (1940) echoes the spectator's desire for the animated puppet to break free from the screen. The emperor's fascination for his automata in *The Emperor's Nightingale* (Jirí Trnka and Miloš Makovec, 1949) doubles the viewer's fascination for the animated puppets.[96] Dolls can also exacerbate our uncertainty between the animate and the inanimate in *Parasite Dolls* (Yoshinaga Naoyuki, Nakazawa Kazuto, 2003) and *9* (Shane Acker, 2009). The *doppelganger* or double evokes feelings of unhomeliness in *Coraline*. The blurring of life and death and automata that look human are two other sources of eeriness identified by Steven Brown in his analysis of *Ghost in the Shell 2: Innocence* (Mamoru Oshii, 2004).[97] The mechanized dolls in *Malice@Doll* also suggest that the uncanny is in the eye of the beholder. The viewers become animated when this reversal of perspective makes them question the limit between the machine and the human.

The sensation of dread can be desirable in some CG animated films and video games, especially in the science fiction and horror genres. For instance, a science fiction film arousing creepy feelings toward mutants can amplify the spectator's anxiety toward research on bodily alterations in bioengineering. This section focuses on sources of the uncanny in the OVA series *Malice@Doll*. The presence of various stylistic devices in this CG animation defamiliarizes the human. *Malice@Doll* conjures up the uncanny by inviting spectators to share the perspectives of machines and automated dolls. Moreover, from the vantage point of the nonhumans, the human inspires fear, since humanness has become closely linked with a deadly infection. While the reversal of perspective may allude to processes of dehumanization in the Internet era, it also provokes visceral reactions toward non-heteronormative couples and characters disfigured by illness.

The Mechanized Dolls

Malice@Doll evokes a sensation of strangeness that relates with unhomeliness and visual aspects of the uncanny associated with CG dolls. The dolls' chilling looks fit the noirish ambience of the dystopian tale, which combines German Expressionism and Gothic esthetic. The presence of sentient dolls also refers to the long history of mechanized dolls in Japan.[98] The main character, Malice@Doll, is named after her e-mail address. She is one of the few sex worker dolls who still stroll the deserted streets of what used to be a vibrant red-light district. The human clients, also called gods, have mysteriously vanished from this world. The system administrator Joe@Admin manages the male robots and the mechanized dolls. Various references to the Internet imply that the self-governed machines and dolls are animated by information technology. According to film scholar Margherita Long, the "story suggests that if men reduce themselves to systems administrators and conduct their relationships entirely on the Internet, according to computer protocols, they become little more than mechanized maintenance crews."[99] Even though it is possible to sense an underlying critic about processes of dehumanization caused by online media, the story remains ambiguous about the reasons behind the disappearance of the humans from that world.

The story focuses on Malice's identity quest. In the beginning, Malice is broken, and she is worried that she may go offline. On her way to the repairer, she discovers a strange natural history museum with rusty skeletons hanging from the walls. During her visit, she stumbles onto a Daliesque statue on display that she at first mistakes for the repairer. A dark green liquid oozes from the statue's eyes, which indicates a malfunction. Unexpectedly, numerous snakelike tentacles spring out from the statue and impale Malice's chest. One of the tentacles has a snake's head. It violently penetrates the space between Malice's open legs. While some have interpreted this rape as gratuitous sexual violence, Long considered this encounter a symbol of the phallus society disguised under the traits of the "phallic mother." The phallic mother represents "the omnipotent, yet-uncastrated being with whom children imagine they were joined prior to the prohibition of the mother's body by the father."[100]

After this gruesome moment of "conception," Malice wakes up with a different anatomy. The frame displays a bird's-eye view of Malice's body curled up in a fetal position, spinning around. When awake, she scrutinizes herself in the mirror. Her complexion, which used to be grayish, has taken warm peach tones. Her pink hair has turned black, and she has lost the painted triangles on her cheeks that were giving her the traits of a sad clown. Malice touches her skin and notices its different texture. She laughs at herself, and expresses surprise to hear her own laughter, an emotional response foreign to a doll. The sequence self-reflexively underlines the alienating effect she experiences while apprehending her new human body with her different senses. What used to be familiar, her body, has now become unfamiliar. The references to *Alice's Adventures in Wonderland* (Lewis Carroll, 1865) and *Through the Looking Glass, and What Alice Found There* (Lewis Carroll, 1871) may signal that Malice's transformation represents a reversal of the humans' transformation into machines.[101]

According to Jentsch, the theme of reanimation and the metamorphosis of a doll into a human, central elements in *Malice@Doll*, may elicit scary feelings. For Freud, however, creative fiction cannot really produce uncanny feelings. As he argues, the creative writer can

> choose a setting which though less imaginary than the world of fairy tales, does yet differ from the real world by admitting superior spiritual beings such as daemonic spirits or ghosts of the dead. So long as they remain within their setting of poetic reality, such figures lose any uncanniness which they might possess.[102]

In *Malice@Doll*, despite the knowledge of the presence of an imaginary world, the contrast between the dolls' soft voices and their expressionless faces may be disturbing to some audience members, as the dolls mix familiar and unfamiliar characteristics. Even though animators used a 3D modeling technique to create the dolls, their faces remain fairly static and their gazes are fixed; only their pupils can move to simulate an electronic mechanism of data acquisition (see Figure 5.6). The disparity between the human likeness of the characters' voices and their doll-like appearances relates to MacDorman's finding on the importance of matching degrees of human likeness in the various facial features to avoid the uncanny valley phenomenon.[103]

In *Malice@Doll*, the jerking body and other uncanny motifs hint at the automaton. Malice's twitching movements before awaking in the stained-glass room at the beginning of the animation and Heather's uncontrolled spasms after Malice's kiss evoke the uncertainty felt in the presence of the inanimate becoming animate and the dead becoming alive. The strings attached to the puppets in Malice's flashback and the open eyes of the dolls sleeping during Malice's visit to her friends are examples of features that reassure about the inanimate nature of the dolls. However, the mechanical dolls or automata are self-animated. They recall the *karakuri ningyō* or mechanical dolls produced for home use and the puppet theater between the 17th and 19th centuries in Japan.[104] The small mechanical puppets called *zashiki karakuri* were based on clockwork or weight-driven mechanisms. They could perform spectacular actions, including shooting arrows with a bow, create calligraphic designs with a brush in one hand and another in the mouth, and serving tea. While the facial expression of the puppet is frozen, the clockwork

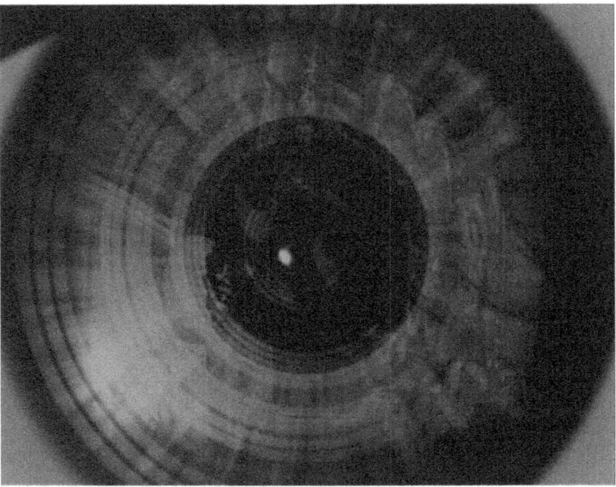

Figure 5.6 Malice's automated pupil and the robotic gaze. *Malice@Doll* (Keitarô Motonaga, 2001).

precision of the gestures fascinates and foregrounds the strangeness of the automated ritual. The life-sized *butai karakuri* were stage mechanical dolls designed to perform in front of an audience during the Edo period. When, for the sake of a demonstration, the *zashiki karakuri* reveal their clockwork mechanisms, they could be disturbing. Nevertheless, the slight jerkiness in the puppet's motion is compensated by the cuteness of its cuddly face and its lavishing costume. In contrast, the mechanized dolls in *Malice@Doll* are not reassuring; on the contrary, they seek to upset sexual norms, revisit human categories, and contest gender discrimination.

The Defamiliarizing Perspectives of Robots and Dolls

By encouraging viewers to share the visual perspectives of nonhuman bodies, *Malice@Doll* creates problematic forms of imaginary transpositions. In a sequence after Malice turned human, spectators are invited to observe Malice's new body from the perspective of the robot Joe@Admin. Disoriented by her metamorphosis, Malice had set out to find an answer to the origin of her physical differences. When she encounters Joe in the street, he does not recognize her even though her physical traits and voice are akin to those she had before her transformation. When he stares at her, a succession of small white bars suggesting bar charts and a moving circular X-ray target overlay Malice's body. Joe's computerized mode of recognition resembles the processes involved in character engagement. Thanks to Joe's sophisticated scanning device, we learn that Malice is no longer a piece of machinery and now possesses an organic body. Although Malice repeatedly tells Joe that she is the same person, he refuses to identify her as Malice. Feeling alienated, Malice starts to cry. She appears to be revolted by her past submission to the gods and momentarily rejects her human body. From Joe's and Malice's personal viewpoints, the familiar has become unfamiliar. According to Freud's insights into this form of estrangement, Malice's new human appearance is uncanny for them.

The suspicious reactions of the various characters to Malice's new body can also self-reflexively illustrate the complex process of character engagement. Malice's metamorphosis interferes with the spectatorial processes of recognition, alignment, and allegiance. The sequence where Joe refuses to recognize Malice confirms that linguistic information is insufficient in the process of reasserting a character's identity; viewers expect the consistency of the external and internal physical parts of a character throughout the plot. Then, before Joe leaves Malice by herself, he claims that something that is neither a doll nor a god will bring chaos to the world. His hostile reaction hints at the lurking dangers that await the new Malice. Later, Doris@Doll, another prostitute doll, rejects Malice because she reminds her of the gods, a term that designates her former clients. Doris's disdainful reaction suggests that the exclusion of someone who looks different is normal for her. The rejection of Malice's nonnormative body mirrors the complicated process of allegiance that some spectators undergo when confronted with computer-animated bodies on the screen.[105]

The subjective alignment with the robotic male gaze in *Malice@Doll* is also problematic. In many sequences, viewers observe the scene from the vantage point of robots that scrutinize or destroy dolls. Devo@ Leukocyte, the alien detector, uses its computerized vision to detect Melissa the Piper. After having identified her as an alien because of her human infection, he slices her body in the middle. In another sequence filled with sexual innuendos, Todd the repairer feels Malice's bare skin with his numerous tweezers-shaped hands. Even though the animation depicts a range of nonnormative bodies, the alignments with patriarchal authority bring to mind what Laura Mulvey famously termed "the male gaze."[106]

While *Malice@Doll* insufficiently questions this oppressive attitude based on gender, it also invites other types of alignments that demonstrate Malice's feminine agency. Before her transformation into a human, Malice was subjected to the sexual fantasies of her clients. In a flashback sequence, she remembers her past as a prostitute and her intimate encounters with clients. At the end of the sequence, she sees her former self uncannily staring back at her. After her transformation, Malice expresses her ardent desire to kiss and infect new partners with humanness. Thanks to imaginary transpositions, spectators can experience desire from Malice's perspective and encounter a variety of partners, including female dolls and masculine machines. The sequences of infection often take advantage of proxemics by presenting the female characters kissing, thus communicating to the viewers a sense of sexual intimacy. In one instance, a close-up displays Malice and Heather's tongues touching. On the soundtrack, we hear a wet licking sound, which sets an enveloping mood rather than an inquisitive one. An extreme close-up of Malice's eye turning red indicates that Heather has been infected. The sequence ends with a close-up on Malice's enigmatic smile. The smile underscores Malice's pleasure, while the canted lips and unexpected framing may represent her satisfaction to have disrupted normativity.

The subjective alignment of the viewer's perspective with the perspectives of dolls and robots enables embodied virtuality, an assemblage between human perception and technology, a topic examined in Chapter 2. The posthuman perspective reveals a continuum of differences and similarities between dolls, humans, and robots. During her stroll in the streets on her way to the repairer, visual effects that symbolize the shift from memories to reality confirm Malice's posthuman anatomy. When her flashback starts and stops, it causes momentarily distortions in the picture reminiscent of those produced by old-fashioned televisions. The translucent, horizontal lines going across the frame are accompanied by static sound effects on the soundtrack. Later, when Malice's perceptual system switches from machinic to human, the images seen through her eyes remain the same for the spectator. When human-Malice has a flashback, color-saturated pictures and glowing objects represent her memories as a doll. In contrast, the male robots' vision is depicted with overlaid charts. The different styles to represent memories and perceptions invite a reevaluation of the models we use to define identities in a world in which the boundaries between the human and the nonhuman are part of the same machinic assemblage.

Malice@Doll employs cross-modal effects to widen the spectator's field of empathic sensations. After Malice's transformation into a human, Heather@Doll, a nice and caring doll, wants to touch base with her friend. She does not follow the advice given by Doris, who has expressly forbidden her to meet up with Malice, whom she calls an imposter. Soon after Malice has given Heather a passionate kiss, Heather starts screaming. Her body jerks frenetically, and she begins to lose control of her arms and legs. The contrast between Heather's impassive face and her spasmodic movements is perturbing. Similarly, research has reported negative responses to jerkiness in the presence of both human-looking robots and animated characters.[107] When Heather falls on the floor, she tells Malice that her body is "going strange." A chaotic montage sequence of fast-paced shots shows streaks of red flesh covered with bumps bursting all over Heather's skin. Streams of uncovered muscles chaotically swirl, expand, and rapidly replace one of her arms. Wet noises of friction and lubrication accompany Heather's violent metamorphosis, which cross-modally supports the disgust evoked at the sight of her exposed bare flesh. Moreover, by avoiding the frontal position and focusing on Heather's shaking body parts, the mise-en-scène disorients viewers and reinforces an alignment with the character's frenzied experience. Although spectators do not actually experience Heather's pain, the visual excess inspires feelings congruent with those someone in Heather's situation could experience, including disgust and disarray. In this sequence, the fast-paced editing and sound effects are cross-modally associated with the frenetic bodily movements. They arouse cognitive and automatic physiological processes that share the general emotive orientation conveyed by the metamorphic narrative.

Malice@Doll blurs the boundaries between the inanimate and the animate and presents a continuum of similarities between the human and the machine. Imaginary transpositions in *Malice@Doll* encourage viewers to see human-Malice from the perspective of nonhumans, including Joe@admin, Doris, Todd the repairer, and Devo@Leucocyte. Cross-modal effects evoke Heather's distress as her mechanical body starts to malfunction. These stylistic devices help translate in the physical domain the process of rejection that the doll-turned-human is experiencing. In a more symbolic level, the "mechanical uncanny" can refer to a social process of marginalization toward physical difference, including people infected by sexually transmitted diseases. The reversal of familiar effects associated with kissing also reflects the problematic rejection in some social spheres of same-sex love. Although some of the traditionally marked "male fantasies" that this animation rehashes are highly questionable, *Malice@Doll* also portrays a variety of gender roles and gazes.

Reversal of Perspectives

By enticing spectators to adopt the perspective of nonhumans, many animations question the motivations behind using the human as a conceptual model of the self. This questioning echoes recent discourses on artificial intelligence and cognition that claim that robots and virtual images have become models for the living.[108] Roboticists Rodney Brooks and Lynn Stein, for instance, use the robot as a model for understanding human thought. In their article "Building Brains for Bodies," they "describe a project to capitalize on newly available levels of computational resources in order to understand human cognition."[109]

Malice@Doll employs a similar reversal of perspectives to exacerbate our anxiety about soon being replaced by machines—or even becoming machines ourselves. The vanishing gap between the human and the nonhuman can amplify our fear of the Other within and without, as synthespians have started replacing humans for many tasks. The possibility of replacing human traits with computer graphic imaging has become technically possible. For some time, films have been substituting synthespians for extras and popular actors lend their traits to cyberstars, as in *Beowulf* (Zemeckis, 2007) and *Assassin's Creed* (Justin Kurzel, 2016), a practice also widespread in video games. In trekking across the uncanny valley, animated films explore the delicate threshold between empathetic responses for likable cyborgs and the instinctive rejection of violent automata.

Malice's new human body embodies these fears. It is on the frontier between the human and the nonhuman. Her appearance disturbs both the inhabitants of the doll world and the human viewers. For the spectators, although she has turned human, her CG body is not verisimilar and instead approaches the uncanny valley. From the machinic perspectives of Doris and Joe, Malice defies the machinic order. For them, she looks strangely abnormal. Hence, Doris rejects Malice and Joe can't help but scrutinize her peculiar body. According to Freud's interpretation, the "human" is the model and the "inanimate" is the uncanny. When the model for the living becomes the robot, the "human" itself can be uncanny when it is too *robot-like*. Because Malice's metamorphosis interferes with Joe's and Doris's recognition subroutines, and this could partly explain their automatic rejection, she may also appear uncanny to them because she is different but still looks too *doll-like*. The film supports this interpretation because her *human* traits remain stiff and the texture of her skin resembles plastic, thereby suggesting the features of a doll. The reversal of the uncanny effects in this animation demonstrates that strangeness lies in the eye of the beholder.

While the reversal of perspective in Brook's research seeks a better understanding of cognition, *Malice@Doll*'s aim is ethical. Through imaginary transpositions, this animation demonstrates that we can learn to reject prejudices based on physical appearance. As seen earlier, evolutionary predispositions may explain uncanny feelings. According to this hypothesis, since bodily mutations can be symptomatic of a disease, responses such as disgust can be considered a self-defense mechanism. The reactions of the dolls to those infected by humanness resemble processes of marginalization of sick people or those who have marks on their bodies. The rejection of people because of their appearance or condition is highly questionable in modern societies. The uncanny, imaginary transpositions and cross-modal effects highlight the thresholds at which these processes of rejection are activated. Unlike a film like *The Curious Case of Benjamin Button*, which carefully camouflages its synthetic mutations, affective responses and emotional disturbances convey the tension at the limits of the human and the nonhuman.

Conclusion

Eerie effects in CG animations can exacerbate our intolerance for deviations from familiarity. According to Jentsch's intellectual principle, dread may arise when one doubts about the animate or inanimate nature of something. For instance, it happens when an apparently lifeless object turns out to be alive or when something alive, such as an automaton, is in fact self-animated. Falling into this category, masks and masklike facial expressions in 2D animation can defamiliarize the appearance of a character and raise doubts. In *Texhnolyze*, an animated series concerned with accessibility to prostheses, the mask evokes uncertainty about the limits between humans and their prosthetic extensions. The masks and masklike expressions could also allude to human insensitivity in Lukuss and the objectification of lower-class people.

In GC animation, the facial movements of synthespians can trigger disturbing responses when they deviate from familiar patterns of expression because we are particularly attuned to the geography of the human face. Scientific studies have shown that uncanny effects are most likely to happen when the highly realistic depiction of some facial regions stands out against regions that are more crudely rendered. This could explain why the glassy eyes of the young boy in *The Polar Express* look peculiar, since the rest of his face looks photorealistic. In contrast, Neytiri's eyes in *Avatar* do not attract as much attention, since the alien proportions of her entire face do not have to follow human standards. This rule, however, appears to have some exceptions. For instance, the disproportionately large eyes of Golum in *The Lord of the Rings* trilogy (Peter Jackson, 2001, 2002, 2003) evoke uneasiness despite his unearthly appearance.

The eerie feelings produced by the incertitude toward liveliness can be desirable in some narratives and unpopular in others. Accordingly, some animations featuring synthespians highlight their technological inscriptions, while others attempt to efface them. These choices may influence the ways that some spectators engage with synthespians. In *The Curious Case of Benjamin Button*, the erasure of technological inscriptions with sophisticated computer imaging helps the viewer's absorption in the narrative. Because it has become increasingly difficult to distinguish the synthespian from the human in some productions, viewers are less distracted by the presence of technological marks. We can appreciate the characters' performances in intimate scenes in *The Curious Case of Benjamin Button*. In contrast, *Final Fantasy: The Spirits Within* spotlights its technical mastery with extremely detailed close-ups of eyes and skin texture. The marks betraying the illusion of photorealism elicit uncanny feelings that support a narrative that promotes an inclusive ecology of biological and nonbiological entities.

Facial distortions can also contribute to expanding and varying the spectators' empathic schemas. For example, facial distortions and masks in the first episode of *Texhnolyze* cause effects of strangeness that are affectively congruent with the off-kilter ambience of the setting. Although the camera does not linger on Ischise's face during the mayhem sequence, as it is usually the case in scenes of empathy, the cross-modal elements vary the flow of affects in ways that initiate cognitive processing, physiological changes, and embodied experiences congruent with Ichise's suffering. While fast-paced editing in certain animated films can desensitize audiences by preventing the complete unfolding of the spectators' empathetic emotions, animation also develops alternative empathic schemas that can expand the audience's sensitivity rather than limit it. The editing techniques in the sequences analyzed from *Texhnolyze* and *Malice@Doll* heighten the synesthetic affect in ways that orient the spectators' responses and help spectators empathize with Ichise and Heather.

Malice@Doll also develops a somber argument about humanity's fate in a cybernetic society where vicious machines prey on innocent robotic dolls. As in *Final Fantasy: The Spirits Within*, the creepy feelings may heighten the audiences' unconscious anxiety of eventually being replaced by artificial forms of intelligence. This animated OVA series appeals to the spectators' emotions to foreground negative reactions toward marginalized people. As the mechanized doll Malice becomes human, she faces rejection from her kind, as the "human" appears uncanny to the other dolls. When she kisses same-sex nonhuman dolls, they suffer from violent convulsions and horrific mutations. Those infected by humanness adopt the form of grotesque creatures. The tension at the border between the human and the nonhuman is examined through imaginary transpositions of oneself into the place of the dolls. The reversal of perspective could be interpreted as an invitation to empathize with those who are physically challenged or those who see the world differently.

As demonstrated in this chapter, the uncanny in animation does not need to be avoided at all cost. Its integration within the structure of engagement can trigger reflections on human obsolescence in cybernetic societies or alert spectators to processes of discrimination toward marginalized people. While doubts can be formative, appearances can also blind us, as *Malice@Doll* suggests. In the final scene, Joe@Admin decides to trust his "feelings" and accepts to open up to Malice's point of view. After Malice transforms into virtual-Malice, she flies back from the heavens to give Joe a final kiss, as he too wanted "to see what Malice sees."

Notes

1 See Travers, "*The Polar Express*" and Noë, "Storytelling and The 'Uncanny Valley.'"
2 On eeriness in *Final Fantasy*, see North, *Performing Illusions*; Mathieson, "Let Me Be Your Fantasy"; Tunison, "Review of *Final Fantasy*"; and Travers, "Review of *Final Fantasy.*"
3 Rosenblum, *See What I'm Saying*, 177.
4 See Rosenblum, *See What I'm Saying* and MacDorman et al., "Too Real for Comfort?"
5 On the influence of composition on visual weight and patterns of looking, consult Freeman, *The Photographer's Eye*, 58–63.
6 Deutsch and Deutsch, "Attention," 84.
7 Rosenblum, *See What I'm Saying*, 179–189.
8 Stafford, *Echo Objects*, 77–89.
9 On the affect-eliciting properties of facial expressions, see Zillmann, "Empathy," 144–145; Kanwisher, "What's in a Face"; Tsao, "A Dedicated System for Processing Faces"; and Ekman, *Emotion in the Human Face*. On facial expressions, see also Tomkins, *Affect, Imagery, and Consciousness* and Izard, *The Face of Emotion*.
10 On facial mimicry in response to iconic representations, see Zillmann, "Empathy," 148.
11 See Hatfield et al., *Emotional Contagion* and Rosenblum, *See What I'm Saying*, 189–194.
12 See Likowski et al., "Facial Mimicry and the Mirror Neuron System" and Nummenmaa, "Is Emotional Contagion Special?"
13 On character responses in melodrama, see Smith, *Engaging Characters*, 166–173.

14 On the representation of the other's suffering in the media, see Zillmann, "Empathy," 161.
15 Zillmann, "Empathy," 161.
16 Stafford, *Echo Objects*, 77–80.
17 Ekman et al., *Facial Action Coding System.*
18 On observational attitudes and emotion in film, see Tan, *Emotion and the Structure of Narrative Film*, 182–189.
19 On the efference hypothesis, which is "the proposal that the universal recognition of facial expression implies an underlying innate emotion 'program' for each of a number of primary emotions," see Plantinga, *The Scene of Empathy*, 242.
20 On empathizing with characters we like, see Hoffner and Cantor, "Perceiving and Responding to Mass Media Characters," 83–91.
21 Zillmann, "Empathy."
22 On the emotional and affective appeal of close-ups in cinema, see, for instance, Bélazs, *Theory of the Film*; Deleuze, chapter 6, *Cinema 1*; and Tan, *Emotion and the Structure of Narrative in Film.*
23 Zillmann, "Empathy," 160.
24 On the salience of close-ups and their influence on empathy, see Grodal, *Embodied Visions*, 201.
25 Jentsch quoted in Freud, "The 'Uncanny,'" 227.
26 The Japanese name of No-face means faceless in English.
27 See Nun, "The Figure of Metamorphosis," 424–425.
28 On masks in Noh theater, see Sakabe, "Mask and Shadow," 245.
29 On cyberpunk culture and postmodernism, see Kellner, "Mapping the Present From the Future"; McCaffery, *Storming the Reality Studio*; and Bukatman, *Terminal Identity.*
30 Marks, "Weak Synesthesia in Perception and Language."
31 I borrow the term synesthetic affect from Plantinga in *Moving Viewers*, 157.
32 Reviews on the eerie effects produced by Tom Hanks' portrayal of the main protagonists in *The Polar Express* suggest that the stiffness of 3D CGI technology can hinder engagement, see Osmond, "Reviews: *The Polar Express*" and Travers, "*The Polar Express.*" On the effects of technology on character engagement in *Final Fantasy: The Spirits Within*, see North, *Performing Illusions*, 150–154.
33 North, *Performing Illusions*, 154.
34 Mori, "The Uncanny Valley."
35 Mori, "The Uncanny Valley."
36 Freud, "The Uncanny."
37 See Royle, *The Uncanny.*
38 Mathieson, "Let Me Be Your Fantasy"; Tunison, "Review of *Final Fantasy*"; and Travers, "Review of *Final Fantasy.*"
39 North, *Performing Illusions*, 155.
40 Creed, "The Cyberstar," 86.
41 Creed, "The Cyberstar," 82.
42 Scientists were invited to discuss the phenomenon of the uncanny valley on the radio program "All Things Considered," York, "Hollywood Eyes."
43 MacDorman et al., "Too Real for Comfort?"
44 The hypothesis is that monkeys increase their looking times of things that they prefer. For a more detailed description of the experiment, see Steckenfinger and Ghazanfar, "Monkey Visual," 18362.
45 Rosenblum, *See What I'm Saying*, 177.
46 MacDorman et al., "Too Real for Comfort?," 696.
47 Ho, "Human Emotion and the Uncanny Valley."

48 Rosenblum, chapter 8, *See What I'm Saying*. See also Green et al., "Sensitivity to the Proportions of Faces that Vary in Human Like-ness"; Kanwisher, "What's in a Face?"; and Laming, quoted in Mathieson, "Let Me Be Your Fantasy."
49 Rosenblum, *See What I'm Saying*, 179.
50 Ge et al., "The Lasting Impression of Chairman Mao."
51 Rosenblum, *See What I'm Saying*, 178.
52 Chaminade et al., "Anthropomorphism" and Krach et al., "Can Machines Think?"
53 Chaminade et al., "Anthropomorphism."
54 Oztop, "Human-Humanoid Interaction."
55 Gazzola et al., "The Anthropomorphic Brain."
56 Rosenthal-von der Pütten and Krämer, "Design Characteristics of Robot."
57 Tinwell, "Universal or Individual Response?" and MacDorman et al., "Individual Differences."
58 On mental schemas and dispositions that influence our allegiance, see Smith, *Engaging Characters*, 192.
59 On the work of iconography on our assumptions, see Smith, chapter 6, *Engaging Characters*.
60 Tinwell et al., "Facial Expression."
61 On the role of physiognomic iconography in the process of allegiance, see Smith, *Engaging Characters*, 191–193.
62 Smith, *Engaging Characters*, 192.
63 MacDorman and colleagues noticed gender differences when observers had to make a decision based on a situation involving CGI characters, see MacDorman et al., "Gender Differences."
64 Canemaker, "A Part-Human, Part-Cartoon Species."
65 Schwind et al., "An Uncanny Valley of Virtual Animal," 49.
66 Canemaker, "A Part-Human, Part-Cartoon Species."
67 Canemaker, "A Part-Human, Part-Cartoon Species."
68 Aida, quoted in Mathieson, "Let Me Be Your Fantasy."
69 Mathieson, "Let Me Be Your Fantasy."
70 See North, *Performing Illusions*, 151.
71 See Smith, *Engaging Characters*, 119.
72 Naremore, *Acting in the Cinema*, 213.
73 North, *Performing Illusions*, 152.
74 See, for instance, "Aki Ross, CGI Goddess" on http://www.angelfire.com/movies/akiross/, last consulted on April 23, 2011.
75 Creed, "The Cyberstar," 84.
76 North, *Performing Illusions*, 203.
77 Tunison, "Review of *Final Fantasy*."
78 North, *Performing Illusions*, 151.
79 Travers, "Review of *Final Fantasy*."
80 Creed, "The Cyberstar," 83–84.
81 York, "The Uncanny Valley." On the uncanny valley, see also Weschler, *Uncanny Valley* and Thompson, "Monsters of Photorealism."
82 Rosenblum, *See What I'm Saying*, 179.
83 Preeg quoted by Rosenblum, *See What I'm Saying*, 179.
84 Preeg, quoted in Rosenblum, *See What I'm Saying*, 178–179.
85 Preeg, quoted in Bradner, "Wizards of Hollywood: Steve Preeg."
86 Preeg, quoted in Bradner, "Wizards of Hollywood: Steve Preeg."
87 For more information on the process of creating photorealistic synthespians, see Bradner, "Wizards of Hollywood: Steve Preeg."

88 Preeg quoted by Rosenblum, *See What I'm Saying*, 184.
89 MacDorman et al., "Too Real for Comfort?" 698.
90 Seyama and Nagayama, "The Uncanny Valley."
91 MacDorman et al., "Too Real for Comfort?" 708.
92 Tinwell et al., "Psychopathy and the Uncanny Valley," 1617.
93 Ferrell, "Life-Treatening Life," 132.
94 Jentsch, "On the Psychology of the Uncanny."
95 Bukatman, "Disobedient Machines," 133 (emphasis in the original).
96 On the use of automata in Japanese and Chinese theater, see Brown, "Machinic Desires," 229–234.
97 For various sources of the uncanny in *Ghost in the Shell 2*, see Brown, "Machinic Desires," 223. On blurring life and death in animation, see also Cholodenko, "Introduction," *The Illusion of Life*. On the animatic automaton, see Cholodenko, "Speculations on the Animatic Automaton," *The Illusion of Life II*.
98 Pate, *Japanese Dolls*.
99 Long, "*Malice@Doll*," 158.
100 Long, "*Malice@Doll*," 167.
101 Long mentions the resemblance of the little Victorian girl in *Malice@Doll* to Alice. Konaka Chiaki, who wrote the script for this series, made "a collection of scripts for *anime*, video games, and live-action films, all of which are more or less overt homage to Lewis Carroll's *Alice's Adventures in Wonderland* (1865) and its sequel, *Through the Looking Glass, and What Alice Found There* (1871)" in Long, "*Malice@Doll*," 159.
102 Freud, "The Uncanny," 250.
103 MacDorman, "Too Real for Comfort?"
104 Pate, *Japanese Dolls*, 224–230.
105 See MacDorman et al., "Gender Differences."
106 On the male gaze, see Mulvey, "Visual Pleasure and Narrative Cinema."
107 On negative evaluation in the presence of human-looking robots, consult MacDorman and Ishiguro, "The Uncanny Advantage" and for the aversive effect of jerkiness in animated characters, see MacDorman et al., "Gender Differences."
108 See, for instance, Viseu, "Simulation and Augmentation."
109 Brooks and Stein, "Building Brains for Bodies," 7.

6 Algorithmic Couplings in Video Games

Introduction

Genetic engineering and biological modifications are at the heart of the video games *BioShock* and *BioShock 2*. The third *BioShock* video game, *BioShock Infinite*, features parallel worlds and explores the strange quirks of quantum mechanics. As the booklet accompanying *BioShock 2* puts it,

> Rapture was founded to allow the best and brightest of humanity to do their brilliant work unfettered by government, religion, or the mediocre. But the "every man for himself" philosophy led to war, fueled by a new substance called ADAM that allowed people to rewrite their DNA.[1]

BioShock and *BioShock 2* are set in the late 1950s and 1960s, before the discovery of recombinant DNA in 1973, a method that enables scientists to alter the genetic material in living organisms.[2] Rapture is a place of decay, filled with debris and trash. Mutilated zombies called "splicers," heavily armored cyborgs, and little girls called Little Sisters populate the underwater city. The players find audiotapes along their path, recorded by evil doctors responsible for a number of scientific experiments that went wrong. For instance, the scientists of Rapture created the Little Sisters. These little girls harvest corpses to recycle ADAM, a substance processed from a deep-sea parasite. When spliced to a host, ADAM produces new stem cells that can allow the host to take on external genetic modifications called Plasmids and Gene Tonics. Examples of Plasmids include Cyclone Trap, Electro Bolt, Incinerate, and Insect Swarm. Gene Tonics provide instant medical cures, esthetical enhancements, and increased hacking abilities. However, the overuse of these "quick fixes" scattered the memories of the inhabitants of Rapture and turned them into aggressive and paranoid zombies. The player's avatar—Jack in *BioShock* and Subject Delta in *BioShock 2*—needs to eliminate the bloodthirsty creatures that will not hesitate to kill him.

BioShock and *BioShock 2* promote their worldviews by engaging the player's body. Avatars in first-person shooters are tools that extend the player's perception.[3] The player adopts the perspective of the avatar and interacts with the various interfaces, which produces a hybrid between body and code. The avatar depends on the player's ability to control its movements. It also responds to the commands of the computer-controlled system that maintains its symbiotic relationship with the player. Because of these possibilities and constraints, playing video games enables varied patterns of sensorimotor experiences. The algorithmic couplings of the player's body and the avatar produce the dynamic forms of engagement with animated bodies that I have termed "becoming-animated."

As seen in the previous chapters, animation spectators can synthesize meaning from the assemblage of affects and technological elements involved in the animation machine. In video games, meaning emerges from constant interactions between the player's perceptual system and the video game components. To demonstrate this point, I analyze *BioShock* and *BioShock 2*, two first-person shooter games in which the player's avatar becomes a genetically enhanced killer. The players improve their fighting abilities by participating in numerous gruesome altercations, thereby undergoing physical transformations that parallel the avatar's mutations. As I argue, these video games not only adapt the player's body schema, but also persuade the player to question the technophilic philosophy of genetic alteration promoted by the denizens of Rapture, a dystopian world submerged under the ocean.

First, the chapter examines how the players accustom themselves to the interface as a first step toward the achievement of a perceptual symbiosis with their avatar. Perceptual symbiosis, however, is not sufficient to master the more complex moves and succeed in these games. The player needs to establish a form of algorithmic synchronism with the interface that requires a physical mastery of the different mappings. In addition, I investigate the mechanisms by which the video games supervise the narrative progression and communicate their message on the power of technology to condition bodies and minds. Notably, the representation of the technological body in these video games inspires the viewers to question the ethics of research on genetic enhancements. In *BioShock*, for instance, the body-technology alliance is presented as a necessity for the survival of the protagonist and by extension the human race. As the player transforms into a Big Daddy, it becomes a cyborg or, in other words, a "body in code." Not surprisingly, the weapons and prosthetic extensions worn by the avatar in the game mirror the physical equipment and interfaces used by the player. The idea of the programmable body conveyed by *BioShock*, and the fantasy of disembodiment it promotes, raises questions about the foundations of transhumanism and the steps we take as a species to preserve human evolution.

Avatars as Tools

The Avatar as a Logical Tool

Players actively explore the constraints of the game world and interact with it by mastering multiple physical interfaces and logical tools.[4] For example, when playing on a computer, the mouse is a physical interface, while the cursor is a logical (or software) interface. In this section, I draw on the article "Towards a Model for a Virtual Reality Experience: The Virtual Subjectiveness" by Narcis Parés and Roc Parés to describe the main components of the virtual environment (VE) and the game world, which is the actualization in real time of the structures of the game. These authors distinguish virtual reality (VR) from VE, because employing these terms interchangeably may cause some confusion.[5] Their definition of VE is an adaptation of an earlier framework established by Stephen Ellis in "Nature and Origins of Virtual Environments" that describes how the structure of the VE is put into action. Ellis distinguishes three major components in the VE: content, geometry, and dynamics.[6] The structural description of "content" stands for the sets of objects and actors in the environment, whereas "geometry" describes the numerical database. "Dynamics" concern the environment's underlying static sets of rules. Parés and Parés propose the term VR for "the case in which the VE is made to evolve over time."[7] According to their definition,

> a VE is not, by itself, associated with the user (in that it does not provide or generate anything) until it is put in action and interfaced with the user, so that it evolves over a period of time, during which the user perceives it and interacts with it.[8]

In my adaptation of Parés and Parés's framework to video games, I use the term "game world" to designate the actualization of the VE, and I replace "user" with "player."[9] Accordingly, the player of a video game "is confronted with a situation of *real time stimuli generation* that is guided by three main components: interfaces, mappings, and model."[10] The model of virtual subjectiveness in video games includes a player and his or her projection within the game world, which often takes the appearance of an avatar. An avatar in a video game is a digital body that allows the player to see objects in the game world from a particular point of view and to interact with this world in real time.[11]

Players intuitively extrapolate experiences of real-world image schemas—or patterns of embodied meaning—to movements their avatar can perform. For example, the SOURCE-PATH-GOAL schema mobilizes sensorimotor skills in the game world that differ from those mobilized in real life. Accordingly, players must manipulate the controller and use objects as points of reference in the game world to control the avatar's movements along a virtual path. Yet, because the game world lacks some sensory information, the interface compensates with maps or directional arrows, as in *BioShock*.

The players can take inspiration from their knowledge of the CONTAINER schema in real life to apply the concept to video games. The containers in the game world provide different types of affordances—possibilities for interaction—than those available in the real world. Even though the player cannot touch the walls and doors, the logical interface usually prevents the avatar from walking through them. In a typical scenario, the avatar is trapped in a locked room. Intuitively, the player understands the necessity to find an escape to reach the goal. More specifically, in *BioShock 2*, it can mean to equip one's avatar with the Electro Bolt Plasmid to successfully hack a door switch. Alternatively, Booker DeWitt, the avatar of *BioShock Infinite*, must gather lock picks along his path and request the help from Elizabeth to pick the locks attached to certain doors. When we play a new video game, the CONTAINER schema takes on a new meaning, one that applies specifically to our sensorimotor exploration of the game world.

Physical and logical interfaces mediate the player's experience and modulate the various movements of the avatar. The physical interfaces include input devices such as keyboards, mouse, sensors, and output devices such as displays and speakers. Some input devices can provide force feedback or tactile feedback.[12] For example, when Booker drinks the Devil's Kiss potion in *BioShock Infinite*, his fingers are set on fire and the controller begins to vibrate to communicate the effect of the Vigor on his body. Additionally, the logical interface fashions the "point of view from which the environment may be constructed."[13] More precisely, the logical interface is a software component that

> may define the viewing direction, field of view, the type of projection, whether it has stereo view, the hearing capacities, force feedback properties, and so on, and it may define its own appearance or representation (as in the case of an avatar).[14]

When the player moves the joystick forward, for instance, the logical interface enables the avatar to walk forward in the game world. Moreover, virtual cameras allow nonlinear exploration of game spaces.[15] Video games utilize them in a variety of ways, and most commercial video games rely on simple camera behaviors, some of which are: a following camera, an overhead view, a first-person point of view, and predefined viewing frames.[16] These camera behaviors provide perspectives that create an impression of presence in the game world depending on the type of game.[17] In the *BioShock* trilogy video games, the camera usually presents a first-person point of view. The player can see the arms of the avatar at the bottom of the screen holding weapons. The animation machine integrates the interfaces, the virtual cameras, and the avatar's behavior within the game structure and narrative, thereby contributing to the player's engagement with the game world and intensifying immersion.

Perceptual Symbiosis

One of the essential elements of a video game, mapping, links the physical interfaces to the logical interface. In doing so, mappings associate the player's motor system with the avatar's point of view. By enabling the player to share the perspective of an avatar over an extended period of time, first-person shooters encourage the development of a strong bond between player and avatar. As this section examines, this bonding facilitates the player's progressive adoption of the avatar's worldview in *BioShock 2*.

When I played *BioShock* 2, I used an Xbox 360 console to control the avatar's first-person point of view with a multidirectional handle. Also set in Rapture, the larger part of the story takes place eight years after the first game. Subject Delta, the main protagonist, is a Big Daddy revived by the Little Sisters. He must retrieve Eleanor, the Little Sister he was protecting before shooting himself while being mind-controlled by the evil Sofia Lamb. The lower halves of the metallic arms of Subject Delta are visible at the bottom left and right of the screen. His gait is clumsy because he wears a heavy metallic diving suit and a large diving helmet. Later in the story, Subject Delta occupies the body of a Little Sister and can observe the world through her eyes. It is as though the Little Sister's body had become Subject Delta's avatar, as she enables him to navigate Sofia Lamb's quarters, a part of Rapture he is forbidden to enter under his Big Daddy appearance. Seeing Rapture through the eyes of a Little Sister requires a different mapping for the same input devices. For instance, the new mapping modifies the haptic feedback provided by the controller and gives the impression that the Little Sister is bouncing around. When she navigates her way around the rooms, she perceives the environment from a low height. The two thin arms of a child replace the metallic arms of Subject Delta. Although the Little Sister is small and can therefore access objects left on the floor more easily than Subject Delta, she has more difficulty to gather scattered money and EVE syringes, perhaps because of the frailty of her body. Moreover, seeing through the Little Sister's eyes provides a strikingly unique perspective on Rapture. From her vantage point, Sofia Lamb's rooms are very colorful, decorated with white velvet drapes, red padded doors, ornamental carpets, swaths of crimson roses, and delicate moldings. However, when she gathers ADAM from a corpse, glimpses of the murky, decaying world of Rapture suddenly replace the glowing simulacrum produced by the merging with her body. The mapping of Subject Delta and the one of the Little Sister provide two very different subjective couplings of the player and the avatar.

Achieving a perceptual symbiosis with an avatar is not instantaneous. Similar to people experiencing *experiential* blindness, beginning players must learn to accustom themselves to the game world by moving around the space.[18] Enactive approaches to perception maintain that the perceiver's ability to perceive is constituted, in part, by the exercise of a range of sensorimotor skills.[19] For instance, we have a practical knowledge of the ways in which movement may bring a thing into view. Through attention, probing, and movement of the eyes, we enact visual content. Similarly, it is by moving the avatar's body around objects and moving the avatar's field of vision that one can acquire general information and depth cues about the space surrounding the avatar.[20]

For players discovering video games with a tridimensional perspective, controlling the motion of the avatar can be physically challenging. The inexperienced players need to master the joystick or the keyboard that will enable them to move around the environment and reach their goal, often under time pressure. The mastery of basic motor actions like walking straight, climbing stairs, and performing steep turns may require a considerable amount of time. When I started playing *BioShock*, for instance, I recorded a few thoughts on my blog. I described my experience of the somatic differences between moving in a real-life space and moving in the game world:

> I feel like a child who has to learn how to walk and orient herself. I am easily immersed in this universe and after some time I feel so dizzy that I need to stop. However, I never experience this sense of fusion with my avatar as I can't properly control it. There is always this frustrating [disconnection] between what I want to do and what I can achieve with the remote control. My jerky movements in the space constantly remind me that there is a divide between me and my avatar.[21]

In this example, I expressed my frustration at being physically challenged by the video game interface. Immersion in the video game universe was exhausting because the spinning and uncooperative body of my avatar made me sick.[22]

After having managed to control the avatar's body, the point of view attached to the avatar's perspective can intensify the impression of presence within the game world. The avatar in the *BioShock* trilogy is human(oid)-centered because it merges the look of the camera lens and the eyes of a character to create the associated "I."[23] While point-of-view shots in cinema display approximately what a character would see, the subjective shot in video games is intended to show the character's exact point of view. This type of shot "results in a rather extreme first-person point-of-view shot, where the camera pans and tracks as if it were mounted on the neck of a character."[24] *BioShock*, as other first-person shooter games, couples the subjective camera perspective with a weapon in the foreground. During the game, there are often so many factors to take into consideration, including keeping your balance, making sure that you do not get killed, reloading your weapon, and heading in the right direction, that the subjective shot amplifies the player's tension. These perceptual strategies reinforce the perception that the player *is* the avatar.

After playing a video game over an extended period of time, players can achieve a sense of perceptual symbiosis with their avatar. For example, after completing *BioShock*, I felt in control of my avatar; I was less under the impression that the game space was controlling me. Yet, when I started to play *BioShock* 2, I was still feeling insecure when I encountered new opponents such as the Brute Splicers. I handled clumsily unfamiliar types of tools, like the heavy drill, but the experience acquired during the first game had made the process of surmounting these difficulties easier. When I finished *BioShock* 2, I had started to enjoy a form of fusion with my avatar. Walking through the labyrinthine corridors and juggling between the numerous tools and weapons had become like a second nature. The discomfort that I used to experience when I was walking in the bulky suit of the Big Daddy in *BioShock* had given way to the feeling of walking "normally."

As in films, video games deploy strategies to dissimulate their posthuman natures. The vision from the point of view of the video game avatar is not interrupted by cuts, which can feel more realistic in a Bazinian sense.[25] On the subjective shots in *Strange Days* (Kathryn Bigelow, 1995), Steven Shaviro writes:

> Events unfold in real time, in a single take, from a single point of view. These sequences are tactile, or haptic, more than they are visual. The subjective camera doesn't just look at a scene. It moves actively through space. It gets jostled, it stops and starts, it pans and tilts, it lurches forward and back. It follows the rhythms of the whole body, not just that of the eyes. This is a presubjective, affective and not cognitive, regime of vision.[26]

As in *Strange Days*, the fact that the subjective perspectives in *BioShock* and other first-person shooters follow the rhythm of the whole body heightens the haptic quality of the medium.[27] However, the moving perspective in video games is caused and directly experienced by the operator. Unless the avatar dies, a cutscene is inserted, or the player decides to halt the game or access a menu, the gameplay is continuous and the interruptions are occasional. Moreover, the action unfolds in the present tense of the avatar. There is seldom questioning, as it is sometimes the case in *Strange Days*, about who is experiencing the events and when they happened.[28]

Although the continuous gameplay in video games enhances perceptual realism, the virtual camera subjectiveness is not like human perception. As the cinematic image, the video game image lacks perceptual effects such as a blinking aperture or better focus in the foveal region of the visual field. Stability and fluidity of the perceptual stimuli during fights depend heavily on the player's skills, as the image may jitter when manipulating guns and shooting targets. Similarly, the movements of the virtual camera in first-person shooters easily betray its machinic origin when one swiftly pushes and releases the toggle button. The mapping between the physical interface and the logical interface (the avatar), which coordinates the impression of seamless perception, is a necessary component of the cyborgean assemblage. Moreover, *BioShock* self-reflexively stresses the posthuman nature of perception in video games, since the avatar literally turns into a cyborg.

Video games present varied kinds of perceptual symbioses. For instance, the third-person perspectives in *Spider-Man 3* (Mark Nau, 2007) and *Lara Croft Tomb Raider: Anniversary* (Jason Botta, 2007) do not merge the perspective of the virtual camera with the point of view of the avatar. Yet, the camera in these games follows closely the movements of the avatar's body. They can simulate the experience of vertiginous nonhuman leaps and catastrophic falls. In *Spider-Man 3*, it is also possible to adjust the camera to see New York City from various angles and at different scales, enabling omniscient bird's-eye view perspectives.

Some remote controls feature vibrating functions, which can enable a more tactile relationship with the VE and the avatar. In *Lara Croft Tomb Raider: Anniversary*, when a huge dinosaur stomps next to her, the remote control vibrates to communicate the reverberations felt by the avatar. Alternatively, the injection of fresh EVE in the arm of the avatar in *BioShock* transmits the surge of energy to the player through a vibration in the remote control. Perceptual symbiosis is heightened by haptic feedback and synchronized perspectives, especially when they occur during life-threatening episodes or highly emotional moments in the narrative.

Adapting the Body Schema

We acknowledge that we have achieved a perceptual symbiosis with our avatar when basic tasks in the game world become second nature. The "remapping" of real-life sensorimotor skills has facilitated elementary actions in the game world such as moving forward, moving backward, and turning right or left. To perform even more complex tasks, including walking through disorienting mazes, fighting enemies, and solving puzzles, the players must remap other physical skills they use in real life to apply them to the game world.

The interactions between the physical interface and the logical interface create a hybrid between body and code. Mark Hansen's concept of "bodies in code" suggests that the systemic coupling between viewers and interactive media may "facilitate the actualization of the organism's potential to extend its bodily boundaries and to expand the scope of its bodily agency."[29] According to Hansen, the "body in code" shifts the focus from the purely informational body, as instantiated by a video game program, to "a body whose embodiment is realized, *and can only be realized*, in conjunction with technics."[30] I consider the "body in code" to emerge from the sensorimotor couplings of the player and the avatar when they perform actions in the diegetic environment. The "body in code" is therefore excluded from ambient acts, nondiegetic operator acts, nondiegetic machinic acts, and times when the avatar's movements are dissociated from the player's control.[31]

As Derrick de Kerckhove notes, "[i]nteractive systems are deeply expanded biofeedback systems. They teach us how we can adapt ourselves [*anpassen können*] to new sensory syntheses, new speeds, and new perceptions."[32] The body image and the body schema are functions that undergird this biofeedback system. The body image "is generated from a primarily visual apprehension of the body as an external object."[33] Body images include the subject's perceptual experience of her body, the subject's emotional attitude toward her own body, and the subject's general conceptual understanding of her body.[34] When the player interacts with other players during a game or explores uncharted game spaces, these representations are altered over time. A player's conceptual understanding of his or her abilities can change as the level of difficulty increases or decreases. For instance, obstacles in a game can be a source of frustration, whereas "gaining access to a coveted new space can create a heightened impression of player/player-character agency and of personal achievement."[35]

Hansen argues that particular artworks technically enable viewers/participants to utilize the excess of the body schema over the body image to increase their agency as embodied beings. In contrast to the body image, the body schema is the internal perspective of the organism. It is the body's power to construct space and world, thanks to its motile, tactile, and visual capability. More precisely, the body schema "is a suite of neural settings that implicitly (and nonconsciously) define a body in terms of its capabilities for action."[36] According to Hansen, the body's coupling with its environment is in excess of the body image. While the external physical envelope of the body image is relatively determined at a given moment, the systemic and sensorimotor couplings of the organism with the VE, by visually extending its reach or through spatial exploration, can momentarily expand the body schema. The player's usage of an avatar to interact with the game world brings to mind Merleau-Ponty's reference to the blind man's stick, since this tool extends his scope by incorporating the stick's range of action within his own boundaries.[37] The avatar can help the player succeed in his or her quest by extending his or her perceptual and physical reach because of its ability to gather objects, walk through mazes, or climb cliffs.

Media scholars Andreas Gregersen and Torben Grodal describe the neural underpinnings that inform these physical remappings and the resulting adaptation of our body schema. Drawing on research on the mirror neuron system to describe our embodied interfacing with video games, they explain that

> modulations in our embodied experiences may come in several interacting streams from the body (somatosensory and proprioceptive) and (audio)visual information related to motor pattern stimuli from outside that activate mirror neurons. Both of these systems may come into play when experiencing embodiment effects in relation to virtual environments. One allows us to feel our own body extending into the virtual environment through a kind of virtual tool-use; the other activates our own motor system as a response to observed motor patterns.[38]

In other words, audiovisual information about an avatar moving in the game world stimulates the players' mirror neuron systems, thereby inducing sensorimotor resonances. As mentioned in Chapter 1, some experiments demonstrate that macaque monkeys can assimilate tools in their body schema through extensive use. Similarly, because of the plasticity of our neural resources, we "automatically take account of new bodily and sensory opportunities."[39] These neural ramifications can be integrated into Parés and Parés's model of virtual subjectiveness because they result from the repetitive use of the physical interface. The body's interacting streams and the various elements that make up the virtual subjectiveness are closely intertwined variables that characterize the experience of the game world. The dynamic process of expanding the body schema via sensorimotor explorations enables players to produce meaningful, embodied remappings. Thanks to this process, they can absorb the narrative knowledge and sensory stimulation provided by the game world.

The integration of new mappings may demand extended practice, especially for inexperienced players. Like learning to play the piano or any other musical instrument, it takes time before the use of plastic neural resources creates and updates the body schema to reflect the newly acquired skills. Once an instrument has been mastered, reading musical notations and playing the corresponding notes become second nature. As Andy Clark puts it, the instrument "become[s] transparent in use."[40] Likewise, the process of mastering various interactions with an avatar induces progressive neural recalibrations and adjustments to the player's body schema. The sustained training of a player also causes deep neural changes, which are "required to fully exploit the new agent-world circuits thus created."[41] When playing a game, the player uses a physical interface such as a controller to maintain the avatar's balance and control its movements. Since the body schema involves patterns of cognitive processes that guide our action and maintain our posture, it helps coordinate the fingers of the player and their movements according to cues given by the environment. Such assemblages link the player and the game world, thereby forming "new systemic wholes."[42]

In video games, as we improve our ability to manipulate the various interfaces, we develop some unconscious automatisms that treat them as seamless extensions. For example, beginners must familiarize themselves with the controller before being able to jump and grab the edge of a cliff without falling in *Lara Croft Tomb Raider: Anniversary*. Because of Lara's particular mapping, it is advisable to consider her built-in physical abilities when overcoming various obstacles and gaining access to difficult areas. Inexperienced gamers must intuitively correlate fine finger movements with their experience of distance within the game world. They must practice throwing the grappling device in order to span gaps that are too wide for her to jump across. Other advanced movements involve jumping onto and perching on the tops of very small platforms. The player's experience and acquired mastery translate into the successful negotiation of obstacles and a quicker completion of the assigned tasks. Players must assimilate her mapping into their body schema to successfully complete the different levels. This process entails both a physical and a cognitive remapping of the player's finger-joystick coupling to the avatar's various movements and tool manipulation. The remapping of the body schema enables novel sensory and muscular experiences that reconfigure the player's agent-world boundary and extend their physical abilities. While Lara utilizes tools to ease her way, the player uses her as a tool to complete the game. The "body in code" in this example mobilizes a remapping of the player's finger-joystick coupling onto Lara's gestures to negotiate obstacles or travel around the game world.

We can think of the assemblage of the player and the avatar in terms of a temporary problem-solving ensemble—or a task-specific device—that is goal-oriented. According to psychologist Geoffrey Bingham, the body draws on various dynamic resources to effectively throw a ball. Part of those resources can be reassembled differently to row a boat.[43] Clark adapts this principle to cognition. He calls "transient extended cognitive systems" (TECSs) the problem-solving ensembles that achieve a specific objective. According to Clark, these

> larger problem solving ensembles are likewise transient creations, geared toward a specific purpose (doing the accounts, writing a play, locating a star in the night sky), and combine core neural resources with temporary add-ons such as pen, paper, diagrams, instruments, and so on.[44]

He maintains that the mind can distinguish between the biological parts of the system and the plug points that the prosthetic extensions are attached to. Further developing his thought about this interfacing, Clark explains that this

> would be analogous to the way the feel of prism goggles on the face has been shown to trigger a learned context-dependent adaptation so that skilled users can don and doff inverting lenses without missing a beat. [...] In sum, then, the existence of well-defined (and perhaps even self-represented) plug points in no way undermines the vision of cognition as embodied and as sometimes extended. For it goes no way at all toward showing that unified information-processing ensembles are not soft assembled across the plug points themselves. In the natural order, interfaces abound. There are interfaces within the brain, between brain/CNS and body, and between organism and world. What counts are not interfaces but systems—systems that may come into being and dissolve on many different timescales but whose operation accounts for much of the distinctive power and scope of human thought and reason.[45]

Adapting this systemic approach to video games, we can consider the player's body and the avatar's body as information-processing ensembles that interact via logical and physical interfaces during a game. The interactions between the player and the video game involve what John Haugeland calls a "low-bandwidth" coupling and "high-bandwidth" forms of agent-environment coupling.[46] On the one hand, the video game interfaces comprise discrete points of interactive contact, namely the buttons on the controller, the content of the screen, the sound effects, the menus, and the positions of the objects located in the game world. On the other hand, the sensory system of the player gets information from these interfaces to coordinate its response. As Clark argues, this extremely high-bandwidth form of coupling can create a "task-specific agent-world circuit."[47] With training, the player becomes able to develop his or her ability to respond to the multiple tasks involved in a game, yielding ongoing adaptive behavior between the player's body and the game world.

From these examples, we discover that an avatar is more than an animated picture joined to a logical interface; it is a tool that extends the self toward the game world via active remappings of the body's boundaries. Interactions with an avatar can enable the dynamic forms of engagement with animated bodies that I have termed "becoming-animated," as players can directly sense the effects of their training on the mutability of the interfaces separating them from the game world.

Algorithmic Couplings of the Player's Body and the Avatar

When one begins to master the physical interface and the logical interface of a video game, one can also notice enhanced reflexes and critical judgment in scenarios that require these skills. As Penny explains, in

> interactive media a user is not simply exposed to images that may contain representations of things and actions. The user is trained in the enaction of behaviors in response to images, and images appear in response to behaviors in the same way that a pilot is trained in a flight simulator.[48]

For instance, a person playing a first-person shooter for the first time must practice for many hours before being comfortable at walking, running, jumping, and aiming a rifle at the targets. The importance of disciplining the body to enhance one's skills is relevant to other types of motor activities, like dancing. However, in video games, as in flight simulators, it is important to establish sensorimotor couplings and algorithmic couplings with the interfaces. The sensorimotor coupling of the player with the video game avatar involves the player's action on the controller. When connected to the console, the controller produces direct effects on the game world. The player can move the avatar and access the menus made available on the screen. These mappings, which match the player's actions with responses in the game world, are realized, thanks to sets of instructions, or algorithms, that restrain the avatar's access to specific areas when certain conditions are met. Furthermore, the algorithms define the physical laws that apply to the game world. While the sensorimotor couplings of the player and the game world control the avatar's movements from the outside to the inside, underlying algorithmic couplings constrain the player's actions within the game world from the inside.[49]

Because the video game interfaces await the user's inputs to respond, players may have the impression that control operates in only one direction: from the player to the video game system. The subjective point of view in a first-person shooter reinforces this idea, giving the player the impression of being a homunculus in the brain of his or her avatar. When explaining the concept of the subjective shot, scholar Alexander Galloway notes that this type of shot "precisely positions itself inside the skull of that character."[50] The homunculus in the brain stands for that entity in control of our actions on the basis of the unitary self. Similarly, when Galloway refers to the player as the operator, he associates the operator with an entity that controls the actions of the avatar. The player, or the operator, uses the interfaces to distribute his or her agency at a distance among the components of the video game.

Yet, video game environments also devise a variety of strategies to "limit degrees of freedom" and control the movements of the player, including "soft" and "hard" boundaries.[51] Hard boundaries restrict the progression of the player in the game world. They are usually motivated by the scenario and may include walls, swamps, islands, and mountains. Soft boundaries are temporary barriers that act as obstacles for the player-avatar. The player can be granted access to these limited spaces under certain conditions. For instance, in *BioShock*, by hacking number locks and security cameras, Jack can gain access to restricted areas. Strategy guides are available online for those interested in overcoming obstacles faster. There are cheat codes for those playing the game on computers. By changing the code written in some files provided with the game, players can change the quantity of ammo they own or increase their power, thus bypassing the limits set by the system and exploiting the system to their advantage.

Additionally, algorithms monitor the interactions between players and the interfaces to anticipate and respond to the various actions of the avatar within the game world with visual, auditory, and haptic feedback. In *BioShock*, a directional arrow frequently appears at the top of the screen to indicate the quickest route to the next goal-oriented task. Although players can choose to ignore these indications—because they prefer to gather more money from corpses or hack a vending machine—these computer-controlled indicators foreground the presence of algorithmic structures that supervise the game's narrative progression and the outcome of the player's interactions within the game world.[52] The algorithmic structure is notably manifest when a player fails to proceed to the next level of a game and needs to painstakingly repeat the same sequence of actions to succeed. This form of disciplining the body pervades video games that center on the development of the avatar's athletic skills, such as *Lara Croft Tomb Raider: Anniversary*. Because of the level of difficulty of some intricate puzzles in this video game, players often need to repeat some bodily movements while tweaking others until they succeed in completely mapping the entire choreographic performance onto their body schema.

First-person shooters and war video games enforce a series of in-game rules that bolster particular behaviors with constraining algorithms. For example, while certain rules of interaction can regiment the protagonist's options when they interact with in-game colleagues and superiors, others may reward patriotic behaviors by awarding "honor" points. These mechanisms incite players to adopt behavioral schemas that accord with determined sets of values, which reflects a form of in-game policing that Ian Bogost has termed "the game's political simulation."[53] The in-game policing is achieved by implementing a set of procedural rhetoric, "a practice of using processes persuasively."[54] By comparing the processes that various games devised to reward the destruction of a target, such as obedience to the hierarchical chain of command and the acquisition of basic skills, one can unveil the game's ideological inclinations. For instance, while "*Counter-Strike* encourages the player to log as many skills as possible, *America's Army* players collaborate in short missions, such as rescuing a prisoner of war, capturing an enemy building, or assaulting an enemy installation."[55] In doing so, *America's Army* reveals its allegiance to strict, orderly military practices, while *Counter-Strike* gives players more freedom of choice in the matter of behavior. Likewise, these video games deploy mechanisms to punish deviant behaviors.

The Kafkaesque maze of rules for political video games or war video games is not all written down though. Instead, as Galloway points out, the player is "learning, internalizing, and becoming intimate with a massive, multipart, global algorithm."[56] Because "winning" is highly desirable, like love and money, this prospect engages players in learning more about their opponent—the computer-controlled engine—to outwit it. As Lev Manovich sums it up in *The Language of New Media*, computer games

> demand that a player execute [sic] an algorithm in order to win. [...] As the player proceeds through the game, she gradually discovers the rules that operate in the universe constructed by this game. She learns its hidden logic—in short, its algorithm.[57]

Video games such as *Civilization III* (2001) and *Sid Meier's Civilization Revolution* (2008) highlight the political realities of the network society, which roots its political and economic exchanges in the pervading networks of the informatic age.[58] While players implicitly interact with the game's algorithm when they deploy their strategy, they also "discover its parallel 'allegorithm.'"[59] As the players infiltrate the algorithmic logic of the system, they progressively reveal the underlying political processes. These video games allegorize the despotism and expansionist logic of civilizations through the ages. As the promotional blurb for *Civilization Revolution* puts it, in

> this game you match wits with the great leaders of human history in a struggle of warfare, diplomacy, commerce and technology. If you fail your civilization will be destroyed, your empire just a pathetic and sad footnote in the annals of history. But if you succeed, your glory will live forever![60]

As Galloway demonstrates, video games like *Civilization Revolution* teach us that a successful conquest of the world comes with the mastery of technology and its hidden politics. In video games, he argues, informatic control brings to the fore allegories of political power.[61] As the players of *BioShock* and *BioShock 2* discover the power of the code, they incidentally learn a tale about the humans' direct rule over the genetic code, a history closely intertwined with "the discourse of information and the technoscientific imaginary of communication and control systems."[62]

These reflections on procedural rhetoric and algorithmic control intimate that reading about a game's story, its strategy, and its multiple interactive options does not replace the acquisition of hands-on knowledge. To further develop Bogost's notion of procedural rhetoric, I argue that embodied concepts acquired by what Mark Johnson calls image schemas strengthen the gain of a detached perspective on the ideologies conveyed by the various structures of behavior and mechanisms of enforcement promoted by a video game. In *BioShock*, for instance, because Ryan Industries implements an individualist ideology rooted in machinic supervision rather than human interactions, it delegates surveillance tasks to a series of automated surveillance systems, especially rotating cameras equipped with movement detectors, DNA authentication mechanisms, and alarms activated by touching hidden triggers. Players progressively adopt paranoid behavioral patterns, notably by taking pictures of splicers with a research camera, enabling them to discover their enemies' vulnerabilities to certain weapons. Cautiously, players must develop the habit of taking pictures of splicers while they are close to their sharp-edged grips. When this pattern of behavior becomes second nature, we know that the system has successfully conditioned our bodies, like those of the evil scientists working for Ryan Industries.

The repetition of gestures and the honing of certain skills in video games and simulators produce new agent-world circuits that may enhance the abilities of the player to interact with similar interfaces in the real world. Because of these leakages from game to reality, military personnel use video games and flight simulators as training tools.[63] As Simon Penny explains in "Representation, Enaction, and the Ethics of Simulation," in

> the mid-90s, it was revealed that the U.S. Marines had licensed *Doom* from Id Software and built "Marine *Doom*," to use as a tactical training tool. The U.S. Army MARKS military training device is manufactured by Nintendo. It is highly reminiscent of *Duck Hunt* except the gun is a plastic M-16, and the targets are images of people, not ducks. More recently the Navy has been using *The Sims* to model the organization of terrorist cells. So in the spirit of "what's good for the goose is good for the gander," we are drawn to the conclusion that what separates the first-person shooter from the high-end battle simulator is the location of one in an adolescent bedroom and the other in a military base.[64]

Drawing on the sociologist Pierre Bourdieu's work, Penny establishes that these technologies of simulation are social technologies that facilitate the learning of bodily discipline and regimes of behavior. In *The Logic of Practice*, Bourdieu has established that we unconsciously internalize certain social behaviors, which, in turn, shape the ways in which a person acts in society. When fully involved in rituals and social practices, individuals are not consciously aware of an underlying quasi-logic that drives their actions. When roaming the labyrinthine corridors and interactive landscapes of video games with their avatar, players register new patterns of behavior that translate into new image schemas. Then, these embodied translations leak from game to reality and inform the way that the player orders the world.

Because players can internalize violent behavior through repetition, Penny claims that video games drill players to kill without discrimination, and like military VR training, they may desensitize players in the real world.[65] Playing games could thus prepare us to become skilled war machines and better strategic decision makers—intentionally or not. Multiple studies have found evidence that exposing children to violent video games can promote aggressive behavior.[66] While these effects are unfortunate, it is necessary to put into perspective the fact that adult players are experienced thinkers, not just acting from instinct, and that many factors besides video games can develop their empathy toward others.

Additionally, the video games *BioShock* and *BioShock 2* explore the ethics of violence in society. They imply that selfishness and addiction to power can turn people into irresponsible and highly aggressive citizens. Bluntly, players who repeatedly choose to harvest the Little Sisters instead of freeing them deserve a dark ending, while the other players can experience a blissful one.[67] However, these video games epitomize barbarity with irony rather than scrutinize the larger impacts of violent behavior and its detrimental effects on society. While violence is necessarily part of first-person shooters, other types of video games are nonviolent and educational. Depending on the type of video game, players can develop a variety of positive skills, including visual attention, puzzle solving, the sense of strategy, the speed of making decisions, the sense of orientation, and memory.[68] Although these cognitive gains do not justify exposing children to violent video games, especially because nonviolent games can provide the same benefits, violence in adult war games is often a necessary component to create a convincing theater of operations. In other words, violent actions can expose underlying ideological structures by engaging players in embodied explorations of meaning, bodily conditioning, negative haptic feedback loops, and corrupted reward systems.

Video games often ask more questions than they provide answers to the problem of ideological coercion.[69] For example, in an interview with the online video game magazine *GameSpy*, Ken Levine, the creative director of *BioShock*, highlights the importance of evaluating the moral implications of killing Little Sisters. Instead of giving players the possibility to shoot them, the game shows a poignant cutscene to deter players from removing the living slug straight from the Little Sister's body, which gives the player "a huge dose of the vital substance—but she will not survive the process."[70] The video game shows a close-up of a Little Sister that highlights her terrified facial expression and prompts the player to choose whether Jack should harvest the girl or not. As Levine notes, "those sequences are either more moving than you would expect, or brutal, depending on which path you take. It's not prurient violence; it's not about the action, but really the decision that you've made."[71] The rhetorical form in this video game appeals to the player's empathy to further his or her "humanism" for posthumans.

Embodied Meaning in Video Games

The transhumanist idea that one day we will be able to upload the content of our brains into thinking machines, or Richard Dawkins' claim that life is the product of executed lines of code, is at odds with phenomenological approaches to life. Video games enable players to experience fantasies of disembodiment and interact with algorithmic logic via deeply embodied alternative forms of subjective perspectives. As players explore the game world, they develop their ability to use cyborgean technology by interacting with the interfaces. Repeated movements introduce new sensorimotor patterns into their body schema and thereby improve the player's chances of survival. When involved in the political worlds created by *BioShock*, the sensorimotor coupling of the player with the interfaces can translate image schemas into embodied knowledge. This concrete knowledge helps players grapple with concepts such as "bodies in code," "survival of the fittest," and "genetic determinism." The bodily pairing between players and avatars enables enactive forms of understanding of the in-game space and world.

The player's dispositions, which include personal character and habits, are important factors to take into consideration when describing the ways that meaning can emerge in the mind of the player. With his psychological model of reception, Persson proposes a multileveled approach to discourse analysis that emphasizes "the *mental* nature of meaning and its production."[72] Although Persson's approach is designed with cinema in mind, the levels that concern the psychology of moving pictures in general can apply to video games. In addition, the player's dispositions contribute to making sense of the textual and procedural cues given by the game. *BioShock*, for example, tests the player's ethics. The player can choose to rescue the Little Sister or harvest her. Yet, even though players draw on their real-life experience to understand the scenarios presented in a video game, as they do in cinema, they do not "make use of identical set of dispositions in both realms (there are discourse-specific dispositions)."[73] For instance, some sets of values and stereotypes that are associated with film and video game genres do not directly match real-life experience. Moreover, the player knows that potentially disastrous consequences for a character in a video game would not apply to a real-life situation.

BioShock draws on iconographic elements from various genres to convey its grim message. Low-key lighting reminiscent of German expressionism, grotesque characters in deranged emotional states, labyrinthine corridors, and skewed designs create the anxiety-ridden atmosphere of Rapture. The explosive piano sequence in *BioShock* reuses mood cues from film noirs, a genre of film particularly popular in the 1940s and 1950s. The noir mood is characterized by anxiety, paranoia, corruption, and violence. Even the music score alternates between lounge and jazz music from that period and a nightmarish fast-paced thriller beat. The combination of stylistic elements supports a discourse that critiques the corrupt and selfish individuals that produced Rapture.

Furthermore, the player's movements and affects can modify the game's emotional impact. There are feedback effects triggered by the player's avatar when certain conditions are met. For example, the players can directly affect the camera framing with their bodily movements. When the players approach a Big Daddy or a Splicer, they heighten their threat and consequently become more concerned for their avatar's life. The disposition-equipped player is not only processing discourses with his or her brain but also producing them. In addition, players can acquire knowledge from information stored in menus and audio diaries in the rooms visited by the player or in the game files. The audio diaries contain personal information recorded by the characters. With their avatar, players can interact with the multifaceted programmable elements composing the logical interfaces and thus participate in the constant and dynamic emergence of meaning.

Optimized Eugenics in Rapture

Playing *BioShock* and *BioShock 2* provides a range of options to somatically apprehend current debates on genetic modification.[74] By implying that human genetic alteration is a process as easy as customizing the pieces of code that compose one's avatar, these video games mirror anxieties over bioengineering technologies found in cultural media.[75] In *How We Became Posthuman*, N. Katherine Hayles examines the influence of the emergence of artificial life on the liberal humanist subject, and for most of the researchers in this field, we must envision "humans as information-processing machines, especially intelligent computers."[76] However, as I argue later, despite the algorithmic structure underlying the concept of life in these video games and the coded nature of the avatar's body, the player's enactment of the survival scenarios complicates Richard Dawkins's idea that "[l]ife is just bytes and bytes and bytes of digital information."[77] Although molecular biology has demonstrated that genes are part of a complex network of biochemical events that specify the phenotypic characteristics of a cell, it also stresses the influence of environmental factors on their expression and the overall development of an organism.[78]

The story of *BioShock* conveys the metaphor "DNA is code" and legitimates genetic determinism, or the idea that humans are the sum of their genes.[79] The proponents of genetic determinism popularize the view that not only phenotypic traits, but also complex behaviors and memory can be hardwired into our DNA.[80] While some scientists in popular films resort to genetic manipulation to change complex behaviors, such as removing animalistic instincts in the case of the three film adaptations of *The Island of Dr. Moreau* (H. G. Wells, 1896), *Island of Lost Souls* (Erle C. Kenton, 1932), *The Island of Dr. Moreau* (Don Taylor, 1977), and *The Island of Dr. Moreau* (John Frankenheimer, 1996), scientists in *BioShock* and *BioShock 2* offer the citizens of Rapture the opportunity to change their genetic makeup with instant gene therapy and superpowers.[81]

At first, the founder of Rapture and Ryan Industries, Andrew Ryan, hoped to solve the problems of humanity with objectivist principles and scientific advancements. Ryan selected the brightest individuals to contribute to his utopian society. After the discovery of ADAM, he embraced the opportunities offered by the new eugenics and built Ryan Amusements to promote the superiority of Rapture to the youth. As demonstrated in the park ride Journey to the Surface, he despised social programs and called Parasites those from the surface who benefited from them. The early proponents of eugenics believed that social programs were inefficient solutions to social inequalities.[82] Rapture's eugenic practices started with the selection of new members among the fittest. They subsequently evolved by developing various methods for improving people's genetic makeup and then producing superior warriors when the Civil War erupted. Although the scientists of Rapture supported the ideology associated with the new eugenics, players are encouraged to discover the limitations of this viewpoint by participating in the various scenarios proposed by the video games.[83] Notably, *BioShock* advocates the importance of an alliance of the human with technology to overcome the supremacy of the gene. This video game uses procedural rhetoric and embodied stimulations to stress the necessity of this alliance.

BioShock's elaborate narrative and evil characters present both positive and negative views on "optimized eugenics." Dr. Steinman's Aesthetic Ideals deploys the rhetoric of technoenchantment to offer the citizens of Rapture a utopian world of heavenly perfection. According to the technoenchantment view, technologies "are represented as the vehicles of ascent to a higher plane, the artifices of divinity, a harnessing of elemental powers."[84] On the walls of the Medical Pavilion, players find multiple posters that promise beauty and symmetry with the help of genetic modifications. In one of his audio diaries, Dr. Steinman states, "Today I had lunch with the Goddess. 'Steinman,' she said... 'I'm here to free you from the tyranny of the commonplace. I'm here to show you a new kind of beauty.' I asked her, 'What do you mean, Goddess?' 'Symmetry, dear Steinman. It's time we did something about symmetry.'" The religious motifs are recurring throughout *BioShock*. For Andrew Ryan, Rapture was a paradise free from the Parasites, the result of his quest for divinity through science. At the end of *BioShock*, the heavily spliced Frank Fontaine is able to summon the elements: fire, ice, and lightning. Before he dies, his body is harnessed to a machine with open arms, a position reminiscent of the Christ on the cross.[85]

Despite its many references to God, Rapture has more the appearance of Hell than Heaven. *BioShock* and *BioShock 2* associate the degradation of the self with genetic alterations. After the Civil War, the posters promoting genetic alterations are exhibited around areas covered with blood. The multiple corpses lying in the vandalized operation rooms in the Surgery allude to gruesome surgical processes instead of blissful flamboyance. After Dr. Steinman started to take ADAM, the multiple splicing scattered his mind, and he became obsessed with his own distorted sense of beauty. Moreover, the mutilated patients of Dr. Steinman who were looking for esthetic improvement must have been disappointed when they started to transform into deformed zombies. The grisly settings reflect the disenchantment view, which purports that "technology will bring about alienation and dehumanization, the erosion of the spiritual essence of humanity."[86] *BioShock* and *BioShock 2* pummel the players' senses with visions of horror and tense musical scores, which remind them of the finite body that controls their virtual self—their own.

Similar to the genetic engineers of Rapture, transhumanists have wished to overcome human finitude and death with the help of technology. For instance, French Anderson, a transhumanist and leading practitioner of gene therapy, claims that genetic engineering only alters our body, not our humanness:

> "since we can only alter the physical hardware, we cannot alter that which is uniquely human by genetic engineering [...]. We cannot alter our soul by genetic engineering." However, much we might manipulate the physical, material components of our living beings, therefore, our essence survives untouched—"the uniquely human, the soul, the image of God in man."[87]

In contrast, *BioShock* challenges the idea that the soul remains unaltered by genetic modifications. After having been genetically modified, the denizens of Rapture become bloodthirsty creatures that act on instinct, not from spiritual motivation. Various stylistic and narrative elements in the game underscore these contradicting discourses on eugenics. On the one hand, the video games suggest that we can transcend physical limitations, thanks to genetic manipulations. On the other hand, these enhanced powers come with a price, as those affected inevitably lose their sanity. As the next sections suggest, the player learns these lessons by transforming into a hybrid between a human and a machine.

Body-Technology Alliance in BioShock

The close encounters between the organic body and the technological body depicted in the three *BioShock* video games are fictive versions of the numerous *vital machines* that cross the boundaries between the organic and mechanical worldviews in our era.[88] In *The Vital Machine*, historian of science David Channell has coined the term "vital machines" to reflect the 20th-century revolutionary developments in systems building, computer science, artificial intelligence, cybernetics, and genetic engineering. There are two main paths that led to the rise of the vital machine. On the one hand, "systems that were predominantly mechanical have been transformed by assimilating elements of the organic, while on the other hand, systems that were essentially organic have been transformed by assimilating elements of the mechanical."[89] Offspring of the vital machine, such as artificial organs, cellular automata, artificial life, and human-made organisms, are systems that blur the line that used to clearly distinguish biology from technology. As Channell demonstrates, the mechanical and organic worldviews of the 19th century were unable to reconcile a series of scientific breakthroughs that upheld that technology was both mechanical and vital, and that a living organism was both vital and mechanical.[90] The new bionic worldview, in which machines can substitute for organic processes and organisms can substitute for machines, accurately describes the futuristic world of Rapture.

BioShock promotes an alliance between body and technology to vanquish Fontaine, the mastermind who invented "optimized eugenics." The perceptual alignment with an avatar is one way for *BioShock* to convey its rhetoric. Achieving a perceptual symbiosis with the first-person shooter avatar is required to survive the numerous threats of Rapture.[91] In real life, the joystick and the video game interfaces must become seamless extensions to the player's body. In the game world, Jack juggles between prosthetic enhancements and genetic augmentations to prevail against his enemies and fulfill his missions. Once the avatar is equipped with biotechnological enhancements and weapons, the player must learn the specific survival techniques and behaviors required by the newly augmented body.

The player enacts the metaphor "man is a machine" as the avatar takes on prosthetic extensions and genetic augmentations to become a Big Daddy. This technological hybridization evokes feelings of strength and conveys erotic connotations. Since Marshall McLuhan's seminal *Understanding Media*, scholars have described the relation between the body and technology with multiple metaphors. In her writing about wearable technology, Anne Cranny-Francis notes that already in the 1980s, the power suits and head-mounted gears that were worn in virtual reality were erotic objects of power produced for male pleasure.[92] Extensions, a concept that described the human-technology relationship in that era, were mainly tools that emphasized phallic dominance. Cyborgs from *Star Trek: Voyager* (1995–2001), the Cybermen episodes of *Doctor Who* (2006), and the James Cameron's *Terminator* characters, Cranny-Francis suggests, borrow the metaphor of prosthetic enhancements to perpetuate erotic fantasies of power. In *The Matrix* trilogy (Lana Wachowski and Lilly Wachowski, 1999, 2003), another trope is evoked, the metaphor of augmentation, to highlight the hybridity of the human and the machine and the ability of this alliance to channel the power of the divine.

In *BioShock*, the profound intermingling of bodies and technology emphasizes the darker side of the cyborg.[93] Instead of evoking the liberatory concept of the cyborg promoted by Donna Haraway in her "Cyborg Manifesto," in which she strives to unite women against the inequalities that developed under patriarchy by making gender obsolete, the cyborg in this video game recalls *The Terminator* (James Cameron, 1984) and *RoboCop* (Paul Verhoeven, 1987), two films representing the cyborg as a weapon of mass destruction. The injection of a serum called EVE gives Jack the ability to use Plasmids and assimilate instant genetic modifications. With the Insect Swarm Plasmid, the protagonist can send a swarm of bees toward an enemy (see Figure 6.1). With the Incinerate Plasmid, the hand can throw a stream of flames to set people on fire. Alternatively, the Winter Blast Plasmid can freeze objects and people instantaneously. In addition to having become a killing tool, the body acts as a surviving tool. Some Gene Tonics enable Jack to boost his body's natural abilities, making it resistant to specific types of damage. Other tonics, such as engineering Gene Tonics, can enhance Jack's intellect and dexterity, allowing him to carry out tasks like hacking Rapture's security systems. The player shares the increased powers acquired by the avatar, as his or her ability for hacking tools and switching between weapons and Plasmids improves over the course of the game.

Even though the avatar's symbiosis with a powerful machine exemplifies godlike powers, it also calls attention to the finitude and limitations of the body. The player must quickly master the rules of the game to maintain his or her avatar alive. With the help of various controls and

Figure 6.1 The Insect Swarm Plasmid. Screen capture from *BioShock* (Ken Levine, 2007).

indicators, the player constantly monitors the physical state of the avatar. Close observation of the surroundings is necessary because even a second of inattentiveness can be fatal. As an example, a review of the game *Burnout* cautioned players: "[Try] not to blink. Blink and you'll almost certainly hit something."[94] The constant monitoring of Jack's vital signs encourages a strong bond between the player and the avatar. This close tie heightens the player's concern for the avatar's safety and modulates the player's flow of affects as the threat increases or decreases. Perceptual symbiosis is one of the many strategies that ensure the player's allegiance and the avatar's survival.

The Programmable Body

In *BioShock* and *BioShock 2*, the players transform into cyborgs and interact with the worldview of Rapture, thanks to the symbiotic relation they develop with their avatar. The technological enhancements and the genetic augmentations in these video games reinforce conceptions about the programmability of the self. Late 20th-century interrelated discourses on evolution and synthetic life have promoted the centrality of "programs" in definitions of life processes and human biology.[95] The idea that the body is programmable is doubly pervasive in Rapture. On the one hand, DNA, with variable sequences of four nitrogenous base pairs, has become a metaphor for a genetic code that is expressed as the phenotype. On the other hand, the video game avatar is a digital body that can be duplicated, copied, and erased: it is a "body in code."

BioShock and *BioShock 2* parallel the body of the future with an electronic gadget that can be upgraded simply by uploading a new plug-in. Rapture's expendable and computerized version of the self supports the postvital view that life is only a playback of encoded sequences of events. Furthering this idea, numerous vending machines sell genetic alterations like cheap add-ons, making these commodities widely available in Rapture (see Figure 6.2).

The digital body simulates the appearance of the living. Some films and animations perpetuate worries about genetic alteration and cloning, as illustrated by *Species* (Roger Donaldson, 1995), *Alien: Resurrection* (Jean-Pierre Jeunet, 1997), *Teknolust* (Lynn Hershman-Leeson, 2002), *Genetic Admiration* (Frances Leeming, 2005), *The Island* (Pavel Lungin, 2006), and *Splice* (Vicenzo Natali, 2009). Film scholar Jackie Stacey contends that the concerns over "the animation of cellular life at the genetic level" appear "at a moment where the mutability of the body coincides with the mutability of the image."[96] As discourses on postvital organisms imply, DNA replicates information and animates the organism.[97] Following a similar pattern, video games program digital organisms and computer-generated animations sew together pieces of code. Thanks to digital cloning, *The Matrix Reloaded* (Lana Wachowski and Lilly Wachowski, 2003) brought an army of virtually cloned Smiths to life in its famous "Burly Brawl" sequence.[98] While

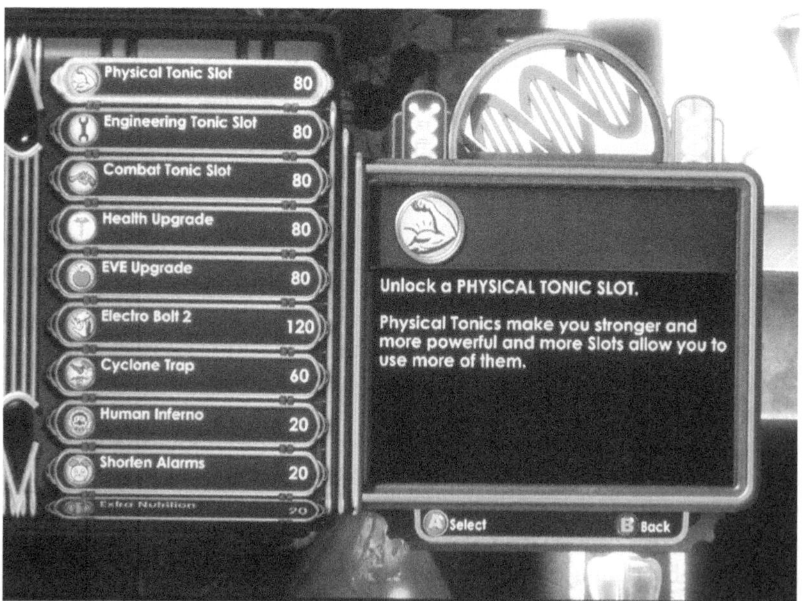

Figure 6.2 Genetic alterations and Physical Tonics are sold like cheap add-ons. Screen capture from *BioShock* (Ken Levine, 2007).

the algorithms of these video games do not model a genome, as genetic algorithms do, they determine the particular behavior and appearance of a digital body—the avatar. Although players can manipulate their avatar in a variety of ways, it only reacts according to predetermined forking paths and options. Similar to an organism that executes code to exist, the avatar corroborates the view that "the postvital organism is nothing but coding."[99]

In *BioShock*, when revived in Vita-Chambers, Jack comes back from the dead with the same possessions, abilities, and data banks. This form of instant cloning or magical reanimation intersects with a background of scientific plausibility. The mysterious process revives the desires of early modern alchemists who wished to give life to inanimate matter.[100] Instant reincarnations in *BioShock* are also recent examples of the fantasies of disembodiment and materialization found in Jeffrey Sconce's *Haunted Media*. Sconce demonstrates that "the shared electrical basis and apparent electrical transmutability of the body's flow of consciousness and flows of information in the media have produced a remarkably consistent series of cultural fantasies."[101] The last thing the players see before reappearing in a nearby Vita-Chamber is an overwhelming flash of white light that dissolves the objects in their field of vision. This visual effect insinuates that the avatar's body disintegrates into coded particles of energy that fly to the closest Vita-Chamber, which could instantaneously clone a replica of information stored in the corpse's DNA molecules. From the player's perspective, the disintegration and duplication of the pixels forming the image correlate with the in-game manipulations of the material body of the protagonist. These fantasies of disintegration and duplication suggest that there is a way to acquire "information" that can replicate an entire body—the DNA molecules for the human body and the computer code for the avatar.

Players not only watch their avatar undergo disembodiment, but also feel transported into cyberspace themselves. In his analysis of corporeal pleasures in video games, Martti Lahti maintains that one of "the most often repeated and taken-for-granted assumptions in much writing on 'cyberspace' is revealed in a tendency to treat new media, games included, as machines to realize desires for bodily transcendence, that is, an 'out-of-body' experience."[102] A sense of ecstasy and liberation may engross characters that jump into cyberspace, for instance, when Case succeeds in penetrating the corporate matrix in the cyberpunk novel *Neuromancer* (William Gibson, 1984). The devices connecting the players to their avatars, especially wires, wireless remote controls, and keyboards, may further the impression of an informational flow streaming from their bodies to the game world. The player's symbiotic relation with the avatar may evoke the idea that the flow of consciousness may exist without an underlying organic body, a notion directly rooted in Descartes's dualism.[103] According to the metaphysical view that separates the material body from the mind, we could identify the player with the soul—or the mind—of the digital body of the avatar. As digital images can be cut, copied, and pasted, avatar bodies can disappear, disintegrate, and rematerialize. During this process, the soul—or the player—is not affected.

With the possibility to rematerialize at will, the *BioShock* video games suggest the possibility to overcome death. Desires for the transgression of human finitude and its physical confines abound in literature about cyberspace. Likewise, the theme of rematerialization pervades animation in general, with its numerous shape-shifting characters that stretch, mutate, or explode and just reappear the way they were before—without even a scratch. More than with animated characters, the avatar in video games highlights the protean nature of the animated body and its function as a stand-in for the programmable body.

In summary, the players of *BioShock* and *BioShock 2* learn the meaning of genetic engineering by experimenting with various scenarios of bodily transformations. These video games imply that human genetic alteration is a process as easy as customizing the pieces of code that compose one's avatar. They rely on various strategies to convey their rhetoric. One of them, the production of a perceptual symbiosis with an avatar that transforms into a Big Daddy heightens character engagement. Perceptual symbiosis also improves the understanding of the narrative and the avatar's feelings. These video games also intimate that the player's body is programmable like the body of the avatar with imagery of instant cloning and digital reincarnations. Yet, as the next section demonstrates, despite the efforts of Ryan Industries to convince the citizens of Rapture that optimized eugenics is the solution to social problems, the player's survival, thanks to the mastery of innovative technologies, may suggest otherwise.

Becoming a Big Daddy

Grim mise-en-scènes and the progressive metamorphoses of the avatar's body into a sanguinary individualist machine somatically persuade the players of *BioShock* to reject Rapture's technophilic philosophy of genetic alteration. While becoming desensitized warriors is not a particularly attractive prospect, this video game instructs players about neo-Darwinian ideology and the survival of the fittest. Players must master an elaborate user interface to quickly learn Rapture's underlying politics, orient themselves in labyrinthine tunnels, and properly handle the various weapons. The mastery of technology and a close collaboration between player and avatar are necessary to ensure the survival of the protagonist in his deadly quest against evil trickery.

At first, Jack, the *BioShock*'s main protagonist, follows an "every man for himself" type of philosophy inspired by Ayn Rand's objectivism.[104]

Simultaneously, this video game employs somatic and visual effects to critique genetic alterations, as well as the corrupt and selfish individuals who rule Rapture. Through procedural rhetoric, the video games encourage players to develop hacking skills to outwit weaker enemies and progress to the next quest. Jack also needs to inject various Plasmids to acquire the superpowers necessary to survive in the hostile neighborhoods of Rapture. Instead of remaining at the level of a concept, the dangers associated with "genetic modifications" are enacted throughout a series of painful scenarios. For instance, in one of the cutscenes, the player is given the option to harvest the Little Sister or rescue her. While Atlas tries to convince Jack that they are no longer human, and he needs the ADAM they carry to survive, Dr. Tenenbaum pleads Jack to spare the life of the innocent child in return for her favors. When the player chooses to harvest the little one, she tries to fight back and pushes Jack away. The sequence is heart wrenching and the wriggling slug extracted from her dead body is disgusting. Mental conditioning is another strategy that the evil Fontaine, posing as Atlas, uses to control Jack. Unwittingly brainwashed, Jack performs the actions dictated by anyone saying the triggering phrase "Would you kindly." While *BioShock* forces players to make various unethical choices to ensure the survival of their avatar—or the success of their enemy—it also teaches the importance of negotiating one's own position within larger debates on free will and genetic determinism.

In addition to playing out scenarios about the risks associated with genetic engineering, the player can experience the laborious transformation into a cyborg. Genetic modifications are not purely informational or transparent processes unnoticed by the organism, but infectious processes that inflict excruciating pain. When Jack injects EVE into his arm, for example, the substance causes black necrotic spots to spread over his skin, concurrently illustrating a gain of strength and decay. When the skin bursts apart, the player's remote control starts vibrating, evoking Jack's pain and his simultaneous surge of energy. Somatic and visual effects representing the effects of genetic modifications on Jack's body draw the player's attention to the effects on his or her own body. The metamorphosis experienced by the player is meant to be particularly painful, unpleasant, and unsettling.

The progressive metamorphosis of Jack into a Big Daddy is paralleled by the player's physical adaptation to the newly acquired mappings. Players benefit from the increased "technical skills" of the avatar, often acquired by drinking Gene Tonics, while they improve their dexterity at hacking turrets and safes. While the repetitive, gruesome altercations hone Jack's fierceness in battle, the players perfect their ability to aim and their weapon-switching speed. As Jack put additional prosthetic devices on his body, he and the player start to experience the surrounding environment from an altered perspective. For instance, after having put on the bulky metallic diving suit, it becomes more difficult to swiftly move around, as the system slows down the pace of the avatar. In addition, each step is accompanied by a thudding echo that reflects the added weight. When the avatar puts on the metallic diving helmet, a circular mask around the screen simulates the opening in front of the helmet (see Figure 6.3). Although these modifications have been "coded" in the system, from the player's perspective, the changes are not only informational: they are directly felt by his or her body.

The world of Rapture depicts the dystopian consequences of the unregulated capitalist exploitation of genetic modifications. At first, with an affordable payment plan from Surgical Savings, everybody could benefit from a cosmetic surgery at Dr. Steinman's Aesthetic Ideals. With Plasmids, consumers could light a cigarette with the tip of their finger or light a lamp by zapping it with electricity. According to Ryan, men should not be slaves from nature but take their future in their own hands. As Ryan explains in one of his diaries,

> What is the difference between a Man and a Parasite? A Man builds. A Parasite asks, "Where is my share?" A Man creates. A Parasite says, "What will the neighbors think?" A Man invents. A Parasite says, "Watch out, or you might tread on the toes of God..."

Although Plasmids were first intended as harmless genetic optimizations, selfishness and widespread corruption led to a genetic arms race. Moreover, the progressive symbiosis between player and avatar in *BioShock* undermines the view that human animals—and other nonhuman

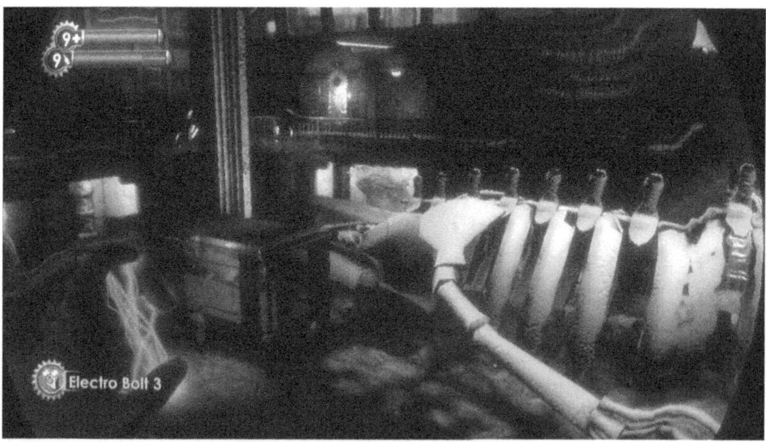

Figure 6.3 Seeing like a Big Daddy. Screen capture from *BioShock* (Ken Levine, 2007).

creatures—are nothing more than their genetic makeup. When playing *BioShock*, the player is given the possibility to experience firsthand the precepts advocated by Ryan Industries. The painful genetic modifications and the sensorimotor experiences of new mappings move the focus away from the idea that it is "genes which evolve and information that lives." Instead, it is by seeking opportunities, adapting to one's environment, learning the world's politics, training our bodies, and taking advantage of technological extensions that one *evolves*. It is by experimenting with puzzling scenarios and ethical dilemmas that complex concepts, such as genetic determinism and free will, can become comprehensible. Since the way one tells a story can itself tell a story, playing *BioShock* and experiencing the world from a genetically optimized organism can also tell us a story about our own becoming-animated.

Yet, the inevitability of the body-technology symbiosis between the player and the avatar is not directly problematized by the video games. As Bukatman notes,

> [i]n cyberpunk the desire to merge with the machine is romanticized as a necessary but voluntary action, the next evolutionary step. In feminist science fiction, this desire to merge with the machine is viewed as aberrant, and is often presented as an act of surrender rather than empowerment.[105]

In *BioShock*, players of various genders have no option but to identify with a white male avatar having hypermasculine characteristics who frequently takes debatable decisions. The avatar's supernatural powers and his lethal weapons may elicit brief feelings of empowerment for the player, but they do not promote any broader commitment to any social causes. In the first *BioShock*, even though rescuing or harvesting the Little Sister is presented as an option to the player, rescuing them is a necessary choice if one wants to unlock the rewarding sequence that presents Jack taking part into the Little Sisters' future. Similarly, although Subject Delta can sacrifice himself in exchange of Eleanor's redemption in one of the alternate endings of *BioShock 2*, the option to herald a monster is not a very satisfying one.

Moreover, the scenarios of *BioShock* often compel the players to give their allegiance to ethically questionable characters. For instance, Atlas pressures the player to harvest the Little Sister, while Dr. Tenenbaum pleads to rescue her. The choice made by the player influences the storyline and leads to one of the alternate endings. Another scenario forces the player to kill Andrew Ryan, the head of Ryan Industries, in order to progress to the next level of the game. Furthermore, after having murdered Ryan at his request, players learn that they have eliminated the wrong guy because Atlas (who is the evil Fontaine), and implicitly the video game interface, had manipulated them like minions. This underpinning framework of choices and constraints reminds us that even though we have overthrown the idea of genetic determinism, it has conveniently been replaced with algorithmic control.

Conclusion

Some video games explore our tight meshing with technology in an era that is witnessing accelerated technological advances in biotechnology. Enacting scenarios that explore the close-fitting intersection of players with avatar technology helps us make sense of the ethics of worldviews that merge the biological, the postvital, and the mechanical. With their references to bodies as machines and machines as bodies, video games like *BioShock* and *BioShock 2* not only reflect a bionic worldview, but also invite players to enact the mutual assimilation of the technological and the biological. By enhancing their avatars—or "bodies in code"—via the logical and physical interfaces, the video game players enact a virtual form of genetic engineering when splicing genes. The various scenarios in these games replace abstract knowledge of the postvital view of life with embodied experience. Becoming-animated is about evaluating the effects of these technological intersections on our body schema, as playing these games develops our physical and mental skills and produces new systemic wholes that remap the body's boundaries.

BioShock and BioShock 2 explore the intricate relationship between the body and the technology via persuasive rhetoric that controls the player's interactions with the game world. By integrating the procedural rhetoric of these games into our patterns of embodied engagement with contemporary society, we can explore contradicting positions on the technological body. On the one hand, the mastery of technology is indispensable to survive Rapture—or could it be about our own survival in a chaotic high-tech world? On the other hand, this same technology is destroying what is left of humanity. The anxiety-ridden mise-en-scène and the displeasing simulations of genetic mutations in these video games help us register their implicit message against genetic alterations (see Figure 6.4). By harnessing these persuasive mechanisms that transform our body-mind, these video games subvert the views that we have been hardwired at birth or should be reprogramed for the benefit of megalomaniacs.

The symbiosis between player and avatar in *BioShock* may raise the specter of becoming a cyborg and a war machine. Distressing scenarios of monstrous transformations elicit fears over the possibility that technology may one day subjugate and transform humanity. As the specialist of Western science fiction J. P. Telotte notes, the overwhelming presence of technological bodies in science fiction texts addresses "our growing anxieties about our own nature in an increasingly technological

Figure 6.4 Anxiety-ridden atmosphere of Rapture. Screen capture from *BioShock* (Ken Levine, 2007).

environment and a kind of evolutionary fear that these artificial selves may presage our own disappearance or termination."[106] Since remaining in control of systems with so many unknown components is not always possible, we run the risk of being overwhelmed by unexpected outcomes. These questions require serious philosophical, cultural, and political considerations about the risks attached to human "enhancements." As Clark maintains, "not all change is for the better, and hybridization (however naturally it may come to us) is neutral rather than an intrinsic good."[107] Despite our biological plasticity and the intrinsic ability of the human body to reconfigure its boundaries to incorporate physical extensions or mental augmentations, we can never be too cautious when deciding to reconfigure our interfaces.

Notes

1 The booklet accompanying *BioShock 2*, 2010, 3.
2 On the history of the recombinant DNA history, see Krimsky, *Genetic Alchemy*.
3 On video game avatars, see, for instance, Waggoner, *My Avatar, My Self* and Galloway, *Gaming*. On avatars in massively multiplayer online games and

synthetic worlds, see, for instance, Castronova, *Synthetic Worlds*; Taylor, *Play Between Worlds*; and Boellstorff, *Coming of Age in Second Life.*

4 On interactivity in video games, see Nitsche, *Video Game Spaces*, 31–65; Wolf, *The Medium of the Video Game*, 107–110; and Burnett, *How Images Think*, 168–170. On ergodic participation in literature and interactive media, see Aarseth, *Cybertext.*

5 Often, video games scholars reserve the term "virtual reality" for games "in which the player is equipped with a head-mounted display that shuts off external sources of sight and sound," King and Krzywinska, *Tomb Raiders & Space Invaders*, 111. This is only one of the many possible physical implementations of a virtual environment.

6 Ellis, "Nature and Origins of Virtual Environments" and Ellis, "Prologue."

7 Parés and Parés, "Towards a Model for a Virtual Reality Experience," 528.

8 Parés and Parés, "Towards a Model for a Virtual Reality Experience," 528.

9 On a historical survey of the relationship between players and different types of characters, see Wolf, chapter 5, *The Medium of the Video Game.*

10 Parés and Parés, "Towards a Model for a Virtual Reality Experience," 529 (emphasis in the original).

11 On controlling the point of view, see Wolf, *The Medium of the Video Game*, 52. On limiting the player's perspective with a virtual camera, see Nitsche, *Video Game Spaces*, 77. On types of virtual cameras, see Nitsche, *Video Game Spaces*, 89–116.

12 On feedback effects, see King and Krzywinska, *Tomb Raiders & Space Invaders*, 109–111.

13 Ellis, "Nature and Origins of Virtual Environments," 322.

14 Parés and Parés, "Towards a Model for a Virtual Reality Experience," 530.

15 For a definition of a virtual camera, see Nitsche, *Video Game Spaces*, 89–92.

16 For a definition of these terms, see Nitsche, *Video Game Spaces*, 93. On the variety of camera movements in video games, see Nitsche, *Video Game Spaces*, 92–116.

17 On effects of presence in video games, see King and Krzywinska, *Tomb Raiders & Space Invaders*, 97–123.

18 Experiential blindness is "blindness due to lack of sensorimotor knowledge rather than to lack of perceptual sensitivity," Noë, *Action in Perception*, 7.

19 On the enactive approach to perception, see Noë, *Action in Perception.* See also other texts that stress the importance of motor activity in perception: O'Regan and Noë, "A Sensorimotor Approach to Vision and Visual Consciousness"; Churchland et al., "A Critique of Pure Vision"; and Clark "Visual Awareness and Visuomotor Action."

20 On perceptual meaning in cinema, see Persson, chapter 1, *Understanding Cinema.* On the impression of depth in space, see Persson, *Understanding Cinema*, 28.

21 Bissonnette, https://pocushocus.wordpress.com/, May 12, 2008.

22 On motion sickness caused by video games, see Thompson, "Victory in Vomit." For a more elaborate discussion on the contribution of proprioceptive senses to perception in video games, see Rambusch, "It's Not Just Hands."

23 The first-person shooter is a gaming genre "invented in the 1970s and perfected by Id Software in the early 1990s with games like *Wolfenstein 3D* and *Doom*," Galloway, *Gaming*, 57.

24 Galloway, *Gaming*, 40.

25 See Bazin, *What is Cinema?*

26 Shaviro, "Regimes of Vision," 62.
27 On subjective perspectives in electronic media and video games, see Galloway, chapter 2, *Gaming*; Sobchack, "The Scene of the Screen"; and Manovich, "Automation of Sight."
28 There are exceptions to this general observation. In *BioShock Infinite*, for example, Elizabeth can open "tears" that enable the player to access alternate worlds, which disturbs the time-space continuum.
29 Hansen, *Bodies in Code*, 20.
30 Hansen, *Bodies in Code*, 20 (emphasis in the original).
31 For definitions of the different types of actions in video games, see Galloway, chapter 1, *Gaming*.
32 Quoted in Hansen, *New Philosophy for New Media*, 195 (emphasis in the original).
33 Hansen, *Bodies in Code*, 38–39.
34 On the difference between body image and body schema, see Gallagher, "Body Schema and Intentionality."
35 King and Krzywinska, *Tomb Raiders & Space Invaders*, 90.
36 Clark, "Re-Inventing Ourselves," 272.
37 Merleau-Ponty, *Phenomenology of Perception*, 165–166.
38 Gregersen and Grodal, "Embodiment and Interface," 69.
39 Clark, *Supersizing the Mind*, 39.
40 Clark, "Re-Inventing Ourselves," 277.
41 On the influence of training on neural change, see Clark, "Re-Inventing Ourselves," 270.
42 Clark, "Re-Inventing Ourselves," 271.
43 Bingham, "Task-Specific Devices."
44 Clark, *Supersizing the Mind*, 158.
45 Clark, *Supersizing the Mind*, 159.
46 Haugeland, "Mind Embodied and Embedded," 207–237.
47 Clark, "Re-Inventing Ourselves," 266.
48 Penny, "Representation, Enaction, and the Ethics of Simulation," 79–80.
49 On algorithmic control in video games, see, for instance, Manovich, *The Language of New Media*, 221–225; Galloway, chapter 4, *Gaming*; and Burnett, *How Images Think*, 183–185. On the balance between freedom and restriction in gamescapes, see King and Krzywinska, chapter 2, *Tomb Raiders & Space Invaders*.
50 Galloway, *Gaming*, 41.
51 For more details on the distinction between "soft" and "hard" boundaries in video games, see King and Krzywinska, chapter 2, *Tomb Raiders & Space Invaders*.
52 On navigational devices and forms of guidance in gamescapes, see King and Krzywinska, *Tomb Raiders & Space Invaders*, 84–89.
53 Bogost, *Persuasive Games*, 76. In chapter 2, Bogost examines a set of games that invite players to experiment with a particular ideology via their interaction with various political processes, including *BioChemFX*, *Counter-Strike*, *America's Army: Operations*, *Force More Powerful*, *Antiwargame*, and many others. For an introduction on ideology and its various meanings, see Eagleton, *Ideology: An Introduction*.
54 Bogost, *Persuasive Games*, 3.
55 Bogost, *Persuasive Games*, 76.
56 Galloway, *Gaming*, 90.
57 Manovich, *The Language of New Media*, 222.
58 On network societies, see Castells, *The Rise of the Network Society*.

59 Galloway, *Gaming*, 91.
60 User's guide, *Civilization Revolution*, 2.
61 On informatic control in video games, see Galloway, *Gaming*, 90–104.
62 Kay, *Who Wrote the Book of Life?*, 11.
63 See, for instance, Lenoir, "Programming Theater of War." On the war simulation game *America's Army: Operations*, which was produced by the U.S. Army, see Bogost, *Persuasive Games*, 75–79. For other analyses of war video games, see Dyer-Witheford and de Peuter, *Games of Empire* and Huntemann and Payne, eds., *Joystick Soldiers*.
64 Penny, "Representation, Enaction, and the Ethics of Simulation," 75–76.
65 Penny draws on David Grossman's experience as an expert at desensitizing soldiers to increase their killing efficiency. See also Grossman and DeGaetano, *Stop Teaching Our Kids to Kill*. Other psychological studies support this hypothesis. See for instance Carnagey et al., "The Effect of Video Game Violence."
66 For a review of these studies, see Barlett, "Video Game Effects."
67 Harvesting a little sister means killing her to recuperate a quantity of ADAM located in her organs.
68 For studies that evaluate the positive outcomes associated with playing video games, see Barlett, "Video Game Effects."
69 On the ideology of *BioShock*, see Cuddy, ed., *BioShock and Philosophy*; Levine, *Gamespy*, "Rationalizing Rapture with *BioShock*'s Ken Levine" and Remo, "Ken Levine on *BioShock*: The Spoiler Interview."
70 From the user's guide of *BioShock 2*, 5.
71 Levine, *GameSpy*, "Rationalizing Rapture with *BioShock*'s Ken Levine."
72 Persson, *Understanding Cinema*, 23 (emphasis in the original).
73 Persson, *Understanding Cinema*, 22.
74 For an overview of the debate over the dangers of future developments in genetic engineering, see Channell, *The Vital Machine*, 146–151. For more background information on the subject, see Goodfield, *Playing God*; Cherfas, *Man-Made Life*; and Watson and Tooze, *The DNA Story*. On the establishment of civil rights for redesigned humans, see Hugues, *Citizen Cyborg*.
75 Sociologists Dorothy Nelkin and Susan Lindee explore the fascination for the gene in popular cultural media from the 1980s and 1990s in *The DNA Mystique*. On genetic in cinema and animated media, see Stacey, *The Cinematic Life of the Gene*; Nottingham, *Screening DNA*; Grau, *Virtual Art*; Holtzman, chapter 4, *Digital Mosaics*; and Kember, "Cyberlife's *Creatures*."
76 Hayles, *How We Became Posthuman*, 246.
77 Dawkins, *River Out of Eden*, 19.
78 For a critical discussion on the influence of environment on gene expression, see Taussig, "The Molecular Revolution in Medicine." For other texts on this topic, see Lewontin, *The Triple Helix* and Oyama, *The Ontogeny of Information*. About using linguistic approximations to describe the process of DNA "coding" for proteins, see Thompson, *Mind in Life* and Moss, "A Kernel of Truth?"
79 On the politics of genetic determinism, see Lewontin et al.,, *Not in Our Genes*, 7.
80 See Nusslein-Volhard, *Coming to Life*.
81 On genetic determinism in the filmic adaptations of *The Island of Dr. Moreau*, see Kirby, "Are We Not Men?".
82 For more details on the history of eugenics, see Kevles, *In the Name of Eugenics*.

83 On the new eugenics in film, see, for instance, Kirby, "The New Eugenics in Cinema."
84 Graham, *Representations of the Post/Human*, 9.
85 See also Cranny-Francis about the hybrid form of the cyborg and its cultural association with the Christ, "From Extension to Engagement."
86 Graham, *Representations of the Post/Human*, 6.
87 Anderson's talk "Can We Alter Our Humanness by Genetic Engineering?" is quoted in Noble, *The Religion of Technology*, 199.
88 On the history of these worldviews and their intersections in the 20th century, see Channell, *The Vital Machine*.
89 Channell, *The Vital Machine*, 113–114.
90 Channell, *The Vital Machine*, 113.
91 On the symbiotic assemblage of player and avatar, see O'Riordan, "Playing with Lara in Virtual Space." On the manifestation of hybrids between humans and nonhumans in computer technology, see Burnett, chapter 8, *How Images Think* and Haraway, *Modest_Witness@Second_Millenium*.
92 Cranny-Francis, "From Extension to Engagement."
93 See Springer, "The Pleasure of the Interface."
94 Anonymous, "*Burnout*," 70.
95 For an overview of the shifts to a rhetoric of "code" in molecular biology, see Doyle, *On Beyond Living* and Kay, *Who Wrote the Book of Life?*
96 Stacey, *The Cinematic Life of the Gene*, 16.
97 On the history of vitalism and postvitalism, see Doyle, *On Beyond Living*.
98 On the "Burly Brawl" sequence, see North, "Virtual Actors, Spectacle and Special Effects."
99 Doyle, *On Beyond Living*, 17.
100 For a brief overview of Hermeticism and the interest of its practitioners in creating artificial beings, see Graham, *Representations of the Post/Human*, 96–97.
101 Sconce, *Haunted Media*, 8.
102 Lahti, "As We Become Machines," 158. For an alternative view on transcendence, see Graham, *Representations of the Post/Human*, 231.
103 See Descartes, *Meditations on First Philosophy*.
104 Ayn Rand describes Objectivism in her novels *Atlas Shrugged* (1957) and *Fountainhead* (1943). Their titles appear to have inspired the name of the villain Fountain, alias Atlas.
105 Bukatman, *Terminal Identity*, 316.
106 Telotte, *Replications*, 170.
107 Clark, "Re-Inventing Ourselves," 278.

7 Becoming-Avatar

Introduction

Various tools, whether RFID technology, prosthetic enhancements, or brain-machine interfaces, extend our physical reach and enable distributed forms of cognition. Wearable technology and computer-mediated interfaces also extend the machinery of mind into the world. For example, the company EMOTIV™ provides different kinds of neuroheadsets to convert brain waves into digital signals that control computer applications and electronic devices.[1] The other way around, the computerized vision system of Second Sight™ provides information about the environment to human neural networks via electronic components.[2] Alternatively, RFID technology introduces a myriad of small sub-cognizers into the cognitive nexus of animal-human-thing, a process that promotes "an animate environment, with agential and communicative powers."[3] As organic brains are increasingly hybridized with the infrastructure of ubiquitous computing, humans are becoming *Robo sapiens*, a term that theorist of science Timothy Lenoir uses to describe the ways that this infrastructure enhances the symbolizing power of the mind.[4] While certain computer-mediated interfaces transform us by getting under our skin, avatars reprogram the rules of social exchanges and remap the patterns of sensorimotor interactions with our environments, both actual and virtual. This chapter argues that avatars in virtual reality-based environments can extend the body's boundaries by reprograming our physical, emotional, and interpersonal skills.[5] Reprograming here means that computer code and scripts interface with the ways that one expresses emotions in synthetic worlds, moves in the virtual space, or demonstrates sensorimotor rehabilitation.

Recent video game avatars are relatively more expressive than the Pac-Man characters from the arcade game of the 1980s but the emotions they express still do not perfectly match ours. Wouldn't it be fun if our avatar in video games or massively multiplayer online games (MMOs) could read our mind and express our feelings? For some time already, businesses and universities have been developing software programs to help us interface emotionally with our avatars. The EMOTIV™ company, for instance, has designed EmoBot, a cute robot avatar that mimics the facial expressions and head movements of the wearer of the neuroheadset. It is possible to train the computer program to detect the brainwaves associated with the specific facial expressions of the wearer and have them reproduced on the face of EmoBot.

The chapter examines the extent to which user interactions with an avatar can be envisaged as a self-reprograming tool, both in fiction and in everyday life. The first section investigates the ways in which we can interface with computers or smartphones and become extended by them. The concepts of extended cognition and distributed agency are then applied to our relation with avatars in synthetic worlds. Our engagement with avatars in fiction and virtual environments shapes our understanding of collaborative agency, multiplicity of selves, and control, as the boundary between the real and the virtual becomes permeable.[6] The programmability of the digital persona also calls attention to discourses about the postvital self. As such, the chapter looks at how synthetic worlds can model the Computational Universe and its autopoietic organization, since both have been used to describe a form of programmability of the natural world and, to some extent, society. As a first case study, the chapter investigates the hypothesis that selfhood could be programmable in *Second Life*. I demonstrate that residents acquire physical, social, and emotional abilities that are at the intersection between the real and the virtual. In synthetic worlds, where algorithms serve to encode virtual living processes, social behaviors, and evolutionary cycles, users learn to behave, think, and act like an avatar—or a "body in code." a concept introduced in the previous chapter. As users actively engage with the simulated environment and expand their virtual horizons, they bring into play new patterns of sensorimotor interactions and emotional abilities at the intersection of the two realms, a process that I call "becoming-avatar." As we develop our virtual selfhood and gain new skills in real life to do so, we also expand the limits of our body to include virtual tools. Finally, the chapter explores the field of virtual reality-based therapy and the healing potential of becoming-avatar.

Finding Ourselves in the Machine

Computerized devices have encouraged us to develop affinities with our machines. For instance, computers that reengineered the genome in the late 20th and the early 21st centuries transformed "our view of ourselves as programed beings."[7] The computer has also challenged the prevailing conception of the liberal humanist subject as a biological, unitary, and rational cognizer. In *Life on the Screen*, Sherry Turkle concludes that multitasking at the computer and sharing agency with online avatars have promoted a conception of "the self as a multiple, distributed system."[8] Likewise, N. Katherine Hayles demonstrates that our sense of subjectivity is increasingly associated with computational processes, to the extent that the high-level cognitive operations traditionally thought to be restricted to embodied humans are now within the domain of posthuman agents who are "seamlessly articulated with intelligent machines."[9] Elaborating on this topic, Andy Clark claims that we are "natural-born cyborgs," since the brain's plasticity enables humans to spread their cognitive processes beyond the bounds of skin and skull, either through internal rewiring or by distributing the cognitive load to external processes and structures.[10] These scholars' views of the self as enmeshed within larger cognitive systems inform my perspective on distributed agency.

The distribution of agency and affect between oneself and an online avatar has evolved with the advent of interactive, graphical avatars. Before the heydays of the Internet, the asynchronous text-based interface Bulletin Board Systems (BBS) allowed people to post messages, play games, and create communities. Already in the mid-1975s, users could engage in real-time multiplayer role-playing games called Multiuser Dungeons (MUDs) and graphical MUDs. Lucasfilm was one of the first to coin the term "avatar" to designate the graphical personas strolling around their multiplayer online virtual environment *Habitat*.[11] In the online-simulated view *Habitat*, the player's avatar was represented by a 2D animated character. The avatars could carry weapons and tools in their hands or pockets, withdraw money from ATMs, and buy objects from vending machines coined Vendroids. Users communicated with each other via text messages displayed above the avatar's body. In this virtual environment, players developed friendship with other avatars, played games, explored the various real-time animated landscapes, and engaged in the kinds of social interactions we find in society. Other examples of MMOs and massive multiplayer online role-playing games (MMORPGs) include: *The Sims Online*, *EVE Online*, *EverQuest*, *Entropia Universe*, and *World of Warcraft*, just to name a few.

The online synthetic world *Second Life* is another example of a way in which we find ourselves in the machine. Operated by the San Francisco-based company Linden Lab, *Second Life* has its own currency, the Linden Dollar, and with a Premium Account, a resident can own a parcel of land. Since the system went live on June 23, 2003, *Second Life* residents have been shopping for new outfits, teleporting to new places, chatting with other avatars, building houses, producing artistic works, and even selling their virtual creations. We not only find bars and imaginary landscapes, but also businesses, nonprofit organizations, libraries, museums, and educational campuses. Some destinations offer information on health and wellness.[12] Residents can receive advice and information on surgical procedures and diseases on HealthInfo Island. The Whole Brain Health landmark on Inspiration Island provides activities to stay fit. If people want to obtain free resources on mental health, they can visit the Virtual Mental Health location. Many of these places are not very populated, but the information displayed on posters located in magical gardens and surreal buildings is more engaging than the plain descriptions found on regular websites. Even though the popularity of *Second Life* has dwindled over the years, the online version of The Globe and Mail reported over half a million users on May 17, 2017.[13] Residents control the actions of their avatars within the virtual environment via a user interface. Clicking with the mouse on certain objects allows the residents to alter their appearance, sit on them, open doors, buy items, or dance. Since the modular building blocks of *Second Life*—the "prims"—are programmable, residents can write scripts with the Linden Scripting Language (LSL) to modify the appearance and behavior of the objects they design. The user, the avatar, and the user interface collaborate so that each performs its part of a set of distributed cognitive tasks that combine low-level and high-level cognitive processes, including walking, teleporting, building, and talking. The transfer of control to algorithmic agents produced by scripts evokes Clark's idea that external resources can relay part of our cognitive tasks.[14]

The conceptual and physical linkages between *Second Life* scripting algorithms and human cognition are central to what I term the "animation machine," a technical ensemble that contains among other things: users, avatars, virtual environments, computer systems, networks, and interfaces. The hybridized assemblage of residents and avatars becomes "a 'soft self,' a constantly negotiable collection of resources easily able to straddle and criss-cross the boundaries between biology and artifact."[15] When programmable environments dovetail with our neural circuits and reconfigure our physical and conceptual boundaries, we envisage ourselves as extended by the animation machine—a process affiliated with becoming-animated.

The encoding of new sensorimotor patterns of interactions proceeds from a two-way process. On the one hand, the algorithmic layer influences the extent to which users can be controlled—and transformed—by the virtual reality system. Media scholar Ted Friedman notably argues that video games can reorganize perception while promoting familiar ideological worldviews.[16] The user interface comprises various built-in commands and functions to control the avatar's movements in space and its gestures. To fully engage with the synthetic world, users must adapt their behavior and become "in sync" with what is expected by the underlying algorithms. This reorganization of perception involves a form of reprograming of the self, a topic that is further examined later in the section "Reprograming the Self in *Second Life*." On the other hand, a user can select an option offered by the user interface to alter the properties of the virtual environment or interact with objects. For instance, the built-in functions provided by the interface can change the display from day to night. A resident can also build a new house or program customized gestures for their avatar with LSL. The underlying algorithms that power the synthetic world enable users to communicate with each other, fashion new objects, and customize their virtual body image.

The user interface distributes cognitive operations such as perception and memory across the real and the virtual. For instance, users can share the same visual perspective as their avatar by choosing the Mouselook view. Residents control the avatar's movements via the arrows on the keyboard or the mouse. The Inventory, a database accessible from a menu option, also helps users memorize and manage information about their virtual possessions, including outfits, a library of gestures and sounds, a photo album, notecards, and landmarks. The sensorimotor interactions afforded by the avatar and the memory offloads provided by the Inventory widen the resident's perceptual scope to include the virtual world and thereby produce "new systemic wholes" that reconfigure the agent-world boundaries.[17]

Thanks to the presence of our digital avatars, we find ourselves in the machine. A computer program automatically detects the resident's virtual presence with a myriad of sub-cognizers, thus modeling a distributed form of cognition involving the resident-avatar-simulation nexus. Algorithms animate the exchange of information between users and their avatars. We learn the numerous rules that apply to *Second Life* via sensorimotor explorations of the user interface and the virtual world. For example, while most objects in *Second Life* are solid, avatars can walk through "phantom" objects. On the one hand, the user interface grants residents partial control over their avatar's movements and actions. I can walk forward or fly up by pressing the right key or combination of keys on my keyboard. On the other hand, the movements performed by the avatar are constrained by the avatar's characteristics of embodiment and the limitations imposed by the virtual environment.[18]

Affective Computing

As we nurture more intertwined relationships with our digital proxies, it may compel some of us to wonder about the extent to which we are becoming (like our) avatars. Players in the area of affective computing have conceived various devices that connect our human emotions with machines. Rosalind Picard has been researching this field for more than 20 years and published the groundbreaking book *Affective Computing* in 1997. She founded the Affective Computing Research Group at the MIT Media Lab in 1997. The applications of affective technologies are wide-ranging and include caregiving robots, sex dolls, digital pets, personalized marketing, wearable devices, autism spectrum detection, and robot-assisted learning.[19] Research in this domain led to a better understanding of how our feelings influence our perception and our level of attention. The development of compression algorithms and facial recognition algorithms based on this knowledge, as well as the production of high-resolution cameras paved the way to systems able to read facial expressions. Among the key elements that helped detect and categorize emotions in pictures were software programs developed by Paul Ekman and his colleagues, such as the Emotional Facial Action Coding System (FACS).[20]

One of the outcomes of experiments on affective computing is that our avatars are progressively becoming like us. For example, the smartphone Samsung Galaxy S9 and the iPhone X feature animated emojis that mimic the user's facial expressions.[21] The iPhone X provides a selection of cute animated emojis named Animojis.[22] The user can pick one of the emojis as a template on which the technology will map facial expressions and movements of the head recorded with the iPhone X True Depth camera system. Then, the user can send an audio message with the Animoji delivering the message for them. The avatar generated by the Samsung application called "AR Emoji" maps over 100 points from the user's face, which were captured by a face-scanning technology. After customizing your avatar's clothes and hairstyle, you can send it in an animated message or perform a karaoke song. According to Brian Heater, an attendee at the Mobile World Congress held in February 2018, the realistic 3D avatars provided by the Samsung Galaxy S9 felt into the uncanny valley, a topic examined in Chapter 5.[23]

The recent usages of the term avatar for mobile devices and online graphical personas are informed by ancient beliefs about the incarnation of a spirit within a remote body.[24] The long history of the avatar tells the story of how one can bypass the physical boundaries of the body.[25] In Hindu mythology, for instance, the Sanskrit word "avatar" refers to a divine incarnation.[26] The divine entity uses a body as a vessel for traveling between different realms of reality. Souls that migrate between bodies in Ovid's *Metamorphoses* allude to this original conception of the avatar. In ancient Egypt, the imagery of a butterfly hatching was a symbolic model for the soul. The Egyptians "figured the body as the chrysalis from which the winged soul is set free, and the Greek word for the pupa, *nekydallos*, means little corpse; *pupa* itself means doll in Latin, suggesting an inanimate, unconscious state."[27] The references to dolls and butterflies are frequent in cyberpunk films and video games, a genre that reflects on the body/mind split involved in our interactions with computer technology.

More recent usages of the term "avatar" are informed by the incarnation of a spirit within a remote body and the problems associated with the fusion or cohabitation of two personalities within one body. In the 19th century, Helena Blavatsky, the cofounder of the Theosophical society, claimed that her body hosted the avatar of a Hindu spiritual master who was known then as Koot Hoomi.[28] This "lodger," as she would call him, would reveal to her information about the Himalayan region and its religious traditions. In the 19th century, Spiritualism in the United States also involved telepathic communication with remote sources of knowledge—in this particular case, the deceased.[29] These three forms of avatars—the Sanskrit physical incarnation of the divine, Mme Blavatsky's lodger, and the Spiritualist mediums' spirits—illustrate alternative ways of interpreting the physical and mental divides between an avatar and its controlling agent. The avatar is a tool or a technology that can provide its users with access to distant worlds and vital information.

Various novels predating the widespread adoption of the Internet explore the permeability of the boundary between the "real" self and one's digital proxy. In Vernor Vinge's *True Names* (1981), two computer geeks named Erythrina and Mr. Slippery meet in the Other Plane through their computer proxies. In William Gibson's *Neuromancer* (1984), computer hacker Case jacks himself into his computer console to access cyberspace, an electronic environment in which thought, body, and information share the same ontology. The main protagonist of Neal Stephenson's *Snow Crash* (1992), Hiro, wears digital goggles to surf the Metaverse, a futuristic version of the Internet in which avatars can interact with each other. This novel popularized the use of the term "avatar" at the end of the 20th century.[30] Inspired by *Snow Crash,* founder of *Second Life*, Philip Rosedale, called "avatars" the residents that inhabit this synthetic world.[31] These narratives about avatars imagine exchanges between consciousness, electricity, and information as a flow that can cross the frontier between the material and the virtual.[32]

Many popular films depict avatarial projections of a living being into surrogates or virtual proxies, including *The Lawnmower Man* (Brett Leonard, 1992), *The Matrix Trilogy* (Lilly Wachowski and Lana Wachowski, 1999, 2003), *eXistenZ* (David Cronenberg, 1999), *Avatar* (James Cameron, 2009), *Surrogates* (Jonathan Mostow, 2009), and *Jumanji: Welcome to the Jungle* (Jake Kasdan, 2017). While the modes of avatarial projections differ in these films, they all evoke an agential connection between viewers in the flesh and virtual avatars. Some films involve multiple users who can share a common perspective in the virtual world, including *The Matrix*, *Tron* (Steven Lisberger, 1982), and *Tron: Legacy* (Joseph Kosinski, 2010). Animated films explore similar topics. *Summer Wars* (Mamoru Hosoda, 2009), for instance, tells a story about people meeting in a virtual world and threatened by a sentient computer system that can disable computerized systems in the real world. The first episode of the TV series *Spicy City* (1997) created by Ralph Bakshi features people dating in a bar located in a synthetic world. The users wear neural headsets to connect with their avatar and can even receive haptic feedback. All these stories do not leave the body behind. Rather, they intimate that the distribution of agency between users and avatars provides pleasure and excitement.

Some films and animations featuring avatars evoke allegories of Foucauldian discipline or a Deleuzean society of control.[33] By adopting the subjective perspective found in first-person shooters, *Gamer* (Mark Neveldine and Brian Taylor, 2009) and *Surrogates* envision a shared visual perspective between viewer and character and a cognitive extension between them. In these new societies of control, the living body (and its underlying self) is either reprogramed to become a puppet in *Gamer* or a meat bag in *Surrogates*. Other films explore the idea of a society of minds meeting inside cyberspace and their social exploitation through avatarial control, including *Sleep Dealer* (Alex Rivera, 2008) and *Gamer*. In their article, "The End of Forgetting," Jonah Bossewitch and Aram Sinnreich examine strategies to control the flow of information in the post-WikiLeaks era. The authors draw on actual events and fiction to divide surveillance strategies into categories such as "souveillance," "total transparency," "off the grid," "black hole," "promiscuous broadcaster," "voracious collector," and "disinformation campaign." Whether through multiplicity of selves, shared perspectives, remote control, or collaborative agency, the animations and films mentioned earlier encourage viewers to imagine the effects of distributing their cognition and affect across the real and the virtual.

The Postvital Self

In addition to referring to the idea of doubling the self, contemporary uses of the term avatar underscore the mutability and programmability of the digital persona. Taking the computer as a virtual model for the living, evolutionary biologist Richard Dawkins argues that it is the gene that evolves and information that lives. When a willow pumps downy seeds into the air, it disseminates genetic programs. In Dawkins's words, "It is raining instructions out there; it's raining programs; it's raining tree-growing, fluff-spreading, algorithms. That is not a metaphor, it is the plain truth. It couldn't be any plainer if it were raining floppy discs."[34] As Richard Doyle demonstrates in *On Beyond Living*, recent accounts of molecular biology have shaped what he calls "the postvital body, a body without life."[35] By recasting the body as an extension of DNA, postvitalism envisages life as a sequence of instructions.

The notion that DNA is a code and the cognitivist assumption that the mind is like a computer in the head have both contributed to the emergence of the Regime of Computation, a concept that permeates synthetic worlds. This concept, which N. Katherine Hayles explores in *My Mother Was a Computer*,

> provides a narrative that accounts for the evolution of the universe, life, mind, and mind reflecting on mind by connecting these emergences with computational processes that operate both in

human-created simulations and in the universe understood as software running on the "Universal Computer" we call reality.[36]

Advocates of this regime, theorists Stephen Wolfram and Harold Morowitz argue that digital algorithms control the behavior of biological organisms and social systems.[37] Their perspectives correspond to what Donna Haraway has termed *god-tricks*, which is a privileged perspective—similar to the perspective of a god—external to the system of observation.[38] The Regime of Computation thus provides a detached and conceptual perspective on biological processes at the origin of life and mind.

Synthetic environments replicate the self-programing from the bottom-up found in biological organisms and remediate a virtual reality-based version of the Computational Universe.[39] *Second Life* evokes the reprograming of the self by the way it affords its residents to reshape their avatar's body bit by bit. The creation of avatars from the bottom-up using "scripts" is reminiscent of Erwin Schrödinger's "code-scripts" to represent life as code.[40] The anthropomorphic vocabulary that pervades the discourse in *Second Life* alludes to postvital approaches to life. For example, *Second Life*'s official guide, *Creating Your World*, introduces residents to the basic and more advanced methods for torturing prims, which is "the sadistic process of morphing prims into exotic new shapes."[41] While the structure of *Second Life* reifies the Regime of Computation, this postvital language associates the building blocks of this synthetic world with living entities.

Skilled residents produce the code for rezzing objects and designing customized gestures. They also program script generators that produce more code, which, in turn, enlivens the residents' social lives and behaviors. The circular organization of this society, with its economic system, communities, and working infrastructure, instantiates the concept of self-organizing social systems developed by sociologist Niklas Luhmann.[42] Luhmann took inspiration from biologists Humberto Maturana and Francisco Varela, who described living systems as autopoietic machines that are autonomous and self-organizing and constantly maintaining their identity. In their own words, the "living organization is a circular organization which secures the production or maintenance of the components that specify it in such a manner that the product of their functioning is the very same organization that produces them."[43] *Second Life* only approximates the circular organization of nonliving autopoietic systems.[44] The synthetic world produces the avatars that interact with itself and they modulate the behavior of the living beings that design them. *Second Life* reprograms the residents' physical skills in Bourdieu's sense of the term habitus and facilitates the usage of new habits and social skills.[45]

The self is also part of an autopoietic system. In his enactive approach to the mind, philosopher Evan Thompson argues that identity formation is a process of differentiation of the self from the environment that happens both at the cellular level and at the sensorimotor level.[46] From the perspective of an enactive approach to mind and life, the phrase "laying down a path in walking," borrowed from neuroscientist Francisco Varela, means that there is no pathway that is predetermined by our genes, since the environments with which our body interacts modify our organization and provide new networks of possibilities.[47] Because what we call our "self" is increasingly influenced by our interactions with digital environments, we must consider the ways that synthetic worlds can alter existing sensorimotor patterns and generate new ones. The symbiotic relationship between residents and avatars has the potential to foster productive interactions among the body, mind, and environment.

When we walk on a path in real life, we maintain our balance and can easily negotiate its imperfections because of our acute perceptual skills. In some ways, as we go along on the path, we do no longer see the path as apart from us; we become one with the path. In contrast, the process of differentiating the self from the synthetic landscape in *Second Life* is dynamically enmeshed with algorithmic procedures. Yet, since real selfhood and virtual selfhood are so closely interrelated, we experience processes of sensorimotor adjustments when walking on virtual paths, just as we do when walking on real paths. While there is no clear separation between path and footsteps when navigating on a real pathway, as Varela and Thompson argue, engaging on a virtual pathway can also evoke similar patterns of reciprocity, as the program's response to user inputs induces feedback loops that modulate the navigation process. By developing fine motor skills and reflexes to select the right keys and thereby respond to changes in the visual scenery, we actively participate in the systemic reprograming of the self.

Reprograming the Self in *Second Life*

The computer code does not regulate the appropriate use of space but it can constrain the user engagement with the virtual space. As Jennifer Stromer-Galley and Rosa Mikeal Martey argue, the rich visual setting of *Second Life* activates spatial schemas that "contribute to the social meaning players attach to that space, which in turn helps shape the social norms that emerge."[48] Norm is defined as the explicit and implicit rules that govern interactions and behavior in online and offline societies. These authors "theorize that behavior is structured via norms established through visual contexts that are constrained and enabled by the code that is used to create a given online world."[49] For example, the visual representation of the users via their avatars activates behaviors informed by interpersonal cues communicated by their online gender and race.[50] The virtual spaces in which the avatars interact, including homes, libraries, museums, churches, schools, and nightclubs also invite the types of social interactions associated with the settings in which they take place. Avatars are more compelled to go to dance and party in a nightclub than in a museum. The residents also draw on both offline and online norms to adjust their behavior according to the social context and visual settings. The next two subsections focus on the ways that computer code shapes the notion of selfhood and the embodied experience of the synthetic world. The avatar—or "body in code"—enables the user to distribute roles across real life and virtual life and alter identity markers such as gender and race.

Digital Bioengineering and Identity Tourism

The understanding that we have of ourselves is shaped by our relationships with others, including virtual others. The roles that we play in our real life and virtual lives also help us articulate our sense of self.[51] The online avatar is instrumental in exploring the various facets of one's persona. Many of the respondents of an ethnographic study "described their avatar personae as symbolically representing their 'authentic inner selves.'"[52] To attain the desired level of authenticity, some residents chose to model their avatar on the appearance of their offline self. While they could possess many avatars, they considered their primary avatar as their default identity. Tom Boellstorff distinguishes "prime" or "primary" avatars and "alts," which are alternatives to the primary avatar.[53] Even though some of the residents attempted to unify their sense of self, their reflections suggest that the idea of a well-defined selfhood with fixed roles and personality traits can be challenging when one possesses multiple virtual selfhoods. Because of all sorts of contingencies, we do not necessarily dare to or have the chance to experiment with all the roles that we would want to adopt in real life. In an ethnographic study, a *Second Life* resident explained that virtual worlds offer this kind of opportunity. According to this resident, *Second Life* "allows you to define your own role instead of being the one you are in RL (in my case, mother, wife)."[54]

For many *Second Life* residents, the online avatar is a tool for programing a new social self. Some studies indicate that our interactions with avatars facilitate behavior change in a wide range of situations.[55] On the one hand, the appearance of the avatars we encounter may improve our self-confidence in performing the same scenarios in real life situations. On the other hand, the way that we represent ourselves in the virtual world may also influence our behavior in real life. One resident mentioned, "I noticed yesterday that I had no problem talking to a complete stranger at the shopping center, simply because I have spent a lot of time in *SL* recently doing the same thing."[56] Additionally, for some residents, their involvement in the choice of the appearance and behavior of their avatar strengthens their impression of control over their social life. In his research, Simon Gottschalk noticed a blurring between real-life self and *Second Life* avatar. One of the people he encountered, Karen, created an avatar named Nina to escape from an abusive relationship. Karen, who felt like a prisoner in her real life, was "[e] ncouraged by the validating encounters and relations Nina/Karen was experiencing in *Second Life*."[57] Karen "decided to model herself after Nina, assuming she would then enjoy the same pleasurable experience in her real life." The online relationships led her to feel much happier. Similar comments from *Second Life* residents reveal that a combination of real-life experiences and virtual ones shape their sense of selfhood.

Since virtual selfhood informs real-life selfhood, the activities we perform under the traits of our virtual selves may influence the conception that we have of our bodily possibilities and appearance—or "body images."[58] In *Second Life*, "our digital-physical appearance is no longer determined by genetic baggage or shaped by habit, age, and other natural biological processes."[59] Changing the hair color and gender of our default avatar is a matter of pointing and clicking. By adjusting the slider that controls the avatar's size, we can metamorphose in "real time" from our thin avatar into one wearing a size XL. But the *Second Life: Official Guide* advises us to keep in mind that appearance also matters in the virtual world:

> While most SL denizens are unbelievably lithe and slender, rather the way we'd all like to be in real life, you might want to nudge the slider up a little—a value 35 to 40 results in a more realistic body shape. Don't worry—your avatar will still appear attractively slim given all the other options.[60]

Technical skills are often required in the presentation of the self in *Second Life*. As Delia Dumitrica and Georgia Garden note from their personal experience, "the range of options for the performance of gender is connected to the individual's level of technical skill."[61] A successful performance of femaleness or maleness often requires advanced customizing of the avatar's body or buying new genitalia from the marketplace. For some skilled residents, this form of tinkering with code entails not only feelings of mastery over their own appearance but also the recognition of affinities with the computer, a psychological process that Turkle explores in *The Second Self*.[62] For others, the overwhelming presence of technology in the presentation of the self is perceived as disempowering.[63] Acquiring the right "body image" is not only associated with dieting or bodybuilding: it has also become a question of shopping savviness and computer skills.

Digital bioengineering and experiments with role-playing can liberate some users from the physical and psychological limitations that their "real" embodiment exerts. These environments sometimes reproduce sexual and gender norms in ways that "objectifies women and marginalizes queer identities."[64] We should consider the implications of what media scholar Lisa Nakamura terms "identity tourism."[65] According to Nakamura, online users "use[d] race and gender as amusing prostheses to be donned and shed without 'real life' consequences."[66] Identity tourism can harbor prejudices toward some communities when the avatar reinforces negative stereotypes. Chicana scholar Carleen D. Sanchez noticed during her exploration of *Second Life* that some of the white residents chose highly sexualized and eroticized Black female avatar bodies "to enact their projected fears and desires to control the exotic female other in a socially sanctioned performance space."[67] While identity tourism provides satisfactory experiences for some *Second Life* residents, for others, certain identity markers are a source of harassment. Black female avatars, as well as avatars wearing religious signs, can be the victim of racism and sexism. Methal Mohammed's avatar "noorelhuda" encountered the hostility of other *Second Life* avatars because she was wearing a *hijab*. During a visit at the beach, a male avatar dressed as a policeman pushed noorelhuda into the sea and drowned her.[68] "By virtue of being physically disembodied from the creator," Beth Simone Noveck argues, "avatars in the theater of the game space may act in antisocial and even pathological ways—ways in which the 'real' person never would—shooting, maiming, and killing in brutal fashion."[69] As these authors contend, we should remember that our actions matter in virtual life, as they do in real life.

The concept of the avatar complicates the idea that our personality is self-contained within our organic boundaries. The coupling of the self with one or multiple avatars entails a multiplicity of selves with multiple roles and social assemblages. The uniqueness of the external appearance is also challenged by the avatar's morphing capability. Easily cloned with just a few points and clicks of the mouse, the avatar's body is a rhizome of fabricated pieces that are dynamically interchangeable, adjustable, and reprogrammable. The shifting assemblage of the avatar's body is not unlike the body without organs envisaged by Gilles Deleuze and Félix Guattari in the way that it connects biological bodies, technologies, and cultural practices.[70] From the process of assembling the body without organs and the experimentation with intensities of affect, we can abstract a new sense of self. Becoming-avatar speaks about the multiplicity of possible assemblages and bodies without organs that are constructed according to the social formations, the places, and the techniques encountered.

Extending One's Sensorimotor Skills

Online virtual worlds influence the sense of embodiment by modulating its "three subcomponents: the sense of self-location, the sense of agency, and the sense of body ownership."[71] Computer code organizes the spatial layout of the synthetic world and regulates the types of interactions that are possible within the synthetic environment. Each online world has its own sets of rules defined by a set of underlying algorithms that limit or enable the users' possibility of actions. For example, *The Sims Online* world prevents avatars from crossing the walls of their houses and they are bound to walk on the ground. In contrast, *Second Life* residents can walk through certain walls and objects depending on the proprieties with which they were designed.

Second Life residents must accustom themselves to the hierarchical organization of the user interface. Recalling an elaborate control board when all the information windows are open, the user interface acts as an augmented space. The numerous drop-down menus often impede the newbies' ability to find the option they want. An underlying layer of code controls the way that an avatar responds to points and clicks of the mouse. It provides the built-in resistance that accompanies each movement performed by the avatar. The effects on the avatar's locomotion, for instance, require adjustments to the image schemas—or patterns of experiential interactions—that are usually associated with walking along a pathway.[72] The symbiotic boundaries between the resident's body and the avatar's body constantly fluctuate and require sensorimotor remapping—an adaptation of the plastic neural resources to reflect new bodily and sensory opportunities.

The avatar is a crucial tool for negotiating the sensorimotor gaps between real experiences and virtual ones. Establishing a symbiotic relationship with one's avatar takes some time, and even controlling one's visual orientation, typically termed "camera movements," can be a challenge in the beginning. In World View, one can adjust the camera perspective, by selecting between the Front View, the Side View, or the Rear View. Certain of the camera adjustments are particularly tiresome, especially if someone wants to zoom in on a character's face. When choosing the Mouselook View, the body of the avatar does not appear on the viewer. With this perspective, which is similar to the filmic "subjective shot," residents can share the visual perspective of their avatar. The virtual camera presents images from the scene that change according to the movements of the avatar's body. The controller-dependent relationship induces affect via the embodied effects of motion in space.

Second Life residents must also remap a range of real-world physical actions by using a series of computer commands. Many preprogramed body movements are associated with menu options, including laughing, bowing, clapping, stretching, moving the head to say yes or no, dancing, shrugging, and expressing boredom. Residents dissatisfied with the options provided can program personalized gestures or buy scripted gestures to extend their avatar's expressivity. Many of the gestures on sale in the marketplace take inspiration from popular films, sitcoms, and animated TV series such as *Austin Powers: International Man of Mystery*

(Jay Roach, 1997), *The Simpsons* (TV series 1989–), and *Family Guy* (TV series 1998–).[73]

In *Second Life*, the avatar challenges the unitary sense of self-location and body ownership. Residents experience computer-generated representations of space and time and interactions with objects in the synthetic world challenge Newtonian physics. Residents can perform impossible feats or fly over buildings. *Second Life* also provides teleportation devices that enable users to instantaneously change location rather than having to travel the entire distance on foot, a feature that shrinks one's sense of space and time. The client-server architecture causes rendering delays and glitches that convey perceptual estrangement. For example, when teleporting to a new location, some of the objects materialize a few prims at a time, which creates odd, incomplete landscapes. While the off-kilter landscape is "rezzing," the unexpected visual perspectives can throw one off balance. Accordingly, one must acquire the necessary reflexes to quickly readjust the posture of the avatar. Residents can also experience a time lag when walking or flying, a frustrating sensation of lack of control over one's body. The difference between moving through virtual space and moving through real space not only reminds us of our own physical constraints, but also reveals new patterns of embodiment that produce a sense of alienation from the self.

As *Second Life* residents transfer part of their agency to a computerized system, they can notice an effacement of the organic self in favor of a human-machine coupling. When we learn to move at the singular pace of our avatars and adopt their limited bodily expressions to convey emotions, we experience the effects of the constraints posed by the underlying algorithms. In the exchange between player and computer, a cyborg consciousness emerges, according to Friedman, when "the line demarcating the end of the player's consciousness and the beginning of the computer's world blurs."[74] Users progressively develop bodily skills and cognitive aptitudes to master the user interface and navigate their way around the synthetic landscape. Drawing on Heidegger's notion of "transparent equipment," Clark explains how the body can become transparent equipment with the development of skills. In the classic example of a skilled carpenter using a hammer, the hammer becomes a transparent piece of equipment as the carpenter shifts attention from correctly handling the hammer to carrying out the task at hand.[75] Likewise, when the user interface becomes transparent equipment in *Second Life*, as in some video games, the avatar becomes an extension of the player's body and any sense of "separateness [is] eventually obliterated."[76] Establishing symbiotic connections with digital avatars catalyzes a distributed form of cognition that is no longer objective and independent from the world, as the liberal humanist view of the subject would have it, but instead is extended by the various interfaces, including the *Second Life* viewer, the keyboard, and the logical interface.

In order to master the interfaces that control the avatar's movements and gestures, residents adapt their body schema, which is "an integrated set of dynamic sensorimotor processes that organize perception and action in a subpersonal and nonconscious manner."[77] Through the repetitive use of these tools, the systemic intersections that connect residents and avatars expand to create new systemic wholes. These systemic wholes are cognitive systems that are constantly being reorganized, since residents can reprogram the avatars' behaviors and *Second Life* administrators can supplement the virtual environment with new functionalities. These structural extensions and molecular adaptations foster the dynamic process of *becoming-avatar* in transforming the body's boundaries.

Emotional Contagion in Virtual Worlds

While participants can build online relationships both via textual and graphical avatars, emotions are arguably heightened by the visual and auditory stimulations available in synthetic worlds such as *Second Life*.[78] This section examines various approaches to increase the authenticity of the emotions conveyed by an avatar. While these methods likely increase emotional engagement, they sometimes miscommunicate the resident's feelings. The perspectives of the residents who attempt to interpret these emotions are also investigated. As argued, the code constrains both the quality of the emotions that are communicated and the process to interpret them.

Virtual Intimacies in Second Life

Several *Second Life* residents have found friendship or even love.[79] As Simon Evans notes from his experience of interviewing *Second Life* residents, "close and intimate bonds are formed by participants, including sexual and familial relationships."[80] To expand their social network and forge new relationships, residents can join groups of like-minded residents, add residents to their Friends list, and swap Calling Cards, which are virtual business cards. These various social modes of interaction help foster a sense of community. Residents can communicate with avatars in close proximity by talking into a microphone or by typing messages in the chat window. They can also send private messages called "ims" to a specific resident.

Second Life provides interactive modes of expressing feelings that cultivate virtual modes of intimacy. The facial expression of emotion can inform our conversation partners about our internal states or shape social interactions.[81] Moreover, the expressiveness of verbal and nonverbal cues "gives communication life."[82] Residents can choose preprogramed gestures available in their Inventory. For example, my avatar starts laughing when I select the gesture "Female - Laugh."[83] I can also type

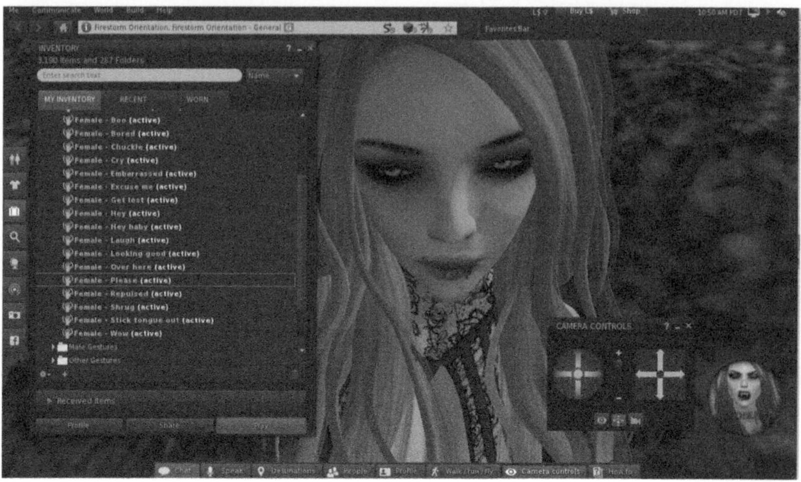

Figure 7.1 Examples of female gestures available in the *Second Life* Inventory. Screenshot from *Second Life*.

"/laugh" in the chat text box. My current avatar, which looks like a female vampire, closes her eyes and shows her teeth when she laughs. While her facial expression is not typical of someone laughing, the giggling sound she makes confirms that she is amused. Other examples of gestures include: bored, cry, boo, embarrassed, shrug, and repulsed (see Figure 7.1). The default options that *Second Life* provides to express emotions only approximate those experienced by the flesh-and-blood residents. As Iris Ophelia, one of the residents of *Second Life*, mentioned:

> This whole world [of *Second Life*] has been created, with so much to see and do and experience, and yet there's so little genuine emotion. The crying gesture is used as a joke 90% of the time. If you were really crying, how could you convey it in *Second Life*?[84]

Acquiring custom avatar animations on the marketplace or designing specific facial expressions and importing them in *Second Life* are some of the ways to improve default gestures. A custom cry or laugh can enhance the emotional connections with other avatars. In a situation mentioned in *Coming of Age in Second Life*, a resident named Vonda needed to be comforted. For her, dancing a slow dance with another avatar made her feel appreciated and loved.[85] Unlike the static avatars in textual chats, the photorealistic appearance of the *Second Life* avatar and the interactive movements can provide more rounded ways to express feelings and develop intimacy. Nevertheless, even though it is now possible to invest in one of the most recent gesture packages, it is challenging to find the gesture that corresponds exactly to one's current mood or to activate the gesture in the instant when the emotion is experienced.

On Avatar Island, a location that used to exist in *Second Life*, residents were able to transform their avatar appearance to match their own with the CyberExtruder software. Some residents chose this option because they aimed to achieve what they considered "a more 'authentic' appearance, one that was more closely aligned to their actual image in their offline lives."[86] For a small fee, the CyberExtruder software fashioned a customized avatar face and skin based on the resident's photograph. The facility where the "operation" took place found inspiration in real-life medical laboratories. The resident first visited the waiting room of the cosmetic surgeon with posters on the walls comparing faces before and after the procedure. Then, the patient entered a large laboratory and lied down into one of the CyberExtruder machines where the surgical procedure was performed. On a *Second Life* forum, Voodoo Bamboo claimed that the CyberExtruder was able to capture the essence of someone, "or at least the persona you wish[ed] to project in *Second Life*."[87] As the gestures an avatar performs in *Second Life* help reflect the residents' real-life emotions, age, gender, and clothing are other aspects of the avatar's persona that can communicate the residents' vision of their authentic self.

Nevertheless, many aspects of the avatar's face diminish the perceived authenticity of the emotions displayed. Proximity of the avatar appearance with the resident's own facial features could potentially draw attention to deviations from them. For avatars displaying a photorealistic face, as in the case of the Samsung Galaxy S9 mentioned earlier, these deviations could elicit uncanny feelings that would divorce the emotions expressed from their intended meaning.[88] Despite efforts to improve the emotional range of the avatars with idle animations, they still display zombie-like features that can disengage residents. The default gestures of my current *Second Life* avatar are not exempt from liveliness. Yet, she possesses inanimate eyes and a hazy gaze, which has been identified as a cause for eeriness in video games.[89] When rezzing, parts of her body and pieces of her clothing are missing, revealing an empty skull, a ragged skirt, and missing hair extensions. Despite the fact that my avatar slightly moves her head, winks, and repeatedly touches her arm with her other arm to display her boredom when she is inactive, her facial muscles remain stiff. Moving the upper region of the face has been identified as an important way for humans to convey nonverbal signals. Lack of movement in the forehead or the eyelids of an avatar can convey ambiguous emotions and increase uncanniness.[90] In the case of my avatar, despite the fact that her forehead participates in the display of various facial expressions, it is easy to mistake the emotion she is supposed to convey with another. For instance, when I select "fear" from the Gesture menu, the center parts of her eyebrows are slightly raised and her lower lip opens, thus revealing her teeth. This demonstration of fear can be easily confused with someone about to cry. Comparatively, sadness is displayed using lowered eyebrows and closing the lips together. In that case, her sadness suggests someone feeling stomach pain. Since my avatar is a vampire, showing the teeth to display anger is appropriate for her role. She rapidly frowns her eyebrows and opens the mouth wide to reveal her long upper incisors. However, unless she plays a role in a machinima, the way she displays her anger seems a little exaggerated for a normal conversation. After comparing the display of emotion from a variety of *Second Life* avatars, I would argue that uncanniness is more related to deadeyes and zombie features than ambiguity in emotional display, a preliminary finding that would require further investigation.

The confusing facial expressions of the *Second Life* avatars can hinder facial mimicry or emotional contagion, a phenomenon identified by the involuntary mimicking of facial affect and emotions in real life or in movies.[91] In most cases, the way that we communicate with our avatars "distorts both the situation-specific moods we normally express and our spontaneous, direct, embodied, way of expressing them."[92] To improve their system, Linden Lab had started to develop an application to enable a webcam to capture the user's expressions and head movements to control the gestures of the avatar.[93] As philosopher Hubert Dreyfus claims, in coupling the "control of one's avatar directly to one's brain or body, [the programmers at Linden Lab] could perhaps draw on the mirror neurons of the users to capture intercorporeality."[94] Usually happening during a direct body-to-body interaction, intercorporeality draws on proxemics and enables the genuine communication of moods. Moreover, avatars would require to be displayed in a close-up to convey their subtle changes of expression. In the meantime, as a post in New World News indicates, it is possible to put "a live webcam stream on a prim, and put that prim on your avatar's head."[95] This hack provides a live broadcast of the resident's facial expressions in *Second Life*. Although the resident's moods are displayed live, the box attached to the body of the avatar remains the catalyst for a sensation of strangeness.

Immersion in High Fidelity *and the Next Generation of Synthetic Worlds*

Wanting to create an even more immersive VR platform, the former CEO of *Second Life*, Philip Rosedale, founded a new synthetic world called *High Fidelity* in 2013. An early demonstration of the new technology was recorded at the Silicon Valley Virtual Reality Meetup in March 2014. Using a facial recognition system based on a PrimeSense depth camera and the Faceshift SDK, Rosedale's avatar was able to reproduce in real time his facial expressions, head gestures, and lip movements. By holding sensors in his hands, the system was able to detect their positions and reproduce his hand gestures in the virtual world. The development team opted for a cartoon-looking avatar. Rosedale explained that they "tried using photorealistic avatars instead, but that combined with the low-latency, expressive features and true-to-life voice turned out to be way too creepy. 'It'll scare the hell out of you,' he said."[96]

One of the key features of the new system is its ability to distribute the server's function and capacity among the users' laptops and smartphones. While performing a test demo, about 20 avatars running on separate servers joined the others in a virtual room where they could all dance together listening to the music played by a DJ. Another interesting feature is the possibility to draw pictures in the synthetic world with colored markers so that other avatars could see them. A lot of work still needed to be invested to improve the speed at which the sound was transmitted to generate smoother conversations. One of the goals of these new developments was to enable easier exchanges between workers interacting via virtual worlds. Rosedale invited the software developers present at the demonstration to participate in the development and the testing of the new software.

High Fidelity, the next-generation platform for synthetic worlds launched Avatar Island in December 2017.[97] *High Fidelity* is employing blockchain technology to oversee transactions in High-Fidelity Coins (HFC) between avatars.[98] Draxtor from The Drax Files Radio Hour made a video of a tour of *High Fidelity* with the blogger Strawberry Singh on March 8, 2018.[99] Draxtor wore the Oculus Rift headset to be able to capture the movements of his hands in real life to interact with a tablet his avatar was holding in virtual life. The principle was that instead of interacting with menus and options on the computer screen in real life, the avatar is the one pushing the buttons on the tablet and making selections. This first trial with the tablet was not an example of what Heidegger calls "transparent equipment." The technology was not particularly responsive and clicking a button appeared very tedious. Even doing a handshake, something that is simple to do in real life, was challenging to the newbies of *High Fidelity*. Once they found the trick, thanks to a tip from a friend from Strawberry's social network, the experience of shaking hands was visually impressive. When Strawberry's avatar touched the hand of Draxtor's avatar, a flash of glowing particles illuminated the space between them, and a message displayed on the screen confirmed that they were effectively connected. Seeing Draxtor struggling with the technology made me realize how transparent in use our fingers, hands, and arms are. We often forget how easily we can turn off the noise that surrounds us when we are in conversation with someone in front of us, something that requires computer savviness in virtual reality. The new decentralized VR platform is still under development as I write these lines. *High Fidelity* is streamlining its technology to improve the environments' response time to provide real-time avatar movements and high-fidelity sound quality in the presence of several users. On November 17th, 2018, they organized a Virtual Reality Festival called Future Lands in *High Fidelity* that involved hundreds of participants.

As the world is increasingly connected, virtual worlds are becoming alternatives to video chats, real-life offices, and real-life classrooms. Since some residents spend their entire days roaming in virtual worlds, we can wonder how the limited exposure to detailed facial emotions may influence our extended selves. Just as constant exposure to violence in video games may desensitize players, could the lack of expressiveness of our online avatars limit our palette of emotions, especially if we start spending most of our time online? While there is certainly a phenomenon of habituation, it is important to remember that *Second Life*, *High Fidelity*, *Sansar*, and other online virtual worlds are rarely the only options that people have to express their feelings and interact socially.[100] These alternatives to real-life modes of communication, while enabling people to express emotions with a limited range of bodily gestures and facial expressions, can also extend our network of relationships, develop our creativity, and teach us new computer skills and communication abilities. The key to developing our sensitivity to others is to engage in a variety of relationships and stimulating experiences, including those we encounter in synthetic worlds.

Virtual Reality-Based Therapies

Virtual reality-based therapies draw on the brain's plasticity and tap into the vivid images displayed in virtual environments to treat various psychological and physical disorders. In the first part of this section, I present some general applications of virtual reality-based therapy, including video capture VR systems and therapies in *Second Life*. The second part examines the use of virtual reality systems in stroke sensorimotor rehabilitation.

Video Capture VR Systems and Therapies in Second Life

For therapists, virtual reality systems are useful to understand, assess, and treat patients with various intellectual disabilities or mental health disorders, including phobias, post-traumatic stress disorder, anxiety disorder, and body image disturbance.[101] The virtual reality systems are categorized by their various degrees of immersion. Systems that involve two-dimensional imagery delivered on flat screens are non-immersive. Devices such as stereoscopic projections or flicker glasses that generate tridimensional presentations with fixed visual perspectives provide semi-immersive experiences. A head-mounted display (HMD) or a computer-animated virtual environment (CAVE) that produces three-dimensional visual information that is updated with head movement induces a higher sense of presence—a state of immersion within the virtual environment.[102] To heighten the sense of presence, certain virtual reality systems provide haptic feedback with data gloves or stimulate additional sensory modalities, including sound and smell.[103] Some of these multisensory virtual reality systems include a motion capture system that reproduces the patient's movements from a first-person perspective in the HMD that the patient wears.[104]

Many virtual reality-based therapies exploit the immersive effects of virtual reality to simulate ecologically valid environments.[105] In the case of situations that elicit phobias, for instance, studies demonstrate that a virtual reality environment can evoke the kind of anxiety responses that occur in real life situations. These environments are as effective as *in vivo* exposure or other forms of alternative treatments.[106] Experimental studies demonstrate the effectiveness of specific virtual therapies in alleviating public speaking anxiety and reducing social phobia.[107] By sensing the presence of avatars in simulations of real life environments, such as elevators, supermarkets, subways, and large auditoriums, patients can negotiate with their fear of public spaces, adopt new image schemas, and develop their communication abilities.

Some therapists also employ non-immersive environments like *Second Life* as tools in the treatment of certain mental health problems.[108] For instance, researchers established a healing center for the US Army veterans.[109] Because the returning soldiers were geographically dispersed, online virtual worlds could "support the formation of social networks, facilitate access to care, and provide social activities."[110] According to scientist Jacquelyn Ford Morie, watching an avatar perform relaxation movements and participate in social activities can have beneficial physiological effects.[111] Jeremy Bailenson and Nick Yee, who conducted related studies at Stanford University's Virtual Humans Interaction Lab, called this effect "The Proteus Effect," a phenomenon "whereby the appearance of one's avatar actually influences the behaviors a person feels that avatar must exhibit in the world."[112] In a subsequent study, Jessie Fox and Bailenson discovered that users in a group who watched an avatar that resembled them exercise produced a form of vicarious reinforcement. The members of the group who watched their avatar exercise were more compelled to exercise in the real world over the next 24 hours than were the people in the group that looked at an inactive avatar or at an avatar that did not resemble them.[113] In the case of the healing center for the veterans, since the psychological connection of the veterans to their avatar was central to the experiment, the design and customization of the avatar by the user and its use over time were expected to foster a strong attachment. Accordingly, the Proteus Effect "can be expected from vicarious activities in the *Second Life* environment even if the physical resemblance is not as pronounced."[114]

Repetitive training during virtual reality-based therapies can also be used for the sensorimotor enhancement of people having impaired motor functions after a stroke or neuromuscular disabilities.[115] Some low-immersive systems find inspiration in the video capture VR systems developed by new media artist Myron Krueger. The artist pioneered the use of this technology and received recognition for his artificial reality laboratory called *Videoplace* in the mid-1970s.[116] This type of low-immersive system differs from the immersive CAVE and HMD. When using the system, the user sits in front of a screen on which he or she can see his or her own silhouette moving. The video capture VR platform extracts the user's silhouette from a video camera output in real time. The system then displays a composite image that merges the user's silhouette with other graphical objects with which the user can interact, live. The video capture VR system can be an effective rehabilitation tool. Research based on this technology draws on a body of literature that attests the positive impact of repetitive training on neural reorganization.[117] For instance, GestureTek Health provides a series of video games to help patients improve their motor function by doing repetitive movements while having fun. They see their silhouette onscreen driving a racing car, juggling with balls, trying to catch soccer balls, and lifting boxes off a conveyor belt.[118] On the performance of these types of systems, Weiss and colleagues note that

> [e]vidence from the literature has demonstrated the feasibility, usability and flexibility of video-capture VR, and there is little doubt that this technology provides a useful tool for rehabilitation intervention. The results of presence questionnaires, reports of user satisfaction, and the sensitivity to differences in user ability as functions of age, gender and disability are all strong indicators of the suitability of this tool.[119]

On the effectiveness of video capture VR systems, scientists Richard Foulds and colleagues explain that "this virtual interaction system promotes the repetitive use of goal directed movements of the arms and body, which are essential to promote cortical reorganization, as well as discourage unwanted changes in muscle tissue that result in contracture."[120] According to the scientists, when individuals voluntarily initiate a movement and attempt to control it, their actions are more likely to encourage healthy neurons to assume the roles of damaged cells than the passive movement of the limbs. Moreover, "[n]eural learning occurs most strongly when intention is confirmed by visual and proprioceptive feedback of movement to the brain."[121]

Since the 1990s, many off-the-shelf systems have been adapted for use in rehabilitation and draw on visual proprioceptive feedback. Platforms adapted for this purpose include the VividGroup's Mandala Gesture

Extreme, Reality Fusion GameCam, Intel's Me2Cam Virtual Game System, and the Sony EyeToy application designed to be combined with the PlayStation 2.[122] Subsequently, systems were designed for the Nintendo Wii and Wii Fit and the Microsoft Kinect. These off-the-shelf systems are easy to use and provide instant feedback to the users on their performance and posture while they perform the exercises and play the games designed for their rehabilitation. Patients with stroke who trained with the Wii demonstrated motor improvement after the intervention.[123] By creating effective feedback loops between brain and body, the virtual reality tools can enhance the user's sensorimotor abilities when integrated with their therapy.

Avatars and the Mirror Neuron System in Stroke Rehabilitation

Studies have demonstrated that the mirror neuron system (MNS) can be employed as a neural substrate for methods used in stroke rehabilitation.[124] As discussed in Chapter 1, research on the MNS has demonstrated that these neurons are activated when performing a movement and when observing others perform that movement.[125] After a stroke, some people cannot move a limb or the voluntary movement of that limb is severely impaired. Because the MNS can be activated without overt movement, some methods in stroke rehabilitation draw on the opportunity offered by the MNS to improve motor functions despite the patient's impairment. The belief that neural changes can be induced by interactions with virtual environments is motivated by the simulation hypothesis, which "suggests that the neural networks of a [sic] action-observation system [...] are not only activated during overt motor execution, but also during observation or imagery of the same motor action."[126] Methods in rehabilitation poststroke based on the MNS include action observation, motor imagery, and imitation. These various methods have been adopted as alternatives to physical therapy or conjointly. As numerous clinical studies demonstrate, "the manipulation of these processes through VR not only can enhance neural activation but improve motor outcomes as well."[127]

Some therapies employing virtual reality platforms and avatars to monitor the patients' progress after a stroke rely on the possibilities offered by the MNS for neuro-rehabilitation. As for the video capture VR platforms, the systems draw on the plasticity of the brain and its potential for neural reorganizations poststroke, which can lead to sensorimotor recovery. As an example, Kynan Eng and his colleagues have designed a virtual reality-based system for the motor neuro-rehabilitation of patients who have suffered from upper limb paresis after a stroke.[128] The patients can control the virtual representation of their arms and hands in real time from a first-person perspective.[129] As the scientists note, the "close correspondence between the real and virtual arms in terms of position, relative orientation and movement is designed to optimally stimulate the patient to treat the virtual arms as their own during the therapy session."[130] The preliminary results indicate that the treatment could facilitate motor relearning and improve functional recovery in the arm with partial paralysis if combined with traditional physiotherapy.

Using Eng's system, Lisa Holper and colleagues tested the actual effects of the neuro-rehabilitation on the brain.[131] They found that observing the movement of a virtual arm and imagining that one's own arm performed the movement yield an increase in the oxygenation of the secondary motor areas of the brain. Although the levels of oxygenation observed in the static task were lower than those registered during the imitation task, the results are consistent with the findings of other fMRI and EEG studies.[132] Given these results, they argue that the "VR system is able to elicit the action-observation system as described by the simulation hypothesis."[133]

By reconfiguring the patient's neural networks linking limb and mind through repeated exercises in the virtual environment, virtual reality-based therapies illustrate Clark's concept of the extended mind, which envisages cognition as being distributed among various extensions, as opposed to being confined within the limits of flesh and skull. Through an embodied engagement with their avatars, some patients can enhance their mobility and the animated body becomes their digital prosthesis. The profound coupling between image and body initiates molecular transformations that invite a constant reevaluation of the subjective boundaries. Harnessing the vicarious effects of virtual reality and avatars, virtual reality-based therapies draw on the mutability of the programmable body's boundaries to facilitate motor relearning and promote neuro-rehabilitation.

Conclusion

We are becoming our avatars and they are becoming us. By increasing the likeness with our machines, digital avatars challenge the rigid boundaries of the liberal humanist self. At once, the concept of the avatar can evoke the multiplicity of embodiments, remote agency, the programmability of the body, affective computing, and a prosthetic extension. Avatars can enable us to distribute our cognition and agency across platforms, notably with the use of EEG headsets. The idea that avatars can enable remote access of knowledge and distributed agency is not new, as references have been found in ancient literature and Hindu mythology. Relatively recently, with the advent of computer technology, we acquired the ability to physically engage with digital avatars. Our smartphones and virtual environments can allow us to distribute images of our proxies that are animated, interactive, and customizable. In *Second Life*, some residents aspire to project a more authentic version of themselves. Others like to experiment with the multiple facets of their personality by engaging in identity tourism. Experiencing digital form of intercorporeality enables new sensorimotor skills and ways of expressing emotions to interact socially with online communities. Because emotions generally make communication more enjoyable, some residents appreciate the possibility of expressing their feelings by selecting specific facial expressions. With the integration of facial recognition systems and sensors, the designers of the synthetic world *High Fidelity* aspire to integrate affective computing in our virtual lives as seamlessly as possible.

Synthetic worlds also influence our understanding of postvital approaches to life. The reshaping of the body bit by bit provides a preview of what scientists and engineers of nanoscience envisage for the future: nothing less than a "shaping of the world atom by atom."[134] As science theorist Colin Milburn puts it, the user-generated worlds of *Second Life* anticipate the radical promises of nanotechnology: "digital control of the structure of matter will enable human beings to rebuild the world according to their every whim, right down to the molecular level, changing it in every infinitesimal detail with the ease of reprogramming pixels on a screen."[135]

Becoming-avatar entails the programing of a digital body, the structural coupling of a resident with an avatar, and the remapping of sensorimotor skills and emotional schemas. As an example, we examined how residents of *Second Life* adapt their patterns of sensorimotor interactions to walk and fly in the virtual world. Achieving fluid motion in *Second Life* requires the acquisition of automatisms in real life to activate the branching structure of the underlying algorithms by selecting the right key at the right time. This embodied form of assimilation to the virtual world is another example of the numerous controller-dependent relationships that we develop with our machines.

Looking at the movements produced by photorealistic avatars can activate the MNS. Thanks to the plasticity of the patients' brains, some virtual reality-based therapies take advantage of the MNS in their treatment. For example, patients suffering from reduced mobility after a stroke can reconfigure their body schema and foster new systemic assemblages by observing their virtual limb move. These various bodily adaptations and symbiotic engagements with avatars are realizations of extended modes of cognition that challenge the unitary conceptions of personhood, embodiment, and agency that prevail in the shifting liberal humanist conception of the subject.

Notes

1 Maskeliunas et al., "Consumer-Grade EEG." For a demo of the EMOTIV™ neuroheadset, see Buhr, "Hack Your Brain."
2 Fischman, "The Blind Can See."
3 Hayles, "RFID: Human Agency," 48.
4 Lenoir, "Contemplating Singularity."

5 On agency in virtual worlds, see Coleman, *Hello Avatar.* On identity in *Second Life* and synthetic worlds, see Au, *The Making of Second Life*; Boellstorff, *Coming of Age in Second Life*; Castronova, *Synthetic Worlds*; Meadows, *I, Avatar*; and Peachey and Childs, eds., *Reinventing Ourselves.*
6 On informatic control and Deleuze's approach to controlled mobility and control society, see Galloway, "Playing the Code."
7 Turkle, *Life on the Screen*, 25.
8 Turkle, *Life on the Screen*, 14.
9 Hayles, *How We Became Posthuman*, 34.
10 Clark, *Natural-Born Cyborgs.*
11 Created in 1985, the promotional video for this multi-player online virtual environment was launched in 1986. On *Habitat*, see Morningstar and Farmer, "The Lessons of Lucasfilm's *Habitat*." For a brief survey of the evolution of the "player character" from role-playing games like *Dungeons & Dragons* to the avatar of MMORPGs like *Habitat*, see Taylor, *Play Between Worlds* and Milburn, "Atoms and Avatars."
12 See Jacobsen Marrapodi, "Improving Health Information Literacy."
13 "Who Still Hangs Out on *Second Life*? More than Half a Million People," www.theglobeandmail.com/life/relationships/who-still-hangs-out-on-second-life-more-than-half-a-million-people/article35019213/
14 Clark, *Supersizing the Mind*, 82.
15 Clark, "Re-Inventing Ourselves," 278.
16 Friedman, "Civilization and Its Discontents."
17 Clark, "Re-Inventing Ourselves," 267. Gregersen and Grodal observe physiological alterations during exchanges between the player's body and the interface in video games, in "Embodiment and Interface." Virtual Reality artworks also put the emphasis on the "dynamic interactive processes from which mindbody and world emerge together" in Hayles, "Flesh and Metal," 320.
18 On various factors that can enhance the sense of embodiment in virtual reality, see Kilteni et al., "The Sense of Embodiment."
19 For a brief history of affective computing and some of its applications, see Yonck, *Heart of the Machine.*
20 Ekman et al., *Facial Action Coding System.*
21 Heater, "Creepy Avatars."
22 Haslam, "How to Use Animoji."
23 Heater, "Creepy Avatars."
24 On the digital avatar, see Apter, "Technics of the Subject"; Case, *Performing Science*; Milburn, "Atoms and Avatars"; Schroder ed., *The Social Life of Avatars*; and Waggoner, *My Avatar.*
25 Warner, *Fantastic Metamorphoses.*
26 Parrinder, *Avatar and Incarnation.*
27 Warner, *Fantastic Metamorphoses*, 92–93.
28 On Helena Blavatsky, see Case, *Performing Science.*
29 On spiritualism, see Sconce, chapter 1, *Haunted Media.*
30 In the acknowledgment section of *Snow Crash*, Stephenson mentions that he was unaware when writing his novel that the term "avatar" had first been used in the virtual reality game *Habitat*, 470.
31 On the making of *Second Life*, see Au, *The Making of Second Life* and Dubner, "Philip Rosedale."
32 Sconce, *Haunted Media.*
33 On films evoking discipline and control, see Davis, "Who's Playing You?" and Shaviro, *Post-Cinematic Affect.* On the society of control, see Deleuze,

"Post-scriptum." For a history of discipline before the networked society, see Foucault, *Discipline and Punish.*

34 Dawkins, *The Blind Watchmaker*, 111. Alternative approaches, such as those of biologist Steven Rose and philosopher of mind Evan Thompson, dispute the idea that we are the sum of our genes. See, for instance, Rose, *Lifelines* and Thompson, *Mind in Life.*

35 Doyle, *On Beyond Living*, 8.

36 Hayles, *My Mother Was a Computer*, 27.

37 See Wolfram, *A New Kind of Science*, and Morowitz, *The Emergence of Everything.*

38 See Haraway, "Situated Knowledges."

39 On representations of life in computer games, see Burnett, chapter 8, *How Images Think.*

40 Schrödinger, *What is Life?*, 21.

41 Weber et al., *Creating Your World*, 44. By searching on the Internet, one can find YouTube videos on prim torture: http://secondlife.wikia.com/wiki/Prim_torture

42 Luhmann, *Social Systems*; Luhmann, "The Autopoiesis of Social Systems"; and Luhmann, *The Reality of the Mass Media.* Guattari examines social systems that qualify as living systems in "Machinic Heterogenesis." Clarke applies systems theory to media theory in *Posthuman Metamorphosis.*

43 Maturana and Varela, *Autopoiesis and Cognition*, 48.

44 It is an approximation of an autopoietic system since it does not fulfill all the criteria for an autopoietic system as defined by Maturana and Varela. Thompson discusses the minimal autopoietic system in *Mind in Life.*

45 Bourdieu, *The Logic of Practice.*

46 Thompson, *Mind in Life.*

47 Varela, "Laying Down a Path."

48 Stromer-Galley and Martey, "Visual Spaces, Norm Governed Places," 1050.

49 Stromer-Galley and Martey, "Visual Spaces, Norm Governed Places," 1043.

50 On gender identity in virtual worlds, see Fizek and Wasilewska, "Embodiment and Gender Identity." For a research that compares the avatar's gender with the resident's own gender, see Mitra and Golz, "Intrisic Gender Identity." On gender stereotypes, see Dumitrica and Gaden, "Gender and Technology in *Second Life.*"

51 For the Symbolic Interaction approach, the concept of person is informed by the multiplicity of roles one performs in various contexts. While Activity Theory also considers context, it puts the emphasis on the idea of the Self as emerging from its goal-oriented actions and social practices. For an application of these approaches to *Second Life*, see Evans, "Virtual Selves."

52 Bloustien and Wood, "Face, Authenticity, Transformations," 52.

53 Boellstorff, *Coming of Age*, 133.

54 Boellstorff, *Coming of Age*, 120.

55 On virtual world experiences that can change residents' real-life behavior and personality traits, see McLeod et al., "When your *Second Life* Comes Knocking" and Wiederhold, "Avatars: Changing Behavior."

56 Boellstorff, *Coming of Age,* 121.

57 Gottschalk, "The Presentation of Avatars in *Second Life*," 513.

58 On the body image in the media in general, see Wykes and Gunter, *The Media and Body Image.*

59 Gottschalk, "The Presentation of Avatars in *Second Life*," 511.

60 Rymaszewski et al., *Second Life*, 93.
61 Dumitrica and Gaden, "Gender and Technology in *Second Life*," 18.
62 In the documentary *Life 2.0* (Jason Spingarn-Koff, 2010), Teasa Copprue/Asri Falcon is a successful designer in *Second Life* and describes how *Second Life* has empowered her.
63 Dumitrica and Gaden, "Gender and Technology in *Second Life*," 15.
64 Brookey and Cannon, "Sex Lives," 145.
65 Nakamura, "Race In/For Cyberspace."
66 Nakamura, *Cybertypes*, 13–14.
67 Sanchez, "My *Second Life*," 69.
68 Mohammed, "A Case Study," 7.
69 Noveck, "Democracy," 269–270.
70 Deleuze and Guattari, *A Thousand Plateaus*, 149–166.
71 On the sense of embodiment in virtual reality, see Kilteni et al., "The Sense of Embodiment," 373.
72 On the frequent analogies between physical and virtual lives for newbies, see Locher et al., "Negotiation of Space in *Second Life*."
73 On the potential of user-defined nonverbal gestures to enhance online interactions, see Antonijevic, "From Text to Gesture Online."
74 Friedman, "Civilization and Its Discontents," 137.
75 Clark refers to the example of the hammer in the hands of the skilled carpenter in Heidegger's *Being and Time* in *Supersizing the Mind*, 10.
76 Kennedy, "Lara Croft."
77 Thompson, *Mind in Life*, 249.
78 Before the advent of *Second Life*, intimacy in virtual chats is discussed in Reid, "Text-Based Virtual Realities."
79 On the story of a real-life couple that met in *Second Life*, see the documentary *Life 2.0* (Jason Spingarn-Koff, 2010).
80 Evans, "The Self and *Second Life*," 49.
81 See Ekman, "Facial Expression" and Keltner et al., "Facial Expression."
82 Planalp, *Communicating Emotion*.
83 On the gendered stereotypes embedded in the nonverbal gestures, see Antonijevic, "From Text to Gesture Online."
84 Quoted in Dreyfus, *On the Internet*, 112.
85 Boellstorff, *Coming of Age*, 159.
86 Bloustien and Wood, "Face, Authenticity, Transformations," 66.
87 "New Way to Get Your Face in SL," posted on August 18, 2007. http://forums-archive.secondlife.com/327/a0/211946/1.html
88 On the phenomenon of the uncanny valley, see Mori, "The Uncanny Valley."
89 See Thompson, "Monsters of Photorealism."
90 Tinwell et al., "Facial Expression of Emotion" and Tinwell et al., "Perception of Psychopathy."
91 Rosenblum examines facial mimicry in real life and in cinema in *What I'm Saying*.
92 Dreyfus, *On the Internet*, 113.
93 Dreyfus, *On the Internet*, 117.
94 Dreyfus, *On the Internet*, 113.
95 Au, "*Second Life* 2.0 Awesomeness."
96 Neal, "Creepily Realistic Avatars."
97 Prisco, "*Second Life* Creator."
98 Rosedale, "Paying Avatars on the Blockchain."
99 Show #173: "Too Many Worlds, Too Many Draxes." *The Draxe Files Radio Hour*, March 11, 2018. https://draxfiles.com/2018/03/11/show-173-too-many-worlds-too-many-draxes/

100 On this topic, see Skoyles, "Socializing in *Second Life*."
101 Standen and Brown, "Rehabilitation of People with Intellectual Disabilities"; Gregg and Tarrier, "Virtual Reality"; Kim et al., "Obsessive-Compulsive Disorder"; Meyerbröker and Emmelkamp, "Anxiety Disorder"; Gershon, et al., "Virtual Reality Exposure Therapy; and Nitsche, *Video Game Spaces*."
102 Meyerbröker and Emmelkamp, "Anxiety Disorder," 57.
103 On the use of sound to increase presence, see Rosati et al., "On the Role of Auditory Feedback."
104 Perez-Marcos et al., "A Fully Immersive Set-up."
105 On aspects of virtual reality that enhance the ecological validity of the environment in social neuroscience, see Parsons et al., "Virtual Reality."
106 Gregg and Tarrier, "Virtual Reality," 350.
107 On public speaking, see North et al., "Fear of Public Speaking." On social phobia, see Klinger et al., "Social Phobia."
108 For reviews of some projects developed in *Second Life*, see Gorini et al., "A *Second Life* for eHealth" and Rehm et al., "What Role Can Avatars Play in e-Mental Health."
109 Morie, "Online Virtual Worlds."
110 Morie, "Online Virtual Worlds," 153.
111 Morie, "Online Virtual Worlds," 157.
112 Morie, "Online Virtual Worlds," 157. On the Proteus effect, see Yee and Bailenson, "The Proteus Effect."
113 See Fox and Bailenson, "Virtual Self-Modeling."
114 Morie, "Online Virtual Worlds," 157.
115 For a review on the use of virtual reality for rehabilitation poststroke, see Bermúdez i Badia et al., "Virtual Reality." On the enhancement of the sensorimotor skills of people with neuromuscular disabilities, see Foulds et al., "Sensory-Motor Enhancement."
116 Krueger, *Artificial Reality II*.
117 For a review of off-the-shelf systems used for virtual rehabilitation, see Bermúdez i Badia et al., "Virtual Reality," 588–589.
118 See examples at www.gesturetekhealth.com under rehabilitation. Last accessed on June 2, 2018.
119 Weiss et al., "Video Capture Virtual Reality," 10.
120 Foulds, "Sensory-Motor Enhancement," 87.
121 Foulds, "Sensory-Motor Enhancement," 87.
122 On EyeToy, see the Gamasutra website, https://www.gamasutra.com/view/news/111925/InDepth_Eye_To_Eye__The_History_Of_EyeToy.php. Last accessed June 2, 2018. For a review of the early developments of video capture VR in therapy and off-the-shelf platforms, see also Weiss, "Video Capture Virtual Reality."
123 Shiner et al., "Wii-Based Movement Therapy." On the positive effects of commercial games such as Dance Dance Revolution and Wii Sports and off-the-shelf systems, see also Lohse et al., "Commercial Games in Therapy."
124 For a review of practical applications of the MNS for stroke recovery, see Garrison et al., "A Neural Substrate."
125 Rizzolatti and Craighero, "The Mirror-Neuron System."
126 Holper et al., "Testing," 58.
127 Bermúdez i Badia et al., "Virtual Reality," 586.
128 Eng et al., "Cognitive Virtual-Reality" and Eng et al., "Interactive Visuo-Motor Therapy."
129 Many video games based on video capture VR platforms have also been adapted for use in rehabilitation, Weiss et al., "Video Capture Virtual Reality."
130 Eng et al., "Interactive Visuo-Motor Therapy," 903.

131 Holper et al., “Testing.”
132 Holper et al., “Testing.”
133 Holper et al., “Testing.”
134 National Science and Technology Council, *Nanotechnology*, 1.
135 Milburn, “Atoms and Avatars,” 72.

Coda

On our trek across the animated landscape, the distorted contours of our animated doubles stimulated our curiosity. A strange mixture of sensual pleasure, uncanny feelings, and muscular pain reverberated through our bodies. But now, it is the end of the road and the picture begins to fade. Before the sunset in cartoon town, let's pause for a moment to reminisce on our journey.

Animated composites and human-animal hybrids render the body's boundaries as porous and malleable. Because we are face experts and attuned to divergences from familiar patterns of embodiment, facial distortions and bodily contortions disrupt our comfort zones. In the world of animated creatures, where these distorted contours abound, collapsing clay figures, muscles about to burst, mutating avatars, and uncanny synthespians matter.

The flow of affects aroused by metamorphic characters is central to our engagement with animated media. By evoking various degrees of eeriness, bedazzlement, or visceral churning, they draw our attention to our own reactions to deviations from expectations. These perceptual encounters offer an opportunity to reevaluate our sets of assumptions about the body's limits, a process that I have called "becoming-animated."

Our embodied relations with animated figures also reveal the permeability of the interfaces that link us to the animated world. By becoming-animated, we enter into an assemblage with the animation machine—a rhizome of alignments, resonances, affects, and conventions that mesh with our corporeal envelopes. The animation machine also reimagines the limits of the body found in media culture by joining biological anatomies, social practices, and technical automatisms.

Moreover, the profoundly embodied configuration of the *Homo sapiens*' body is preadapted to be extended by technological tools thanks to its flexible agent-world boundary. Working as technological extensions, the animation's automatisms stimulate the spectator's neural networks. With their focus on perceptual effects, some animations can even reveal the inner workings of human perception. *Spheres* (René Jodoin and Norman McLaren, 1969), for example, accentuates some of the gestalt laws of perceptual organization with geometrical patterns of moving pearls. Alternatively, *The Cabinet of Jan Švankmajer* (Stephen Quay and Timothy Quay, 1984) teaches the principles of apparent motion to the viewer. Each in their own way, these animated films highlight the systemic intersections between the spectator's visual system and the animation machine.

The structure of engagement strengthens the assemblages of affects, technical automatisms, and conventions orchestrated by the animation machine. This structure draws on the viewers' innate attraction to anthropomorphism and natural inclination to decode facial expressions. It notably sustains the audiences' absorption with strategies that elicit a combination of "feeling with" and "feeling for" the main protagonists. Other low-road mechanisms produce bodily couplings at the neural level, the affective level, and the level of the body schema that inform the esthetic experience. Animation taps into our built-in mirroring mechanisms—the mirror neuron system—to elicit empathic reverberations, some of which are: muscular mimicry, facial mimicry, and embodied simulations.

Research on the embodied mind and the conceptual metaphor theory demonstrates that our understanding of audiovisual metaphors is partly grounded in sensorimotor experiences and empathic mechanisms. An orientational metaphor such as HAPPY IS UP can imbue an animated sequence with a cheering mood. The visual manifestation of this image schema in *Boundin'* (Bud Luckey, 2003) helps make comprehensible the subjective perspective of the bouncing sheep. While we understand the world because of the body that we have, we can also rely on our experience of sensorimotor interactions with real spaces to interpret virtual patterns of interactions with imaginary places. The characters in the animation *Antagonia* (Nicolas Brault, 2002) respond to different laws of physics and thereby new force schemas apply. Thanks to their peculiar patterns of sensorimotor exploration of the animated space, we can appreciate their topsy-turvy world.

The imaginary transposition of oneself into the place of an animated character is an important aspect of the structure of engagement. It initiates a merging of the spectator's perspective with the character's perspective in ways that blur the strict separation between self and animated other. By aligning the gaze of the spectator with the gaze of the monstrous animated hybrid, the animation machine composites the spectator's perception into the animated world. In other words, the spectator's perceptual system actively participates in the process of reanimating living-dead cartoons.

In their use of perceptual alignments, cyberpunk animations raise many questions about the limits of the human and its intersections with computer technology. The viewers' imaginary transpositions into the place of cyborgs remind them that spectatorship is not organism-bound, but is preadapted to be extended by any technology we may think of, and thus hint at what I call "posthuman perception." Various forms of subjectivity are powered by the technology of animation and enacted by an embodied viewer in cyberpunk animation. For instance, some sequences of *Final Fantasy: The Spirits Within* (Hironobu Sakaguchi, 2001) feature composited interfaces that represent augmented perception. Thanks to Eadweard Muybridge's flickering images of bodies in motion, *Immortal Ad Vitam* (Enki Bilal, 2004) reveals Jill's humanness by showing the perceptual hybridization between the human viewer and the animation technology. The merging of subjectivities is an example of embodied virtuality. In *Ghost in the Shell* (Mamoru Oshii, 1995), Kusanagi and the Puppet Master's "ghosts" merge into a new body. Following their physical and mental fusion, the ending suggests the spectators' transmutation into an electronic entity that could transport them into the animated world. Finally, the proprioceptive mimicry of Kusanagi's posthuman condition or the subjective alignments with cyberstars enables viewers to explore alternative subject positions via empathic mechanisms.

Character design is another crucial aspect of character engagement. Physical characteristics provided by age, gender, class, and race influence our interpretation of the character's personality and aspirations. Form and modes of production are other factors to consider when we analyze an animation. The shape-shifting nature of the animated cartoon unsettles the IN-OUT schema, a schema that we rest on to understand the bounded nature of the body. This liminality in terms of form can carry over into the political domain. Metamorphic creatures are able to transgress the limits between categories and defy the status quo. This attribute partly explains why stories featuring *grylli* and hybrids often promote diversity, personal growth, or social change. In *Corpse Bride* (Tim Burton and Mike Johnson, 2005), various references to transgressions of the IN-OUT schema allude to the feelings of captivity or alienation experienced in the strict Victorian society. The partially decomposed flesh of Emily, the Corpse Bride, suggests that she is caught between two worlds. In contrast, the malleability of the clay bodies of the workers in *The Death of Stalinism in Bohemia* (Jan Švankmajer, 1990) alludes to their exploitation during Stalinism. The modes of production may also acquire political significance in *Princess Mononoke* (Hayao Myazaki, 1997). This animation champions cross-cultural understanding and respect for all living creatures. The Tatari-gami curse symbolizes the hatred that is destroying the forest and consuming Ashitaka, San, Lady Eboshi, and the villagers of Irontown. The combination of cel animation and digital techniques to design the cursed arm represents the clash between the traditional and the modern, a recurring trope in the narrative.

The metamorphic transformations of animated characters in *Princess Mononoke* and *Howl's Moving Castle* (Hayao Miyazaki, 2004) can also mirror the molecular transformations happening to the viewer. The glowing feelers that crawl on Ashitaka's arm reflect the turbulent flow of affects that characterizes the human body in general. In *Howl's Moving Castle*, the metamorphosis of Howl arouses empathic reverberations that disturb the body's chemical balance. Howl's becoming-animal brings to mind the effects of war on soldiers as they turn into insensitive war machines. In these metamorphic narratives, hybrids, malleable puppets, and shape-shifting characters defy the unitary body of liberal humanism to decry marginalization, oppression, and alienation.

Mimicry of the film's body can also manipulate the viewer's affective experience in persuasive ways. When animated characters move across the frame, they activate muscular memories. Even though every animation can revive muscular memories, some genres and styles are more conducive to mimicry. While the rushing locomotive in *The Polar Express* (Robert Zemeckis, 2003) and the feeling of swinging across Times Square in the video game *Spider-Man 3* (2007) are pleasurable in and of themselves, martial arts films showcase the muscularity of the body to empower viewers. In animation, the hyperbolized movements of martial artists rely on cartoonal logic and often parody extravagant abilities depicted in films. Viper and Mulan are two female warriors who defy cultural traditions and empower viewers with their strength and feminine fighting styles.

The modes of production can evoke defamiliarizing muscular sensations that contribute to the discourse of an animated film. For example, the revulsion for abnormality induced by pixilation and stop motion in *The Club of the Laid Off* (Jiří Barta, 1989) and *The Secret Adventures of Tom Thumb* (Dave Borthwick, 1993) reflects anxieties about technological progress and modernization. The rotoscope technology can also contribute to sociocultural associations. When Koko the Clown performs his skits in the Fleischer's animations, our innate life-detector recognizes the realism of human motion produced by the rotoscope. In contrast, *Minnie the Moocher* (Dave Fleischer, 1932) and *Betty Boop's Snow White* (Dave Fleischer, 1933) echo the rotoscoped gestures of Cab Calloway in uncanny ways. For instance, the grotesque walrus in *Minnie the Moocher* and the haunted scenery invite racist associations between African Americans and criminality. The representations of superhumans in *Black Jack: The Movie* (Osamu Dezaki and Fumihiro Yoshimura, 1996) and muscular cyclists in *The Triplets of Belleville* (Sylvain Chomet, 2003) approach the idea of the posthuman from an embodied perspective. Adopting the vantage point of victimized athletes and sharing their pain is a means to understand the negative effects of bodily enhancement from a first-person perspective. By extending the spectator's audiovisual experience to the muscular domain, these animated films compel the spectator to engage in debates about the transforming effects of technology on the body.

Uncanniness is a feeling that underscores the tension between the human and the nonhuman. When used in conjunction with the structure of engagement, uncanny effects can inspire reflections on the future of the human. Various modes of production and techniques contribute to the eeriness of an animation. Masks and masklike facial expressions can defamiliarize character appearance and cause incertitude about the subject-object dyad. This doubt is particularly relevant in *Texhnolyze* (Hiroshi Hamasaki, 2003), an animated TV series featuring the city of Lukuss, a place where the inhabitants are increasingly fitted with cybernetic prostheses. The causes of the mixed feelings evoked by human-looking synthespians range from poor character design to innate evolutionary mechanisms to avoid the threat of corpses. The apprehension toward aliveness can be desirable in animations concerned about the obsolescence of the body in futuristic societies. In *Final Fantasy: The Spirits Within*, the uncanny pervades a narrative about a world where the respect of all life forms, including alien ones, has become a necessity for human survival. The mechanical uncanny is another source of dread. It arises when self-animated dolls and automata project a semblance of life. The revulsion elicited by the uncanny in *Malice@Doll* (Keitarô Motonaga, 2001) is associated with processes of discrimination toward marginalized people. Moreover, from the perspective of the mechanized dolls, it is the doll turned human who looks strange. The reversal of the usual perspective on the uncanny and the perceptual alignment with dolls compel viewers to empathize with those who see the world differently, humans or otherwise.

Some video games demonstrate the contribution of bodily experiences to the comprehension of abstract concepts. Understanding the politics and debates conveyed by the video games *BioShock* (2007) and *BioShock 2* (2010) requires an embodied exploration of the game world. These quests of adventures in Rapture reveal the necessity of forging an alliance between body and technology to survive. Hence, they put to the test the adaptability of the player's perceptual system. The players must continuously improve their skills and find technological means to bypass physical limitations. In extending the perceptual scope through the physical and logical interfaces, the symbiotic relationship of the player and the avatar can produce new systemic wholes that augment the body's reach. By playing different scenarios, the players enact the continuous reshaping of the limits of the human enabled by cultural media. The repeated sequences of movements translate image schemas into embodied knowledge. For example, enacting survival scenarios helps the players grapple with concepts such as "survival of the fittest" and "free will." The players of *BioShock* also experience the ideology of optimized eugenics promoted by Rapture when they are progressively transforming into a killing cyborg. In addition, the video game avatar evokes the idea that the body is like code. For example, after dying, the avatar's instant reincarnation into Vita chambers illustrates the concept of postvitalism in a concrete way. Additionally, the video games integrate procedural rhetoric and informatic control into the players' body schemas, constraining their movements and behaviors within a web of deterministic laws. When taking pictures of splicers or hacking turrets has become second nature, we know that the system has sufficiently drilled our bodies to behave like evil scientists and readied us to join the ranks of Ryan Industries.

In synthetic worlds, virtual selfhood is intricately meshed with technology. The computer-powered world of *Second Life* offers the possibility of experimenting with alternative forms of intercorporeality. By exploring the virtual landscape at the singular pace of their avatar, residents can acquire patterns of sensorimotor interactions and emotional abilities adapted for the virtual environment, a process that I call "becoming-avatar." This transformation progressively happens as the residents familiarize themselves with the interfaces and the tools become transparent equipment. By becoming in sync with their avatar, residents assimilate the computerized regime of vision into their body schema. As the ramifications of the real extend toward the virtual, our engagement with avatars in virtual worlds informs our understanding of distributed cognition, collaborative agency, and identity tourism. The latter concept concerns the opportunity to design the physical appearance of our second selves to portray a different gender or race. Alternatively, some users aspire to present a more authentic image of the person they really are inside. However, identity quests and relationships in synthetic worlds can be challenging. For example, conveying one's emotions with meaningful gestures is an operation that can require computer savviness. Moreover, using an avatar to inform interlocutors about our internal states and intentions is not always evident, as its facial expressions can be confusing or creepy. With the development of affective computing technologies, such as facial recognition systems and sensors, the next-generation platforms for synthetic worlds such as *High Fidelity* hope to enable easier exchanges between remote workers and more immersive virtual intimacies. In the sphere of virtual reality-based therapies, avatar engagement can stimulate the mirror neuron system to promote neuro-rehabilitation and improve the recovery of motor mobility after a stroke.

These diverse experiences of perspective-sharing and symbiotic engagement invite us to envisage a continuum of embodiments, which shifts the focus away from a strict division between the human and the nonhuman or the real and the animated. By adopting the perspectives of animated entities, in a world in which the human and the nonhuman become part of the same machinic assemblage, we are invited to reevaluate the relevance of the models that we have always used to attribute identities. These posthuman explorations contribute to our understanding of the new relations we develop with avatars and synthespians in a society in which they are increasingly recruited for establishing business relations, working in the entertainment industry, and assisting in medical treatments.

Engaging with the animated world can activate new circuits of thought, enhance our sensorimotor abilities, and fine-tune our empathic understanding. Because of the plastic nature of our neural resources and the body's aptitude for initiating symbiotic relationships, animated media develop our selfhood in a variety of ways, from embodied learning to creative reshaping of one's personal image. These dynamic connections open up new pathways that animate the tips of our nerves and power up technological collaborations in both real and virtual communities. However, we must remain careful when we select our extensions and our symbiotic partners. Becoming-inanimate or becoming-animated? In the end, the choice is all yours.

That's All Folks!

References

Aarseth, Espen. *Cybertext: Perspectives on Ergodic Literature*. Baltimore, MD: Johns Hopkins University Press, 1997.

Adolphs, Ralph. "Cognitive Neuroscience of Human Behavior." *Nature Reviews* 4, no. 3 (2003): 165–178.

Akatsuka, Wakagi. "The Wager of a Militant Surrealist: On Jan Švankmajer's *The Death of Stalinism in Bohemia*." 1998. Accessed January 23, 2011. http://srch.slav.hokudai.ac.jp/publictn/45/akatsuka/akatsuka-E.html.

Aksentijevic, Aleksandar. "Consciousness and Apparent Motion: Paradox Resolved." *Theory and Psychology* 26, no. 1 (2015): 44–57.

Anderson, Aaron. "Violent Dances in Martial Arts Films." *Jump Cut*, no. 44 (2001): 1–3. Accessed October 17, 2011. www.ejumpcut.org/archive/jc44.2001/aarona/aaron1.html.

Anderson, Aaron. "Action in Motion: Kinesthesia in Martial Arts Films." *Jump Cut*, no. 42 (1998): 1–11, 83.

Anderson, Joseph, and Barbara Anderson. "The Myth of Persistence of Vision Revisited." *Journal of Film and Video* 45, no. 1 (1993): 3–12.

Anonymous. "Hanks Fears Hollywood Stars to Be Replaced by Robots." *The Internet Movie Database* (IMDB), Movie/TV News. Accessed July 9, 2001. www.imdb.com/news/ni0058281/.

Anonymous. "*Burnout*." *Edge* 104 (December 2001): 70–71.

Antonijevic, Smiljana. "From Text to Gesture Online: A Microethnographic Analysis of Nonverbal Communication in the *Second Life* Virtual Environment." *Information, Communication, and Society* 11, no. 2 (2008): 221–238.

Apter, Emily. "Technics of the Subject: The Avatar-Drive." *Postmodern Culture* 18, no. 2 (2008). http://muse.jhu.edu/journals/postmodern_culture/v018/18.2.apter.html.

Arnheim, Rudolf. *Film as Art*. Berkeley and Los Angeles: University of California Press, 1974.

Arnheim, Rudolf. *Visual Thinking*. Berkeley and Los Angeles: University of California Press, 1969.

Arnheim, Rudolf. *Art and Visual Perception: A Psychology of the Creative Eye*. Berkeley and Los Angeles: University of California Press, 1954.

Ashby, W. Ross. *Design for a Brain*. London: Chapman and Hall, 1952.

Atwood, Margaret. *Survival: A Thematic Guide to Canadian Literature*. Toronto, ON: House of Anansi Press, 1972.

Au, Wagner James. *The Making of Second Life: Notes from the New World*. New York: Collins, 2008.

Au, Wagner James. "*Second Life* 2.0 Awesomeness: Stream Live Webcam Video of Your Real Head on Your *Second Life* Avatar!," *New World Notes* (blog). February 26, 2010. http://nwn.blogs.com/nwn/2010/02/shared-media-awesomeness.html.

Balázs, Béla. *Theory of the Film: Character and Growth of a New Art.* New York: Arno Press, 1972.

Barker, Jennifer. *The Tactile Eye: Touch and the Cinematic Experience.* Berkeley and Los Angeles: University of California Press, 2009.

Barlett, Christopher P. "Video Game Effects—Confirmed, Suspected, and Speculative: A Review of the Evidence." *Simulation and Gaming* 40, no. 3 (2009): 377–403.

Barrier, Michael. *Hollywood Cartoons: American Animation in Its Golden Age.* Oxford and New York: Oxford University Press, 2003.

Baudrillard, Jean. "Prophylaxis and Virulence." In *Posthumanism*, edited by Neil Badmington, 34–41. New York: Palgrave, 2000.

Bavelas, Janet Beavin, Alex Black, Charles R. Lemery, and Jennifer Mullett. "Motor Mimicry as Primitive Empathy." In *Empathy and Its Development*, edited by Nancy Eisenberg and Janet Strayer, 317–338. Cambridge: Cambridge University Press, 1987.

Bazin, André. *What Is Cinema?* Translated by Hugh Gray. Berkeley and Los Angeles: University of California Press, 1967.

Bell, David, and Barbara M. Kennedy, eds. *The Cybercultures Reader*, 2nd ed. London and New York: Routledge, 2007.

Bellmore, Kate. "Who Is This Girl I See?: Reflecting on Female Representation in Disney's *Mulan*." June 22, 2014. https://reelclub.wordpress.com/2014/06/22/who-is-this-girl-i-see-reflecting-on-female-representation-in-disneys-mulan/.

Benedikt, Michael. "Cyberspace: First Steps." In *The Cybercultures Reader*, 2nd ed., edited by David Bell and Barbara M. Kennedy, 19–33. London and New York: Routledge, 2007.

Berenson, Bernard. *The Florentine Painters of the Renaissance.* New York and London: G. P. Putnam's Sons, 1909.

Bergson, Henri. *Matter and Memory.* Translated by N. M. Paul and W. S. Palmer. New York: Cosimo, 2007.

Bermúdez i Badia, Sergi, Gerard G. Fluet, Roberto Llorens, and Judith E. Deutsch. "Virtual Reality for Sensorimotor Rehabilitation Post Stroke: Design Principles and Evidence." In *Neurorehabilitation Technology*, 2nd ed., edited by David J. Reinkensmeyer and Volker Dietz, 573–603. New York: Springer, 2016.

Berti, Anna, and Frassineti, Francesca. "When Far Becomes Near: Re-Mapping of Space by Tool Use." *Journal of Cognitive Neuroscience* 12 (2000): 415–420.

Bigelow, Susan J. "Technologies of Perception: Miyazaki in Theory and Practice." *Animation* 4 (2009): 55–75.

Bingham, Geoffrey P. "Task-Specific Devices and the Perceptual Bottleneck." *Human Movement Science* 7 (1988): 225–264.

Blackmore, Susan J., Gavin Brelstaff, Kay Nelson, and Tom Trościanko. "Is the Richness of Our Visual World an Illusion? Transsaccadic Memory for Complex Scenes." *Perception* 24, no. 9 (1995): 1075–1081.

Blake, Randolphe, and Maggie Shiffrar. "Perception of Human Motion." *Annual Review of Psychology* 15, no. 8 (2007): 12.1–12.27.

Blakeslee, Sandra. "Cells That Read Minds." *New York Times*. (2016). January 16. D1, D4.

Bloustien, Geraldine F., and Denise Wood. "Face, Authenticity, Transformations, and Aesthetics in *Second Life*." *Body & Society* 19, no. 1 (2013): 52–81.

Boellstorff, Tom. *Coming of Age in Second Life: An Anthropologist Explores the Virtually Human*. Princeton, NJ: Princeton University Press, 2008.

Bogost, Ian. *Persuasive Games: The Expressive Power of Videogames*. Cambridge, MA: The MIT Press, 2007.

Bois, Yve-Alain, and Rosalind Krauss. *Formless: A User's Guide*. New York: Zone Books, 1997.

Bolton, Christopher, Istvan Csicsery-Ronay, and Takayuki Tatsumi, eds. *Robot Ghosts and Wired Dreams: Japanese Science Fiction from Origins to Anime*. Minneapolis: University of Minnesota Press, 2007.

Bordwell, David, and Kristin Thompson. *Film Art: An Introduction*, 9th ed. New York: McGraw-Hill, 2010.

Bordwell, David. "Aesthetics in Action: Kung Fu, Gunplay, and Cinematic Expressivity." In *Fifty Years of Electric Shadows*, edited by Law Kar, 81–89. Hong Kong: Urban Council, 1997.

Bordwell, David. *Making Meaning: Inference and Rhetoric in the Interpretation of Cinema*. Cambridge, MA: Harvard University Press, 1989.

Bordwell, David. *Narration in the Fiction Film*. Madison, WIS: University of Wisconsin Press, 1985.

Bordwell, David. "The Part-Time Cognitivist: A View from Film Studies." *Projections* 4, no. 2 (2010): 1–18.

Bordwell, David. "A Case for Cognitivism." *Iris* 9 (1989): 11–40.

Bossewitch, Jonah, and Aram Sinnreich. "The End of Forgetting: Strategic Agency Beyond the Panopticon." *New Media & Society* 15, no. 2 (2013): 224–242.

Bouldin, Joanna. *The Animated and the Actual: Toward a Theory of Animation, Live-Action, and Everyday Life*. Dissertation, University of California, Irvine, 2004.

Bourdieu, Pierre. *The Logic of Practice*. Translated by Richard Nice. Cambridge: Polity, 1990.

Boyd, James, and Tetsuya Nishimura. "Shinto Perspectives in Miyazaki's Anime Film *Spirited Away*." *Journal of Religion and Film* 8, no. 2 (2004) www.unomaha.edu/jrf/Vol8No2/boydShinto.htm.

Bradner, Liesl. "Brad Pitt Becomes 'Button': Steve Preeg Explains the Magic. Wizards of Hollywood: Steve Preeg." Accessed February 12, 2009. herocomplex.latimes.com/uncategorized/brad-pitt-becom/.

Branigan, Edward. *Narrative Comprehension and Film*. London and New York: Routledge, 1992.

Brennan, Theresa. *The Transmission of Affect*. Ithaca, NY: Cornell University Press, 2004.

Brookey, Robert Alan, and Kristopher L. Cannon. "Sex Lives in *Second Life*." *Critical Studies in Media Communication* 26, no. 2 (2009): 145–164.

Brooks, Rodney A., and Lynn Andrea Stein. "Building Brains for Bodies." *Autonomous Robots* 1 (1994): 7–25.

Brown, Steven T. *Tokyo Cyber-Punk: Posthumanism in Japanese Culture*. New York: Palgrave Macmillan, 2010.

Brown, Steven T. "Machinic Desires: Hans Bellmer's Dolls and the Technological Uncanny in *Ghost in the Shell 2: Innocence*." In *Mechademia 3: Limits of the Human*, edited by Frenchy Lunning, 222–253. Minneapolis: University of Minnesota Press, 2008.

Buchan, Suzanne. "Animation Spectatorship: The Quay Brothers' Animated 'Worlds.'" *Entertext* 4, no. 1 (2004/5): 97–125.

Buckland, Warren, ed. *Puzzle Films: Complex Storytelling in Contemporary Cinema*. Hoboken, NJ: Wiley-Blackwell, 2009.

Buckland, Warren. *The Cognitive Semiotics of Film*. Cambridge: Cambridge University Press, 2000.

Buhr, Sarah. "Hack Your Brain with a Machine That Reads Minds." *Tech Crunch*, June 30, 2014, https://techcrunch.com/2014/06/30/hack-your-brain-with-a-machine-that-reads-minds/.

Bukatman, Scott. "Disobedient Machines: Animation and Autonomy." In *Beyond the Finite: The Sublime in Art and Science*, edited by Roald Hoffmann and Iain Boyd Whyte, 128–148. Oxford and New York: Oxford University Press, 2011.

Bukatman, Scott. "Taking Shape: Morphing and the Performance of Self." In *Meta-Morphing: Visual Transformation and the Culture of Quick-Change*, edited by Vivian Sobchack, 225–249. Minneapolis: University of Minnesota Press, 2000.

Bukatman, Scott. *Terminal Identity: The Virtual Subject in Postmodern Science Fiction*. Durham, NC: Duke University Press, 2005 (1993).

Burnett, Ron. *How Images Think*. Cambridge, MA: The MIT Press, 2004.

Cabarga, Leslie. *The Fleischer Story*. New York: DaCapo Press, 1988.

Canemaker, John. "A Part-Human, Part-Cartoon Species." *The New York Times*. October 3, 2004. www.nytimes.com/2004/10/03/movies/03cane.html.

Canemaker, John. "Winsor McCay." In *The American Animated Cartoon: A Critial Anthology*, edited by Danny Preary and Gerald Preary, 15–26. New York: Dutton, 1980.

Carmena, Jose M., et al. "Learning to Control a Brain-Machine Interface for Reaching and Grasping by Primates." *PLoS Biology* 1, no. 2 (2003): 193–208.

Carnagey, Nicholas L., Craig A. Anderson, and Brad J. Bushman. "The Effect of Video Game Violence on Physiological Desensitization to Real-Life Violence." *Journal of Experimental Social Psychology* 43, no. 3 (2007): 489–496.

Carroll, Noël. *The Philosophy of Motion Pictures*. Malden, MA: Blackwell Publishing, 2008.

Carroll, Noël. *The Philosophy of Horror; or Paradoxes of the Heart*. London and New York: Routledge, 1990.

Case, Sue-Ellen. *Performing Science and the Virtual*. London and New York: Routledge, 2007.

Casetti, Francesco. *Inside the Gaze: The Fiction Film and Its Spectator*. Translated by Nell Andrew. Bloomington and Indianapolis: Indiana University Press, 1998.

Castells, Manuel. *The Rise of the Network Society*. Cambridge, MA: Blackwell Publishers, 1996.

Castronova, Edward. *Synthetic Worlds: The Business and Culture of Online Games*. Chicago, IL: The University of Chicago Press, 2005.

Cavallaro, Dani. *The Animé Art of Hayao Miyazaki*. Jefferson, NC: McFarland, 2006.

Cavallaro, Dani. *Cyberpunk and Cyberculture: Science Fiction and the Work of William Gibson*. London: The Athlone Press, 2000.

Cavallaro, Dani. "The Brain in a Vat in Cyberpunk: The Persistence of the Flesh." *Studies in History and Philosophy of Biological and Biomedical Sciences* 35, no. 2 (2004): 287–305.

Cavell, Stanley. *The World Viewed: Reflections on the Ontology of Film*. Cambridge, MA: Harvard University Press, 1979.

Chaminade, Thierry, Jessica Hodgins, and Mitsuo Kawato. "Anthropomorphism Influences Perception of Computer-Animated Characters' Actions." *Social Cognitive and Affective Neuroscience* 2, no. 3 (2007): 206–216.

Channell, David F. *The Vital Machine: A Study of Technology and Organic Life*. Oxford and New York: Oxford University Press, 1991.

Chao, Linda L., and Alex Martin. "Representation of Manipulable Man-Made Objects in the Dorsal Stream." *Neuroimage* 12, no. 4 (2000): 478–484.

Chen, Ya-Chen. *Women in Chinese Martial Arts Films of the New Millenium*. Lanham, MD: Lexington Books, 2012.

Cherfas, Jeremy. *Man-Made Life*. New York: Pantheon, 1982.

Cholodenko, Alan, ed. *The Illusion of Life II: More Essays on Animation*. Sydney, NSW: Power Publications, 2007.

Cholodenko, Alan, ed. *The Illusion of Life: Essays on Animation*. Sydney, NSW: Power Publications, 1991.

Christensen, Thomas A., ed. *Methods in Insect Sensory Neuroscience*. Boca Raton, FL: CRC Press, 2004.

Churchland, Patricia S., Vilayanur S. Ramachandran, and Terrence J. Sejnowski. "A Critique of Pure Vision." In *Large-Scale Neuronal Theories of the Brain*, edited by Christof Koch and Joel L. Davis, 23–61. Cambridge, MA: The MIT Press, 1994.

Churchland, Paul M. *A Neurocomputational Perspective: The Nature of Mind and the Structure of Science*. Cambridge, MA: The MIT Press, 1992.

Ciment, Gilles. "Sylvain Chomet : Faire flotter des bateaux impossibles." *Positif* 508 (2003): 78–82.

Clark, Andy. *Supersizing the Mind: Embodiment, Action, and Cognitive Extension*. Oxford and New York: Oxford University Press, 2008.

Clark, Andy. *Natural-Born Cyborgs: Minds, Technologies, and the Future of Human Intelligence*. Oxford and New York: Oxford University Press, 2003.

Clark, Andy. *Being There: Putting Brain, Body, and World Together Again*. Cambridge, MA: The MIT Press, 1996.

Clark, Andy. "Re-Inventing Ourselves: The Plasticity of Embodiment, Sensing, and Mind." *Journal of Medicine and Philosophy* 32, no. 3 (2007): 263–282.

Clark, Andy. "Visual Awareness and Visuomotor Action." *Journal of Consciousness Studies* 6, no. 11–12 (1999): 1–18.

Clarke, Bruce. *Posthuman Metamorphosis: Narrative and Systems*. New York: Fordham University Press, 2008.

Clarke, Julie. *The Paradox of the Posthuman: Science Fiction Techno-Horror Films and Visual Media*. Saarbrüken: VDM Verlag Dr. Müller, 2009.

Clynes, Manfred, and Nathan Kline. "Cyborgs and Space." In *The Cyborg Handbook*, edited by Chris Hables Gray, 29–33. London and New York: Routledge, 1995.

Coëgnarts, Maarten, and Peter Kravanja, eds. *Embodied Cognition and Cinema.* Leuven: Leuven University Press, 2015.

Coëgnarts, Maarten, and Peter Kravanja. "Embodied Visual Meaning: Image Schemas in Film." *Projections: The Journal for Movies and Mind* 6, no. 2 (2012): 84–101.

Coleman, Beth. *Hello Avatar: Rise of the Networked Generation.* Cambridge, MA: The MIT Press, 2011.

Collins, K. Austin. "Race Is the Past and Future of Horror Movies." *The Ringer*, October 31, 2016. www.theringer.com/2016/10/31/16039122/race-is-the-past-and-future-of-horror-movies-17f561d72918.

Cook, Richard, Geoffrey Bird, Caroline Catmur, Clare Press, Cecilia Heyes. "Mirror Neurons: From Origin to Function." *Behavioral and Brain Sciences* 37, no. 2 (2014): 177–241.

Coplan, Amy. "Empathetic Engagement with Narrative Fictions." *Journal of Aesthetic and Art Criticism* 62, no. 2 (Spring 2004): 141–152.

Crafton, Donald. *Shadow of a Mouse: Performance, Belief, and World-Making in Animation.* Berkeley and Los Angeles: University of California Press, 2012.

Crafton, Donald. *Emile Cohl, Caricature, and Film.* Princeton, NJ: Princeton University Press, 1990.

Crafton, Donald. *Before Mickey: The Animated Film 1898–1928.* Cambridge, MA: The MIT Press, 1982.

Cranny-Francis, Anne. "From Extension to Engagement: Mapping the Imaginary of Wearable Technology." *Visual Communications* 7, no. 3 (2008): 363–382.

Crary, Jonathan. *Techniques of the Observer: On Vision and Modernity in the Nineteenth Century.* Cambridge, MA: The MIT Press, 1992 (1990).

Creed, Barbara. "The Cyberstar: Digital Pleasures and the End of the Unconscious." *Screen* 41, no. 1 (2000): 79–86.

Crenshaw, Kimberlé. "Mapping the Margins: Intersectionality, Identity Politics and Violence Against Women of Color." *Stanford Law Review* 43, no. 6 (1991): 2141–1299.

Cuddy, Luke, ed. *BioShock and Philosophy: Irrational Game, Rational Book.* West Sussex: Wiley Blackwell, 2015.

Culhane, Shamus. *Talking Animals and Other People.* New York: St. Martin's, 1986.

Currie, Gregory. *Image and Mind: Film, Philosophy, and Cognitive Science.* Cambridge: Cambridge University Press, 1995.

Damasio, Antonio. *Descartes' Error: Emotion, Reason, and the Human Brain.* New York: Putnam, 1994.

Darley, Andrew. "Bones of Contention: Thoughts on the Study of Animation." *Animation* 2 (2007): 63–76.

Davis, Adam. "Who's Playing You? Allegories of Discipline and Control in Avatar Films." *The Journal of New Media and Culture* 8, no. 1 (2012). Accessed April 29, 2018. www.ibiblio.org/nmediac/summer2012/Articles/whois_playing.html.

Dawkins, Richard. *River out of Eden: A Darwinian View of Life.* New York: Basic Books, 1995.

Dawkins, Richard. *The Blind Watchmaker.* London: Penguin Books, 2006 (1986).

Decety, Jean. "Motor Cognition and Mental Simulation." In *Cognitive Psychology: Mind and Brain*, edited by Edward E. Smith and Stephen M. Kosslyn, 451–481. New York and London: Pearson, 2006.

Decety, Jean. "Do Imagined and Executed Actions Share the Same Neural Substrate?" *Cognitive Brain Research* 3, no. 2 (1996): 87–93.

Deleuze, Gilles. *Cinema 2: The Time-Image.* Translated by Hugh Tomlison and Robert Galeta. London and New York: Continuum, 2009 (1985).

Deleuze, Gilles. *Cinema 1: The Movement-Image.* Translated by Hugh Tomlison and Barbara Habberjam. London and New York: Continuum Impacts, 2009 (1983).

Deleuze, Gilles. "Post-scriptum sur les sociétés de contrôle." *L'Autre Journal*, no. 1 (mai 1990). Translation available at: www.nadir.org/nadir/archiv/netzkritik/societyofcontrol.html.

Deleuze, Gilles, and Félix Guattari. *A Thousand Plateaus: Capitalism and Schizophrenia.* Translated by Brian Massumi. London and New York: Continuum, 2007.

Descartes, René. "Meditations on First Philosophy." In *The Philosophical Works of Descartes*, Vol. 1, translated by Elizabeth Haldane and G. R. T. Ross. Cambridge: Cambridge University Press, 1975.

Deutsch, J. Anthony, and Diana Deutsch. "Attention: Some Theoretical Considerations." *Psychological Review* 70, no. 1 (1963): 80–90.

Dimberg, Ulf. "Facial Reactions to Facial Expressions." *Psychophysiology* 19 (1982): 643–647.

Doyle, Richard. *On Beyond Living: Rhetorical Transformations of the Life Sciences.* Stanford, CA: Stanford University Press, 1997.

Dreyfus, Hubert L. *On the Internet*, 2nd ed. London and New York: Routledge, 2009.

Dubner, Stephen J. "Philip Rosedale Answers Your *Second Life* Questions." *The New York Times: Freakonomics—Opinion Blog.* Accessed December 13, 2007. http://freakonomics.com/2007/12/13/philip-rosedale-answers-your-second-life-questions/.

Dumitrica, Delia, and Georgia Gaden. "Knee-High Boots and Six Pack Abs: Autoethnographic Reflections on Gender and Technology in *Second Life.*" *Journal of Virtual Worlds Research* 1, no. 3 (2009): 1–23. doi: 10.4101/jvwr.v1i3.323.

Dyer-Witheford, Nick, and Greig de Peuter. *Games of Empire: Global Capitalism and Video Games.* Minneapolis: University of Minnesota Press, 2009.

Edelman, Gerald. *Bright Air, Brillant Fire: On the Matter of Mind.* New York: Basic Books, 1992.

Eisenstein, Sergei. *Eisenstein on Disney.* Edited by Jay Leyda. Translated by Alan Upchurch. Calcutta: Seagull Books, 1986.

Eisenstein, Sergei and Sergei Tretyakov. "Expressive Movement." In *Meyerboyld, Eisenstein and Biomechanics: Actor Training in Revolutionary Russia*, edited by Alma Law and Mel Gordon, 173–191. Jefferson, NC: McFarland, 1996.

Ekman, Paul, Wallace V. Friesen, and Joseph C. Hager. *Facial Action Coding System.* Salt Lake City, UT: A Human Face, 2002.

Ekman, Paul. *Emotion in the Human Face*, 2nd ed. Cambridge: Cambridge University Press, 1982.

Ekman, Paul. "Facial Expression and Emotion," *American Psychologist* 48, no. 4 (1993): 384–392.

Elkins, James. *Pictures of the Body: Pain and Metamorphosis.* Stanford, CA: Stanford University Press, 1999.

Ellis, Stephen R. "Prologue." In *Pictorial Communication in Virtual and Real Environments*, 2nd ed., edited by Stephen R. Ellis, 3–11. London: Taylor & Francis, 1993.

Ellis, Stephen R. "Nature and Origins of Virtual Environments: A Bibliographical Essay." *Computing Systems in Engineering* 2, no. 4 (1991): 321–347.

Elsaesser, Thomas, and Malte Hagener, *Film Theory: An Introduction Through the Senses.* London and New York: Routledge, 2010.

Eng, Kynan, Ewa Siekierka, Monica Cameirao, Lukas Zimmerli, Pawel Pyk, Armin Duff, F. Erol, Corina Schuster, Claudio Basseti, Daniel Kiper, and Paul Verschure. "Cognitive Virtual-Reality Based Stroke Rehabilitation." *IFMBE Proceedings* 14, no. 5 (2007a): 2839–2843.

Eng, Kynan, Ewa Siekierka, Pawel Pyk, Edith Chevrier, Yves Hauser, Monica Cameirao, Lisa Holper, Karin Hägni, Lukas Zimmerli, Armin Duff, Corina Schuster, Claudio Bassetti, Paul Verschure, and Daniel Kiper. "Interactive Visuo-Motor Therapy System for Stroke Rehabilitation." *Medical and Biological Engineering and Computing* 45, no. 9 (2007b): 901–907.

Evans, Simon. "The Self and *Second Life*: A Case Study Exploring the Emergence of Virtual Selves." In *Reinventing Ourselves: Contemporary Concepts of Identity in Virtual Worlds*, edited by Anna Peachey and Mark Childs, 33–57. London: Springer, 2011.

Evans, Simon. "Virtual Selves, Real Relationships: An Exploration of the Context and Role for Social Interactions in the Emergence of Self in Virtual Environments." *Integrative Psychological Behavioral Science* 46, no. 4 (2012): 512–528.

Fahlenbrach, Kathrin, ed. *Embodied Metaphors in Film, Television, and Video Games.* London and New York: Routledge, 2016.

Fahlenbrach, Kathrin, and Felix Schröter. "Embodied Avatars in Video Games: Audiovisual Metaphors in the Interactive Design of Player Characters." In *Embodied Metaphors in Film, Television, and Video Games: Cognitive Approaches*, edited by Kathrin Fahlenbrach, 251–268. London and New York: Routledge, 2016.

Fauvel, Maryse. "Nostalgia and Digital Technology: *The Gleaners and I* (Varda, 2000) and *The Triplets of Belleville* (Chomet, 2003) as Reflective Genres." *Studies in French Cinema* 5, no. 3 (2005): 219–229.

Featherstone, Mike, and Roger Burrows, eds. *Cyberspace, Cyberbodies, Cyberpunk: Cultures of Technological Embodiment.* London: Sage, 2000.

Fehsenfeld, Lisa. "Motion Analysis Overview." Paper presented at "Narration, Imagination, and Emotion in the Moving Image Media," Grand Rapids, MI, July 2004.

Ferrell, Robyn. "Life-Treatening Life: Angela Carter and the Uncanny." In *The Illusion of Life. Essays on Animation*, edited by Alan Cholodenko, 131–143. Sydney, NSW: Powers Publications, 1991.

Fischman, Josh. "The Blind Can See, a One-Armed Woman Can Fold Her Skirts." *National Geographics* 217, no. 1 (January 2010): 34–53.

Fisher, Kevin. "Tracing the Tesseract: A Conceptual Prehistory of the Morph." In *Meta-Morphing: Visual Transformation and the Culture of Quick-Change*, edited by Vivian Sobchack, 103–129. Minneapolis: University of Minnesota Press, 2000.

Fizek, Sonia, and Monika Wasilewska. "Embodiment and Gender Identity in Virtual Worlds: Reconfiguring Our 'Volatile Bodies.'" In *Creating Second Lives. Community, Identity and Spatiality as Constructions of the Virtual*, edited by Astrid Ensslin and Eben Muse, 75–98. London and New York: Routledge, 2011.

Fleischer, Max. "Method of Producing Moving Picture Cartoons." United States Patent Office, October 9, 1917. https://patents.google.com/patent/US1242674A/en

Fleischer, Richard. *Out of the Inkwell: Max Fleischer and the Animation Revolution*. Lexington: University Press of Kentucky, 2005.

Fodor, Jerry. *The Language of Thought*. New York: Thomas Y. Crowel Co., 1975.

Forbes Irving, Paul M. C. *Metamorphosis in Greek Myths*. Oxford and New York: Oxford University Press, 1990.

Forceville, Charles J. "From Image Schema to Metaphor in Discourse: The FORCE Schema in Animation Films." In *Metaphor: Embodied Cognition and Discourse*, edited by Beate Hampe, 239–256. Cambridge: Cambridge University Press, 2017.

Forceville, Charles, and Marloes Jeulink. "The Flesh and Blood of Embodied Understanding: The Source-Path-Goal Schema in Animation Film." *Pragmatics & Cognition* 19, no. 1 (2011): 37–59.

Ford, John M. *Web of Angels*. New York: Tor Books, 1980.

Fordham, Joe. "Pete Kozachik on *Corpse Bride*." *Cinefex* 104 (2006): 25–30.

Foucault, Michel. *Discipline and Punish*. Translated by Alan Sheridan. New York: Vintage Books, 1995 (1975).

Foulds, Richard A., David M. Saxe, Arthur W. Joyce III, and Sergei Adamovich. "Sensory-Motor Enhancement in a Virtual Therapeutic Environment." *Virtual Reality* 12, no. 2 (2008): 87–97.

Fox, Jessie, and Jeremy Bailenson. "Virtual Self-Modeling: The Effects of Vicarious Reinforcement and Identification on Exercise Behaviors." *Media Psychology* 12 (2009): 1–25.

Freedberg, David, and Vittorio Gallese. "Motion, Emotion and Empathy in Esthetic Experience." *Trends in Cognitive Science* 11, no. 5 (2007): 197–203.

Freeman, Michael. *The Photographer's Eye*. Burlington, MA: Focal Press, 2007.

Freud, Sigmund. "The 'Uncanny.'" In *The Standard Edition of the Complete Psychological Works of Sigmund Freud*, Vol. 17, translated by James Strachey, 217–256. London: The Hogarth Press, 1955. (Originally published in *Imago* 5–6 (1919): 297–324).

Friedman, Ted. "Civilization and Its Discontents: Simulation, Subjectivity, and Space." In *On a Silver Platter: CD-ROMs and the Promises of a New Technology*, edited by Greg M. Smith, 132–150. New York and London: New York University Press, 1999.

Frijda, Nico. *The Emotions*. Cambridge: Cambridge University Press, 1986.

Fung, Juliane. "Feminist and Queer Analysis of Disney's *Mulan*." 1998. Accessed September 2, 2018. http://mulananalysis.weebly.com/.

Gallagher, Shaun. "Body Schema and Intentionality." In *The Body and the Self*, edited by José Bermúdez, 225–244. Cambridge, MA: The MIT Press, 1998.

Gallese, Vittorio. "Mirror Neurons and Art." In *Art and the Senses*, edited by Francesca Bacci and David Melcher, 455–463. Oxford and New York: Oxford University Press, 2010.

Gallese, Vittorio, and David Freedberg. "Mirror and Canonical Neurons and Crucial Elements in Esthetic Response." *Trends in Cognitive Science* 11, no. 7 (2007): 6.

Gallese, Vittorio, and George Lakoff. "The Brain's Concepts: The Role of the Sensory-Motor System in Conceptual Knowledge." *Cognitive Neuropsychology* 22, no. 3 (2005): 455–479.

Galloway, Alexander R. *Gaming: Essays on Algorithmic Culture*. Minneapolis: University of Minnesota Press, 2006.

Galloway, Alexander R. "Playing the Code: Allegories of Control in *Civilization*." *Radical Philosophy*, no. 128 (2004): 33–40.

Garrison Kathleen A., Carolee J. Winstein, and Lisa Aziz-Zadeh. "The Mirror Neuron System: A Neural Substrate for Methods in Stroke Rehabilitation." *Neuroreabilitation Neural Repair* 24, no. 5 (2010): 404–412.

Gazzola, Valeria, Giacomo Rizzolatti, Bruno Wicker, and Christian Keysers. "The Anthropomorphic Brain: The Mirror Neuron System Responds to Human and Robotic Actions." *Neuroimage* 35, no. 4 (2007): 1674–1684.

Ge, Liezhong, Jing Luo, Mayu Nishimura, and Kang Lee. "The Lasting Impression of Chairman Mao: Hyperfidelity of Familiar-Face Memory." *Perception* 32, no. 5 (2003): 601–614.

Gershon, Jonathan, Page Anderson, Ken Graap, Elana Zimand, Larry Hodges, and Barbara O. Rothbaum. "Virtual Reality Exposure Therapy in the Treatment of Anxiety Disorders." *Scientific Review of Mental Health Practices* 1, no. 1 (2002): 76–81.

Gibson, William. *Neuromancer*. New York: Ace Books, 2000.

Gibson, William. "Burning Chrome." *Omni*, July 1982.

Gibson, William. "Johnny Mnemonic." *Omni*, May 1981.

Gillis, Stacy. *The Matrix Trilogy: Cyberpunk Reloaded*. London and New York: Wallflower Press, 2005.

Gillis, Stacy. "Cyber Noir: Cyberspace, (Post)Feminism and the Femme Fatale." In *The Matrix Trilogy: Cyberpunk Reloaded*, edited by Stacy Gillis, 74–85. London and New York: Wallflower Press, 2005.

Goh, Diana. "(Mis)representation of the Chinese Culture in *Mulan*." November 1, 2016. https://savethosethoughts.wordpress.com/2016/11/01/misrepresentation-of-the-chinese-culture-in-mulan-1998/.

Goodfield, June. *Playing God: Genetic Engineering and the Manipulation of Life*. New York: Harper and Row, 1977.

Gorini, Alessandra, Andrea Gaggioli, Cinzia Vigna, and Giuseppe Riva. "A Second Life for eHealth: Prospects for the Use of 3-D Virtual Worlds in Clinical Psychology." *Journal of Medical Internet Research* 10, no. 3 (2008): e21. www.jmir.org/2008/3/e21.

Gottschalk, Simon. "The Presentation of Avatars in *Second Life*: Self and Interaction in Social Virtual Spaces." *Symbolic Interaction* 33, no. 4 (2010): 501–525.

Grady, Joseph. "A Typology of Motivation for Conceptual Metaphor: Correlation vs. Resemblance." In *Metaphor in Cognitive Linguistics: Selected Papers from the 5th Cognitive Linguistics Conference, Amsterdam, 1997*, edited by Raymond W. Gibbs Jr. and Gerard J. Steen, 79–100. Amsterdam: John Benjamins Publishing, 1999.

Graham, Elaine L. *Representations of the Post/Human: Monsters, Aliens and Others in Popular Culture.* New Brunswick, NJ: Rutgers University Press, 2002.

Grandinetti, Fred M. *Popeye: An Illustrated Cultural History*, 2nd ed. Jefferson, NC: McFarland, 2004.

Grau, Olivier. *Virtual Art: From Illusion to Immersion.* Cambridge, MA: The MIT Press, 2004.

Gray, Chris Hable, ed. *The Cyborg Handbook.* London and New York: Routledge, 1995.

Green, Robert D., Karl F. MacDorman, Chin-Chang Ho, and Sandosh Vasudevan. "Sensitivity to the Proportions of Faces that Vary in Human Likeness." *Computers in Human Behavior* 24, no. 5 (2008): 2456–2474.

Gregersen, Andreas, and Torben Grodal. "Embodiment and Interface." In *The Video Game Theory Reader 2*, edited by Bernard Perron and Mark J. P. Wolf, 65–83. London and New York: Routledge, 2003.

Gregg, Lynsey, and Nicholas Tarrier. "Virtual Reality in Mental Health: A Review of the Literature." *Social Psychiatry and Psychiatric Episdemiology* 42, no. 5 (2007): 343–354.

Grèzes, Julie, and Jean Decety. "Functional Anatomy of Execution, Mental Simulation, Observation, and Verb Generation of Actions: A Meta-Analysis." *Human-Brain Mapping* 12, no. 1 (2001): 1–19.

Grodal, Torben. *Embodied Visions: Evolution, Emotion, Culture, and Film.* Oxford and New York: Oxford University Press, 2009.

Grossman, David, and Gloria DeGaetano. *Stop Teaching Our Kids to Kill: A Call to Action Against TV, Movie & Video Game Violence.* New York: Random House, 1999.

Guattari, Félix. "Machinic Heterogenesis." In *Chaosmosis: An Ethico-Aesthetic Paradigm*, translated by Paul Bains and Julian Pefanis, 33–57. Bloomington and Indianapolis: University of Indiana Press, 1995 (1992).

Gunning, Tom. "The Cinema of Attractions: Early Film, Its Spectator, and the Avant-Garde." *Wide Angle* 8, no. 3–4 (1986): 63–70.

Hagendoorn, Ivar. "The Dancing Brain." *From Cerebrum: The Dana Forum on Brain Science* 5, no. 2 (2003): 19–34.

Halberstam, Judith. *Skin Shows: Gothic Horror and the Technology of Monsters.* Durham, NC: Duke University Press, 1995.

Hall, Edward T. *The Hidden Dimension.* Garden City, NJ: Doubleday, 1966.

Hames, Peter. "Interview with Jan Švankmajer." In *Dark Alchemy: The Films of Jan Švankmajer*, edited by Peter Hames, 96–118. Westport, CT: Greenwood Press, 1995.

Hampe, Beate. "Image Schemas in Cognitive Linguistics: Introduction." In *From Perception to Meaning: Image Schemas in Cognitive Linguistics*, edited by Beate Hampe, 2–12. Berlin: De Gruyter Mouton, 2005.

Hansen, Mark B. N. *Bodies in Code: Interfaces with Digital Media.* London and New York: Routledge, 2006.

Hansen, Mark B. N. *New Philosophy for New Media*. Cambridge, MA: The MIT Press, 2004.

Haraway, Donna. *Modest_Witness@Second_Millenium. FemaleMan©_Meets_OncoMouse*. London and New York: Routledge, 1997.

Haraway, Donna. *Simians, Cyborgs, and Women: The Reinvention of Nature*. London and New York: Routledge, 1991.

Haraway, Donna. "A Cyborg Manifesto: Science, Technology and Socialist-Feminism in the Late Twentieth Century." In *The Cybercultures Reader*, 2nd ed., edited by David Bell and Barbara M. Kennedy, 34–65. London and New York: Routledge, 2007.

Haraway, Donna. "Situated Knowledges: The Science Question in Feminism and the Privilege of Partial Perspective." *Feminist Studies* 14, no. 3 (1988): 575–599.

Haslam, Karen. "How to Use Animoji: Send, Save, and Share Animoji with (and without) iPhone X." *MacWorld*. Accessed December 4, 2017. www.macworld.co.uk/how-to/iphone/how-use-animoji-3668491/.

Hatfield, Elaine, John T. Cacioppo, and Richard L. Rapson. *Emotional Contagion*. Cambridge: Cambridge University Press, 1994.

Haugeland, John. "Mind Embodied and Embedded." Chap 9. in *Having Thought: Essays in the Metaphysics of Mind*. Cambridge, MA: The MIT Press, 1998.

Hayles, N. Katherine. *My Mother Was a Computer: Digital Subjects and Literary Texts*. Chicago, IL: The University of Chicago Press, 2005.

Hayles, N. Katherine. *How We Became Posthuman: Virtual Bodies in Cybernetics, Literature, and Informatics*. Chicago, IL: The University of Chicago Press, 1999.

Hayles, N. Katherine. "RFID: Human Agency and Meaning in Information-Intensive Environments." *Theory, Culture & Society* 26, no. 2–3 (2009): 47–72.

Hayles, N. Katherine. "Flesh and Metal: Reconfiguring the Mindbody in Virtual Environments." *Configurations* 10, no. 2 (2002): 297–320.

Heater, Brian. "Samsung's AR Emoji Taps Creepy Avatars and Disney Characters to Compete with Animoji." *Tech Crunch*. Accessed February 25, 2018. https://techcrunch.com/2018/02/25/samsungs-ar-emoji-taps-creepy-avatars-and-disney-characters-to-compete-with-animoji/.

Heidegger, Martin. *Being and Time*. Translated by John Macquarrie and Edward Robinson. New York: Harper & Row, 1962 (1927).

Heider, Fritz, and Marianne Simmel. "An Experimental Study of Apparent Behavior." *American Journal of Psychology* 57, no. 2 (1944): 243–259.

Ho, Chin-Chang, Karl F. MacDorman, and Zacharias Pramono. "Human Emotion and the Uncanny Valley: A GLM, MDS, and Isomap Analysis of Robot Video Ratings." In *Proceedings of the 3rd ACM/IEEE International Conference on Human–Robot Interaction* (2008): 169–176. doi: 10.1145/1349822.1349845.

Hoffner, Cynthia, and Joanne Cantor. "Perceiving and Responding to Mass Media Characters." In *Responding to the Screen: Reception and Reaction Processes*, edited by Jennings Bryant and Dolf Zillmann, 63–101. Hillsdale, MI: Lawrence Erlbaum Associates, 1991.

Holper, Lisa, Thomas Muehlemann, Felix Scholkmann, Kynan Eng, Daniel Kiper and Martin Wolf. "Testing the Potential of a Virtual Reality Neurorehabilitation System During Performance of Observation, Imagery and Imitation of

Motor Actions Recorded by Wireless Functional Near-Infrared Spectroscopy (fNIRS)." *Journal of NeuroEngineering and Rehabilitation* 7, no. 1 (2010): 57.

Holtzman, Steven. *Digital Mosaics: The Aesthetics of Cyberspace.* New York: Simon & Schuster, 1997.

Hooks, Ed. *Acting in Animation: A Look at 12 Films.* Portsmouth, NH: Heinemann, 2005.

Hugues, James. *Citizen Cyborg: Why Democratic Societies Must Respond to the Redesigned Human of the Future.* Boulder, CO: Westview Press, 2004.

Hume, David. *Enquiries Concerning the Human Understanding and Concerning the Principles of Morals*, 2nd ed. Oxford: Claredon Press, 1966 (1777).

Hunt, Leon. *Kung Fu Cult Masters: From Bruce Lee to Crouching Tiger.* London and New York: Wallflower Press, 2003.

Huntemann, Nina B., and Matthew Thomas Payne, eds. *Joystick Soldiers: The Politics of Play in Military Video Games.* London and New York: Routledge, 2010.

Hutchings, Peter J. "The Work-Shop of Filthy Animation." In *The Illusion of Life: Essays on Animation*, edited by Alan Cholodenko, 161–181. Sydney, NSW: Powers Publications, 1991.

Hutchins, Edwin. *Cognition in the Wild.* Cambridge, MA: The MIT Press, 1995.

Hutchinson, W. D., Kourtney Davis, Andres M. Lozano, R. R. Tasker, and Jonathan O. Dostrovsky. "Pain-Related Neurons in the Human Cingulate Cortex." *Nature Neuroscience* 2, no. 5 (1999): 403–405.

Izard, Carroll E. *Human Emotions.* New York: Plenum Press, 1977.

Izard, Carroll E. *The Face of Emotion.* New York: Appleton-Century-Crofts, 1971.

Jacobsen Marrapodi, Elisabeth. "Improving Health Information Literacy with Games in the Virtual World *Second Life*." In *Virtual, Augmented Reality and Serious Games for Healthcare 1*, edited by Minhua Ma, Lakhmi C. Jain, and Paul Anderson, 175–189. Berlin: Springer, 2014.

James, William. *The Principles of Psychology.* New York: Dover, 1950 (1890).

Jenkins, Eric. *Special Affects: Cinema, Animation, and the Translation of Consumer Culture.* Edinburgh: Edinburgh University Press, 2014.

Jentsch, Ernst. "On the Psychology of the Uncanny (1906)." *Angelaki* 2, no. 1 (2008): 7–16. (Originally published in "Zur Psychologie des Unheimlichen" *Psychiatrisch-Neurologische Wochenschrift* 8, no. 22 (1906): 195–198 and 8, no. 23 (1906): 203–205).

Johansson, Gunnar. "Visual Perception of Biological Motion and a Model for Its Analysis." *Perception & Psychophysics* 14, no. 2 (1973): 201–211.

Johnson, Mark. *The Meaning of the Body: Aesthetics of Human Understanding.* Chicago, IL: The University of Chicago Press, 2008 (2007).

Johnson, Mark. *The Body in the Mind: The Bodily Basis of Meaning, Imagination, and Reason.* Chicago, IL: The University of Chicago Press, 1987.

Johnson, Mark H. "Biological Motion: A Perceptual Life Detector?" *Current Biology* 16, no. 10 (2006): R376–R377.

Johnston, John. *The Allure of Machinic Life: Cybernetics, Artificial Life, and the New AI.* Cambridge, MA: The MIT Press, 2008.

Johnston, John. "Machinic Vision." *Critical Inquiry* 26, no. 1 (1999): 27–48.

Kanwisher, Nancy. "What's in a Face?" *Science* 311, no. 5761 (February 2006): 617–618.

Kay, Lili E. *Who Wrote the Book of Life? A History of the Genetic Code*. Stanford, CA: Stanford University Press, 2000.

Kellner, Douglas. "Mapping the Present from the Future. From Baudrillard to Cyberpunk." Chap. 9 in *Media Culture: Cultural Studies, Identity and Politics, between the Modern and the Postmodern*. London and New York: Routledge, 2003.

Kelso, J. A. Scott. *Dynamic Patterns: The Self-Organization of Brain and Behavior*. Cambridge, MA: The MIT Press, 1997.

Keltner, Dacher, Paul Ekman, Gian C. Gonzaga, and Jennifer Beer, "Facial Expression of Emotion." In *Handbook of Affective Sciences*, edited by Richard J. Davidson, Klaus R. Scherer, and H. Hill Goldsmith, 415–432. Oxford and New York: Oxford University Press, 2003.

Kember, Sarah. "Cyberlife's *Creatures*." In *The Cybercultures Reader*, 2nd ed., edited by David Bell and Barbara M. Kennedy, 516–546. London and New York: Routledge, 2007.

Kennedy, Helen. "Lara Croft: Feminist Icon or Cyberbimbo? On the Limits of Textual Analysis." *Game Studies* 2, no. 2 (2002). Accessed June 5, 2011. www.gamestudies.org.

Kevles, Daniel J. *In the Name of Eugenics: Genetics and the Uses of Human Heredity*. New York: Knopf, 1985.

Keysers, Christian. *The Empathic Brain: How the Discovery of Mirror Neurons Change Our Understanding of Human Nature*. Amsterdam: Social Brain Press, 2011.

Kilteni, Konstantina, Raphaela Groten, and Mel Slater. "The Sense of Embodiment in Virtual Reality." *Presence: Teleoperators and Virtual Environments* 21, no. 4 (2012): 373–387.

Kim, Kwanguk, Chan-Hyung Kim, So-Yeon Kim, Daeyoung Roh, and Sun I. Kim. "Virtual Reality for Obsessive-Compulsive Disorder: Past and Future." *Psychiatry Investigation* 6, no. 3 (2009): 115–121.

King, Geoff. *Spectacular Narratives: Hollywood in the Age of the Blockbuster*. London and New York: I.B. Tauris, 2000.

King, Geoff, and Tanya Krzywinska. *Tomb Raiders & Space Invaders: Videogame Forms and Contexts*. London and New York: I.B. Tauris, 2006.

Kirby, David A. "Are We Not Men? The Horror of Eugenics in *The Island of Dr. Moreau*." *ParaDoxa* 17 (2002): 93–108.

Kirby, David A. "The New Eugenics in Cinema: Genetic Determinism and Gene Therapy in *GATTACA*." *Science Fiction Studies* 27, no. 2 (2000): 193–215.

Kirsh, David, and Paul P. Maglio. "Reaction and Reflection in *Tetris*." In *Artificial Intelligence Planning Systems: Proceedings of the First Annual Conference AIPS*, edited by J. Hendler. San Mateo, 283–284. Burlington, MA: Morgan Kaufmann, 1992.

Klein, Norman. "Animation and Animorphs." In *Meta-Morphing: Visual Transformation and the Culture of Quick-Change*, edited by Vivian Sobchack, 21–40. Minneapolis: University of Minnesota Press, 2000.

Klinger, Evelyne, Patrick Légeron, Stéphane Roy, Isabelle Chemin, Françoise Lauer, and Pierre Nugues. "Virtual Reality Exposure in the Treatment of Social Phobia." *Studies in Health Technology and Informatics* 99 (2004): 91–119.

Kozachik, Pete. "Reanimated Romance: Director of Photography/Visual-Effects Supervisor Pete Kozachik Outlines His Approach to Tim Burton's

Corpse Bride, the First Stop-Motion Feature Shot with Digital Still Cameras." *American Cinematographer – The International Journal of Film & Digital Production Techniques* 86, no. 10 (2005): 48–52, 54–57.

Krach, Sören, Frank Hegel, Britta Wrede, Gerhard Sagerer, Ferdinand Binkofski, and Tilo Kircher. "Can Machines Think? Interaction and Perspective Taking with Robots Investigated via fMRI." *PLOS ONE* 3, no. 7 (2008): e2597. doi: 10.1371/journal.pone.0002597.

Krimsky, Sheldon. *Genetic Alchemy: The Social History of the Recombinant DNA Controversy*. Cambridge, MA: The MIT Press, 1983.

Kristeva, Julia. *Powers of Horror: An Essay on Abjection*. Translated by Leon S. Roudiez. New York: Columbia University Press, 1982.

Krueger, Myron. *Artificial Reality II*. Reading: Addison-Wesley, 1991.

Kurzweil, Ray. *The Age of Spiritual Machines: When Computer Exceed Human Intelligence*. New York: Viking, 1999.

Lahti, Martti. "As We Become Machines: Corporealized Pleasures in Video Games." In *The Video Game Theory Reader*, edited by Mark J. P. Wolf and Bernard Perron, 157–169. London and New York: Routledge, 2003.

Lakoff, George. "Mapping the Brain's Metaphor Circuitry: Metaphorical Thought in Everyday Reason." *Frontiers in Human Neuroscience* 8 (2014): 958. doi: 10.3389/fnhum.2014.00958.

Lakoff, George, and Mark Johnson. *Philosophy in the Flesh: The Embodied Mind and Its Challenge to Western Thought*. New York: Basic Books, 1999.

Lakoff, George, and Mark Johnson. *Metaphors We Live By*. Chicago, IL: The University of Chicago Press, 2003 (1980).

Lamarre, Thomas. *The Anime Machine: A Media Theory of Animation*. Minneapolis: University of Minnesota Press, 2009.

Lamarre, Thomas. "Speciesism, Part I: Translating Races into Animals in Wartime Animation." In *Mechademia 3: Limits of the Human*, edited by Frenchy Lunning, 75–95. Minneapolis: University of Minnesota Press, 2008.

Langer, Mark. "Cyborgs Before Computers: The Rotoscope as Prosthesis." Paper presented at 11th Annual Society for Animation Studies Conference, Brisbane, Australia, August 3, 1999.

Leder, Drew. *The Absent Body*. Chicago, IL: The University of Chicago Press, 1990.

Lenoir, Timothy. "Contemplating Singularity." Accessed August 4, 2009. https://nationalhumanitiescenter.org/on-the-human/2009/08/contemplating-singularity/.

Lenoir, Timothy. "Programming Theaters of War: Gamemakers as Soldiers." In *Bomb and Bandwidth: The Emerging Relationship Between Information Technology and Security*, edited by Robert Latham, 175–198. New York: The New Press, 2003.

Leslie, Esther. *Hollywood Flatlands: Animation, Critical Theory and the Avant-Garde*. London and New York: Verso, 2002.

Levi, Antonia. "*Howl's Moving Castle*." In *Mechademia 3: Limits of the Human*, edited by Frenchy Lunning, 261–263. Minneapolis: University of Minnesota Press, 2008.

Levine, Kevin. "Rationalizing Rapture with *BioShock*'s Ken Levine," interview by Patrick and Sterling. *GameSpy*, June 25, 2007.

Lewis, Marc D. "Bridging Emotion Theory and Neurobiology Through Dynamic Systems Modeling." *Behavioral and Brain Sciences* 28, no. 2 (2005): 169–194. doi: 10.1017/S0140525X0500004X.

Lewontin, Richard. *The Triple Helix: Gene, Organism, and Environment.* Cambridge, MA: Harvard University Press, 2002.
Lewontin, Richard, Steven Rose, and Leon Kamin. *Not in Our Genes: Biology, Ideology, and Human Nature.* New York: Pantheon Books, 1984.
Likowski, Katja, Andreas Mühlberger, Antje B. M. Gerdes, Matthias J. Wieser, Paul Pauli, and Peter Weyers. "Facial Mimicry and the Mirror Neuron System: Simultaneous Acquisition of Facial Electromyography and Functional Magnetic Resonance Imaging." *Frontiers in Human Neuroscience* 6 (2012): 1–10.
Lipps, Theodor. "Einfühlung, innere Nachahmung, und Organempfindungen." *Archiv für die gesamte Psychologie* 1 (1903): 185–204.
Livingstone, Margaret. *Vision and Art: The Biology of Seeing.* New York: Harry N. Abrams, 2002.
Locher, Miriam A., Andreas H. Jucker, and Manuel Berger. "Negotiation of Space in *Second Life* Newbie Interaction." *Discourse, Context, & Media* 9 (2015): 34–45.
Lohse, Keith R., Courtney G. E. Hilderman, Katharine L. Cheung, Sandy Tatla, and H. F. Machiel Van der Loos. "Systematic Review and Meta-Analysis Exploring Virtual Environments and Commercial Games in Therapy." *PLOS ONE* 9, no. 3 (2014): e93318. doi: 10.1371/journal.pone.0093318.
Long, Margherita. "*Malice@Doll*: Konaka, Specularization, and the Virtual Feminine." In *Mechademia 2: Networks of Desire*, edited by Frenchy Lunning, 157–173. Minneapolis: Minnesota University Press, 2007.
Luhmann, Niklas. *The Reality of the Mass Media.* Translated by Kathleen Cross. Stanford, CA: Stanford University Press, 2000.
Luhmann, Niklas. *Social Systems.* Translated by John Bednarz Jr. and Dirk Baecker. Stanford, CA: Stanford University Press, 1995.
Luhmann, Niklas. "The Autopoiesis of Social Systems." In *Sociocybernetics Paradoxes: Observation, Control and Evolution of Self-Steering Systems*, edited by Felix Geyer and Johannes van der Zouwen, 172–192. London: Sage, 1986.
Lunning, Frenchy, ed. *Mechademia 3: Limits of the Human.* Minneapolis: University of Minnesota Press, 2008.
Lyons, Williams. *Emotion.* Cambridge: Cambridge University Press, 1985.
MacDorman, Karl F., Joseph A. Coram, Chin-Chang Ho, and Himalaya Patel. "Gender Differences in the Impact of Presentational Factors in Human Character Animations on Decisions in Ethical Dilemmas." *Presence* 19, no. 3 (2010): 213–229.
MacDorman, Karl F., and Steven O. Entezari. "Individual Differences Predict Sensitivity to the Uncanny Valley." *Interaction Studies* 16, no. 2 (2015): 141–172.
MacDorman, Karl F., Robert D. Green, Chin-Chang Ho, and Clinton T. Koch. "Too Real for Comfort? Uncanny Responses to Computer Generated Faces." *Computers in Human Behavior* 25, no. 3 (2009): 695–710.
MacDorman, Karl F., and Hiroshi Ishiguro, "The Uncanny Advantage of Using Androids in Cognitive and Social Science Research." *Interaction Studies* 7, no. 3 (2006): 297–337.
Magnee, Maurice J., Jeroen J. Stekelnburg, Chantal Kemner, and Beatrice de Gelder. "Similar Facial Electromyographic Responses to Faces, Voices, and Body Expressions." *NeuroReport* 18, no. 4 (2007): 369–372.

Manovich, Lev. *The Language of New Media*. Cambridge, MA: The MIT Press, 2001.

Manovich, Lev. "Automation of Sight from Photography to Computer Vision." In *Electronic Culture: Technology and Visual Representation*, edited by Timothy Druckrey and Michael Sand, 229–239. New York: Aperture, 1996.

Maravita, Angelo, and Atsushi Iriki. "Tools for the Body (Schema)." *Trends in Cognitive Sciences* 8, no. 2 (2004): 79–86.

Marks, Lawrence E. "Weak Synesthesia in Perception and Language." In *The Oxford Handbook of Synesthesia*, edited by Julia Simner and Edward Hubbard, 761–789. Oxford and New York: Oxford University Press, 2013.

Marr, David. *Vision: A Computational Investigation into the Human Representation and Processing of Visual Information*. New York: Freeman, 1982.

Martin, John. *The Modern Dance*. New York: A. S. Barnes and Company, 1933.

Maskeliunas, Rytis, Robertas Damasevicius, Ignas Martisius, and Mindaugas Vasiljevas. "Consumer-Grade EEG Devices: Are They Usable for Control Tasks?" *PeerJ* 4 (2016): e1746. doi: 10.7717/peerj.1746.

Mathieson, S. A. "Let Me Be Your Fantasy." *The Guardian*. Accessed April 26, 2001. www.theguardian.com/technology/2001/apr/26/onlinesupplement5.

Maturana, Humberto R., and Francisco J. Varela. *The Tree of Knowledge: The Biological Roots of Human Understanding*. Translated by Robert Paolucci. Boston, MA: Shambhala Publications, 1998 (1984).

Maturana, Humberto R., and Francisco J. Varela. *De máquinas y seres vivos*. Santiago de Chile: Editorial Universitaria, 1972. Translated and reprinted in English under *Autopoiesis and Cognition: The Realization of the Living*. Dirdrecht: D. Reidel Publishing Company, 1980.

McCaffery, Larry, ed. *Storming the Reality Studio: A Casebook of Cyberpunk and Postmodern Fiction*. Durham, NC: Duke University Press, 2003.

McCarty, John. *Splatter Movies: Breaking the Last Taboo of the Screen*. New York: St. Martin's, 1984.

McClamrock, Ron. *Existential Cognition: Computational Minds in the World*. Chicago, IL: The University of Chicago Press, 1995.

McHale, Brian. *Constructing Postmodernism*. London and New York: Routledge, 1992.

McHale, Brian. "Towards a Poetics of Cyberpunk." In *Beyond Cyberpunk: New Critical Perspectives*, edited by Graham J. Murphy and Sherryl Vint, 3–28. New York and London: Routledge, 2010.

McLeod, Poppy-Lauretta, Yi-Ching Liu, and Jill Elizabetth Axline. "When Your *Second Life* Comes Knocking: Effects of Personality on Changes to Real Life from Virtual World Experiences." *Computers in Human Behavior* 39 (2014): 59–70.

McLuhan, Marshall. *Understanding Media: The Extensions of Man*. Cambridge, MA: The MIT Press, 1995 (1964).

McMahan, Alison. *The Films of Tim Burton: Animating Live Action in Contemporary Hollywood*. New York and London: Continuum, 2005.

McManus, Ian Christopher, J. Stoker, and Baljit Cheema. "The Aesthetics of Composition: A Study of Mondrian." *Empirical Study in Arts* 11, no. 2 (1993): 83–94.

Meadows, Mark Stephen. *I, Avatar: The Culture and Consequences of Having a Second Life*. Berkeley, CA: New Riders Press, 2008.

Meltzoff, Andrew, and M. Keith Moore. "Infants' Understanding of People and Things: From Body Imitation to Folk Psychology." In *The Body and the Self*, edited by Jose Luis Bermúdez, Anthony Marcel, and Naomi Eilan, 43–69. Cambridge, MA: The MIT Press, 1998.

Meltzoff, Andrew, and M. Keith Moore. "Newborn Infants Imitate Adult Facial Gestures." *Child Development* 54, no. 3 (1983): 702–709.

Merleau-Ponty, Maurice. *Phenomenology of Perception*. Translated by Colin Smith. London and New York: Routledge, 2005 (1945).

Metz, Christian. *The Imaginary Signifier: Psychoanalysis and the Cinema*. Translated by Celia Britton, Annwyl Williams, Ben Brewster, and Alfred Guzzetti. Bloomington and Indianapolis: Indiana University Press, 1982.

Meyerbröker, Katharina, and Paul M. G. Emmelkamp. "Virtual Reality Exposure Therapy for Anxiety Disorder: The State if the Art." In *Studies in Computational Intelligence*, Vol. 337, edited by Sheryl Brahnam and Lakhmi C. Jain, 47–62. Berlin: Springer-Verlag, 2011.

Milburn, Colin. "Atoms and Avatars: Virtual Worlds as Massively-Multiplayer Laboratories." *Spontaneous Generations* 2, no. 1 (2008): 63–89.

Mitra, Barbara Maria and Paul Golz. "Exploring Intrinsic Gender Identity Using *Second Life*." *Journal of Virtual Worlds Research* 9, no. 2 (2016): 1–17. doi: 10.4101/jvwr.v9i2.7202.

Mohammed, Methal. "Cultural Identity in Virtual Reality (VR): A Case Study of a Woman With Hijab in *Second Life* (SL)." *Journal of Virtual World Research* 2, no. 2, (2009): 1–10. doi: 10.4101/jvwr.v2i2.435.

Moody, Eric J., Daniel N. McIntosh, Laura J. Mann, and Kimberly R. Weisser. "More Than Mere Mimicry? The Influence of Emotion on Rapid Facial Reactions to Faces." *Emotions* 7, no. 2 (2007): 447–457.

Moravec, Hans. *Mind Children: The Future of Human Robot Intelligence*. Cambridge, MA: Harvard University Press, 1988.

Mori, Masahiro. "The Uncanny Valley." Translated by Karl F. MacDorman and Norri Kageki. *Energy* 7, no. 4 (1970): 33–35. Accessed April 5, 2018. https://spectrum.ieee.org/automaton/robotics/humanoids/the-uncanny-valley.

Morie, Jacquelyn Ford. "The Healing Potential of Online Virtual Worlds." In *Studies in Computational Intelligence*, Vol. 337, edited by Sheryl Brahnam and Lakhmi C. Jain, 149–166. Berlin: Springer-Verlag, 2011.

Morningstar, Chip, and F. Randall Farmer. "The Lessons of Lucasfilm's Habitat." In *Cyberspace: First Steps*, edited by Michael Benedikt, 273–301. Cambridge, MA: The MIT Press, 1991.

Morowitz, Harold. *The Emergence of Everything: How the World Became Complex*. Oxford and New York: Oxford University Press, 2002.

Moss, Lenny. "A Kernel of Truth? On the Reality of the Genetic Program." In *Proceedings of the Philosophy of Science Association*, Vol. 1, edited by D. Hull, M. Forbes, and K. Okruhlik, 335–348. Chicago, IL: The University of Chicago Press, 1992. www.jstor.org/stable/192766.

Mulvey, Laura. "Visual Pleasure and Narrative Cinema." *Screen* 16, no. 3 (1975): 6–18.

Münsterberg, Hugo. *Hugo Münsterberg on Film: The Photoplay: A Psychological Study and Other Writings*. London and NewYork: Routledge, 2001.

Murata, Asuka, Vittorio Gallese, Giuseppe Luppino, Misato Kaseda and Hiroyuki Sakata. "Selectivity for the Shape, Size, and Orientation of Objects for

Grasping in Neurons of Monkey Parietal Area AIP." *Journal of Neurophysiology* 83, no. 5 (2000): 2580–2601.

Nakamura, Lisa. "Race In/For Cyberspace: Identity Tourism and Racial Passing on the Internet." In *The Cybercultures Reader*, 2nd ed., edited by David Bell and Barbara M. Kennedy, 297–304. London and New York: Routledge, 2007.

Nakamura, Lisa. *Cybertypes: Race, Ethnicity, Identity on the Internet*. London and New York: Routledge, 2002.

Napier, Susan J. *Anime from Akira to Howl's Moving Castle: Experiencing Contemporary Japanese Animation*. New York: Palgrave Macmillan, 2005.

Naremore, James. *Acting in the Cinema*. Berkeley and Los Angeles: University of California Press, 1988.

National Science and Technology Council. *Nanotechnology: Shaping the World Atom by Atom*. Washington, DC: National Science and Technology Council, 1999.

Neal, Megan. "Creepily Realistic Avatars Are Giving *Second Life* a Second Life. 'It'll Scare the Hell Out of You.'" *Motherboard*, April 25, 2014. https://motherboard.vice.com/en_us/article/9akabd/creepily-realistic-avatars-are-giving-second-life-a-second-life.

Neill, Alex. "Empathy and (Film) Fiction." In *Post-Theory: Reconstruction Film Studies*, edited by David Bordwell and Noël Carroll, 175–194. Madison: University of Wisconsin Press, 1996.

Nelkin, Dorothy, and Susan Lindee. *The DNA Mystique: The Gene as a Cultural Icon*. New York: Freeman, 1995.

Neumann, Hanns-Peter. "Machina Machinarum: The Clock as a Concept and Metaphor Between 1450 and 1750." *Early Science and Medicine* 15, no. 1–2 (2010): 122–191.

Nichols, Bill. *Ideology and the Image: Social Representation in the Cinema and Other Media*. Bloomington and Indianapolis: Indiana University Press, 1981.

Nitsche, Michael. *Video Game Spaces: Image, Play, and Structure in 3D Game Worlds*. Cambridge, MA: The MIT Press, 2008.

Noble, David F. *The Religion of Technology: The Divinity of Man and the Spirit of Invention*. New York: Penguin, 1999.

Noë, Alva. *Varieties of Presence*. Cambridge, MA: Harvard University Press, 2012.

Noë, Alva. *Action in Perception*. Cambridge, MA: The MIT Press, 2004.

Noë, Alva. "Storytelling and The 'Uncanny Valley.'" *Cosmos and Culture* no. 7 (2012): 13. Accessed April 15, 2017. www.npr.org/sections/13.7/2012/01/20/145504032/story-telling-and-the-uncanny-valley.

North, Dan. *Performing Illusions: Cinema, Special Effects and the Virtual Actor*. London and New York: Wallflower Press, 2008.

North, Dan. "Virtual Actors, Spectacle and Special Effects: Kung Fu Meets 'All That CGI Bullshit.'" In *The Matrix Trilogy: Cyberpunk Reloaded*, edited by Stacy Gillis, 48–61. London and New York: Wallflower Press, 2005.

North, Max M., Sarah M. North, and Joseph R. Coble. "Virtual Reality Therapy: An Effective Treatment for the Fear of Public Speaking." *International Journal of Virtual Reality* 3, no. 3 (1998): 1–6.

Nottingham, Stephen. *Screening DNA: Exploring the Cinema-Genetics Interface*. Book on CD. DNA Books, 1999.

Noveck, Beth Simone. "Democracy—the Video Game: Virtual Worlds and the Future of Collective Action." In *State of Play: Law, Games, and Virtual Worlds*, edited by Jack M. Balkin and Beth Simone Noveck, 257–282. New York: New York University Press, 2006.

Nummenmaa Lauri, Jussi Hirvonen, Riitta Parkkola, Jari K. Hietanen. "Is Emotional Contagion Special? An fMRI Study on Neural Systems for Affective and Cognitive Empathy." *NeuroImage* 43, no. 3 (2008): 571–580. doi: 10.1016/j.neuroimage.2008.08.014.

Nun, Yael Ben. "The Figure of Metamorphosis in Japanese Animation: When Aesthetics, Technique, and Culture Meet." In *Conference Proceedings of Avanca Cinema*, 2011, 421–428.

Nusslein-Volhard, Christiane. *Coming to Life: How Genes Drive Development*. San Diego, CA: Kales Press, 2006.

Odin, Roger. *De la fiction* (*It is Fiction*). Bruxelles: De Boeck Université, 2000.

Oehlert, Mark. "From Captain America to Wolverine: Cyborgs in Comic Books, Alternative Images of Cybernetic Heroes and Villains" In *The Cyborg Handbook*, edited by Chris Hable Gray, 219–232. London and New York: Routledge, 1995.

O'Pray, Michael. "Jan Švankmajer: A Mannerist Surrealist." In *Dark Alchemy: The Films of Jan Švankmajer*, edited by Peter Hames, 48–77. Westport, CT: Greenwood Press, 1995.

O'Regan, J. Kevin, Ronald A. Rensink, and James J. Clark. "Change-Blindness as a Result of 'Mudsplashes.'" *Nature* 398 (1999): 34. doi: 10.1038/17953.

O'Regan, J. K. and Noë, Alva. "A Sensorimotor Approach to Vision and Visual Consciousness." *Behavioral and Brain Sciences* 24, no. 5 (2001): 883–975.

Orbaugh, Sharalyn. "Emotional Infectivity: Cyborg Affect and the Limits of the Human." In *Mechademia 3: Limits of the Human*, edited by Frenchy Lunning, 150–172. Minneapolis: University of Minnesota Press, 2008.

Orbaugh, Sharalyn. "Sex and the Single Cyborg: Japanese Popular Culture Experiments in Subjectivity." *Science Fiction Studies* 29, no. 3 (2002): 436–452.

Orgs, Guido, Sven Bestmann, Friederike Schuur, and Patrick Haggard. "From Body Form to Biological Motion: Apparent Velocity of Human Movement Biases Subjective Time." *Psychological Science* 22, no. 6 (2011): 712–717.

O'Riordan, Kate. "Playing with Lara in Virtual Space." In *Technospaces: Inside the New Media*, edited by Sally Munt, 224–237. London and New York: Continuum, 2001.

Ortony, Andrew, Gerald L. Clore, and Allan Collins. *The Cognitive Structure of Emotion*. Cambridge: Cambridge University Press, 1988.

Osmond, Andrew. "Reviews: *The Polar Express*." *Sight and Sound* 15, no. 1 (2005): 62.

Ōtsuka, Eiji. "Disarming Atom: Tezuka Osamu's Manga at War and Peace." Translated by Thomas Lamarre. In *Mechademia 3: Limits of the Human*, edited by Frenchy Lunning, 111–125. Minneapolis: University of Minnesota Press, 2008.

Oyama, Susan. *The Ontogeny of Information: Developmental Systems and Evolution*, 2nd ed. Durham, NC: Duke University Press, 2000 (1985).

Oztop, Erhan, David W. Franklin, Thierry Chaminade, and Gordon Cheng. "Human-Humanoid Interaction: Is a Humanoid Robot Perceived as a Human." *International Journal of Humanoid Robotics* 2, no. 4 (2005): 537–559.

Page, Edwin. *Gothic Fantasy: The Films of Tim Burton*. London and New York: Marion Boyars, 2007.

Palmer, Stephen E. *Vision Science: Photons to Phenomenology*. Cambridge, MA: MIT Press, 1999.

Parés, Narcis, and Roc Parés. "Towards a Model for a Virtual Reality Experience: The Virtual Subjectiveness." *Presence* 15, no. 5 (2006): 524–538.

Parrinder, Geoffrey. *Avatar and Incarnation*. Oxford: Oneworld Publications, 1997.

Parsons, Thomas T., Andrea Gaggioli, and Giuseppe Riva. "Virtual Reality for Research in Social Neuroscience." *Brain Sciences* 7, no. 42 (2017): 1–21.

Pate, Alan Scott. *Ningyo: The Art of Japanese Dolls*. North Clarendon, VT: Tuttle, 2005.

Peachey, Anna, and Mark Childs, eds. *Reinventing Ourselves: Contemporary Concepts of Identity in Virtual Worlds*. Berlin: Springer, 2011.

Penny, Simon. "Representation, Enaction, and the Ethics of Simulation." In *First Person: New Media as Story, Performance, and Game*, edited by Noah Wardrip-Fruin and Pat Harrigan, 73–84. Cambridge, MA: The MIT Press, 2004.

Perez-Marcos, Daniel, Massimiliano Solazzi, William Steptoe, Oyewole Oyekoya, Antonio Frisoli, Tim Weyrich, Athony Steed, Franco Tecchia, Mel Slater, and Maria V. Sanchez-Vives. "A Fully Immersive Set-up for Remote Interaction and Neurorehabilitation Based on Virtual Body Ownership." *Frontiers in Neurology* 3 (2012): 110. doi: 10.3389/fneur.2012.00110.

Perron, Bernard, and Felix Schröter, eds. *Video Games and the Mind: Essays on Cognition, Affect and Emotion*. Jefferson, NC: McFarland, 2016.

Person, Lawrence. "Notes Toward a Postcyberpunk Manifesto." *Slashdot*, 1998. http://slashdot.org/features/99/10/08/2123255.shtml.

Persson, Per. *Understanding Cinema: A Psychological Theory of Moving Imagery*. Cambridge: Cambridge University Press, 2003.

Petersik, J. Timothy. "The Two-Process Distinction in Apparent Motion." *Psychological Bulletin* 106, no. 1 (1989): 107–127.

Picard, Rosalind. *Affective Computing*. Cambridge, MA: The MIT Press, 1997.

Pickering, Andrew. *The Cybernetic Brain: Sketches of Another Future*. Chicago, IL: The University of Chicago Press, 2011.

Piechowski-Jozwiak, Bartlomiej, François Boller, and Julien Bogousslavsky. "Universal Connection Through Art: Role of Mirror Neurons in Art Production and Reception." *Behavioral Sciences* 7, no. 2 (2017): 29–39.

Planalp, Sally. *Communicating Emotions: Social, Moral, and Cultural Processes*. Cambridge: Cambridge University Press, 1999.

Plantinga, Carl. *Moving Viewers: American Film and the Spectator's Experience*. Berkeley and Los Angeles: University of California Press, 2009.

Plantinga, Carl. "Cognitive Film Theory: An Insider's Appraisal." *Cinemas* 12, no. 2 (2002): 15–37.

Plantinga, Carl. "The Scene of Empathy and the Human Face on Film." In *Passionate Views: Film, Cognition, and Emotion*, edited by Carl Plantinga and Greg M. Smith, 239–255. Baltimore, MD: Johns Hopkins University Press, 1999.

Plantinga, Carl, and Greg M. Smith, eds. *Passionate Views: Film, Cognition, and Emotion*. Baltimore, MD: Johns Hopkins University Press, 1999.

Pointer, Ray. *The Art and Inventions of Max Fleischer: American Animation Pioneer.* Jefferson, NC: McFarland, 2017.

Port, Robert F., and Timothy van Gelder, eds. *Mind as Motion: Explorations in the Dynamics of Cognition.* Cambridge, MA: The MIT Press, 1995.

Prisco, Giulio. "*Second Life* Creator: *High Fidelity*'s HFC Is a Social Cryptocurrency for VR." *Bitcoin Magazine.* March 20, 2018. https://bitcoinmagazine.com/articles/second-life-creator-high-fidelitys-hfc-social-cryptocurrency-vr/.

Putnam, Hilary. *Representation and Reality.* Cambridge: Cambridge University Press, 1988.

Ramachandran, Vilayanur S. and William Hirstein. "The Science of Art: A Neurological Theory of Aesthetic Experience." *Journal of Consciousness Studies* 6, no. 6–7, (1999): 15–51.

Rambusch, Jana. "It's Not Just Hands. Embodiment Aspects in Gameplay." In *Video Games and the Mind: Essays on Cognition, Affect and Emotion*, edited by Bernard Perron and Felix Schröter, 73–87. Jefferson, NC: McFarland, 2016.

Raos, Vassilis, Maria-Alessandra Umiltá, Akira Murata, Leonardo Fogassi, and Vittorio Gallese. "Functional Properties of Grasping-Related Neurons in the Ventral Premotor Area F5 of the Macaque Monkey." *Journal Neurophysiology* 95, no. 2 (2006): 709–729.

Rehm, Imogen C., Emily Foenander, Klaire Wallace, Jo-Anne M. Abbott, Michael Kyrios, and Neil Thomas. "What Role Can Avatars Play in e-Mental Health Interventions: Exploring New Models of Client-Therapist Interaction." *Frontiers in Psychiatry* 7 (2016): 186. doi: 10.3389/fpsyt.2016.00186.

Reid, Elizabeth M. "Text-Based Virtual Realities: Identity and the Cyborg Body." In *High Noon on the Electronic Frontier: Conceptual Issues in Cyberspace*, edited by Peter Ludlow, 327–345. Cambridge, MA: The MIT Press, 1996.

Remo, Chris. "Ken Levine on *BioShock*: The Spoiler Interview." *Shacknews*, August 30, 2007.

Ribot, Théodule-Armand. *The Psychology of the Emotions.* London: Walter Scott, 1897.

Richmond, Scott C. *Cinema's Bodily Illusions: Flying, Floating, and Hallucinating.* Minneapolis: University of Minnesota Press, 2016.

Rifelj, Carol de Dobay. "Minds, Computers, and Hadaly." In *Jeering Dreamers: Villier de l'Isle-Adam's L'Eve Future at Our Fin de Siècle: A Collection of Essays*," edited by John Anzalone, 127–139. Amsterdam: Editions Rodopi, 1996.

Rizzolatti, Giacomo, and Laila Craighero. "The Mirror-Neuron System." *Annual Review of Neuroscience* 27 (2004): 169–182.

Rizzolatti, Giacomo, Leonardo Fogassi, and Vittorio Gallese. "Mirrors in the Mind." *Scientific American* 295, no. 5 (2006): 54–61.

Roberts, Robert. *Emotions: An Essay in Aid of Moral Psychology.* Cambridge: Cambridge University Press, 2003.

Rosati, Giulio, Antonio Rodà, Frederico Avanzini, and Stefano Masiero. "On the Role of Auditory Feedback in Robot-Assisted Movement Training After Stroke: Review of the Literature." *Computational Intelligence and Neuroscience* 2013 (2013): Article ID 586138. doi: 10.1155/2013/586138.

Rose, Steven. *Lifelines: Life Beyond the Gene.* Oxford and New York: Oxford University Press, 2003. (1997)

Rosedale, Philip. "Paying Avatars on the Blockchain." *High Fidelity* (blog). January 31, 2018. https://blog.highfidelity.com/paying-avatars-on-the-blockchain-95756be3479f.

Rosenblum, Lawrence D. *See What I'm Saying: The Extraordinary Powers of Our Five Senses*. New York: W. W. Norton & Company, 2010.

Rosenthal-von der Pütten, Astrid M., and Nicole C. Krämer. "How Design Characteristics of Robot Determine Evaluation and Uncanny Valley Related Responses." *Computers in Human Behavior* 36 (2014): 422–439.

Rouyer, Phillipe. "*Les Triplettes de Belleville* : Un Tour de France... et d'Amérique." *Positif*, no. 508 (2003): 76–77.

Royle, Nicholas. *The Uncanny*. London and New York: Routledge, 2003.

Russett, Robert, and Cecile Starr, eds. *Experimental Animation: An Illustrated Anthology*. New York: Van Nostrand Reinhold Company, 1976.

Rymaszewski, Michael, Wagner James Au, Cory Ondrejka, Richard Platel, Sara Van Gorden, Jeannette Cézanne, Paul Cézanne, Ben Batstone-Cunningham, Aleks Krotoski, Celebrity Trollop, Jim Rossignol, and *Second Life* residents from around the world, eds. *Second Life: The Official Guide*, 2nd ed. Indianapolis: Wiley Publishing, 2008.

Sakabe, Megumi. "Mask and Shadow in Japanese Culture: Implicit Ontology in Japanese Thought." In *Modern Japanese Aesthetics: A Reader*, edited by Michelle Marra, 242–250. Honolulu: University of Hawaii Press, 1999.

Sakata, Hideo, Masato Taira, Akira Murata, and Seiichiro Mine. "Neural Mechanisms of Visual Guidance of Hand Action in the Parietal Cortex of the Monkey." *Cerebral Cortex* 5, no. 5 (1995): 429–438. doi: 10.1093/cercor/5.5.429.

Sanchez, Carleen D. "Cyber Border Crosser." In *Women and Second Life: Essays on Virtual Identity, Work and Play*, edited by Julie Achterberg and Dianna Baldwin, 63–76. Jefferson, NC: McFarland, 2013.

Scheler, Max. *The Nature of Sympathy*. Translated by Peter Heath. London and New York: Routledge and K.O, 1954.

Scherer, Klaus R. "Affect Bursts." In *Emotions: Essays on Emotion Theory*, edited by Stephanie H. M. van Goozen, Nann E. van de Poll, and Joseph A. Sergeant, 161–193. Hillsdale, NJ: Erlbaum, 1994.

Schivelbusch, Wolfgang. *The Railway Journey: The Industrialization of Time and Space in the Nineteenth Century*. Berkeley and Los Angeles: University of California Press, 1986 (1977).

Schroeder, Ralph, ed. *The Social Life of Avatars: Presence and Interaction in Shared Virtual Environments*. London: Springer, 2002.

Schrödinger, Erwin. *What is Life? The Physical Aspect of the Living Cell & Mind and Matter*. Reprint. Cambridge: Cambridge University Press, 1967. (1944).

Schwind, Valentin, Katharina Leicht, Solveigh Jäger, Katrin Wolf, and Niels Henze. "Is There An Uncanny Valley of Virtual Animal? A Quantitative and Qualitative Investigation." *International Journal of Human-Computer Studies* 111 (2018): 49–61.

Sconce, Jeffrey. *Haunted Media: Electronic Presence from Telegraphy to Television*. Durham, NC: Duke University Press, 2000.

Seyama, Jun'ichiro, and Ruth S. Nagayama. "The Uncanny Valley: The Effect of Realism on the Impression of Artificial Human Faces." *Presence: Teleoperators and Virtual Environments* 16, no. 4 (2007): 337–351.

Shannon, Claude E. "Presentation of a Maze-Solving Machine." In *Cybernetics: Circular Causal and Feedback Mechanisms in Biological and Social Systems, Transactions of the Eighth Conference*, March 15–16, 1951. New York: Josiah Macy Jr. Foundation, 1952.

Shapiro, Lawrence. *Embodied Cognition.* London and New York: Routledge, 2011.

Shaviro, Steven. *Post-Cinematic Affect.* Winchester: Zero Books, 2010.

Shaviro, Steven. *The Cinematic Body: Theory Out of Bounds.* Minneapolis: University of Minnesota Press, 2006 (1993).

Shaviro, Steven. "Regimes of Vision: Kathryn Bigelow, *Strange Days.*" *Polygraph* 13 (2001): 59–68.

Shiffrar, Maggie, and Freyd, Jennifer. "Timing and Apparent Motion Path Choice with Human Body Photographs." *Psychological Science* 4, no. 6 (1993): 379–384.

Shiner, Christine T., Winston D. Byblow, Penelope A. McNulty. "Bilateral Priming Before Wii-Based Movement Therapy Enhances Upper Limb Rehabilitation and Its Retention After Stroke a Case-Controlled Study." *Neurorehabilitation Neural Repair* 28, no. 9 (2014): 828–838.

Short, Sue. *Cyborg Cinema and Contemporary Subjectivity.* New York: Palgrave Macmillan, 2005.

Silberstein, Michael, and Chemero, Anthony. "Complexity and Extended Phenomenological-Cognitive Systems." *Topics in Cognitive Science* 4 (2012): 35–50.

Silverman, Kaja. *The Subject of Semiotics.* Oxford and New York: Oxford University Press, 1983.

Silvio, Carl. "Refiguring the Radical Cyborg in Mamoru Oshii's *Ghost in the Shell.*" *Science Fiction Studies* 26, no. 1 (1999): 54–70.

Simondon, Gilbert. *Du mode d'existence des objets techniques.* [*On the Mode of Existence of Technical Objects*]. Paris: Éditions Aubier, 1958.

Singer, Tania, Ben Seymour, John O'Doherty, Holger Kaube, Raymond J. Dolan, Chris D. Frith. "Empathy for Pain Involves the Affective but not Sensory Components of Pain." *Science* 30 (2004): 1157–1162.

Skoyles, Chris. "Does Time Spent Socializing in *Second Life* Tend to Enhance or Degrade 'Real Life' Social Skills." *Quora* (blog). September 12, 2011. www.quora.com/Does-time-spent-socializing-in-Second-Life-tend-to-enhance-or-degrade-real-world-social-skills#ans741799.

Skulsky, Harold. *Metamorphosis: The Mind in Exile.* Cambridge, MA: Harvard University Press, 1981.

Smelik, Anneke. "Cinematic Fantasies of Becoming-Cyborg." In *The Scientific Imaginary in Visual Culture*, edited by Anneke Smelik, 89–104. Göttingen: V&R Unipress, 2010.

Smith, Adam. *The Theory of Moral Sentiments.* New York: Augustus M. Kelley, 1966 (1759).

Smith, Greg. *Film Structure and the Emotion System.* Cambridge: Cambridge University Press, 2003.

Smith, Murray. *Engaging Characters: Fiction, Emotion, and the Cinema.* Oxford and New York: Oxford University Press, 1995.

Sobchack, Vivian. *Carnal Thoughts: Embodiment and Moving Image Culture.* Berkeley and Los Angeles: University of California Press, 2004.

Sobchack, Vivian, ed. *Meta-Morphing: Visual Transformation and the Culture of Quick-Change*. Minneapolis: University of Minnesota Press, 2000.

Sobchack, Vivian. *The Address of the Eye: A Phenomenology of Film Experience*. Princeton, NJ: Princeton University Press, 1992.

Sobchack, Vivian. "The Scene of the Screen: Envisioning Cinematic and Electronic 'Presence.'" In *Electronic Media and Technoculture*, edited by John Caldwell, 137–155. New Brunswick, NJ: Rutgers University Press, 2000.

Sobchack, Vivian. "Animation and Automation, or, the Incredible Effortfulness of Being." *Screen* 50, no. 4 (2009): 375–391.

Solso, Robert L. *Cognition and the Visual Arts*. Cambridge, MA: The MIT Press, 1996.

Springer, Claudia. "The Pleasure of the Interface." In *Technology and Culture: The Film Reader*, edited by Andrew Utterson, 71–85. London and New York: Routledge, 2005.

Stacey, Jackie. *The Cinematic Life of the Gene*. Durham, NC: Duke University Press, 2010.

Stadler, Harald. "Film as Experience: Phenomenological Concepts in Cinema and Television Studies." *Quarterly Review of Film and Video* 12, no. 3 (1990): 37–50.

Stafford, Barbara Maria. *Echo Objects: The Cognitive Work of Images*. Chicago, IL: The University of Chicago Press, 2007.

Standen, Penny J., and David J. Brown. "Virtual Reality in the Rehabilitation of People with Intellectual Disabilities: Review." *Cyberpsychology Behavior* 8 (2005): 272–282; discussion 283–288.

Steckenfinger, Shawn A., and Asif A. Ghazanfar. "Monkey Visual Behavior Falls Into the Uncanny Valley." *PNAS* 106, no. 43 (2009): 18362–18366.

Stein, Nancy L., Tom Trabasso, and Maria Liwag. "A Goal Appraisal Theory of Emotional Understanding: Implications for Development and Learning." In *Handbook of Emotions*, 2nd ed., edited by Michael Lewis and Jeannette M. Haviland, 436–457. New York: Guilford Press, 2000.

Stein, Nancy L., Tom Trabasso, and Maria Liwag. "The Representation and Organization of Emotional Experience: Unfolding the Emotion Episode." In *Handbook of Emotions*, edited by Michael Lewis and Jeannette M. Haviland, 279–300. New York: Guilford Press, 1993.

Stephenson, Neal. *Snow Crash*. New York: Bantam Books, 2003 (1992).

Stevens, Jennifer A., et al. "New Aspects of Motion Perception: Selective Neural Encoding of Apparent Human Movements." *NeuroReport* 11 (2000): 109–115.

Stromer-Galley, Jennifer, and Rosa Mikeal Martey. "Visual Spaces, Norm Governed Places: The Influence of Spatial Context Online." *New Media & Society* 11, no. 6 (2009): 1041–1060.

Tan, Ed S. *Emotion and the Structure of Narrative Film: Film as an Emotion Machine*. Mahwah, NJ: Lawrence Erlbaum, 1996.

Taussig, Karen-Sue. "The Molecular Revolution in Medicine: Promise, Reality, and Social Organization." In *Complexities: Beyond Nature and Nurture*, edited by Susan McKinnon and Sydel Silverman, 223–247. Chicago, IL: The University of Chicago Press, 2005.

Taylor, T. L. *Play Between Worlds: Exploring Online Game Culture*. Cambridge, MA: The MIT Press, 2006.

Telotte, J. P. *Replications: A Robotic History of the Science Fiction Film*. Urbana and Chicago: University of Illinois Press, 1995.

Thomas, David. *Vertov, Snow, Farocki: Machine Vision and the Posthuman*. New York: Bloomsbury Academic, 2013.

Thompson, Clive. "Victory in Vomit: The Sickening Secret of Mirror's Edge." *Wired*, November 16, 2008. http://archive.wired.com/gaming/gamingreviews/commentary/games/2008/11/gamesfrontiers_1117.

Thompson, Clive. "Monsters of Photorealism." *Wired*, December 5, 2005. www.wired.com/2005/12/monsters-of-photorealism/.

Thompson, Evan. *Mind in Life: Biology, Phenomenology, and the Sciences of Mind*. Cambridge, MA: The Belknap Press of Harvard University Press, 2007.

Tiemersma, Douwe. *Body Schema and Body Image: An Interdisciplinary and Philosophical Study*. Amsterdam: Swets & Zeitlinger, 1989.

Tinwell, Angela. "Is the Uncanny Valley a Universal or Individual Response?" *Interaction Studies* 16, no. 2 (2015): 180–185.

Tinwell, Angela, Deborah Abdel Nabi, and John P. Charlton. "Perception of Psychopathy and the Uncanny Valley in Virtual Characters." *Computers in Human Behavior* 29, no. 4 (2013): 1617–1625.

Tinwell, Angela, Mark Grimshaw, Debbie Abdel Nabi, and Andrew Williams. "Facial Expression of Emotion and Perception of the Uncanny Valley." *Computers in Human Behavior* 27, no. 2 (2011): 741–749.

Todorov, Tzvetan. *The Fantastic: A Structural Approach to a Literary Genre*. Translated by Richard Howard. Ithaca, NY: Cornell University Press, 1975.

Tomkins, Silvan S. *Affect, Imagery, Consciousness*. New York: Springer, 1962.

Travers, Peter. "*The Polar Express*." *Rolling Stone Reviews*, November 18, 2004. www.rollingstone.com/movies/reviews/the-polar-express-20041118.

Travers, Peter. "*Final Fantasy*." *Rolling Stone*, July 6, 2001. www.rollingstone.com/movies/reviews/final-fantasy-20010706.

Troje, Nikolaus F., and Cord Westhoff. "The Inversion Effect in Biological Motion Perception: Evidence for a 'Life Detector'?" *Current Biology* 16, no. 8 (2006): 821–824.

Tsao, Doris. "A Dedicated System for Processing Faces." *Science* 314, no. 5796 (October 2006): 72–73. doi: 10.1126/science.1135163.

Tunison, Michael. "Review of *Final Fantasy: The Spirits Within*." *Box Office Online*, July 11, 2001. www.boxofficemagazine.com/reviews/2008-08-final-fantasythe-spirits-withi?q=final+fantasy.

Turkle, Sherry. *Life on the Screen: Identity in the Age of the Internet*. New York: Simon & Schuster, 1995.

Turkle, Sherry. *The Second Self: Computers and the Human Spirit*. New York: Simon & Schuster, 2005 (1984).

Uhde, Jan. "Jan Švankmajer: Genius Loci as a Source of Surrealist Inspiration." In *The Unsilvered Screen: Surrealism on Film*, edited by Graeme Harper and Rob Stone, 60–71. London and New York: Wallflower Press, 2007.

Uva, Christian. "La performance numérique entre corps et ultracorps." In *Body Images in the Post-Cinematic Scenario: The Digitization of Bodies*, edited by Alberto Brodesco and Frederico Giordano, 37–50. Milan: Mimesis International, 2017.

Varela, Francisco. "Laying Down a Path in Walking." In *Gaia: A Way of Knowing: Political Implications of the New Biology*, edited by William I. Thompson, 48–64. Great Barrington, MA: Lindisfarne Press, 1987.

Varela, Francisco J., Eleanor Rosch, and Evan Thompson. *The Embodied Mind: Cognitive Science and Human Experience.* Cambridge, MA: The MIT Press, 1993.

Vinge, Vernor. "True Names." In *True Names and the Opening of the Cyberspace Frontier*, edited by James Frenkel, 239–330. New York: Tom Doherty Associates Book, 2001.

Virilio, Paul. *Pure War*, 2nd ed. New York: Semiotext(e), 1997.

Virilio, Paul. *The Vision Machine.* Translated by Julie Ross. London: British Film Institute, 1994.

Vischer, Robert. "On the Optical Sense of Form: A Contribution to Aesthetics." In *Empathy, Form, and Space. Problems in German Aesthetics, 1873–1893*, translated and edited by Harry Francis Mallgrave and Eleftherios Ikonomou, 89–123. Santa Monica, CA: Getty Center for the History of Art and the Humanities, 1994 (1873).

Viseu, Ana. "Simulation and Augmentation: Issues of Wearable Computers." *Ethics and Information Technology* 5, no. 1 (2003): 17–26.

von Neumann, John. *The Computer and the Brain.* New Haven, CT: Yale University Press, 1958.

Waggoner, Zach. *My Avatar, My Self: Identity in Video Role-Playing Games.* Jefferson, NC: McFarland, 2009.

Warburg, Aby. *The Renewal of Pagan Antiquity: Contributions to the Cultural History of the European Renaissance.* Translated by David Britt. Los Angeles, CA: Getty Research Institute for the History of Art and the Humanities, 1999.

Warner, Marina. *Fantastic Metamorphoses, Other Worlds: Ways of Telling the Self.* Oxford and New York: Oxford University Press, 2002.

Watkins, Mel. *On the Real Side.* New York: Simon & Schuster, 1995.

Watson, James D., and John Tooze. *The DNA Story: A Documentary History of Gene Cloning.* San Francisco, CA: W. H. Freeman, 1981.

Weber, Aimee, Kimberly Rufer-Bach, and Richard Platel. *Creating Your World: The Official Guide to Advanced Content Creation for Second Life.* Indianapolis: Wiley, 2007.

Weiss, Gail. *Body Images: Embodiment as Intercorporeality.* London and New York: Routledge, 1999.

Weiss, Patrice L., Debbie Rand, Noomi Katz, and Rachel Kizony. "Video Capture Virtual Reality as a Flexible and Effective Rehabilitation Tool." *Journal of NeuroEngineering and Rehabilitation* 1, no. 1 (2004): 12. doi: 10.1186/1743-0003-1-12.

Wells, Paul. *Understanding Animation.* London and New York: Routledge, 1998.

Weschler, Lawrence. *Uncanny Valley: Adventures in the Narrative.* Berkeley, CA: Counterpoint, 2011.

Wiederhold, Brenda K. "Avatars: Changing Behavior for Better or for Worse." *Cyberpsychology* 16, no. 5 (2013): 319–320.

Wiener, Norbert. *Cybernetics; or, Control and Communication in the Animal and the Machine.* Cambridge, MA: The MIT Press, 1948.

Williams, Linda. "Film Bodies: Gender, Genre, and Excess." *Film Quarterly* 44, no. 4 (1991): 2–13.

Wilson, Margaret. "Six Views of Embodied Cognition." *Psychonomic Bulletin & Review* 9, no. 4 (2002): 625–636.

Wilson, Robert. *Boundaries of the Mind: The Individual in the Fragile Sciences*. Cambridge: Cambridge University Press, 2004.

Wolf, Mark J. *The Medium of the Video Game*. Austin: University of Texas Press, 2001.

Wölfflin, Heinrich. *Prolegomena zu einer Psychologie der Architektur*. Doctoral dissertation, University of Munich, 1886. (Republished in Berlin: Gebr. Mann, 1998).

Wolfram, Steven. *A New Kind of Science*. Champaign, IL: Wolfram Media, 2002.

Wollheim, Richard. *The Thread of Life*. Cambridge, MA: Harvard University Press, 1984.

Wood, Aylish. *Digital Encounters*. London and New York: Routledge, 2007.

Wykes, Maggie, and Barrie Gunter. *The Media and Body Image*. London: Sage, 2005.

Yee, Nick, and Jeremy Bailenson. "The Proteus Effect: The Effect of Transformed Self-Representation on Behavior." *Human Communication Research* 33, no. 3 (2007): 271–290.

Yonck, Richard. *Heart of the Machine: Our Future in a World of Artificial Emotional Intelligence*. New York: Arcade Publishing, 2017.

York, Jamie. "Hollywood Eyes Uncanny Valley in Animation," "All Things Considered," NPR radio program, radio broadcast and transcript, March 5, 2010. www.npr.org/templates/story/story.php?storyId=124371580.

York, Jamie. "The Uncanny Valley." "On the Media," NPR radio program, radio broadcast and transcript, March 5, 2010. www.wnycstudios.org/story/132702-the-uncanny-valley.

Zeki, Semir. *Inner Vision: An Exploration of Art and the Brain*. Oxford and New York: Oxford University Press, 1999.

Zeki, Semir. "Neural Concept Formation and Art: Dante, Michelangelo, Wagner." *Journal of Consciousness Studies* 9, no. 3 (2002): 53–76.

Zillmann, Dolf. "Empathy: Affect from Bearing Witness to the Emotions of Others." In *Responding to the Screen: Reception and Reaction Processes*, edited by Jennings Bryant and Dolf Zillmann, 135–167. Hillsdale, MI: Lawrence Erlbaum Associates, 1991.

Index

3D rendering *119*, 120
8 Man After 69, 74, 92n30
9 189
The 101 Dalmatians 181
2001: A Space Odyssey 136

abstract animation 41, 55; *see also* *Spheres*
acentral imagining 123, 131n80; *see also* central imagining
Acting in Animation 108
Aeon Flux 63
affect, affects: "affect bursts" 36; and bottom-up responses 98; and chemical balance 118, 272; flow of 42, 98–99, 109, 128, 169–170, 197, 225, 269; and "low road" mechanisms 36, 102, 270; *see also* acentral imagining; affective mimicry; central imagining; direct affect; embodied simulation; emotion; emotional contagion; observational attitudes; movements on the screen; personal-space invasion; proprioception; synesthetic affect; the transmission of affect
Affective Computing 242
affective mimicry: defining 125; and *Howl's Moving Castle* 125; and *Prisoners* 14; *see also* emotional contagion; facial mimicry; motor mimicry
affective resonances *see* empathic resonances
agency: collaborative 245; distributed 239–240, 244, 262; feminine 193; and sense of embodiment 250; sharing with avatars 239, 262; in video games 210, 214; in *Second Life* 252
Akatsuka, Wakagi 113
Akira 62
Alan Wake 176
Alberti, Leon Battista 34
algorithms 215, 241–243; algorithmic control 70, 217, 232, 241, 246–247, 251–252; algorithmic couplings 203, 214, 217, 241–242, 263; algorithmic logic 216, 239; allegorithm 19, 216; and living systems 219–221, 227, 239, 245–246; political simulation 215; *see also* procedural rhetoric
Alice's Adventures in Wonderland 190
Alien: Resurrection 226
America's Army 216, 235n53, 236n63
Anderson, Aaron 140–141, 145
Anderson, French 222
Anémic Cinéma 69
anger 45, 109, 118, 125, 170, 175, 256
animation *see* abstract animation; cel animation; computer-generated animation; hand-drawn animation; puppet animation; stop-motion animation; pixilation
animation machine 9, 51, 54–55, 57, 65, 76, 90, 97, 121, 123–124, 128, 269–270; definition 8; in video games 203, 205; in virtual reality 241
Antagonia 48–50, 57, 270
antipathy 100, 109, 115, 151, 172, 181; *see also* "feeling against"
Appleseed Ex Machina 16, 65, 81–83, 90, 138
Appleseed Alpha 181
Armitage III: Polymatrix 88
Armitage: Dual Matrix 88
artifact emotion 183–184
Ashby, Ross 70

Assassin's Creed 195
assemblage: and the animation machine 9, 54, 57, 65, 77, 84, 90–91, 269; and affects 118, 120–121, 124; and avatars 212, 241, 250; and becoming 124, 127; and empathy 128; and meaning-making 203; and modes of production 80; and rotoscope 153; and subjective perspective 164, 193; *see also* Deleuze, Gilles and Guattari, Félix
athletes: skater 147; cyclist 17, 154, 156–157, 272; runner 159, *160*; *see also* martial arts; *Modeling*; *The Triplets of Belleville*; *Black Jack: The Movie*
Atwood, Margaret 153–154, 157, 163
Austin Powers: International Man of Mystery 252
automatisms 6, 8, 52–53, 55, 76, 84, 90, 121, 212, 263, 269–270
autonomic reflexes 134
autopoiesis 239, 246–247, 265n44
Avalon 74
Avatar 80, 176, 244
avatars: and affect 209, 225; and agency 239; and algorithmic coupling 203, 215; in animation 244–245; and becoming-animated 213; and "body in code" 220, 225–227, 232; and body schema 211–212; definition 204; EmoBot 239; and emotion 238, 220; and first-person point of view 205, 207, 214; history of 243–244; in literature 90, 244; and logical interface 205, 209, 213; on mobile devices 243; online 238; and perceptual alignment 223; and problem-solving ensemble 212–213; and third-person perspective 209; as tool 204, 210–212; *see also* *BioShock*; *Habitat*; mappings; perceptual symbiosis; *Second Life* avatars; empathic resonances; video games

Bailenson, Jeremy 259
Bakshi, Ralph 244; *see also Spicy City*
Ballet mécanique 67
ballistic vision 123
Barker, Jennifer 13, 135
Barta, Jiří 142; *see also The Club of the Laid Off*
basic stress response 134
Batman 172
Baudrillard, Jean 160
becoming-animal: Deleuze, Gilles and Guattari, Félix on 124, 126; in *Howl's Moving Castle* 17, 97, 122, 124–127, 272; in *Princess Mononoke* 127–128
becoming-animated 127–128; and algorithmic couplings 203; and augmented perception 77–80; and change blindness 3–5; definition 3, 5, 15; and disquieting motion 142–145, 164; and embodied virtuality 76; and empathic resonances 124–125, 128, 164; and flickering images 81–84; and hyperbolized movements 140–141, 164; and intersubjective alignment 76; and perceptual assemblage 53, 57, 86; and rotoscoped motion 152–153, 164; and the uncanny 168; in video games 203, 213, 231–232, 241, 269, 275
becoming-avatar: and affective computing 240–241, 253–256, 258, 263; and authentic self 255; definition 239; and distributed agency 240–242; and extended cognition 242, 262–263; and reprograming the self 250–253, 263; and sensorimotor skills 241, 251–253, 263; and virtual-reality based therapies 261–262; *see also* avatars; *Second Life*; *Second* Life avatar; virtual reality-based therapies
Beowulf 195
Bergson, Henri 6, 68
Berenson, Bernard 33
Betty Boop's Bamboo Isle 150
Betty Boop's Snow White 146, 151–153, 163, 272
On Beyond Living 245
Bigelow Susan, 118
bionic worldview 223, 232
BioShock: and affect 207–208, 217, 220, 222, 225, 232; and allegiance 229–230; and becoming cyborg 229–230; and Big Daddy 203, 208, 220, 224, 228–230; and body-technology symbiosis 230–231; and genetic determinism 221, 229; and hacking 229; and haptic

feedback 209; and mad scientists 221–222, 229–230; and mental conditioning 229; and objectivism 228; and optimized eugenics 18, 221–223, 228, 273; and pain 229, 231; *see also* genetic modifications; postvitalism; procedural rhetoric
BioShock 2 202–203, 205–206, 208, 216; and genetic alteration 222; and hacking 205; and haptic feedback 206; and Little Sister's mapping 206; and multiple endings 231; and programmable body 225–226
BioShock Infinite 20n4, 202, 205, 235n28
Bird, Brad 182; *see also The Incredibles*
Birth of the Dragon 140
Black Jack: The Movie 153, 158–164
Blade Runner 62, 70, 74, 87, 179
Blade Runner 2049 179
Blavatsky, Helena 243–244
body image 20n3, 128, 210, 249, 258; in animation 104; defining 210; in the media 265n58; virtual 242, 249; *see also* "body in code"; body schema
"body in code" 203, 210, 225, 239, 248
body schema: vs. body image 20n3, 210; defining 3, 42, 210, 253; effects of animated figure on 29; and renegotiating boundaries 25, 212; and *Second Life* 253; and tool use 27–28, 211, 253; and video games 19, 203, 209–212, 215; and virtual reality-based therapies 263; *see also* "body in code"; perceptual symbiosis; sensorimotor coupling
body's interior (pictures of the): blood 159–160; blurring inside and outside 111, 118–119; bowels 113–114; cells 160; heart 159; flesh 194; medical imagery 163; operating room 159; porous membranes 119; responses to the sight of the 159–160; as a sign of death 114; X-ray vision 159–160
Boellstorff, Tom 248
Bogost, Ian 14, 18, 215, 217
Bordwell, David 13, 93n41, 139
Bossewitch, Jonah 245
Bouldin, Joanna 86
Boundin' 46, 50, 56, 136, 270
Bourdieu, Pierre 217–218, 246
brain's plasticity 9, 27, 58n25, 240, 258
Brennan, Theresa 119
Brooks, Rodney 42, 195
Brown, Steven 189
Brunelleschi, Filippo 34
A Bug's Life 182
Bukatman, Scott 231
Buñuel, Luis 113
Burnout 225
Burton, Tim 106–107; *see also Corpse Bride*; *Charlie and the Chocolate Factory*

The Cabinet of Jan Švankmajer 51–53, 57
Calloway, Cab 17, 134, 145–146, 150–153, 163, 272
camera movements 142; in depth 135, 137; digital 136–137; and effortless travel 136; impossible 137–138; *see also* digital effects
Cameron, James 224; *see also Avatar*; *The Terminator*; *Terminator 2*
Canemaker, John 182
canonical neurons 30, 58n39
Captain America 106
Cardinal, Roger 75
Carmena, Jose 28
Carrey, Jim 171
Cars 133, 182
Cartesianism 13, 227–228
Casetti, Francesco 66–67
Catwoman 172
Cavallaro, Dani 116
Cavell, Stanley 6
cel animation 120, 176, 178, 271
centers of indetermination 6, 8, 68
central imagining 123, 131n80; *see also* acentral imagining
change blindness 3–7, 20n6
Channell, David 223
Chaplin, Charlie 171
character design 14, 16, 97, 105, 122, 162, 171; spectator's response to 106, 108, 176, 181, 273; and facial distortions 181; and metaphors 106, 108, 112, 122, 130n40; and values 106; *see also* character engagement; synthespians; iconography
character engagement 87–88, 98–99, 102, 124; and genre 170; and physical appearance 170; and technology 176–177

character simulation 131n79, 100, 102, 169; defining 13, 102
Charlie and the Chocolate Factory 106
Un chien andalou 113
Children's Dreams 95
A Christmas Carol (Zemeckis) 136–137, 171–172
Chrysalis 65
Cinema 1 6, 68
Cinema's Bodily Illusions 7
The Cinematic Body 72
cinematism: Virilio on 123, 137; and bomb's-eye view 124
City Lights 171
Civilization III 216
Clair, René 67; *see also Entr'acte*
Clark, Andy 9, 15, 24–25; on agent-world circuits 213; on grades of embodiment 25; on farming out reasoning processes 26; on human-centered products 77; on hybridization 233; on natural-born cyborgs 9, 72, 240; on new systemic wholes 27; on spreading the cognitive load 78, 241; *see also* brain's plasticity; extended mind; soft self; transient extended cognitive system; transparent in use
classic conditioning 134
close-up: in *Black Jack: The Movie* 159; in *Un chien andalou* 113; in *City Lights* 171; in *Corpse Bride* 109–110; and eeriness 188; in *Howl's Moving Castle* 100, 125; of nonhuman eyes 74, 88, 184, *191*; and pain 175; in *Malice@Doll* 193; in *The Passion of Joan of Arc* 171; in *Princess Mononoke* 118; and sadness 173; in scenes of empathy 169; in *Texhnolyze* 172, 174–175
The Club of the Laid Off 17, 142–145, 162, 272
Clynes, Manfred 150
Coëgnarts, Maarten 11–12, 45
cognition: cybernetics 70; information processing as 70–71; robot as a model for 195; *see also* Clark, Andy; embodied mind; enactive perception; situated cognition; visual perception
Cohl, Émile 95–96, 103
Collins, Austin 152
comic book characters 172
Coming of Age in Second Life 254
Communism 40, 97, 113
compositing 17, 63, 74–75, 77, 80, 90, 119–120, 260, 271
Computational Universe 19, 84, 94n70, 239, 246
computer-generated animation 18, 79, 136, 226; CGI in *Princess Mononoke* 120; *see also Appleseed Ex Machina*; *A Christmas Carol*; *Final Fantasy: The Spirits Within*; *The Incredibles*; *Malice@Doll*; *The Polar Express*; synthespians; *WALL-E*
computer-generated effects *see* digital effects
conceptual metaphor theory (CMT) 24, 38, 44–45, 270; and embodied mind 43; *see also* image schemas; metaphors
concern 13, 36, 98–99, 102, 175; concern-based construals 129n10
The Congress 178
contrapposto: Alberti on the 34; in *Howl's Moving Castle* 35–36; in *SoulCalibur IV* 34–36
Coraline 178, 189
Corpse Bride 16, 112, 115, 127–128, 178, 271; blurring life and death 111; Emily's splitting 110–111; empathy with Emily 108–110; empathy with Victor 107–108; facial expressiveness 108; and IN-OUT schema 105–106; self-reflexivity 111; state of alienation 107
correlation-based metaphor 44
Cosmic Voyage 136
Counter-Strike 216, 235n53
Cranny-Francis, Anne 224
Crary, Jonathan 6–7
Creating Your World 246
Creed, Barbara 88, 178, 183, 185
Crouching Tiger, Hidden Dragon 140–141, 162
The Curious Case of Benjamin Button 18, 80, 185–188, 196–197
Currie, Gregory 53
cybernetics 16, 70, 93n36, 223; *see also* Macy Conferences on Cybernetics
cyberpunk genre 91n1; in animation 16, 64, 173; and avatarial experience 64, 72, 74; and character

engagement 65, 69, 73, 87; in film 65, 72–73; and gender 63; and hacking 63–64; and identity 71; in literature 62, 70; and motifs 16, 64–65, 70, 73; and perceptual extensions 16, 63–64, 70, 72; and point-of-view shots 63–64, 73; *see also* cyborg; posthuman; posthuman perception; visual perception
cyberstars 79, 89, 176, 178, 183, 195, 271
cyborg 91n2; in animation 62–63, 65, 72–74, 115, 182; the animator as a 150; categories 156; Cybermen 224; Donna Haraway on the, 10, 63, 150, 224; empathy with 17, 86–87, 195; and prosthetic enhancement 224; and the rotoscope 150; subjective perspective 7, 16, 73, 86, 90; term's origins 150; transforming into 3, 19, 203, 209, 228–232; in video games 34–35; *see also 8 Man After*; *Appleseed Ex Machina*; *BioShock*; *BioShock 2*; Clark, Andy; cyborg viewer; *Ghost in the Shell*; *RoboCop* (Padilha); *RoboCop* (Verhoeven); *The Terminator*; *Terminator 2*
cyborg viewer 10, 16, 75–77, 90–91, 145; and electronic transmutation 86; as human-technology symbionts 24, 56; and "machinic vision" 71; and mind-melding with cyborgs 83; and mixed-reality environments 77; and the multiplication of perspectives 72; and the rotoscope 134, 150–151, 153; and the uncanny 178
Czech Republic 113
Czech Surrealism 113
Czechoslovakia 40, 97, 113

Dalí, Salvadore 113
Damasio, Antonio 121
Dawkins, Richard 219–220, 245
Dawn of the Planet of the Apes 80
The Death of Stalinism in Bohemia: 17, 97, 112–115, 128, 271; clay figures in 113–114; and disgust 114; Stalinism in 114
Deleuze, Gilles 6, 68
Deleuze, Gilles and Guattari, Félix: on assemblage 20n21, 122, 124; on the body without organs 250; on molecular becoming 124, 157; *see also* becoming-animal
Descartes, René 227; *see also* Cartesianism
Descartes' Error 121; *see also* Damasio, Antonio
Despicable Me 136
Deutsch, J. Anthony 169
Deutsch, Diana 169
Diagonal Symphony see Symphonie Diagonale
Dick, Philip K. 62
digital effects 17, 120; in *Corpse Bride* 112; as the enemy within 119; as infection 118, 120; and proprioceptive effects 136–138; as reflection on technology 138; and the uncanny 171; *see also* compositing; morphing
direct affect 134, 163, 164n4; *see also* autonomic reflexes; basic stress response; camera movements; classic conditioning; dizziness; facial mimicry; flickering images; mimicry of the film's body; motion sickness; motor mimicry; movements on the screen; muscular empathy; nausea; personal-space invasion; stroboscopic effects
disease: and nonhumans 120–121; and queerness 194–195; and superhumans 159–161; and the uncanny 179, 195–196; in virtual worlds 240
disgust 37, 113–115, 159, 180–181, 194, 196, 229
Disney, Walt 20n2, 131n59, 176
distributed cognition 26, 29, 70, 91, 93n35, 262; in virtual reality 238, 241–242, 274
dizziness 134, 136
Do Androids Dream of Electric Sheep? 62
Doctor Who 224
Dog 144
doll: and appearance 190–191, 196; *butai karakuri* 192; and cyberpunk 243; and human likeness 191; mechanized 75, 168, 189, 198, 273; and prostitute 192; sex 242; and the uncanny 178, 187–190, 198; violence against 192, 197; and voice 190–191; *zashiki karakuri* 191–192; *see also Malice@Doll*; mechanical uncanny

Donatello 34
Doom 217, 234n23
doppelganger see doubling
double *see* doubling
doubling 104–105, 111, 137, 144, 171–172, 189, 245, 270 *see also* avatars
Dough for the Do-Do 68
Doyle, Richard 245
Dr. No 106
Draxtor 257
Dreyer, Carl 171
Dreyfus, Hubert 256
Du Bos, Jean-Baptiste 37
Duchamp, Marcel 69
Duck Amuck 68
Dumitrica, Delia 249

Echo Objects 12, 38
Edelman, Gerald 42
Eisenstein, Sergei 89; on expressive movement 139; on plasmaticness 105; on motor mimicry 141
Ekman, Paul 170, 243
Elastigirl 1, 12, 46–48, 56, 112
Ellis, Stephen 204
Elkins, James 34, 97, 114
Elsaesser, Thomas 13
Elysium 65
embodied cognition *see* embodied mind
embodied meaning: in animation 11, 38–45; in video game 3, 219–220, 224–225, 228–230; *see also* conceptual metaphor theory; embodied mind; image schemas; metaphors
embodied mind 10, 21n30, 24, 31, 42–43, 60n80, 270; in cinema 15, 21n31
The Embodied Mind 68
embodied perception: in animation 10–14, 38, 41–42, 51, 53–54, 64–65, 90; in audiovisual media 68–69; augmented perception 77–78, 91; extended embodiment 76, 90; perceptual effects 82, 84, 86, 136; in video games 203, 207, 209–210; *see also* affect; change blindness; embodied meaning; embodied mind; enactive perception; extended mind; gestalt laws; mirror neuron system; optical toys; posthuman perception; proprioception; situated cognition
embodied simulation 32–36, 97, 102, 125, 134, 138, 144, 270; in animation 32, 128, 157, 163; defining 33; and meaning 38; and mirroring mechanisms 36; in sculpture 34; *see also* contrapposto; muscular empathy; psychomania; *Sisyphus*; *The Triplets of Belleville*
embodied virtuality 16, 63, 84, 90–91, 93n56, 193, 271; defining 76
Engaging Characters 16, 98, 123
emoji 243
emotion, emotions: and action films 170; in audiovisual media 38, 39, 50, 56, 59n59, 108–109; and audiovisual technique 98, 122, 134, 137, 139–140; and automatic responses 36, 38; and bodily states 98, 109; character 139, 168–170; and character engagement 98–99, 109, 123; and close-up 125; 169, 171; and cognition 42, 98; and cyberpunk genre 65, 91; defining 36; and facial expression 108–109, 118, 125; and facial feedback 125, 169; and film genre 98–99, 135, 169–170; and horror genre 98; as a flow 36, 59n57, 98–99, 109; "high road" 36; and interpretation 67; lack of 87–88, 108, 173–174; loss of control over one's 118; metaphors about 45; in movie theaters 120, 169; and music 107; and pan-cultural similarities 170; perception of 31, 33; and persuasion 128; and physical appearance 125; and posthumans 64, 87; proper 36; in psychology 37, 169–170; range of 108; in response to technique 122; in response to bodily distortions 115; and romantic comedies 99; and spectator's behavior 170; as theme 122; and understanding 38, 41–43; *see also* affect; "affect bursts"; anger; antipathy; character simulation; disgust; emotional contagion; empathy; fear; gore; happiness; interest; love; mood; observational attitudes; pain; personal-space invasion; sadness; scene of empathy; suspense; sympathy; the transmission of affect; the uncanny

emotional contagion 12, 14, 38, 56, 102; and close-up 169; and mirror neurons 169; in virtual worlds 256
emotional simulation *see* character simulation
EMOTIV™ 28–29, 238
empathic resonances 12–13, 15, 17, 56, 122, 127–128, 164, 270; and avatar 210, 214, 219; defining 12, 56
empathic reverberations *see* empathic resonances
empathy: in action films 170; in animation 18; and character design 105–106, 112; and character personality 108, 125; for characters in pain 161, 164; in cinema 37; and close-up 125, 171, 175; cognitive 169; cognitive vs. physical 33; and continuity editing 101; defining 109; and emotional range 108; in esthetic experience 12, 31; and expressive looks 176; and genre 135, 169; as human trait 88; lack of 87–88, 182; and mechanisms of mediation 106, 112; and melodrama 169–170; and metamorphosis 125; and mirror neuron system 10, 12, 31, 56, 97, 106; and muscular effort 154; and pain 155; for posthumans 219; for robots 179; and star persona 100; and structure of engagement 97; for suffering cyborgs 82; vs. sympathy 109; and uncanninness 168, 177; for victims 154; *see also* affective mimicry; embodied simulation; emotional contagion; empathic resonances; facial empathy; facial mimicry; "feeling with"; imaginary transposition; motor mimicry; muscular empathy; scene of empathy
The Emperor's Nightingale 112, 188
Employees Leaving the Lumière Factory 134
enactive perception 3–5, 10, 25, 69, 92n24, 207, 247; in animation 4, 7, 16, 41, 62, 65; and spectator 62; in video games 207; in synthetic worlds 247; *see also* embodied perception; Noë, Alva; visual perception
Eng, Kynan 261–262
Enter the Dragon 140–141
Entr'acte 67
Entropia Universe 240
epistemic action 27
eugenics 158, 168n78, 221, 223; in *Black Jack: The Movie* 158; *see also* new eugenics; *BioShock*
Eureka 77
EVE Online 240
EverQuest 240
eXistenZ 72, 74
experiential blindness 207, 234n18
extended cognition *see* extended mind
extended mind 9–10, 15, 24–25, 78, 84, 262

Facial Action Coding System (FACS) 170, 243
facial empathy 168–171; *see also* affective mimicry; character engagement; close-up; emotional contagion; empathy; facial feedback; facial mimicry; mirror neuron system; observational attitudes; scene of empathy
facial feedback 169; defining 125; *see also* facial mimicry
facial mimicry 169; and close-up 169; defining 125; *Howl's Moving Castle* and 125; mirror neurons and 169, 270; *Second Life* and 256; *Texhnolyze* and 174; *see also* affective mimicry; emotional contagion; facial feedback
Family Guy 252
Fantasmagoria 103–104, 127; morphing 95–96; shape-shifting characters 96
Fantasmagorie see Fantasmagoria
The Fantastic 104
Fantastic Planet 188
Father and Daughter 44
fear 36, 98, 112, 117, 123, 125, 179–180, 255–256, 259
"feeling against" 109
"feeling for" 109, 130n48, 270
"feeling with" 109, 130n48, 270
Felix Finds Out 103
Felix in Hollywood 103
Felix the Cat 103–104
Felix the Cat Switches Witches: and the *gryllus* 103–104
Fehsenfeld, Lisa 134
Ferrell, Robyn 188

film noir 163, 170, 189; affect in 173, 220
film studies 10–11, 44, 101; *see also* haptic film theories; film theories; phenomenology
film theories 10, 13, 16, 21n29, 66–67, 72, 90, 92n15; *see also* film studies; haptic film theories; phenomenology
Final Fantasy: The Spirits Within 1, 16, 64–65, 71, 76–80, 88, 90, 167–168, 178, 188, 197, 271, 273; motion capture in 182–183; photorealism in 181–185; and production 182–183; and star system 183
Finding Nemo 182
first-person shooters 13, 203, 206–209, 214–215, 217–218, 223, 234n23, 245
Fischman, Josh 83
Flat Hatting 45
Fleets of Stren'th 149
Fleischer, Dave 145, 149, 152
Fleischer, Joe 145
Fleischer, Max 17, 145–147, 149
flickering images: causing health problems 82; in change blindness experiments 4, 6; and flicker fusion 53, 61n108; perception of 82–84, 90; and posthuman assemblage 91, 271; and mental breakdown 82; and pain 81; *see also* stroboscopic effects
flip book 23–24
Flora 113
Fodor, Jerry 41, 60n80
Food 113
Forceville, Charles 11, 39, 44
France 154, 156
Frankenstein; or, the Modern Prometheus 75
Freedberg, David 12, 30, 32–33
Freud, Sigmund 168, 177–178, 190, 192, 195
Freyd, Jennifer 143
Frijda, Nico 36
Fullmetal Alchemist 96

Gallese, Vittorio 12, 30, 32–33, 42
Galloway, Alexander 214, 216
game world 3, 9, 204–207; camera perspective 207–209; directional arrows 205; empathic resonances 210–211; haptic feedback 205–206, 209; "hard" boundaries 215, 235n51; logical interfaces 204–205, 273; physical interfaces 204–205, 273; "soft" boundaries 215, 235n51; subjective shot 207; *see also* algorithmic couplings; avatars; video games; virtual environment; virtual reality
Gamer 245
Garden, Georgia 249
Gattaca 158
gender 14, 39, 102, 105, 115–116, 144, 153, 180; and avatars 249–250; and cyborg trope 150; in martial arts animations 139–140; and motherhood 85; roles 195; and same sex intimacy 193; stereotypes 63, 140, 152; and victimization 63–64; in video games 231
Genetic Admiration 226
genetic modifications: in *BioShock* 19, 202–203, 220, 222–224, 229–230; in *Black Jack: The Movie* 158; as commodities 226; dangers of 229–230; and digital body 228, 232; in film 161, 221, 226; and pain 231; in *The Secret Adventures of Tom Thumb* 163; and transhumanism 222
gestalt laws of perception 15, 39, 51, 54, 57, 59n73; law of symmetry 54, law of proximity 55
Ghost in the Shell (Oshii) 62–64, 84–87, 271
Ghost in the Shell 2: Innocence 64, 74, 189
Ghost in the Shell: Stand Alone Complex – The Laughing Man 65
Gibson, William 70, 91n1, 93n34, 93n35, 93n48, 94n74, 244
Golum 188, 197
gore 158–159, 161, 163
Gottwald, Klement 113
Goya, Francisco 33
Gravity 136
Gregersen, Andreas 211
Grodal, Torben 211
gryllus 116, 271; defining 103
Guardians of the Galaxy 80
Guattari, Félix 8, 20n21

Habitat 240, 264n11, 264n30
Hagener, Malte 13
The Hand 39–40
hand-drawn animation 112, 119
Hanks, Tom 79
Hansen, Mark 209–210; on embodiment in media 68; on perception 69; on technicity 9; *see also* "body in code"
happiness 46, 125, 270
haptic feedback 205–206, 209, 215; in virtual reality 259; in *Spicy City* 244
haptic film theories 13, 21n41, 67, 208; *see also* embodied meaning; phenomenology
Haraway, Donna 10, 63, 150, 224, 246
The Hasher's Delirium 95
Haunted Media 227
Hayles, N. Katherine 10, 19, 65, 76, 84, 90, 220, 239, 245
Heater, Brian 243
Heidegger, Martin 252, 257
Hello Dolly! 171
High Fidelity 256–258
Hoffmann, E. T. A. 177
Holper, Lisa 262
Hooks, Ed 108
horror 98, 125–126, 135, 145, 152, 159, 161, 176, 189, 222
How We Became Posthuman 65, 220
Howl's Moving Castle: becoming-animal 124, 126–127; character engagement 98–101; empathic resonances 125, 128, 272; Howl's metamorphosis 17, 116, 124–125; iconography 99–100; imaginary transposition 123; personal-space invasion 122–123; personality growth 127; scene of empathy 125; Sophie's transformation 122; subjective perspective 123; war machine 126–127; *see also* close-up; contrapposto
Hume, David 37
Hutchings, Peter 74–75
Hutchins, Edwin 42
hybrids 17, 75, 82, 95, 115, 117, 126, 269–270; and cross-cultural exchange 117; and digital effects 120; and identity 115, 120–121, 128; in Miyazaki's work 116; and the rotoscope 150
I Never Change My Altitude 133
Iacoboni, Marco 29, 31
iconography 100, 163, 181, 200n59, 200n61; defining 99
identification: with avatars 72; and challenges 69, 72, 86, 88; with cyberstars 88, 178; vs. engagement 100, 102, 127; and liberal humanist subject 66; with metamorphic characters 102, 110; Metz on 66–67, 101–102; with stars 183; and suture theory 66; *see also* character engagement; psychological realism; spectator; structure of engagement
identity tourism 19, 250, 263, 274
ideology 19, 145, 153, 175, 215–218, 228
illusion 101, 123; of continuous motion 6, 15, 23, 51–53, 57, 61n106; Gregory Currie on 53; optical 24; *see also* identification; optical toys; proprioception; psychological realism
Image and Mind 53
image schemas 11; in animation 45–50, 98, 111; in audiovisual media 44, 56; BALANCE 11, 44; CENTRAL-PERIPHERAL 46; CONTAINER/CONTAINMENT 11, 43–44, 47, 95, 106, 130n39; 205; COVER 47–48; defining 21n32, 43; and distinctive qualities 44; ENABLEMENT 44, 46; expanding the repertoire of 138; FLEXIBILITY 46–48; IN-OUT 16, 43, 46, 95, 97, 105–106, 112, 127–128, 130n39, 271; inventory of 11, 44; FRONT-BACK 46; and qualities of bodily movement 44; and metaphorical meaning 14–15, 38, 43–44, 95, 106; and mirror neuron system 11–12; SOURCE-PATH-GOAL 11, 44, 95, 204; UNDER 47–48; UP-DOWN 44, 46, 48; VERTICALITY 11, 47–48; *see also* conceptual metaphor theory; metaphors
The Imaginary Signifier 101
imaginary transposition 14, 102, 154, 196, 270; defining 13; with dolls 193, 198; with Howl 123; in *Malice@Doll* 193–194, 196; with a robot 192

immersion: in animation 68, 87, 136–137; in video games 206–207; in virtual reality 256, 258–260, 274; *see also* presence; sense of embodiment
impact aesthetic 135
Inside the Gaze 66
intellectual uncertainty principle 171, 178
intercorporeality 256
interest 87, 98–99, 109, 144, 184
interface, interfaces 204; animation 2–3, 7–8, 15, 29, 56, 62–63, 76–77, 89; augmented 77, 80, 90; brain-machine (BMI) 28, 238; Clark on 212–213; and communication system 66; composited 77–78, 271; computer 19, 28, 238; and cyborgean assemblage 84, 164; estrangement of the 144; and extension 86, 164; heads-up display systems 77; neural 70; perceptual entanglement with 3, 10, 77; perceptual hybridization with 80, 90; permeability of the 9, 48, 57, 120, 269; sensory coupling at the 10, 69, 97; *see also* game world; haptic feedback; *Second Life*; video games
iPhone X 243
Iriki, Atsushi 27
Iron Man 172
Iron Man 77
The Island (2006)
The Island of Dr. Moreau (Frankenheimer) 158, 221
The Island of Dr. Moreau (Taylor) 161, 221
The Island of Dr. Moreau (Wells) 161, 221
Island of Lost Souls 221
Immortal Ad Vitam 16, 76, 83–84, 90, 181, 271
The Incredibles 1, 12, 46–48, 50, 56, 106, 112, 133

James, William 42
James Bond 106
Jentsch, Ernst 171, 177–179, 188, 190, 196; *see also* intellectual uncertainty principle
Jeulink, Marloes 11, 44
Jodoin, René 54, *55; see also Spheres*
Johansson, Gunnar: visual vector analysis model 53–55; biological motion 143, 148
Johnson, Mark: on embodied meaning 41–43, 45; on image schemas 43–44
Johnson, Mike 106; *see also Corpse Bride*
Johnston, John 71
Jumanji: Welcome to the Jungle 244
Jungle Drums 150

The Karate Kid 140
de Kerckhove, Derrick 210
Keysers, Christian 106, 179
Kinect 261
kineograph *see* flip book
Klein, Norman 151
Kline, Nathan 150
Kozacik, Pete 108
Krauss, Rosalind 69
Kravanja, Peter 11–12, 45
Krueger, Myron 260
Kung Fu Panda (trilogy) 138
Kung Fu Panda 3 140, 162
Kung Fu Panda: Secrets of the Furious Five 17, 138–139, 141, 162
Kurzweil, Ray 70

Lahti, Martti 227
Laing, R. D. 87
Lakoff, George 11, 40, 42
Lakoff, George and Johnson, Mark: 60n94; on conceptual metaphors 11; on image schemas 43–44; on orientational metaphors 46; *see also* metaphors
Lamarre, Thomas 8, 123–124
Lara Croft Tomb Raider: Anniversary 209, 212, 215
The Lawnmower Man 244
Leder, Drew 42
Lee, Bruce 141
Léger, Fernand 67
Lenoir, Timothy 238
Leonarduv deník 113
levels of perceptual understanding *see* Persson, Per
Levi, Antonia 126
liberal humanist subject 3, 10, 16, 20, 66, 72, 220, 239
life detector 147–148, 151–152, 163, 272

limits of the human: and androids 74, 97, 181; and animals 103, 115, 117, 120; and becoming-animated 15, 57, 162; and the body in pain 153; and hybrids 14; and infections 118; and machines 73, 194; and marginalization 196; and masks 172–173, 196; and metamorphoses 96, 103, 105; and monsters 97, 115; and morphing 121; and muscular effects 17, 133, 163; and posthumans 87, 89–91, 161, 270–271; and superhumans 162; and the uncanny 89; in wartime 126
Lipps, Theodor 33
Long, Margherita 189
The Lord of the Rings 80, 188, 197
Los desastres de la guerra 33
love: in animation 31, 99, 110, 128, 140, 149, 171, 195; in synthetic worlds 253–254
Lucas, George 80
Lucy 65
Luhmann, Niklas 246
Lumière brothers 134

MacDorman, Karl 179, 187, 191
Macy Conferences on Cybernetics 70
Mad Max: Fury Road 135
Makovek, Miloš 112
Malice@Doll: and character engagement 192, 198; cross-modal effects in 194; and disgust 194, 196; depiction of pain in 194; and gender politics 193, 195; Japanese mechanized dolls (*karakuri*) in 189, 191–192; the phallic mother in 190; reference to *Alice's Adventures in Wonderland* (book) in 190; reversal of perspectives in 168, 195, 198; the robotic male gaze in 192–193; same sex desire in 193–194, 198; sexual innuendos in 190, 195; subjective alignments in 193; *see also* close-up; dolls; imaginary transposition; the uncanny
Manovich, Lev 216
mappings: defining 206; in *BioShock* 229, 231; in *BioShock 2* 206; and body schema 211, 215; in *Lara Croft Tomb Raider: Anniversary* 212; in video games 203–204, 209, 213–214; in virtual reality 251, 263
Maravita, Angelo 27
Marr, David 70
Martey, Rosa Mikeal 247
martial arts: in animation 135, 139–141, 162; and empowerment 140; female warriors 139–141, 162; kung fu 135, 138–140, 162
Martin, John 145
masculinity 149, 153, 156, 231
The Mask 121
masks: 116; in *A Christmas Carol* 171; and eeriness 168, 171, 273; and secret identity 172; in *Spirited Away* 172; in *Texhnolyze* 168, 172–174, 196, 273; *see also* limits of the human
The Matrix: 72, 74, 133, 244; Trilogy 65, 224
The Matrix Reloaded 226
Maturana Humberto 42, 246
McCay, Winsor 23
McHale, Brian 72, 84
McLaren, Norman 54; *see also Spheres*
McLuhan, Marshall 28–29, 224
mechanical uncanny 188, 195, 273
melodrama 135, 169–170, 198n13
Meltzoff, Andrew 29
Merleau-Ponty, Maurice 8–9, 210
Messmer, Otto 103; *see also* Felix the Cat
metamorphic creatures 96, 103; alien 176, 188; androids 74, 89; automata 112, 145, 178, 188–189; blob men 35, 101, 112; chimeras 96; corpses 105–106, 108–109, 111; demons 17, 103, 116–118, 128; ghosts 75, 146, 151–152, 164, 171, 176; marionettes 39, 188; No-Face 116, 172, 199n26; phantoms 77; robots 74, 89; spirits 99, 115, 118; splicers (*BioShock*) 202, 208, 274; Tatari-gami 117–118, 121, 271; witches 35, 104, 122; wizards 115, 122, 124, 126; zombies 72, 103–105, 202; *see also* cyborg; dolls; *gryllus*; hybrids
metamorphoses: in animation 95, 97, 103–104, 106, 127; in *anime* 115–116; in *BioShock* 3, 228–229, 232; in *Black Jack: The Movie* 159–160; classification of 104; and doubling 104, 171, 172; and

effects on viewers 2–3, 7, 12, 121, 125, 127, 198, 203, 229; Emily in *Corpse Bride* 111–112, 128; in *Fantasmagoria* 96; and Felix the Cat 103; hatching 104, 243; Howl in *Howl's Moving Castle* 97, 116, 122–126, 128, 272; and identity crisis 116; and limits of the human 96–97, 103, 126; in *Malice@Doll* 190, 192, 194, 196; and marginalization 96; and mutating 3, 104, 116; and No-face in *Spirited Away* 116–117; in *Princess Mononoke* 120–121; and *Second Life* avatar 249; and Sophie in *Howl's Moving Castle* 122; and splitting 104, 110; and subject position 105; *see also gryllus*; empathic resonances
Metamorphoses (Ovid) 103
metaphors: embodied 11; AFFECTION IS WARMTH 45; APPEARANCE IS PHYSICAL FORCE 47; augmentation 224; BAD IS DOWN 45; BEING IN CONTROL IS BEING ABOVE 40; BEING SUBJECTED TO CONTROL IS DOWN 47; BODY IS A CAGE 112, 128; BODY IS A MACHINE 112, 128; CONTRARIES ATTRACT EACH OTHER 48, 50; CONTROL IS CONTROL BY THE HANDS 40; DIFFICULTIES ARE BURDENS 45; EMOTION IS HEAT 45; HAPPY IS UP 45–46, 50, 56, 270; HAVING CONTROL IS UP 47; HEART IS A CLOCK 112, 128; KNOWLEDGE IS A BURDEN 11; MOVING TIME 45; HUMAN IS AN ANIMAL 122; HUMAN IS A WAR MACHINE 122; "man is a machine" 224; PHYSICAL APPEARANCE IS PHYSICAL FORCE 47; GOOD IS UP 47; prosthetic enhancement 224; SIGNIFICANT IS BIG 45; SOCIAL CONTROL IS PHYSICAL CONTROL 40; TIME IS SPACE 11, 45; "undercover" 47; VIRTUE IS UP 47; *see also* correlation-based metaphor; orientational metaphor; primary metaphor; resemblance metaphor
Metz, Christian 66–67, 101
Michelangelo 12, 33
The Mighty Navy 149
mimicry of the film's body 134–136, 272
Minnie the Moocher 134, 146, 151–153, 163, 272
mirror neuron system: and animation 30–31, 56; defining 29, 155; and embodied understanding 29–30, 56, 106; and human motion 180; in humans 30; and image schemas 11; and innate mimetic ability 29; in monkeys 30; and motor mimicry 36, 38, 56; and moving images 30, 39; and neuroesthetics 32; and positioning 170; and robot motion 180; and still images 30; and video games 211; and virtual reality 30, 256; *see also* canonical neurons; empathy; facial mimicry; uncanny valley
mirroring effects *see* empathic resonances
Miyazaki, Hayao 116–118, 127; *see also Howl's Moving Castle*; *Nausicaä of the Valley of the Wind*; *Princess Mononoke*; *Spirited Away*
MMO 238, 240
MMORPG 240, 264n11
mobility of the observer 6–7; *see also* Crary, Jonathan
Modeling 146–147, 163
Mohammed, Methal 250
molecular becoming 157
Monsters, Inc. 4–5, 182
mood 34, 38, 125, 169, 188, 220; anguish 171–174; deflated 110; eeriness 172, 175; and character engagement 107, 136, 169; frightening 125, 176
Moore, M. Keith 29
Moravec, Hans 70
Mori, Masahori 177
Morie, Jacquelyn Ford 259
morphing 68, 95, 116, 121–122, 125, 246, 250; defining 121; in *Princess Mononoke* 120–121
motion capture 79–80, 147–148, 166n46, 182–183, 259; Contour Reality Capture 186; *see also The Curious Case of Benjamin Button*; *Final Fantasy: The Spirits Within*
motion sickness 134; in animation 136; in video games 234n22
motor disability 260–262
motor imagery 154–155, 261
motor mimicry 34, 36–38, 56, 102, 125, 138–139; with the film's

body 136; and framing 139, 163; in martial arts films 141; and the nature of the movement 144
movements on the screen: direct physiological effects 134; technical movements 134; physical movements 134; *see also* camera movements
The Moving Picture World 146
Mr. Incredible 12, 47–48, 56
MUD 240
Mulan 138, 140–141, 162, 170
Mulan II 17, 138, 140–141, 162
Mulvey, Laura 193
muscular augmentation: and athletic performances 146–147, 150, 154–155, 159; and cyborg trope 150, 156; and empowerment 138–139, 141, 162; and ethics 134, 153, 156, 158, 161; and martial arts animation 139–140; and Popeye 133–134, 149–150; and racial prejudice 150–153; and rotoscope motion 134, 151; and Superman 149; and uncanny feelings 134, 143–144, 146, 151; and viewers' muscularity 136, 139, 141, 143, 145, 147, 154, 157–158; *see also* motor mimicry; muscular empathy
muscular empathy 14, 38, 135; in animation 12, 17, 56, 142, 154, 156, 158; and character engagement 36; defining 33–34; hindering 142–143; and vertigo 34; and visceral discomfort 34; *see also* affect; embodied simulation; mirror neuron system; motor mimicry; proprioception; psychomania; revulsion for abnormality
muscular memory 133–138
Muybridge, Eadweard 83, 90, 271

Napier, Susan 115
Naremore, James 183
narrative: and absorption 77, 87, 188, 197; and character engagement 17, 102, 170; cyclical 111; cyberpunk 65, 70, 72, 76, 84–86, 89–91; and embodied simulation 36; emotion in 108–110, 125, 175, 194, 209, 228; and facial mimicry 169; metamorphic 16, 95–97, 100, 111–112, 115, 127–128, 272; and muscular memories 17; and spatiotemporal manipulations 68, 84, 95–96; and the structure of engagement 98–100, 105, 111; about technological bodies 7; and technological inscriptions 78, 188, 197; and themes 116, 127–128, 197, 223, 244; and the uncanny 18, 197, 273; in video games 203, 206, 215, 221, 223, 228, 244; *see also* Persson, Per; scene of empathy
nausea 134
Nausicaä of the Valley of the Wind 116
von Neumann, John 70
neuroesthetics 32, 59n46
Neuromancer 70, 80, 84, 93n34, 94n74, 227, 244
new eugenics 158–159, 166n79, 237n83; in *BioShock* 221
New York 154, 209
Noë, Alva 4; on models 15, 24; on enactive perception 25–26, 58n16, 60n89, 69; on the uncanny 18

O 11, 44
Oculus Rift 257
O'Regan, J. Kevin 5
observational attitudes 199n18; *attitude en-face* 170; *attitude en-profil* 170
Oehlert, Mark 156
The Old Man of the Mountain 152
optical toys 23, 56; *see also* flip book; thaumatrope
Orbaugh, Sharalyn 120
orientational metaphor 43, 46–47; *see also* metaphors
On the Origin of Species 103
Out of the Inkwell 145, 147, 165n41
Oztop, Erhan 180

pain: and empathy 164; and mirror neurons 31, 33; and motor mimicry 37; muscular 33–34, 154–156; representation of the body in 17, 34–35, 65, 81–82, 88, 124–127, 161, 163, 175, 194, 229; spectators sharing the 31, 33, 46, 110, 158, 272; *see also* contrapposto; muscular empathy
Palmer, Steven 70
Parasite Dolls 74–75, 77, 189
Parés, Narcis 204, 211
Parés Roc 204, 211

The Passion of Joan of Arc 171
The Pendulum, the Pit and Hope 113
Penny, Simon 214, 217–218
perception *see* posthuman perception; visual perception
perceptual symbiosis 124, 203, 206–207; and avatar's perspective 207–209; and body schema 209–211; and mapping 206, 209, 211–212; and systemic coupling 210; *see also* "body in code"
person schema 116
personal-space invasion 102; defining 122–123; and intimacy 123; and threat 48; *see also Howl's Moving Castle*
Persson, Per: on the levels of meaningfulness 39–41, 43, 50, 54, 99–100, 219; on the preferred levels 40, 60n77; on personal space 122; on understanding cinema 39, 67
Persuasive Games: The Expressive Power of Videogames 14
phenomenology 8, 9; in cinema 6, 21n41
pheromones *see* the transmission of affect
Philosophy in the Flesh 11
Picard, Rosalind 242
Pinocchio 104, 188
Pitt, Brad 185, 188
pity 109, 114, 159
Pixar 47, 182
pixilation 1–2, 6, 17, 134, 144–145
Plantinga, Carl 125, 169
plasmaticness 20n2, 105, 126
player 203–204; and algorithmic couplings 203, 214–215, 227; and body schema 19, 203, 210–211; and effects of technology 19; and emotions 208, 220, 225, 229; and embodied meaning 203–205, 216, 218–220, 224, 231–232; and ethics 218, 229, 231–232; and extended perception 203; and extended reach 9, 210; and perceptual symbiosis 203, 206, 208–209, 225, 228; and persuasion 14, 19, 203, 215, 225, 228, 232; and strategy 27; physical adaptation of the 229–230; *see also* avatars; video games; symbiotic relationship
PlayStation 2 261
point-of-view shot 63, 66, 73, 85, 91, 101–102, 123, 129n22, 135, 207
The Polar Express 167–169, 176, 186, 188, 197, 199n32, 272; motion capture in 182; *see also* close-up; the uncanny
Popeye 96, 133, 149–150, 153, 166n55
Popeye the Sailor Meets Sinbad the Sailor 149–150
Possible Worlds 74
posthuman, posthumans: and centrifugal self 84–85; defining 240; and discrimination 76, 89; and embodied virtualities 84, 193; and embodiment 271–272; and empathy 18, 76, 87, 271; Hayles on 10, 65, 84; and identification 65, 91; representations of 16, 65, 70, 72–75, 89–90, 159–161, 193–194; and vision 71, 73–75, 76; *see also* cyberpunk; cyborg; posthuman perception; posthumanism
posthuman perception 28, 53; in animation 3, 16, 65, 69–70, 77, 90–91, 143; and cyborgean assemblages 90; and cyberpunk 16, 69–70, 73, 270–271; defining 84; and embodied virtualities 63, 193; and extension 53, 91; as a theme 86; and intersubjective alignments 63, 76, 86, 193; and perceptual entanglement 3, 10; in video games 209, 229; *see also* becoming-animated
posthumanism 62, 161
postvitalism 226, 237n97, 245; in *BioShock* 226–227, 232, 273; defining 19; and postvital body 115, 226–227, 245; and postvital self 239, 245–246; and *Second Life* 19, 246, 263
Preeg, Steve 185–186
presence: character 48, 101, 129n15, 151; of the medium 73–74, 121; and models 24; in video games 205, 207, 234n17; in virtual reality 259–260, 267n103; *see also* immersion; sense of embodiment
primary metaphor 40, 45, 48, 50, 56
Princess Mononoke: becoming-animal in 127–128; crossings between species in 117–118; digital effects

118–120; molecular assemblages 120–121; supernatural motion in 117; themes in 17, 128, 271
Prisoners 12, 14, 33
procedural rhetoric 18, 217; in *BioShock* and *BioShock 2* 19, 221–223, 229, 232; defining 215
programmable body: 245–246; digital bioengineering 249–250; in video games 225–228; in virtual reality 246–247
propositional attitude 41
proprioception 32–34; in animation 2, 46, 87, 89, 99, 122, 124, 128, 271; in cinema 7, 81; defining 7, 29; Richmond on 136; in video games 211, 234n22; in virtual reality 260
prosthetic extensions: in animation 77; and avatars 262; in *BioShock* 203, 223–224, 229; and distributed cognition 238; erotic connotations of 224; as fantasy of power 224; as motif 77, 196; the player's adjustment to 3, 230; in systems 213
The Proteus Effect 259
proxemic patterns 48, 122, 193, 256
psychological typage 112
psychological realism: in moving images 48, 66, 74–75, 89, 101–102, 147; in video games 208–209
psychomania 34
puppet animation 1, 16, 39–40, 51–52, 67, 108–112, 133–134, 142–145, 164, 188–189; *see also Corpse Bride*; *Dog*; *The Emperor's Nightingale*; *The Hand*; *The Secret Adventures of Tom Thumb*; *Street of Crocodiles*
The Puppet's Nightmare 95

Quay Brothers 51
Quest 44

race 14, 39, 153, 271; and stereotypes 18, 146, 150–152; and representation online 248, 250; and blackness 18, 151–152, 163; and sexuality 152–153; and slavery 152
The Railway Journey 6
Rand, Ayn 228, 237n104
Regime of Computation 84–85, 245–246
La Région Centrale 134
reprograming the self: and avatar 238–239, 246–247; defining 238; and virtual selfhood 248–249; *see also* avatar, identity tourism; programmable body
resemblance metaphor 44–45, 112, 122, 128
revulsion for abnormality 145, 156, 272
Rhythmus 41
Rise of the Planet of the Apes 80
Rizzolatti, Giacomo 36
RoboCop (Padilha) 65
RoboCop (Verhoeven) 65, 72–74, 224
Rosedale, Philip 244, 256–257; *see also Second Life*; *High Fidelity*
Rosenblum, Lawrence 37, 179–180
rotoscope: and Cab Calloway 17, 134, 142, 150; description 145; and effects 135, 146; vs. motion capture 147; and phantom presence 151–153; as prosthesis 150; and realism 147, 150, 152, 163, 272; and the structure of engagement 145–146; in Superman cartoons 149, 152; and the uncanny 146, 151–152, 163, 272; *see also* race

sadness 36, 46, 107, 109–110, 173, 256
Samsung Galaxy S9 243, 255
Sanchez, Carleen D. 250
scene of empathy 169, 197; defining 125
Scherer, Klaus 36
science fiction 172–176; *see also Avatar*; *Final Fantasy: The Spirits Within*; *RoboCop*; *The Terminator*; *Westworld*; *World Record*
Schivelbush, Wolfgang 6
Sconce, Jeffrey 227
Second Life: activities in 240; and algorithms 241–242, 251; as autopoietic system 246; client-server architecture 252; currency of 240; destinations in 240; and distributed cognition 241; and image schemas 251, 259; and interfaces 252–253; and LSL 242; and norms 248; and Regime of Computation 246; and residents 242, 246, 249; resources in 240; rezzing 252; rules 242, 250;

scripts 246; and use of space 247; user interface in 241–242, 251–253, 274; *see also Second Life* avatar
Second Life avatar 240–242; and affect 240, 242; and agency 250; alts 248; and authentic self 246–247, 255; and behavior 247; and body ownership 251–252; and body schema 253; and camera view 251; characteristic of embodiment 242, 249–250; as computer code 248–249; and emotions 253–255; and facial mimicry 256; and gender 248–250; and gestures 242, 246, 251, 253–255; impossible motion 252; and multiplicity of selves 250; and persona 248; and photorealism 254; and prime 248; and race 248; and religion 250; and rezzing 255; and roles 248–249; and self-location 250–252; and sensorimotor interactions 242, 247, 250–251; and social life 248–249, 253; and uncanniness 255–256; and virtual intimacy 254; and virtual selfhood 239, 247–249; *see also* identity tourism; postvitalism; reprograming the self
The Secret Adventures of Tom Thumb 1, 2, 6, 134, 144–145, 162–163
self-reflexivity: in *BioShock* 209; in *The Cabinet of Jan Švankmajer* 53; in *Corpse Bride* 108; about modes of production 104, 108, 120, 178, 190; about perception 16, 64, 209; about spectatorship 83, 154, 156–157, 163, 192; in *The Triplets of Belleville* 154, 156–157, 163; in *WALL-E* 31
sense of embodiment 250–251; *see also* presence
sensorimotor couplings *see* empathic resonances
Shannon, Claude 70
shape-shifting characters *see* metamorphic creatures
Shapiro, Lawrence 60n80; on the conceptualization tenet 43
Shaviro, Steven 13, 72, 208
Schrödinger, Erwin 246
Sheehan, Gordon 149
Shelley, Mary 75
Shiffrar, Maggie 143
shock 37, 128, 159, 180
Shrek 182
Sid Meier's Civilization Revolution 216
Singh, Strawberry 257
Silvio, Carl 85
Simondon, Gilbert 8–9
The Simpsons 252
The Sims Online 251
Sinnreich, Aram 245
Sisyphus 32, 36, 56, 134
situated cognition 10; *see also* cognition; embodied mind
The Six Million Dollar Man 6
Sleep Dealer 72, 245
Small Soldiers 74
Smith, Adam 37
Smith, Murray 16, 96, 98, 100, 102, 105
Snow Crash 244, 264n30
Sobchack, Vivian 13
"soft self" 21n26; in animation 9; in virtual reality 241
SoulCalibur IV 34, 36, 56
Soviet Union 113
Spartacus 11
special effects *see* visual effects
Species 226
spectator: biological 66; defining 98; ideal 66–67; *see also* character engagement; identification; interface; point-of-view shot; psychological realism; spectator's body; the structure of engagement
the spectator's body 2, 8, 12, 76, 82, 84, 88, 115, 133
Spheres 15, 24, 51, 54–55, 57, 269
Spicy City 244
Spider-Man 172
Spider-Man (film) *3* 137, 209, 272
Spider-Man (trilogy) 138
Spirited Away 116, 172
splatter films 159, 161
Splice 226
sports *see* athletes
Stacey, Jackie 226
Stadler, Harald 87
Stafford, Barbara 12, 36, 38, 170
Stalinism 113–115
star persona 100, 183
Stelarc 27, 58n21
Stephenson, Neal 244, 264n30; *see also Snow Crash*

stop-motion animation: 1, 17, 51–53, 83, 106, 112, 142–145, 153, 272; *see also The Cabinet of Jan Švankmajer*; *The Death of Stalinism in Bohemia*; *Dog*; *The Club of the Laid Off*; *The Emperor's Nightingale*; *The Hand*; *The Secret Adventures of Tom Thumb*
Strange Case of Dr. Jekyll and Mr. Hyde (Stevenson) 103
Strange Days 80, 90, 208
Star Trek: Voyager 224
Stein, Lynn 195
Stevens, Jennifer 143
Street of Crocodiles 67
stroboscopic effects 82, 94n67
Stromer-Galley, Jennifer 247
the structure of engagement 96–102, 127, 270, 192; and alignment 100; and allegiance 98, 102, 115, 170, 181; and concern 98–99, 102; disrupting 111; emotions and 98–99; and empathic responses 102; and interest 98–99; and recognition 100, 107, 181; *see also* character engagement; imaginary transposition
the structure of sympathy 96, 100
Studio Ghibli 120; *see also Howl's Moving Castle*; *Princess Mononoke*; *Spirited Away*
Summer Wars 244
superheroes 47, 56, 106, 153, 156, 172; *see also* Captain America; Catwoman; Elastigirl; *The Incredibles*; Iron-Man; Mr. Incredible; Spider-Man; Superman
superhuman, superhumans: in *Black Jack: The Movie* 158–161, 272; spectators as 162; vision 160; *see also* posthuman
Superman 104, 106, 146, 149–150, 152–153, 166n55
Superman (1941) 149
Surrogates 244–245
suspense 99, 159
Švankmajer, Jan 113–114; *see also The Death of Stalinism in Bohemia*; *Flora*; *Food*; *Leonarduv deník*; *The Pendulum, the Pit and Hope*
symbiotic relationship 275; in animation 3, 76, 86, 117, 122, 127, 158; in video games 203, 273; in *Second Life* 247, 251
sympathy: and character design 181; for characters 65, 88, 98, 100, 102, 109, 130n46, 175; and close-up 171–172; vs. empathy 109; and facial mimicry 169; as innate 175; and personal-space invasion 122; and technique 157; *see also* "feeling for"; structure of empathy; structure of sympathy
Symphonie Diagonale 41
synesthetic affect 175, 197, 199n31
synthespians 197; in *Alan Wake* 176; and artifact emotion 183–184; in *Avatar* 176; as competing with actors 79–80, 178–179, 195; in *The Curious Case of Benjamin Button* 18, 181, 185–186; and digital captures 186–187; and emotions 168; in *Final Fantasy: The Spirits Within* 1, 16, 79, 168, 181, 183, 188; in *Malice@Doll* 168; and photorealism 185; in *The Polar Express* 168; response to 18, 176, 178, 180–181, 196, 273; in *Shrek* 182; *see also* cyberstars; uncanny valley
synthetic worlds *see Habitat*; *High Fidelity*; *Second Life*

The Tactile Eye 135
Tan, Ed 170
Technics of the Observer 6
technoenchantment 221–222
Teknolust 226
Telotte, J. P. 232
The Terminator 87, 92n31, 224
Terminator 2
Tetris 26
Texhnolyze 63, 74, 77, 168, 196–197, 273; cross-modal effects in 175; depiction of pain in 175; lack of emotions in 173–174; *see also* close-up; masks
thaumatrope 23–24, 57n2
third-person perspective 37, 209
The Thirteenth Floor 72, 74, 77
Thompson, Clive 185
Thompson, Evan 42, 247
Through the Looking Glass, and What Alice Found There 190
A Thousand Plateaus 157
Tinker Bell 137
Todorov, Tzvetan 104

Tour de France 154–155
Toy Story 3 177
transformations *see* metamorphoses
The Transmission of Affect 119
the transmission of affect 119
transient extended cognitive system (TECS) 212
transparent equipment *see* transparent in use
transparent in use 27, 211, 252, 257; *see also* Heidegger, Martin
The Triplets of Belleville 17, 153–158, 162–164, 272
Trnka, Jiří 40, 112; *see also The Emperor's Nightingale*; *The Hand*
Troje, Nikolaus 147–148, 152
Tron 244
Tron: Legacy 244
True Names 244
Turkle, Sherry 19, 239, 249

Uhde, Jan 113
Ulbrich, Ed 185
"The 'Uncanny'" 177
the uncanny: in 2D animation 168, 173; Freud on 177–179, 190; and animistic beliefs 177; and automata 177–178, 188–189; and castration complex 177; and *doppelgangers* 171, 189; in *A Christmas Carol* (Zemeckis) 171; and dolls 178, 188–189; and facial distortions 197; in *Final Fantasy: The Spirits Within* 167–168; in *Ghost in the Shell 2: Innocence* 189; Jentsch on 177–178; and jerkiness 194; and lifeless eyes 167, 169, 176, 184, 186; and limited expressions 168, 173, 181; in *Malice@Doll* 189, 191, 197; in *The Polar Express* 167–168; and Tiwa in *Fantastic Planet* 188; and voice synchronization 168; and wax figures 178; and zombie-like appearances 176, 179; *see also* Golum; MacDorman, Karl; masks; Noë, Alva; North, Dan; Weschler, Lawrence
uncanny valley: and animals 179; strategies to avoid 181–184; defining 168, 177; and evolution 179–180; and face perception 180; and human-machine hybrid 179; and the mirror neuron system 180; and mortality 179; overcoming 176, 185–188; and realistic virtual pets 182; and scientific explanations 168, 179–180, 187–188, 196–197; and synthespians 177–178
Understanding Cinema 67
Understanding Media 28, 224
Uva, Christian 147

Vanilla Sky 74
Varela, Francisco 42, 68, 246–247
Varieties of Presence 24
"Velvet Revolution" 113
victim positions: Atwood's defining for 153–154, 163, 166n68; in *The Triplets of Belleville* 157; in *Black Jack: The Movie* 163–164
Victorian 105–106, 201n101
video games: and affect 220, 225, 229; and avatar 209, 238; and cognition 9; and concern 220, 225; and image schemas 204–205, 217–219; and interface 203–207, 209, 212–214; and technological extensions 3; *see also* algorithms; agency; avatars; *BioShock*; *BioShock 2*; *BioShock Infinite*; *Burnout*; body schema; *Civilization III*; *Doom*; first-person shooters; game world; image schemas; *Lara Croft Tomb Raider: Anniversary*; player; procedural rhetoric; proprioception; psychological realism; *SoulCalibur IV*; *Sid Meier's Civilization Revolution*; *Spider-Man 3*; symbiotic relationship; *Tetris*
viewer *see* spectator
Virilio, Paul 73, 123, 137
virtual environment: defining 204, 211, 234n5, 239
virtual reality 234n5; CAVE 258, 260; defining 204; HDM 258–260; immersion 258; *see also* game world; *Habitat*; *High Fidelity*; *Second Life*; virtual reality-based therapies
virtual reality-based therapies 258; and mirror neuron system 261–262; and neuro-rehabilitation poststroke 261–263, 274; and *Second Life* 259; and video capture VR systems 260–261
Vischer, Robert 33

The Vision Machine 73
Vision Science: Photons to Phenomenology 70
visual effects: and scalar travel 138; and slow motion 6, 137; and superhuman speed 138; and supporting wires 138; and X-ray vision 159; *see also* compositing; digital effects
visual perception: of biological motion 53–54, 143, 147–148; in cinema 66–69; definition 70–71; disembodied 82; full VR 71; machinic vision 71; psychology of 67; vision 70; *see also* embodied perception; enactive perception; Johansson, Gunnar
vital machines 223
The Vital Machine 223

Waking Life 135
WALL-E 1, 30–31, 56, 171, 182
War for the Planet of the Apes 80
Warburg, Aby 33
Warner, Marina 104
Watkins, Mel 152
weak synesthesia 175
Wells, H. G. 161
Wells, Paul 95, 149, 152
Weschler, Lawrence 18, 185
Westoff, Cord 147–148, 152
Westworld 73
Wiener, Norbert 70
Wii 261
Wii Fit 261
Williams, Linda 135
Wölfflin, Heinrich 33
Wood, Aylish 68, 144
World Record 87–88
World of Warcraft 240
WWII 70, 149, 153

XBox 360 206

Yee, Nick 259

Zemeckis, Robert 171; *see also* *Beowulf*; *A Christmas Carol*; *The Polar Express*
Zillmann, Dolf 37, 170